CANOEING &
KAYAKING
WEST
VIRGINIA

30th Anniversary Edition

CANOEING & KAYAKING WEST VIRGINIA

30th Anniversary Edition

BY PAUL DAVIDSON, WARD EISTER, DIRK DAVIDSON
REVISED BY CHARLIE WALBRIDGE
WITH BOBBY MILLER AND TURNER SHARP

MENASHA RIDGE PRESS
Birmingham, Alabama

Canoeing & Kayaking West Virginia

Published by Menasha Ridge Press
Printed in the United States of America
Distributed by Publishers Group West
Fifth edition 2003

Library of Congress Cataloging in Publication Data

Walbridge, Charles C., 1948–
    Canoeing and kayaking West Virginia /revised by Charlie
Walbridge; with Paul Davidson, Ward Eister, Dirk Davidson,
Turner Sharp, and Bobby Miller.—5th ed.
    Previously published: Wildwater West Virginia / Paul Davidson.
1985. Includes index.
ISBN 978-0-89732-545-5 (pbk. : alk. paper)
ISBN 978-0-89732-825-8 (ebook);
ISBN 978-1-63404-250-5 (hardcover)
    1. Canoes and canoeing—West Virginia—Guidebooks.
2. Kayaking—West Virginia—Guidebooks. 3. West Virginia—
Guidebooks. I. Davidson, Paul, 1931 Dec. 12– Wildwater West
Virginia. II. Title.

GV776.W4 W35 2003
917.54'044—dc21

                                        2002154291

Menasha Ridge Press
An imprint of AdventureKEEN
2204 First Avenue South, Suite 102
Birmingham, Alabama 35233
www.menasharidge.com

Table *of* Contents

part**One**

**GEORGE WASHINGTON'S RIVER AND ITS TRIBUTARIES:
THE POTOMAC DRAINAGE**

part Two

THE BIG MOUNTAIN RIVER—THE MIGHTY CHEAT

part**Three**

FASTEST WATER TO THE NORTH—THE TYGART SUB-BASIN

part**Four**

THE NORTHWEST QUADRANT—THE OHIO BASIN

part**Five**

THE BEAUTIFUL VALLEY RIVER—THE GREENBRIER

part**Six**

WILDEST WATER FROM THE CENTRAL HEARTLAND

part**Seven**

BIG WATER FROM THE SOUTH—THE NEW AND THE BLUESTONE

part**Eight**

TROUBLED WATERS DRAINING THE WEST

part**Nine**

AND A COUPLE FROM NEIGHBORING STATES

Index

Map Index

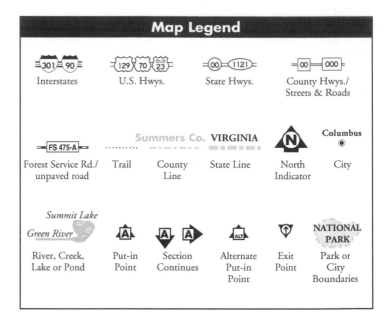

Disclaimer

CAUTION!

While every effort has been made to insure the accuracy of this guidebook, river and road conditions can change greatly from year to year. The descriptions in this book should be used as a general guide only. A decision to attempt a run can be made only after an on-the-spot inspection of the river. The authors and publishers are not responsible for any personal injury or property damage that may result from your activities. As always, you paddle at your own risk.

The publishers of *A Canoeing and Kayaking Guide to West Virginia* are always interested in hearing from our readers. If you find our descriptions and maps to be inaccurate or incomplete, please send your observations to:

Charlie Walbridge
A Canoeing and Kayaking Guide to West Virginia
PO Box 43673
Birmingham, Alabama 35243

Preface

This is the 30th anniversary of *A Canoeing and Kayaking Guide to West Virginia,* formerly *Wildwater West Virginia.* I remember the excitement of getting the first edition in the mail; I snuck away from my job as canoe counselor at a boys' summer camp and read it cover to cover! The year 2003 is also my 34th of running the rivers of the Mountain State. I started coming to the Petersburg Races on the upper Potomac when I was still in college, and for many years thereafter commuted from my home in Philadelphia. Now, after many years of making long weekend drives, my wife and I are living in Bruceton Mills. Like many area paddlers, I carry a worn copy of *Wildwater West Virginia* (now *A Canoeing and Kayaking Guide to West Virginia*) in the glove compartment of my car. It has served me well for hundred of river miles, and I still consult it before trying new runs. This new and updated version will serve you as well.

In updating this book I've tried to respect the style of the original authors, both of whom I paddled with years ago. Bob Burrell and Paul Davidson, the creators of this guidebook, introduced me to many of the rivers described here. Although they are no longer active in the Mountain State, the sport they loved has blossomed since those early days. Their efforts jump-started the adventure-travel side of the tourist business here, creating jobs and opportunities in formerly depressed areas. In earlier revisions Doc Davidson was assisted by Ward Eister and his son, Dirk. Later Risa Shimoda described the changes wrought by the 1985 flood.

Although I'd have liked to run every river profiled in this guide, it's just not possible for anyone to do this. Fortunately, others have gone where I have not. Ed Evangelidi, Ed Gertler, Ed Grove, and Turner Sharp read the book carefully and checked it against their vast personal knowledge of West Virginia rivers. Each sent me piles of papers crammed with corrections and updates that have been incorporated into the book. Bobby Miller, creek boater extraordinaire, has improved the write-ups of the region's most difficult runs and added a bunch of new ones. Lastly, Carl Bolyard from the West Virginia Rivers Coalition brought me up-to-date on the state's most pressing conservation issues. Without them this revision would have never happened.

Most of the rivers in this guide were originally explored between 1960 and 1980. The wonderful tales of this era were recorded in newsletters published by the Canoe Cruiser's Association of Washington, DC *(The Cruiser)* and the West

Virginia Wildwater Association *(Splashes)*. In this edition we
have included interludes, trip reports, philosophy, and other
musings taken from these pages. Thanks for this go to Ed Gertler,
who allowed me to borrow his complete collection of these
publications.

Thanks, guys! See you on the river!

Charlie Walbridge
Bruceton Mills, West Virginia

Introduction

This guide began as a collective effort by members of the West
Virginia Wildwater Association, who had been exploring the
creeks, streams, and rivers of West Virginia since 1965. Bob
Burrell and Paul Davidson published the first edition in 1972.
Now, over 30 years later, *A Canoeing and Kayaking Guide to West
Virginia*, formerly *Wildwater West Virginia*, remains the most
complete, up-to-date paddlers guide to Mountain State rivers. It
has been revised frequently, incorporating comments from dozens
of active paddlers. In addition to covering the state's classic
whitewater trips, it also describes a broad selection of flatwater
and mildwater touring rivers. And, to keep pace with the cutting
edge of whitewater sport, noted steep-creek expert Bobby Miller
has written up many recently discovered hardcore creek runs.
There is truly something for everyone here.

Since this guide was first published, the number of paddlers on
West Virginia's rivers has exploded. The Mountain State is now a
mainstay for canoe and kayak enthusiasts from around the world.
A vibrant and progressive commercial rafting industry gives less
experienced people the opportunity to see our rivers as well.
Roughly 200,000 people travel down the New River Gorge each
year, and the famous Gauley River sees over 80,000 visitors during its 6-week fall season. Some people may think West Virginia
rivers are getting a little *too* popular! But while a few other whitewater runs see intense use on a few choice spring weekends, you
can still run most of the wild and beautiful rivers in the state
without seeing another soul.

This guidebook notes with sadness the destruction of life and
property caused by flooding. In 1985 Hurricane Juan unleashed
a deluge of rain on the Cheat and Potomac River watersheds.
The result was a massive flood of geological proportions. For the
residents of West Virginia, this unprecedented high water had
tragic results: 40 dead, 2,600 homeless, and property damage

totaling $500 million. Entire towns were wiped out, dozens of bridges were destroyed, and some communities were cut off for weeks. In June and July of 2001 a similar disaster hit communities in the southern part of the state. Many roads, including all of the access roads into the popular New River Gorge, were closed for weeks. Some rivers and creeks were changed, and we have made note of this in our guide. Other scars will remain for decades, both on the land and in the minds of those who experienced the disasters.

We hope that this guide will help you to appreciate West Virginia's magnificent rivers. If you're a paddler, angler, or hiker, we can direct you to some stunningly beautiful places that few people have seen. If you love the sight and sound of moving water, we'll lead you to some of the most spectacular whitewater rapids in the country. And for federal and state legislators, we bear witness to the treasures that exist here and that some unenlightened special interests seek to destroy. If this book helps you appreciate our state's rivers and understand what is happening to them, we have succeeded.

Using This Guide

Each chapter opens with an introduction to the watershed it covers, followed by individual river descriptions. Each river description begins with headings listing the following data: river difficulty, river length, river gauge, water level, river gradient, river volume, solitude, and scenery. The descriptions are followed by notes outlining unusual difficulties, shuttle directions, maps covering the area, and gauge information.

River Difficulty—Our river difficulty classification is adapted from the system used by American Whitewater. For detailed information, refer to the Rating River Difficulty section on page 5.

Distance and Time—Each description provides the river miles traversed between the put-in and take-out. We then provide conservative paddling times (3 mph) for the runs we have clocked without allowing for lunch, scouting, playing, napping, etc. Wind, flips, pins, water levels, and rescuing can alter these times. Unless otherwise specified, right and left refer to these directions as you look downstream.

Water Levels—Each section of river has its own personality when it comes to "too high" or "too low." We indicate a useful range, indicating a comfortable minimum and a reasonable maximum. Rivers can be run at much higher levels by experts who know

them well and at significantly lower levels by determined rock bashers who don't mind wading and lifting over shallow places. Where we don't have a specific figure we list the level as "NA," meaning not available.

Government agencies like the United States Geological Survey (USGS) or the US Army Corps of Engineers (USCOE) measure river flows at gauging stations throughout the country. This information is collected and recorded hourly. You'll find pertinent websites and phone numbers listed in the discussion of river gauges on page 7.

You'll also encounter "paddlers gauges" painted on bridge piers and rocks. Although not reported anywhere, they remain in wide use.

Gradient—This is the average drop of the river in feet per mile (fpm). If parts of the river drop at a value significantly different from the average, we indicate this by parentheses. For example, 40(3@60) means that while the river drops at an average rate of 40 fpm, 3 miles of it drop at 60 fpm.

Remember: the difficulty of a river's rapids is not determined by gradient alone. Some rivers drop evenly over continuous rapids of roughly the same difficulty. Others alternate between long pools and drops that are steeper than the gradient would indicate. Waterfalls are an extreme example of this. Geological peculiarities, such as huge boulders, high ledges, and gorges must also be considered. Our river descriptions will give some insight.

Volume—Because knowing the gradient isn't enough information, we also consider the size of the stream. A steep, high-volume river is generally much more difficult than a small stream with the same gradient. We have used the annual mean discharge in cubic feet per second (cfs) as an index of volume. Four hundred cfs is the division between small (S) and medium (M), and 1,500 cfs is the division between medium and large (L). Where the volume is significantly below 400 cfs, the letter designation is "VS," which stands for very small. If good data is available, a number is given in the text. If not, a letter designation of the volume indicates our best guess.

Knowing the mean annual discharge gives you a rough idea of what water levels are on rivers you haven't seen. Rivers are generally runable when the flow equals or exceeds their annual mean discharge. Rivers should usually be avoided during seasons when they fall below this figure and approached with caution when they rise to three times that number. Small rivers are early spring and very late fall runs. Larger rivers have a longer season, but with dangerous midseason high levels.

Scenery—Scenery is ranked on an A to D scale:

   A—remote wilderness areas with little sign of civilization

   B—more settled, but still beautiful pastoral countryside

   C—lots of development (cities or industry)

   D—pollution, strip mines, tipples, slag-heaps, rundown buildings, and other forms of landscape abuse

The quality of the scenery along a river can change quickly. For example, the Elk River below Sutton is usually considered B, even A at times, but immediately becomes D when it passes through Clay. Cities and manufactured settings are not necessarily eyesores. Parsons, Philippi, Petersburg, and Harpers Ferry are all very attractive when viewed from the river, but Morgantown and Charleston are not.

Solitude—Some people don't mind seeing other paddlers, while others prefer not to. Much depends on the season. Winter and early spring rivers are lightly traveled everywhere. Some seasonal rivers have a few popular weekends as the weather warms up. Some runs, especially those with reliable summer dam releases, get very crowded. We provide some general guidelines:

   A—very popular, and crowded at times

   B—not crowded, but may be busy at times

   C—other groups are seldom seen

Rating River Difficulty

American Whitewater's River Classification System provides a good framework for discussing river difficulty. However, there are considerable variations in how this system is interpreted nationwide. Some expert paddlers tend to underrate everything, and an inexperienced paddler may go the other way and overestimate the difficulty. What seems horrendous to one person may be quite manageable to a more skilled paddler. We've tried to see that the rivers of comparable difficulty carry similar ratings, but because so many people have contributed to this guide there may well be unintended variations. If you have any doubts about your ability to handle a run, talk to paddlers who have done it before or allow some extra time to scout.

For years there's been pressure to downgrade rivers in response to innovations in boat design and technique. Because we've chosen not to do this, some rivers in this guide may seem overrated to expert paddlers. This makes this book an "old school" guide. Paddlers who consult "new school" guidebooks like *Colorado*

Rivers and Creeks, or the *Guide to the Best Whitewater in California* will find comparable rivers rated lower than they would be here. Don't expect to finesse a Class-5 "new-school" creek just because you've run the Upper Gauley a few times! Recently a number of steeper, more demanding runs have been discovered which redefine the limits of whitewater sport. They are really a full grade higher than our "standard" Class 5 run. We rate them as Class 5+ or 6 to distinguish them from the other Class 5s that, although not easy, are less demanding.

Flat Water

Class A—Standing or slow-flowing water not more than 2.5 mph.

Class B—Current between 2.5 and 4.5 mph, but back-paddling effectively neutralizes it.

Class C—Current more than 4.5 mph. Back-paddling cannot neutralize the speed of the current. Simple obstacles may require a certain amount of boat control.

Whitewater

Class 1—Easy. Occasional small riffles consisting of low, regular wave patterns. About what you might encounter on a lake on a mildly windy day.

Class 2—Medium difficulty. Rapids occur more frequently, usually retaining a regular wave pattern as on a lake with a fairly vigorous wind (enough to cause whitecaps). Although there may be more than one route, the most practical one is easily determined. There may be simple, uncomplicated chutes over ledge up to 3 feet high.

Class 3—Difficult. Numerous rapids, with higher, irregular standing waves, hydraulics, and eddies. In Class-3 rapids you must maneuver. The most practical route may not be obvious, and you'll find that you have to work a little. Expect ledges up to 4 feet, waves up to 3 feet, overhanging branches, and deeper water.

Class 4—More difficult. Long, extensive stretches of rapids with high, irregular standing waves and difficult hydraulics, holes, eddies, and crosscurrents. Good boat control is essential, and you are working very hard. Class 4 requires plenty of fast decision making because the most practical route may not be obvious. Difficult ledges with irregular passages, "stopper" waves, or souse holes may block the way.

Class 5—Extremely difficult. It's not always easy to tell where Class 4 ends and Class 5 begins. These rapids are not only quite

difficult but they are long and continuous. Irregular stoppers and souse holes are unavoidable; partially submerged boulders and ledges are everywhere; very complex eddies and crosscurrents are not only present but occur in long, dazzling combinations. Common usage also refers to short, very intense rapids as Class 5 if they require a lot of skill and courage to run.

Class 6—Utmost difficulty. This isn't a hard class to define, but in recent years there's been a tendency to ignore the definition. It's supposed to mean the utmost limit of navigability, with its chief distinguishing characteristic being *unusual risk of life*. Mistakes made here can be fatal. No one should ever be urged or taunted into running a 6 (or anything else for that manner).

When the difficulty of a river falls between two grades, two numbers will be used, i.e., Class 2–3. If most of the river is of one classification except for one or two spots, it is referred to as, say, Class 3(4). These ratings are for normal water levels, and classifications may change drastically in high water. Similarly, river ratings usually drop about a class in low water. If you run a few Class 4s in low-water conditions, don't assume you are a Class 4 paddler.

Using River Gauges

The Water Resources Division of the USGS measures water flows on most rivers in the United States at frequent intervals. The USCOE and various power companies collect similar information. These flows are recorded in cubic feet per second (cfs) and are available to everyone.

The key variable is the height of the river at a fixed point. Gauge houses, situated on most rivers, consist of a well at the river's edge with a float attached to a recording clock. The gauge reads in hundredths of feet. Rating tables are constructed for each gauge to get a cfs reading for each level.

This information is very useful for paddlers who are planning a trip. In the "old days," paddlers had to phone various government offices and listen to recorded messages. They also contacted outfitters and private individuals who kept track of nearby paddler gauges. Nowadays we can get this information quickly at various websites, along with the weather! A few clicks gather information that would have taken us dozens of phone calls to obtain. Multiple websites provide backup when a single site goes down. The most important sites for the Mountain State area are:

WATER-LEVEL SITES

USGS—Realtime Water Levels; water.usgs.gov/nwis/rt

The US Coast and Geologic Survey has compiled a remarkable website. Hundreds of gauges are updated continually, and graphs showing recent flow trends are now available at the touch of a mouse. This is the greatest thing for paddlers since sprayskirts were invented, so remember to support these folks at appropriations time.

American Whitewater; www.americanwhitewater.org

This site collects USGS gauge readings for whitewater rivers throughout the country and automatically extrapolates water levels on rivers not covered by these gauges. Their "gaugebot" service can be set up to e-mail selected river readings to you each morning. Their site also contains many other resources of interest to paddlers.

USCOE-Pittsburgh; wmw.lrp.usace.army.mil

This very functional site covers the Cheat, Tygart, and Yough drainages as well as the reservoirs that they manage on these rivers.

USCOE-Huntington;
www.lrh-wc.usace.army.mil/wc/whitewater.html

Their "whitewater page" covers readings on the Elk, New, Gauley, and Russell Fork, plus releases and release schedules from dams under their control.

2 Lines Deep Creek Hydro; www.deepcreekhydro.com

This site has the latest information on scheduled and unscheduled releases into the Upper Yough from Deep Creek Lake.

PHONE SOURCES

Gauge readings can also be obtained by phone from various offices. Recorded messages are usually updated once a day, at about 9 a.m.

For the Potomac, Rappahanock, and Shenandoah Basins: Call the National Weather Service in Maryland at (703) 260-0305 for a taped message.

For the Monongahela Basin (including the Cheat, the Tygart, and the Yough): Call the National Weather Service in Pittsburgh at (412) 262-5290 for a taped message.

For the Kanawha Basin (including the Greenbrier, New, Gauley, Meadow, Cranberry and Elk Rivers): Call The National Weather

Service in Charleston from 8 a.m. to 4:30 p.m. at (304) 746-0180. A live person will answer your questions.

Phone numbers for specific gauges:

Release schedules for the Upper Youghiogheny River are available a few days in advance from the Deep Creek Hydro Project (call (814) 533-8911). From there, you can get the daily operations tape, which is updated as water is released, and the weekly operations tape, which lists scheduled releases.

The USCOE at Summersville Lake provides readings of the Mt. Lookout gauge on the Meadow, the Craigsville Gauge (inflow), and the Summersville Dam release (outflow) on the Gauley; call (304) 872-5809.

The USCOE at Bluestone Dam provides the dam outflow in cfs and readings for the Alderson gauge on the Greenbriar, the Pipestem gauge on the Bluestone, and the Hinton gauge on the New. Call (304) 466-0156 for a taped message.

The National Park Service's New River Gorge Visitors Center also provides river levels for the New and Gauley. Call (304) 574-2115.

Gauge readings for the Elk River at Webster Springs can be obtained by calling (304) 847-5532.

THE WATERLINE SERVICE

Waterline is a free, 24-hour phone service covering most of the USGS gauges mentioned in this book. Their figures are continuously updated every few hours, 24 hours a day, 7 days a week. They can be accessed by phone, without a computer. This is very useful when you're on the road.

To get a reading, call (800) 452-1737. This gets you into an automated menu; you then dial the code number of the river gauge you want. You'll get the current reading and a number of prior readings. For more information, call Waterline at (800) 945-3376 or check their website at www.h2oline.com.

Waterline's West Virginia gauge codes are as follows:

The Big Sandy (Preston County)	541155 Parsons
541126 Rockville	541161 Rowlesburg
The Blackwater	Clear Fork
541132 Davis	541161 Clear Fork
Buckhannon River	Coal River
545115 Buckhannon	541164 Tornado
Cheat River	Cranberry
545114 Albright Power Station	541172 Richwood

Waterline's West Virginia gauge codes continued:

Dry Fork of Cheat
  543116 Gladwin
  541183 Hendricks
Elk River
  541213 Frametown
  541199 Queen Shoals
  541212 Webster Springs
Gauley River
  541221 Belva
  541223 Camden on Gauley
  541226 Craigsville
  541225 Summersville
Greenbrier River
  541235 Buckeye
  541237 Hilldale
Guyandotte
  541242 Branchland
  541246 Below Bailey Dam
Kanawha River
  541264 Charleston
  541266 Kanawha Falls
Little Kanawha River
  541296 Burnsville
  541311 Burnsville Dam
  541297 Glenville
  541298 Grantsville
  541299 Palestine

  541281 Wildcat
  541478 West Fork at Rocksdale
Meadow River
  541318 Mt. Lookout
New River
  541337 Hinton
  541338 Thurmond
Potomac River
  545111 Paw Paw
North Branch Potomac
  541331 Luke
  541332 Pinto
  241236 Barnum
  241237 Kitzmiller
South Branch Potomac
  541412 Springfield
Shaver's Fork of the Cheat
  541389 Bemis
Tygart River
  541471 Belington
  541472 Colfax
  541475 Dailey
  541476 Elkins
  541469 Tygart Dam
  541474 Philippi
  541319 the Middle Fork at Audra

Weather Information

They say that if you don't like mountain weather, just wait a minute! Forecasting the weather in West Virginia is often difficult, but there are a number of online resources to help you.

NOAA Rainfall Page for West Virginia;
www.afws.net/states/wv/wv.htm

Know exactly where rain has fallen! Each county has 6 to 24 sites that monitor rainfall. Accumulations for the last 15 minutes, 30 minutes, 1 hour, 3 hours, 6 hours, 12 hours, and 24 hours are displayed here. This is especially useful in the summer, when rainfall can be heavy, but spotty.

National Weather Service for West Virginia;
weather.noaa.gov/weather/wv_cc_us.html

This site provides excellent local forecasts for West Virginia by
county. These are often more accurate for remote mountain areas
than forecasts provided by the commercial services listed below.

Accu-Weather; www.accuweather.com

Intellicast; www.intellicast.com

Weather Underground; www.weatherunderground.com

Finding Your Way in West Virginia

Finding take-outs and put-ins in whitewater country can be difficult for visitors. Secondary roads are not numbered on the official
state road map, and important shuttle roads are not shown.
Topographical maps can be quite helpful for geographical features
but are cumbersome and often outdated. County road maps and
the *Delorme State Topographic Atlas* are the best choice when setting remote shuttles.

Most put-ins and take-outs can be reached with ordinary cars,
providing there is no snow. A few are rather rough, requiring
high-clearance, 4-wheel-drive vehicles. Some roads are privately
owned and permission should always be obtained beforehand.
Occasionally there is no road access at all! Here avid paddlers dis-
cover that their two lower appendages are not as useless as they
thought!

For most of the rivers in this guide we provide a map showing
the shuttle. Under the shuttle directions for each river, federal
highways are prefixed with US as in US 220; major state highways
with WV as in WV 39; and forest service roads with FS as in FS
92. County roads appear with the prefix CR as in CR 6, or they
may appear in quotes as "6." At some intersections you will find
a green sign naming the county, followed by an encircled number,
i.e., Preston 6. This doesn't mean that it is 6 miles to Preston; 6 is
the number of the secondary road, and Preston is the county.

Map Resources

County road maps or USGS topographic maps are useful sup-
plements to the maps in this guide. Each river description gives
the county or counties where the river is located, as well as the

appropriate 7.5 minute (1:24,000 scale) USGS topo maps. The 1:100,000-scale USGS topo maps cover a much wider area and are easier to use, but their 20-meter (75 foot) contour intervals (as opposed to the 20-foot intervals on the 1:24,000 maps) are not as convenient for determining river gradients.

USGS maps may be purchased from the West Virginia Geologic and Economic Survey, PO Box 879, Morgantown, WV 26507-0879; call (304) 594-2331. Their headquarters is in the Mont Chateau building on Cheat Lake. You may also contact the USGS directly: write to Mapping Distribution, USGS Information Services, Box 25286, Building 810, Federal Center, Denver, CO 80225, or call (888) 275-8747. Ask for the index and catalog of topographic and other published maps. USGS topographic maps can also be viewed on the internet at www. topozone.com.

Individual county road maps can be ordered from the West Virginia Department of Transportation Division of Highways, Planning and Research Division, 1900 Kanawha Boulevard East, Building 5, Charleston, WV 25305-0430, or call (304) 558-2868. A book including all West Virginia county road maps is available for $16.85 by mail from County Maps, Puetz Place, N2454 County Road HH, Lindon Station, WI 53944. Phone orders are accepted at (608) 666-3331.

The *Delorme Topographic Atlas for West Virginia* (and for most other states) can be found in many bookstores or ordered at PO Box 298, Yarmouth, ME 04096; call (207) 846-7000; or visit www.delorme.com. Delorme also sells CDs, which allow you to view all the topo maps in the United States on your computer; the 3D *TopoQuads* provide the most detail.

The *Monongahela National Forest Recreation Map* is a topo map detailing roads and trails not shown on state highway or county road maps. It's useful for finding the remoter put-ins in the National Forest or the lands contiguous with it and for locating hiking trails and campsites. For a copy of the map, send $6 to the Forest Supervisor, 200 Sycamore Street, Elkins, WV 26261 (No phone orders, please). You can also purchase copies at their Elkins headquarters, their Cranberry Glades Nature Center, and their Seneca Rocks Discovery Center.

Interacting with Local Residents

Those of us who paddle throughout the United States sometimes encounter problems with local residents. Such hassles are extremely rare in West Virginia. The people of this state are almost

uniformly honest, hard working, and friendly. They view our sport with attitudes ranging from studied indifference to real interest. In many areas rafting has become an important component of the local economy and boaters are welcome. Crime in rural areas is quite rare. Unless you go looking for trouble you're unlikely to find it.

Nonetheless, some advice on etiquette is in order. Changing clothes or relieving oneself in public is unacceptable behavior anywhere; often people see a lot more than you think and they become offended. Usually one end of the shuttle is isolated, and these activities can be performed there without irritating anyone. In populated areas it's wise to utilize public rest rooms and changing areas. Whitewater paddlers sometimes feel pretty rowdy after a good run. Remember that loud, boisterous conduct and public drinking is frowned upon in quiet country towns, so tone down your activities accordingly.

Many secondary roads, even paved ones, are quite narrow and have blind curves. There may be long sections where two cars cannot comfortably pass each other. Paddlers still wired from long drives on interstates or highways often drive secondary roads too fast, terrifying local residents. The kayaks and canoes on your roof clearly identify you as boaters. Because I live along the shuttle road for the Big Sandy, many of my neighbors complain to me about their all-too-close encounters with kayakers. On these roads you should drive under 35 miles per hour and yield to oncoming traffic. The person nearest a wide spot pulls over and allows the other car to pass. Keep an eye out for ATVs on back roads. Often piloted much too fast by kids, they come out of nowhere fast!

Other important issues include river access and parking. If you need to cross private property, ask permission first. Consent is usually given freely, but failure to follow this procedure may result in a parking ticket or vandalism to your vehicle. Never block any road or driveway, even a small dirt track, for any reason. This includes loading and unloading. People live way back in the hills on marginal roads, and your thoughtlessness may cause them substantial inconvenience. When in doubt, ask. You can often find an appropriate space and walk a short distance to the river.

As the river outfitting business has grown, rafting companies have purchased access areas. These facilities are often open to "private" boaters who have the good sense to follow a few rules. Outfitters need considerable space to maneuver their trucks and busses. Their access and parking requirements should be respected, even if that means less convenient parking and a longer walk to the river. It will help to maintain a positive relationship if you assist them with dropped paddles or swimming guests on the

river. During high-use periods there may be traffic jams. Expect delays and be patient. Often a good strategy is to follow a bus or truck to the river; most are radio equipped and move ahead only when the road is clear.

One last thing. Some local boaters run tough whitewater rivers very aggressively. They like to move really fast and run Class 5+ drops without scouting. Before you try to emulate them, remember that these folks make 20 to 50 runs on a given stream each year and they know it extremely well. Let them pass, then continue at your own pace.

Paddling Organizations

AMERICAN WHITEWATER

The mission of American Whitewater (AW) is to conserve and restore America's whitewater resources and enhance opportunities to enjoy them safely. They have a full-time staff of eight that works to protect whitewater every day of the year!

Their activities fall into five main areas:

Education—Through its magazine, *American Whitewater,* and its website, AW provides information and education about whitewater rivers, boating safety, technique, and equipment.

Conservation—AW maintains a complete national inventory of whitewater rivers, monitors threats to those rivers, publishes information on river conservation, provides technical advice to local groups, works with government agencies, and—when necessary—takes legal action to prevent river abuse.

Events—AW organizes sporting events, contests, and festivals to raise funds for river conservation. They run the annual Gauley River Festival in West Virginia, the largest gathering of whitewater boaters in the nation.

Safety—AW promotes paddling safety, publishes reports on whitewater accidents, and maintains both a uniform national rating system for whitewater rivers (the International Scale of Whitewater Difficulty) and an internationally recognized whitewater safety code.

River Access—To assure public access to whitewater rivers AW arranges for river access through private lands by negotiation or purchase, seeks to protect the right of public passage on all rivers and streams navigable by kayak or canoe, and resists unjustified restrictions on government-managed whitewater rivers.

AW Membership is $35 and includes:

•A full year (six issues) of the journal, *American Whitewater*

•A free Safety Code and American Whitewater sticker

•Discounts on paddling gear at selected retailers around the country

•The satisfaction of helping to improve paddling opportunities everywhere.

American Whitewater
1424 Fenwick Lane
Silver Spring, MD 20910
Or join on their website: www.americanwhitewater.org

THE WEST VIRGINIA WILDWATER ASSOCIATION

The West Virginia Wildwater Association (WVWA) was founded in 1965 to promote the use and enjoyment of West Virginia rivers. It has grown from a handful of members into a major recreational and conservation organization. They are dedicated to helping others enjoy, understand, and appreciate the joy of paddling. They sponsor clinics for new boaters throughout the year, schedule trips during the paddling season, and work to keep paddlers aware of conservation and access concerns.

The WVWA holds monthly meetings on the second Tuesday of each month at the Dunbar Public Library at 7 p.m. Their newsletter, *Splashes,* is published six times a year. The WVWA is always looking for new club members and paddling partners.

Please write to:

West Virginia Wildwater Association
PO Box 8413
South Charleston, WV 25303
www.wvanet.net

THE WEST VIRGINIA RIVERS COALITION

The rivers of the Mountain State provide a fabulous paddling playground unparalleled in the East. During the past several years we have seen successes as well as new problems arise for many of our favorite rivers. The threats include:

A 90-acre human and agricultural waste treatment pond located above the Potomac Trough that lacks both leak protection and detection systems.

Channelization and dredging by bulldozers on the North Fork and South Branch of the Potomac, Red Creek, and Seneca Creek.

Mining impacts on the Blackwater, Tygart, Cheat, Tug, and Big Sandy rivers.

Nitrogen and fecal contamination in the Potomac watershed due to industrial poultry farming.

Superhighway construction in progress that will have devastating impacts on the pristine headwaters of the Cheat, Potomac, and Cacapon rivers.

Mountaintop removal projects that have buried over 1,000 miles of headwater streams in West Virginia, and unsafe coal slurry ponds that threaten population centers and water quality.

A newly proposed power plant and surface mine in Upshur County that will send AMD (acid mine drainage) into the Middle Fork and Buckhannon rivers and sulfur dioxide into the Monongahela National Forest.

To respond effectively to these and other issues, in 1989 paddlers formed the West Virginia Rivers Coalition (WVRC). WVRC has grown to 2,800 members and provides assistance to over 90 watershed groups statewide. Three full-time employees and three part-time employees concerned with the state's rivers and streams now staff the office in Elkins, West Virginia.

WVRC has worked hard to promote permanent protection for 13 classic whitewater streams in the Monongahela National Forest under the Wild and Scenic Rivers Act. The US Forest Service has agreed that all of the streams fit the criteria for protection. Currently these nominated rivers receive Wild and Scenic protection; WVRC awaits a political climate receptive to full Wild and Scenic designation.

Since 1998 WVRC has drawn attention to West Virginia's compliance with the Federal Clean Water Act and has implemented change using the CWA as a tool to comment on pollution discharge permits and to question surface mining practices. Other projects include:

Stopping agricultural waste from entering Potomac headwaters.

Monitoring state and federal agencies that permit road construction, valley fills, and mining.

Advocating for state rivers to be maintained for high drinking water standards and trout habitat.

Advocating expansion of the Gauley National Recreation Area to include a midcanyon access point, and providing a shuttle to private boaters as an interim solution.

To succeed with these and other projects, WVRC needs the support of paddlers who enjoy and appreciate West Virginia streams. Membership is $25 and includes a bumper sticker, quarterly newsletter, and the option of an e-mail listserve alert to keep you aware of threats to your favorite rivers. To join, write to West Virginia Rivers Coalition, 801 North Randolph Avenue, Elkins, West Virginia 26241, or call (304) 637-7201.

Check out the WVRC website and its boater-friendly resources at www.wvrivers.org.

part**One**

GEORGE WASHINGTON'S RIVER AND
ITS TRIBUTARIES: THE POTOMAC DRAINAGE

Of all the rivers in West Virginia, the mighty Potomac and its tributaries are by far the most historic. Sometimes referred to as the Nation's River, the Potomac witnessed and was a central factor in our country's birth and early growth. Much of the upper drainage remains almost the same as it was in George Washington's day. It's a watershed of outstanding beauty that offers a great variety of whitewater adventures. It's truly canoe and kayak country at its best.

Immense cliffs and rock formations characterize most of the headwaters of the Potomac, especially the Cacapon and the South Branch tributaries. They provide some of the most breathtaking scenery in West Virginia. Caudy's Castle, Royal Glen or Petersburg Gap, Seneca, Eagle, and Champe Rocks are, of course, known well enough to have their own names, but there aren't enough names in the book to give to all such formations, many of which can only be seen by the whitewater paddler. Underground rivers have eroded the sedimentary limestone layers of the South Branch highlands for centuries, creating a spelunker's bonanza underground. These caves contain as much variety, beauty, and challenge as that offered to the paddlers and rock climbers above ground. Smoke Hole and Seneca Caverns are, well known to the public, but Cave Mountain, Schoolhouse, Hell Hole, and the like are examples of caves known intimately only by the skilled spelunker. Few areas in the country can boast that they look as good below the ground as above.

The main stem of the Potomac is formed near Green Spring, West Virginia where its two major branches join. Here the beautiful water of the South Branch, straight from the mountains of Highland County, Virginia, meets the ugly, acid-polluted water of the North Branch, coming from where the southwestern tip of Maryland cuts into West Virginia. Later on, near Berkeley Springs, the Potomac picks up the Cacapon system, and then a little farther, it merges with the Shenandoah to form West Virginia's easternmost tip, Harper's Ferry.

The North Branch has a long history of degradation. The area saw some of the worst clear-cutting and strip mining in the state,

and highly visible scars remain. Air pollution from the Westvaco paper mill in Luke, Maryland killed all the vegetation on a near-by mountainside, and its disgusting sulfur smell carried for miles! But while not pristine, the river has recovered somewhat. A pollution abatement program at the paper mill, combined with the demise of a number of large factories in the Cumberland area, has improved air and water quality significantly. Trees are returning to the formerly dead mountainsides. The Luke mill is not in full compliance yet, and the American Canoe Association has filed suit to bring them into line.

Although upper headwaters of the North Branch are badly polluted with silt and acid, the section just downstream of Jennings Randolph Lake and Dam actually supports trout. The scenery can be pretty and even striking, but many of the towns are poor and worn down. Charles Morrison wrote: "Some scars of . . . early industrialization are still to be found along the North Branch. The by-products of modern industry—air and water pollution and defacement of the land—are more evident along the North Branch than anywhere else in the valleys of the Potomac. But there is a danger in other parts of the Valley as well. Either we will cherish the 'Cradle of the Republic' as Gutheim called it, or we let it become stifled by the refuse of unplanned and uncontrolled exploitation."

The South Branch can be thought of as a collection of three main tributaries—the South Branch proper, the North Fork, and the South Fork or Moorefield River. The distance separating the two streams farthest from each other at potential put-ins (Circleville and Fort Seybert) is only 17 miles. Each stream rests in its own beautiful valley separated from its neighbor by a single high mountain ridge. All begin as clear, cold trout streams, gradually drawing warmth from the South Branch Valley. When they reach the area below Petersburg and Moorefield, they mingle to form some of the finest warm-water fishing in the eastern United States. Bald eagles feed on the fish and are commonly seen in the Trough, Smoke Hole, and Hopeville canyons. Waste from factory farming along the South Branch, especially gigantic chicken farms, is a serious and growing threat. The West Virginia Rivers Coalition worked hard to stop a 90-acre chicken-manure lagoon and spray field near Moorefield.

Because the early explorations of this area followed the rivers, the Potomac tributaries have seen much history. Early settlers traced them in their quest for freedom and independence. George Washington himself helped to explore the area; at age 16, he placed the Fairfax Stone near the southwest corner of Maryland to mark the boundary between the Potomac and Ohio

drainage. His later disregard for this marker, which separated French and British interests, led to the ambush at Jumonville Glen that started the French and Indian War. After the revolution the Potomac became a main transportation route for people and goods. The Chesapeake and Ohio (C&O) Canal operated until surprisingly recent times. Political boundaries were often drawn at the rivers themselves or at the edge of watersheds. Washington spent much time and effort trying to find a way to connect the Potomac and Ohio River basins by waterways. He did not succeed, but what he learned from his travels and recorded in his journals influenced many subsequent events.

Little action from the French and Indian or Revolutionary Wars actually penetrated the Potomac Highlands due to the transportation difficulties, but a few sites are memorable. Chief among these is Old Fields, just north of Moorefield near the head of the Trough. Here American Indians first burned away the forest to form fields. One of the first white settlements in the area was annihilated in 1756 in an American Indian battle. Old Fields later became an important stop on various transportation routes, situated as it was on the South Branch and also at the intersection of the Seneca Trail and McCullough's Path, two of West Virginia's earliest highways. Several frontier defense forts were located in this area. In addition to Fort Pleasant at Old Fields, there were some 30 others, 2 of which, Fort Ashby and Fort Seybert, still exist in whitewater country. Terrible massacres of whites led by Killbuck and his warriors occurred within 24 hours of each other, at Fort Seybert and at Upper Tract.

The Civil War probably started in Harper's Ferry, where a national park displays some of the original buildings and fortifications near the mouth of the Shenandoah. This would make an interesting lunch stop, but (to alleviate congestion) the Park Service has barred all river travelers from landing here. Although no major Civil War battles were actually fought along the Potomac, sectionalism tore the highlands apart politically and militarily. There were a few memorable "minor" skirmishes. Romney, for example, changed hands 56 times, and there were wild chases through Franklin and Old Fields. Fort Mulligan, located high above the river just west of Petersburg, was occupied by northern troops. The trenches and gun emplacements are still visible, with a water tank of more recent vintage squarely within the outline of the fort. Keyser, then called New Creek (they should have left it that way), was an important outpost, as was Moorefield. Saltpeter, an important component of gunpowder, was mined in Cave Mountain in the Smoke Hole. Moorefield keeps some of this heritage alive in late September, when many of the antebellum homes in the area are opened for public display.

A number of camping areas exist in the area, but aside from Big Bend, few are near rivers. The 1985 flood destroyed campgrounds at Seneca Creek and Smoke Hole. The rest of the land is either privately owned or inaccessible. Camping can be found along the Savage River in Maryland and near Jennings Randolph Lake on the North Branch.

Potomac streams are known throughout the East for fine bass and trout fishing. Suckers, muskies, bluegills, redeyes, and fallfish are commonly caught. The Shenandoah is well known for its many different species of catfish. All of the lower Potomac and the Cacapon also produce eels. The forest communities and the prevalence of pulpwood production on family farms help sustain a large population of deer and wild turkey. Hunter success is very high for these animals. A large number of squirrels live in the abundant oak forests. The black bear finds refuge in the high, isolated areas, such as North Fork Mountain, but a paddler is not likely to see one. Beaver and muskrats are common, especially along the Moorefield and Cacapon Rivers. Being close to the Atlantic flyway, an impressive variety and number of waterfowl can be seen. The shale barrens of the Panhandle contain unusual plant communities—perhaps the most unique member of which is the prickly pear cactus, a plant well adapted to the summer droughts common to this area. The Panhandle is well known for its apple orchards, grazing, and poultry productions. Most of the farms are well kept and attractive. But as you near Washington, DC, the farms begin to give way to rapacious suburban development—a real threat to the lower river.

Few dams exist on the Potomac. Among the most interesting are those built below Cumberland on the Potomac for maintenance of the famous C&O Canal. Begun in 1828 and completed in 1850, the system consisted of 74 locks, which had to lift or lower a mule-drawn barge a total of 605 feet. The barges moved at only 2 mph, or slower than a canoe against the wind, so it was a rather leisurely form of transportation. The canal actually ran until 1924, and many of these dams still impound water. There are power company dams on the Shenandoah above Millville, on the Potomac below Williamsport, on the Stony River in Mount Storm, and on the Cacapon near its mouth. There are also several dams on the North Branch in the Cumberland area. Jennings Randolph Lake, a USCOE project on the North Branch of the Potomac, creates a sizeable reservoir. Conservationists predicted an environmental disaster here which, fortunately, failed to materialize. Acid runoff actually settles out in here, and the water quality of the lake and outflow is good. Paddlers now enjoy weekend releases from the dam in the spring and early summer.

NORTH BRANCH OF THE POTOMAC RIVER

The North Branch defines the border between Maryland and West Virginia until its confluence with the South Branch in Old Town, creating the main branch of the Potomac River. This branch of the Potomac has something for all levels of paddlers, a long Class-4+ run, a delightful Class 2–3 trip, and a mostly swift-water paddle that has beautiful scenery mixed in with more developed areas, including the industrial city of Cumberland.

MAPS: USGS: Davis, Table Rock, Gorman, Mount Storm, Kitzmiller, Westernport, Keyser, Lonaconing, Cresapstown, Cumberland, Pattison Creek, Old Town (USGS); Grant, Mineral, Hampshire (County); Maryland and West Virginia State Road Maps.

CLASS	1–3
LENGTH	9
TIME	2
GRADIENT	40
VOLUME	159
GAUGE	PHONE
LEVEL	4.8–7 FT. (KITZMILLER)
FLOW	FREE FLOWING
SOLITUDE	A
SCENERY	B

A — HENRY TO STEYER

DESCRIPTION: This run starts in the shadow of Fairfax Stone, a historic survey mark that divides Maryland and the Old Dominion and indicates the farthest headwaters of the Potomac. This section is an easy run with only one good whitewater section about 1 mile below Wilson. Look for a 6-foot slide.

SHUTTLE: WV 90 parallels the run.

GAUGE: The Kitzmiller gauge is 13 miles downstream. It must be unusually high for this little headwater run. Call (703) 260-0305. You'll need a reading between 4.8–7 feet to be runable.

CLASS	3–4
LENGTH	13
TIME	4
GAUGE	PHONE
LEVEL	4–8 FT. + AT KITZMILLER
FLOW	FREE FLOWING
GRADIENT	51
VOLUME	159
SOLITUDE	A
SCENERY	A–C

B — STEYER TO SHALMAR

DESCRIPTION: Yee-hah! This is one of the longest and most continuously difficult runs in this part of the country. It descends rather steeply for its size, which accounts for the constant rapids, turbulent drops, and excellent action. The water is polluted with mine acids, usually muddy from the surrounding strip mines, and isn't much to look at. The scenery is mostly beautiful until you reach the garbage-laden banks, unpainted houses, and barren strip mines near Kitzmiller.

This is the ledgiest river you will ever encounter, and there must be at least a thousand hydraulics. The first mile below

Steyer is a very peaceful descent over Class 1–2 rapids. Every once in a while, a rather juicy drop through a narrow channel dampens your navel, until, without much warning, you are into it up to your eyeballs, and you realize that the gradient is really picking up. Almost all of the rapids have at least one ledge, usually made more complicated by sinister turbulence. It is very narrow and rocky all the way to the mouth of the Stony, where the volume of the river typically doubles.

A half-mile beyond the mouth of the Stony below a railroad bridge is the first in a series of really big drops. After this the river broadens into a continuous series of open, haystack-filled rapids. But then the river narrows and the rapids become more difficult. Padded boulders, powerful souse holes, and difficult crosscurrents add spice to the run. This continues for mile after mile. You'll rarely encounter a stretch of quiet water longer than 50 yards.

The North Branch of the Potomac flooded badly in 1985. This didn't change the big ledges, but the entire riverbed was badly scoured. Several miles of railroad track were undermined or washed away entirely, and bulldozers were driven in the river to repair the damage. Some drops, particularly those around islands, are still unstable. Many are steep, rocky, and choked with debris. Caution is advised.

DIFFICULTIES: Run the first island below Steyer on the right; it contains a nice drop into a hole. The left side of the second island leads to the horseshoe-shaped Corkscrew Ledge, made for entering left of center, heading right. This is scoutable from river left. At low water, the river channels to the right of the island into a fairly big but punchable hydraulic. From here on to the mouth of the Stony, the river is continuously ledgy. In high water it gets pushy and the holes get pretty mean.

A half-mile below the Stony, a railroad bridge marks the first of three 5–6-foot ledges which occur within the next half-mile. The first is called Rattlesnake Ledge, and you'll see its namesake on warm, sunny days. It's the most complex of the three big drops but is easily scouted on the left. Once you enter left of center, move farther left to skirt a roostertail, and avoid Lady Kenmore Hole on the bottom. At 4.8 feet on the Kitzmiller gauge, an alternate route opens up on the right. The second ledge is the steepest, but it's just a straight shot down the center into a big wave. The third ledge has a jagged, complicated route down the far right side. At low levels this has been run far left with a turn to the right. Take time to scout, especially at high water. Over 5.5 feet, the holes become beefy, and keepers appear above 6.5 feet. A bit below here, an innocuous set of ledges lures the unwary paddler into several ledge holes. Sneak on the right.

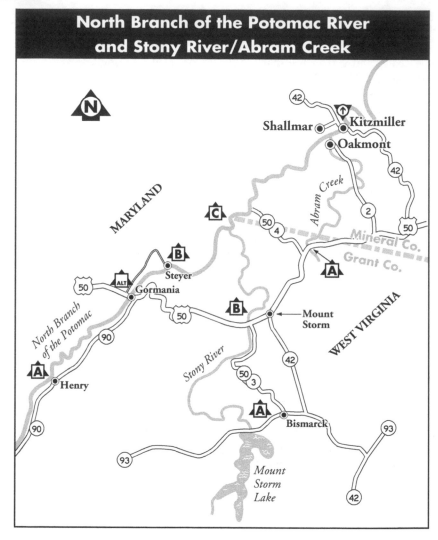

North Branch of the Potomac River and Stony River/Abram Creek

A little more than 9 miles into the run, the remains of a concrete bridge stand in the river. Run far left. Below here, a tall, sheer rock cliff marks the rapids just downstream, appropriately named Maytag for the number of paddlers who have experienced an extended rinse cycle here. The rapid consists of a set of powerful holes is followed by a series of large, offset breaking waves. Scout to pick the best route, but a run to the far left misses the holes.

The whole run is long and challenging. You will be working every minute. This is one of the coldest areas in the state, and the icy, cold conditions that often accompany high water are very

taxing. It's not a good river to test out intermediates because there are no midway take-outs—only a long walk along the railroad tracks. Paddlers in the party should be competent and capable of taking care of themselves.

SHUTTLE: The put-in can be reached from US 50 at Gormania by taking a dirt road down the Maryland side of the river for 2 miles to Steyer. A put-in can also be made on the Stony River at the US 50 bridge (see section B of Stony River below). To reach the take-out, travel east on US 50, pick up WV 42 at Elk Gardens and drive to the bridge in Kitzmiller, Maryland. To save 2 miles of less interesting whitewater at the end, drive upstream from Kitzmiller, on river left, to the old mining community of Shallmar, Maryland. This is opposite where Abram Creek joins the North Branch on river right.

GAUGE: Call the Baltimore-Washington office of the National Weather Service (703) 260-0305 for a reading, updated twice a day (late morning and early evening). This is a Class 3–4 run up to about from 4.7 to 5.5 feet, becoming solid big-water Class 4+ from 5.5 to 6.5 feet.

BARNUM TO BLOOMINGTON, MARYLAND

CLASS	I –3
LENGTH	8.2
TIME	3
GAUGE	PHONE
LEVEL	OVER 4OO CFS
FLOW	DAM RELEASE
GRADIENT	38
VOLUME	I 59
SOLITUDE	B–C
SCENERY	A–D

DESCRIPTION: Before the dam was built, the run from Kitzmiller to Bloomington offered almost 17 miles of fast intermediate whitewater. When the dam went up in the late 1970s, the water quality in both the lake and river below actually improved. The strip mine and railroad-bed scars are healing nicely, giving the lake and river an attractive appearance except at the put-in and take-out.

The run below Kitzmiller is now broken up into several shorter sections. There's roughly 3 miles of interesting Class 3 upstream above the headwaters of Jennings Randolph Lake, but then it's 5.5 miles of flatwater to the nearest access point: the Howell Branch Launch Area. Portaging the dam would be very strenuous! The next 1.5 miles of rapids can only be reached this way, because the road to the dam tailwaters is not open to the public. That brings us to Barnum, the start of this trip.

The stretch from Barnum to Bloomington is a delightful Class 2–3 run. Most rapids are cobble bars, with a few ledges thrown in for variety. One ledge, found at the end of a series of islands halfway through the run, creates a surprisingly deep and nasty

hole that catches many boaters off guard. So watch out! Scheduled water releases, strongly supported by local business interests, have become quite popular. They happen each year on weekends in April and May.

DIFFICULTIES: Aside from the above mentioned ledge, the biggest risk comes from the fast-moving, aggressively driven coal and lumber trucks and the huge clouds of dust found on the steep, potholed shuttle road.

SHUTTLE: Barnum can be reached by a winding dirt road from WV 46. The usual take-out is at 135 near the mouth of the Savage River or on WV 46 at the Potomac River Bridge. Both of these roads are heavily used by coal and logging trucks, so stay alert. Take out above the mouth of the Savage River at the Bloomington Park/Treatment Plant on Hammil Avenue. There is also a small parking area just downstream of the Savage on river left.

GAUGE: Normally the USCOE conserves lake water, releasing it gradually for downstream needs. Their normal flows are less than 400 cfs, the minimum needed for paddling. A series of four weekend releases are scheduled for April and May, and there are periodic "flushes" to improve downstream water quality. These 900–1,200 cfs flows raise the river to a very enjoyable level. Daily flows are available from the Baltimore Office of the USCOE, (410) 962-7687, or from the Jennings Randolph Dam, (304) 355-2346, from 7 a.m.–4:30 p.m. on weekdays. The Barnum Gauge, available online, also shows this flow.

CLASS	1–2
LENGTH	8
TIME	3
GAUGE	PHONE
LEVEL	3.5
FLOW	NATURAL & DAM RELEASE
GRADIENT	22
VOLUME	MEDIUM
SOLITUDE	A–B
SCENERY	B–C

BLOOMINGTON TO THE RT. 220 BRIDGE S. OF KEYSER

DESCRIPTION: This is a pleasant Class-2 run. All the rapids are straightforward, unobstructed descents over cobble-bar rapids with a few low ledges thrown in for variety. Occasionally the river is split by islands, creating enjoyable wave trains at higher levels. The right channel of an island near Westernport contains a "surprise hole" similar in size to those found on the Barnum run. Below here, the North Branch cuts a deep valley through Dan's Mountain. The scenery, which is rather industrial through Luke and Westernport, improves just downstream and stays nice all the way to Keyser. The scenery starts to deteriorate again near Keyser,

but there's no easy take-out until the Route 220 Bridge is reached.

DIFFICULTIES: A half mile below the mouth of the Savage River the immense Westvaco Paper Mill sprawls along both sides of the river for over a mile. It's an impressive example of large-scale industry and is fascinating to see from the water. Don't gawk until you spot the horizon line of a low-head dam. There's a short, miserable portage on the right. The paper mill smell, while much improved, is very noticeable. The water, formerly an emerald green, deteriorates noticeably below here. This is courtesy of the Westernport sewage treatment plant and the Westvaco paper mill.

SHUTTLE: From the water plant in Bloomington, MD, drive down Rt. 135 towards Keyser. At McCool, MD, turn south on US 220, crossing the North Branch to Keyser, WV. After crossing the bridge, turn left on WV 46 and drive back through a residential area towards the 220 bridge. The take-out is just beneath it.

GAUGE: This section is often up even when dams on the Potomac and Savage River are not releasing much. The Luke, MD, gauge available on the USGS website, should read between 400 and 2,000 cfs. The Pinto gauge should read 3 feet or more. If the level is over 1,200 cfs, you can make the run in conjunction with a recreational release from Jennings Randolph Lake in about 2 hours.

KEYSER, WV TO PINTO, MD

CLASS	A–1
LENGTH	8
TIME	2.5
GAUGE	PHONE
LEVEL	3.5
FLOW	NATURAL & DAM RELEASE
GRADIENT	9
VOLUME	MEDIUM
SOLITUDE	A
SCENERY	A

DESCRIPTION: This section has become a very desirable novice run ever since air and water quality downstream of the Westvaco Paper Mill improved. The river winds gracefully through an unspoiled valley decorated with gorgeous shale cliffs. The current here is steady, but the rapids are mostly Class-1 gravel bars.

SHUTTLE: From Keyser, drive North on 220. The easiest take-out is at an old bridge site just upstream of the Route 9 bridge, which has rather steep banks. Turn off 220 about a half-mile past the Rt. 9 turnoff, and go about 0.25 miles to a dead end.

GAUGE: This section is often up even when dams on the Potomac and Savage River are not releasing much. The gauge in Pinto, MD, available on the USGS website, should read 3 feet or more.

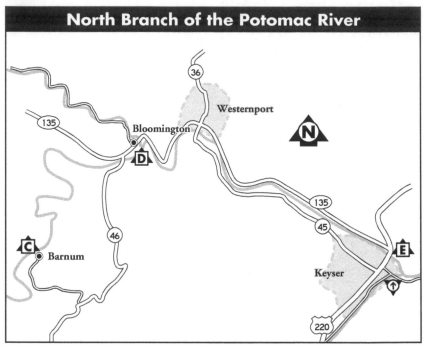

North Branch of the Potomac River

CLASS	A–1
GRADIENT	4
VOLUME	MEDIUM
LENGTH	30.5
TIME	2 DAYS
GAUGE	WEB
LEVEL	2.8+
AT PINTO, MD	
FLOW	DAMS & NATURAL
SOLITUDE	A
SCENERY	A–D

PINTO, MD TO OLD TOWN, MD

DESCRIPTION: This section contains the good, the bad, and the ugly. It gets off to a good start, passing more high cliffs before running into the visual blight of downtown Cumberland. There's a 5-foot (runable) rubble dam at the old Celanese plant, and below here the area starts to get built. The pools get longer and the riffles shorter. The river through Cumberland has been channelized for flood control, and there's a 15-foot-high dam under a bridge that must be carried on the right. Below Cumberland, the river is very wide and becomes shallow and tedious in low water. Below Wiley Ford, the river flows into nice country once again. It is mostly flat except for a 3-foot high dam. Take out on the South Branch of the Potomac just above its mouth.

SHUTTLE: There are a number of possible put-ins in both Maryland and West Virginia. To get to the take-out, take the toll bridge from Old Town, MD. Into West Virginia, pass under the

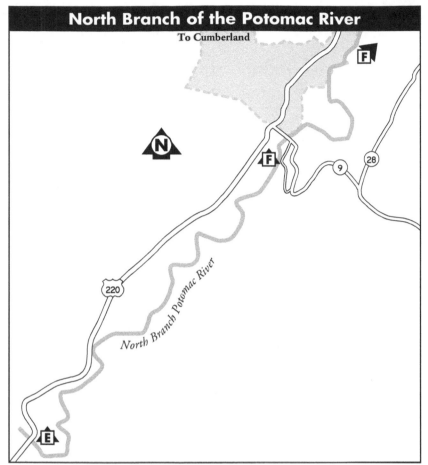

North Branch of the Potomac River

To Cumberland

railroad, and turn left on Arnold Stickley Road. It's about 1.5 miles to the South Branch, just above its mouth.

GAUGE: This section of the river is usually "up" in summer except during prolonged dry spells. Check the USGS website for a reading at Pinto, MD, of over 2.8 feet.

STONY RIVER

The upper section of the Stony River is a small creek. Like the Cheat and the Savage, the lower section of the Stony is well named. In addition to a constant, steep gradient, many boulders and ledges require

paddlers to constantly maneuver. You'll need plenty of water to make this run.

MAPS: Mount Storm Lake, Gorman, Mount Storm, Kitzmiller (USGS); Grant, Mineral (County)

CLASS	2–4
GRADIENT	7 l
VOLUME	83
LENGTH	7.6
TIME	3
GAUGE	PHONE
LEVEL	6 FT.+ AT KITZMILLER
FLOW	DAM
SOLITUDE	A
SCENERY	A

VIRGINIA POWER DAM TO US 50

DESCRIPTION: The river starts in a fairly easy manner but picks up to Class-4 action in the middle of the run. The rapids are steep, boulder-strewn, and often blind. Then the gradient evens out, and rapids become longer and less severe toward US 50.

DIFFICULTIES: Precise boat control is needed in many of the steeper, more congested rapids. Also, the small size of this stream demands constant vigilance for fallen trees.

SHUTTLE: Take the road to Bismarck "50/3" leading from the bridge and drive to WV 93. Turn right and drive to the sluice at the Virginia Power dam. It's a long, steep carry from the road down to the put-in on the right side of the sluice. Put in on the pool below the turbulence. Take out at the US 50 bridge.

GAUGE: None. Examine the water at the put-in and take-out. You'll probably need over 5.5 feet at Kitzmiller to have a good chance at this run.

CLASS	3+–4
LENGTH	6
TIME	2
GAUGE	PHONE
LEVEL	5 FT.+ AT KITZMILLER
FLOW	DAM
GRADIENT	76
VOLUME	83
SOLITUDE	A
SCENERY	A

US 50 TO NORTH BRANCH OF THE POTOMAC

DESCRIPTION: Beginning placidly at the US 50 bridge, this little brawler heads downhill fast. Not only is the gradient steep throughout with no slack water, but also the maneuvering among boulders, over ledges, and through complicated drops is extremely difficult and physically taxing. At low water, the maneuvering is extreme and the run somewhat easier. High water makes the maneuvering easier, but the rapids get turbulent and very pushy (at anything but the lowest water levels). This is a much harder run than the upper section. Although the river passes pleasant woods, high cliffs, and picturesque falls, it also runs through strip mines, spoil piles, and mine dumps. The water is clear but polluted with mine acids.

DIFFICULTIES: The whole cotton-picking run is hard! The Class-4 designation relates more to constant, intricate maneuvering in low water, but many of the drops get nasty at high flows. Mining and timbering activity have pushed numerous trees into the river, creating hazards that led to the death of a kayaker, so stay sharp. There are several vigorous drops as you approach the North Branch. Just above the junction, there's a steep sliding ledge that must be run down the center through several large holes. Sneaking on either side results in pitoning.

SHUTTLE: Put in under US 50 bridge. A take-out can be reached by turning north on the "Kuhn Mine Road" (US 50/4) just east of Mount Storm. This hard road eventually splits. Keep to the left to avoid ending up in a strip mine. The last mile of road is bad for low-clearance vehicles. Take out just above the falls and bridge. Most paddlers prefer to combine this trip with a run on the best part of the North Branch down to Kitzmiller, Maryland, 2 hours and 9 miles downstream.

GAUGE: None. Examine the water at the Rt. 50 put-in. The Kitzmiller gauge on the Potomac should be at least 5 feet

Burrell on Growth

The thing that annoys me is the unquestioned premise that whitewater sport has to grow. The hell it does. I like it the way it is. As a matter of fact what attracted me to the sport in the first place was that it was something that few people did. Since our sport was sort of far out and takes a lot of effort to learn and get in to, it attracts a very interesting type of person. If you are a river rat, you can't help but notice a certain flair for the cuckoo, the nut, and the joker that seems to permeate our members. Do you think it would be this way if the sport were too easy, if it were "in," if it were the thing to do? Look what happened to skiing and camping. Manufacturers, hucksters, and gadgeteers have ruined both sports. Where once they attracted independent, do-it-yourself, pioneering types, now both are over populated with people with no inherent interest in the sport or the out-of-doors, and the ski slopes and camp grounds are overpopulated and either outrageously expensive or grossly overused.

Can't the mess we are in today largely be a product of the let's make more, let's make it bigger, let's get more members, let's raise the Gross National Product, let's dig more coal, burn more electricity, build bigger dams, make bigger reservoirs syndrome? These are all symptoms of our national psyche which once viewed nature as a formidable object, which must be conquered and subdued in order for us to grow, grow, grow. Let's make it difficult for new members to join. Insult them, throw rocks at them, drill holes in their hulls—anybody that survives is bound to be interested and have a great sense of humor! Who cares if we have the smallest whitewater club in the world as long as it is made up of the best people. 'Nuff said.

Bob Burrell

Reprinted from West Virginia Wildwater Association
Splashes, November 1971.

ABRAM CREEK

This is one exciting little stream. It's hard to catch up, and when it is up, everything else is screaming. The scenery alternates between pleasant woods and coal mines, haul roads, railroad tracks, and old houses.

MAPS: Mount Storm, Kitzmiller (USGS); Grant, Mineral (County)

CLASS	2–4+
LENGTH	8.5
TIME	3
GAUGE	Visual
LEVEL	6.5 at Kitzmiller
FLOW	Free Flowing
GRADIENT	47 (1 @ 110)
VOLUME	60
SOLITUDE	A
SCENERY	A–D

US 50 to Shallmar

DESCRIPTION: The first mile is the hardest part and compares with such streams as the Upper Yough and the Lower Stony. It starts off fast below US 50, moving into a 1-mile stretch with a 110 fpm gradient. There are no big drops here, but it's good Class 4+ and plenty of maneuvering is required. Most of the middle section is milder (up to Class 3+), but at low levels the rapids are complex and require constant attention. This part is actually easier with more water. There is also a low-water bridge in the middle of a rapid, which must be portaged.

In the last mile, there's much less maneuvering around boulders and more big waves and complex currents. Toward the end, watch for the coal mine on the left bank. One or two rapids below here there's a big sliding ledge, a last drop into the Potomac that's visible from the take-out in Shallmar. Most people will need to scout this.

SHUTTLE: Put in at the US 50 bridge east of Mount Storm. To preview the creek on the way to the take-out, go east on US 50 for 3 miles, turn left to Emoryville, and follow the creek through Oakmont to a railroad fork at the mouth. Or you can simply drive to Kitzmiller, then up the river to Shallmar.

GAUGE: None. One paddler reported plenty of water when the river was even with the top of the base of the concrete abutment at US 50. Inspection here and at the take-out should give you a good idea of what's happening. The North Branch of the Potomac needs to be running close to 6.5 feet for this creek to be up. Call the Baltimore-Washington office of the National Weather Service at (703) 260-0305 for this reading.

OTHER STREAMS OF THE NORTH BRANCH OF THE POTOMAC RIVER

NEW CREEK

Don't hold your breath on this one! This may be about the absolute lower limit as far as size goes. When there is enough water on this tiny stream to float a boat, everything else has to be in flood stage.

MAPS: Antioch, Westernport, Keyser (USGS); Mineral (County)

NEW CREEK

CLASS	1–2
LENGTH	9
TIME	3
GAUGE	VISUAL
LEVEL	NA
FLOW	FREE FLOWING
GRADIENT	NA
VOLUME	VS
SOLITUDE	A
SCENERY	A

DESCRIPTION: It's a straightforward Class 1–2 stream following major highways through a largely pastoral setting. Other than the usual mundane stream difficulties, there are two low-water bridges and a 3-foot dam at the Keyser Water Works.

SHUTTLE: Put in near the intersection of WV 93 and US 50 or anywhere else upstream or downstream, as the highway is always nearby. Take-out on US 220 in Keyser near the Potomac State campus.

GAUGE: None. Inspect the level on site. This is a very small stream that's only runable during high-water periods.

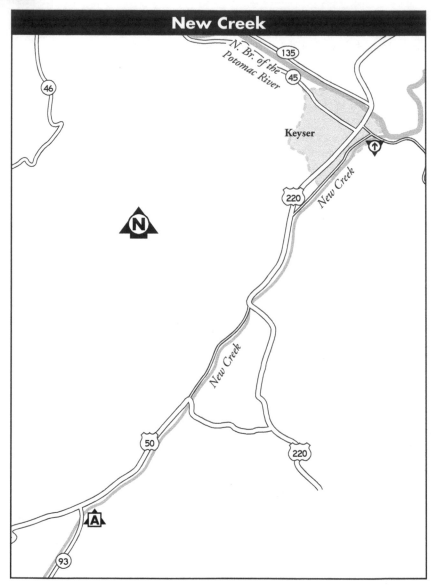

PATTERSON CREEK

This is an interesting stream passing through a very fertile, historic valley. It has been inhabited for centuries, and a wealth of American Indian artifacts may still be collected in the area. It is one of the richest areas of the state for game; deer, squirrels, and wild turkey are especially plentiful. The small stream is also a great bass fishery and, surprisingly, contains muskies.

MAPS: Burlington, Headsville, Cresaptown, Patterson Creek (USGS); Grant, Mineral (County)

BURLINGTON TO THE NORTH BRANCH OF THE POTOMAC

CLASS	I
LENGTH	23
TIME	5
GAUGE	VISUAL
LEVEL	NA
FLOW	FREE FLOWING/DAM
GRADIENT	NA
VOLUME	S
SOLITUDE	A
SCENERY	A

DESCRIPTION: Patterson Creek is runable only when everything else is up, but the riffles do not add up to any particular difficulty. As usual, fences, dangling wires, etc., must be considered. A potentially interesting open-boat run could be made at high water between Burlington on US 50 and Fort Ashby at the intersection of WV 46 and WV 28, a distance of about 18 miles. It is another 5 miles to its mouth on the North Branch. There is a 4-foot dam just above WV 28 that is runable on the left, and a second 2-foot-high dam about 2 miles downstream.

GAUGE: None. It's runable during high-water periods.

NORTH FORK OF PATTERSON CREEK

THROUGH GREENLAND GAP

CLASS	I-2
LENGTH	6.5MI.
TIME	2
GAUGE	VISUAL
LEVEL	NA
FLOW	FREE FLOWING
GRADIENT	70
VOLUME	VS
SOLITUDE	A
SCENERY	A

MAPS: Greenland Gap (USGS); Grant (County)

DESCRIPTION: The North Fork of Patterson Creek is very tiny, but at high water it affords a fast Class 2+ run through Greenland Gap. The put-in is at a gravel pit above the Gap. Below here the stream rushes continuously over ledges and boulders. Not surprisingly, trees could be a hazard here. There is a falls where the rock anticline of the Gap dips to the river. (Visible from the road through the Gap.) Take out 50 yards above, carry on the road, and put in at the bridge below. Below the Gap, the river rushes over almost continuous gravel rapids through a beautiful pastoral valley. Besides many fences, there is a Soil Conservation Service impoundment just above the confluence with Patterson Creek. End your trip above the dam (6.5 miles from the put-in) unless you plan to continue down Patterson Creek.

SHUTTLE: WV 42 runs north between Petersburg and Mount Storm. At the town of Scherr, turn onto CR3-3 towards Greenland, which leads through the gap. Drive through to the take-out.

GAUGE: None. Inspect on site. You'll need lots of water to run this steep, tiny stream.

SOUTH BRANCH OF THE POTOMAC RIVER

The South Branch starts just inside Virginia with the confluence of Straight Creek and the East Branch Potomac River. From here, the water drifts, rumbles, and rolls for 130+ miles to its confluence with the North Branch of the Potomac.

MAPS: Moatstown, Sugar Grove, Franklin, Upper Tract, Hopeville, Petersburg West, Petersburg East, Rig, Moorefield, Old Fields, Sector, Romney, Augusta, Springfield, Headsville, Levels, Oldtown (USGS); Pendleton, Grant, Hardy, Hampshire (County); Monongahela National Forest Map

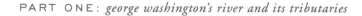

CLASS	1−2
LENGTH	30+
TIME	2−3 DAYS
GAUGE	PHONE
LEVEL	4 FT. + AT PETERSBURG
FLOW	FREE FLOWING/DAM
GRADIENT	NA
VOLUME	S
SOLITUDE	A
SCENERY	B

ABOVE THE US 220 BRIDGE NEAR UPPER TRACT

DESCRIPTION: Both Strait Creek and the East Branch Potomac River, which create the South Branch, are navigable by radical paddlers willing to portage dozens of fences, but reasonable boaters start at the forks. En route to Thorn Creek, the stream is fairly busy, dropping gently over gravel bars, rock gardens, and a few ledges. At low levels, boats may scrape a few diagonal gravel bars. The pools are short. You will encounter several fences and a few low-water bridges. The river flows through a pretty, rural valley with many old houses and farm structures. From Thorn Creek to US 220, there are four low-water bridges and two fences. There's a beautiful short canyon called "River Gap" just below Franklin. Watch out for an old washed-out dam in the canyon. There's a 5-foot dam just below the canyon, which should be carried. From this point on there are still many riffles, though the pools are longer. Franklin is an extremely attractive rural town with splendid overnight and eating facilities. It is the spelunking capital of West Virginia.

GAUGE: The minimum level is about 4 feet on the Petersburg gauge, 3 feet at Franklin. From Thorn Creek to US 220, the minimum level would be about 3.5 feet at Petersburg. Call the Baltimore-Washington office of the National Weather Service at (703) 260-0305.

SMOKE HOLE CANYON—US 220 TO PETERSBURG

CLASS	1–3
LENGTH	25
TIME	8.5
GAUGE	PHONE
LEVEL	3 FT. + AT FRANKLIN
FLOW	FREE FLOWING
GRADIENT	5@35/ 20@16
VOLUME	160
SOLITUDE	A
SCENERY	A

DESCRIPTION: This is a very long run, perhaps too much for one day, but it has been described collectively because it represents an identifiable unit. Many paddlers make a two-day overnighter of it. The first 5 miles have the best whitewater on the South Branch and are among the most beautiful of the whole Potomac. The scouring effect of the 1985 flood is still visible two decades later! Some people believe that the rugged mountains forming the lower Smoke Hole Canyon are even more beautiful. Don't argue, just enjoy.

The river begins to pick up speed and action as it leaves the broad valley below Franklin, passes under the US 220 bridge, and crosses a ford. It quickly turns a corner and enters a magnificent canyon. The rapids through here are very closely spaced and fairly steep. Those looking only for action will end their run after 5 miles at the Smoke Hole picnic area, but most will want to continue. Everyone should spend some time in this unique area, as there are many attractive sights and trails. Cave Mountain and Eagle Rock are two very noteworthy natural monuments.

Leaving the Smoke Hole picnic area, you enter the most scenic, historic, and famous areas in West Virginia. This is the land of whiskey stills, American Indian wars, and Civil War battles. The river runs mostly through an isolated canyon of unparalleled grandeur. Abandoned mountaineer farms and homesteads add charm to the run and recall the fortitude and austerity of the early settlers. They also tell of a tragic paradox. In order to protect the river from trash-laden riverbanks, fishing shanties, and the like, the Forest Service acquired this land to incorporate it into the Spruce Knob—Seneca Rocks National Recreation Area. As a result, these independent farmers were displaced. It was unfortunate that their way of life and clean, well-kept farms could not be preserved.

The rapids are not as heavy as those upstream and seldom exceed a Class-2 rating unless the water is very high. Big Bend Campgrounds, operated by the Forest Service, is a convenient overnight spot because cars may be left here. It will be your last contact point until Royal Glen is reached miles below. From Big Bend there are few signs of civilization. Several excellent primitive campsites can be found alongside the deep pools. As the miles progress, the canyon and the gradient decrease, and the

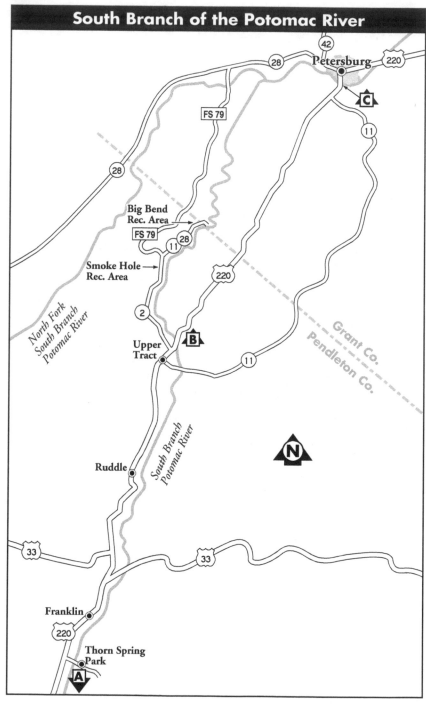

South Branch of the Potomac River

pools between the rapids get longer and longer. Soon the North Fork rushes in to join its parent stream, and together they head east toward Petersburg, 4 miles away.

DIFFICULTIES: The hardest rapid, Chimney Rock Slide, is found at the canyon entrance. An old rockslide once blocked the river with huge boulders, but this drop keeps getting easier. Now the whole rapid is easily scouted from a cobble bar just upstream on river left; run it on the left over a double ledge through a chute to a pool below. The rest of this section is an easy float over cobble bars and bulldozed channels. Royal Glen Dam is almost completely washed out and is easily run on the left. The best rapid on the run is right above the US 220 bridge near Petersburg, where sloping ledges create some interesting play holes.

SHUTTLE: If you plan on making the entire run straight through or with an overnight, the shuttle is simple. Just put in at the US 220 bridge below Upper Tract and take out at the next one in Petersburg, 15 miles away by car. A simpler put-in can be had by driving down to the ford just beyond the bridge. For a 5-mile run, leave a car at the Smoke Hole picnic area; for a 9-mile run, leave it at the Big Bend Campground. Arranging a take-out at Royal Glen involves a horrendous shuttle, driving clear over the mountain on WV 74, turning on WV 4/28 to the right, and right again at the Department of Highway's maintenance yard. Great scenery up there, but you may as well paddle the remaining 3.5 miles into Petersburg.

GAUGE: A good one is visible. A minimum of 3 feet at Franklin is required to descend, and whitewater boaters will want a bit more for a fun run.

PETERSBURG TO OLD FIELDS

DESCRIPTION: This is a flatter section of the upper Potomac, traversing some of the finest agricultural land in West Virginia. The pools are long, and the gentle rapids (Class 1, occasionally 2) are few and far between. This is a good open-boat run through excellent fishing water. Bass and trout may be taken year-round.

The river branches many times below the US 220 bridge between Petersburg and Moorefield. In one of the major branches, known locally as "Buzzard's Fork," high rock formations on the left are populated with what appear to be wild goats. To see them

CLASS	1–2
LENGTH	17
TIME	4
GAUGE	PHONE
LEVEL	3+ FT
FLOW	FREE FLOWING
GRADIENT	8
VOLUME	672
SOLITUDE	A
SCENERY	B

run up and down the sheer cliffs is worth the trip itself. Just below here on the left are three large pools of backwater than can be explored by canoe and short portages. Known as the "Sloughs," they are popular for bass fishing.

DIFFICULTIES: The only hazards to watch out for are peculiar local laws and a few strange landowners. Apparently titles to the land in this area extend under the river, giving landowners ownership of anything solid under the surface. This means if you flip, stop to dump, wade a riffle, or otherwise have to get out of your canoe, you are trespassing, and at least one person will have you arrested by a conservation officer if he catches you. It is pointless to test this strange situation, so please cooperate by staying in your boat.

SHUTTLE: Put in at the city parking lot in Petersburg and take out at the Old Fields bridge just north of Moorefield on US 220.

GAUGE: See Section E.

THE TROUGH—OLD FIELDS TO HARMISON'S LANDING

CLASS	C, 1–2
LENGTH	11
TIME	3
GAUGE	PHONE
LEVEL	3+ FT
FLOW	FREE FLOWING
GRADIENT	5
VOLUME	1,226
SOLITUDE	B–C
SCENERY	A+

DESCRIPTION: This trip is a must for everyone who loves the West Virginia outdoors. The Trough is a beautiful and popular canoeing river, and many organizations sponsor large float trips on it. It's OK for novices or even non-canoeists to run.

The first 4 miles of the trip pass through very scenic farmland and actually contain most of the rapids. The approach of the railroad bridge at the end of this stretch is tricky and marks the beginning of the Trough. As you make a wide, right-hand turn in the river, you are on the left side and must quickly get over to the right 50 yards above the bridge in order to avoid an exposed ledge. In high water, there will be good-sized standing waves below the bridge for nearly 100 yards. You will find yourself entering the serenity of a deep canyon with 1,500-foot mountain walls rising steeply from each side of the river. The vistas are ever-changing and provide spectacular scenery, especially in the spring and fall when seasonal colors are at their peak. There is very little whitewater in the Trough itself, but the scenery more than makes up for this lack. This river also provides some of the best bass fishing in the state, and one can find many primitive campsites along the sandy banks. There are a few more riffles as the Potomac leaves the Trough, and the river widens considerably. Other than a

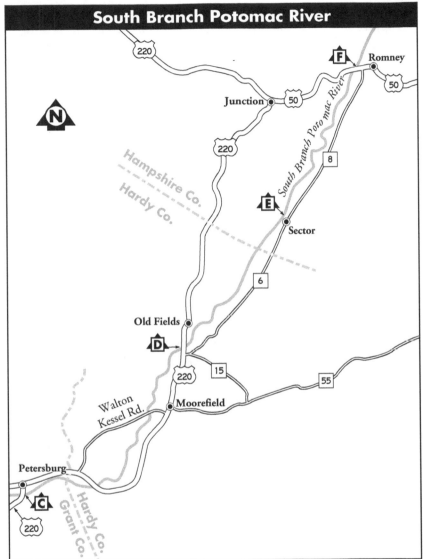

South Branch Potomac River

reasonable amount of caution at the railroad bridge rapid, there are no difficulties.

SHUTTLE: Put in where US 220 crosses the South Branch just south of Old Fields. Finding the take-out at the end of the Trough isn't easy. Take a secondary road leading due east from the put-in bridge, cross the railroad tracks, and turn left on the road at the farmhouse. This road is called "6" in Hardy County

and "8" in Hampshire County. Continue until the river comes back into view. Harmison's Landing is poorly marked.

GAUGE: See Section E.

E

HARMISON'S LANDING TO US 50 AT ROMNEY

CLASS	I
LENGTH	I 3
TIME	4
GAUGE	PHONE
LEVEL	3+ FT. AT FRANKLIN
FLOW	FREE FLOWING
GRADIENT	5
VOLUME	I,226
SOLITUDE	A
SCENERY	A–B

DESCRIPTION: The river widens and slows considerably after leaving the Trough. Within the next 10 miles, it passes through verdant farmlands and is characterized by extremely long, placid pools punctuated by short riffles. It is an ideal float-fishing stream and a good place to catch trophy bass. Near Romney, 200-foot-high shale cliffs rise from the right bank and extend for over a mile. But the scene is spoiled by the profusion of camps and cottages perched atop the precipice. The trip from Harmison's Landing is ideal for novices, johnboats, and weekend campers. A popular, 2-day, open-boat camping trip starts by putting in at the US 220 bridge, camping overnight at Harmison's, and then continuing on to Romney the next day. There are no difficulties in this lower part except that an angry bull might chase you if you get out at the wrong place.

SHUTTLE: See section D for directions to Harmison's Landing. To reach the take-out, continue on the road past landing, eventually reaching US 50. Take out at the old bridge pier on the right bank, 100 yards upstream from the present span.

GAUGE: You want a level of 3 feet or more on the Franklin gauge. Call the Baltimore-Washington office of the National Weather Service at (703) 260-0303.

F

THE SOUTH BRANCH BELOW ROMNEY

CLASS	A
LENGTH	34
TIME	I–2 DAYS
GAUGE	VISUAL
LEVEL	RUNABLE YEAR-ROUND
FLOW	FREE FLOWING
GRADIENT	NA
VOLUME	L
SOLITUDE	A
SCENERY	C–D

DESCRIPTION: There is little whitewater in this long, slow, 34-mile stretch of the South Branch from Romney to the junction with the North Branch at Green Spring. The banks are pretty muddy, and the scenery consists of developed farmland or fishing shanties. It is a good float-fishing stream, highly recommended for bass. It may get dangerous at high-water stages.

SHUTTLE: There are many possible access points on this section. For a good take-out, head towards Old Town, Maryland,

and, about a mile before the bridge, turn onto Arnold Stickley Road. A mile and a half later it reaches the to the South Branch, just above its mouth.

GAUGE: It's up most of the year, except during long dry periods.

MOOREFIELD RIVER

All of the headwaters of the Potomac are characterized by massive, awe-inspiring rock formations; the upper section of the Moorefield (also called the South Fork of the South Branch of the Potomac) ranks among the best. Wildlife is abundant: on a single trip you might see ducks, turkeys, beaver, kingfishers, woodchucks, and deer. The lower section between Milam and Moorefield is a delightful open-boat trip through some of the most charming farmland in West Virginia.

MAPS: Fort Seybert, Mozer, Milam, Petersburg East, Lost River State Park, Moorefield (USGS); Pendleton, Hardy (County)

FORT SEYBERT TO MILAM BRIDGE

CLASS	2–3
LENGTH	10
TIME	3.5
GAUGE	PHONE
LEVEL	4.5–6 FT. AT SPRINGFIELD
FLOW	FREE FLOWING
GRADIENT	25/4 @40
VOLUME	204
SOLITUDE	A
SCENERY	A–B

DESCRIPTION: The entire run is fantastically beautiful. The water is magnificently clear and the banks unspoiled. The first half of the run is not difficult, but the gradient picks up during the last half of the run as the river cuts through Moorefield Gorge. Most rapids in this section are now pretty open, but a few are tight and clogged by boulders. These can be scouted or eddy-scouted easily by competent intermediates.

After a couple of miles from the put-in and just past a little church on the right, the river divides into three channels. There's a pretty mean rapid, choked with boulders, where these channels come together. If you don't like this, quit now, because it is only a prelude to what lies ahead in the canyon.

Afterwards, there's a pleasant cruise through a farm valley (Class 2). The farms, though isolated, are well kept and progressive. At the end of the valley a massive rock formation on the right stands as a sentinel, guarding the entrance of the Moorefield Gorge. For the next 4 miles the rapids are steeper than the gradient indicates because of the long, flat pools in between each set. Several drops have a nasty disposition. Often large boulders block a paddler's view of the rapid ahead. Scouting, in boat or on shore, is recommended. Take your time through here, for safety's sake as well as to enjoy the incredible beauty of this river.

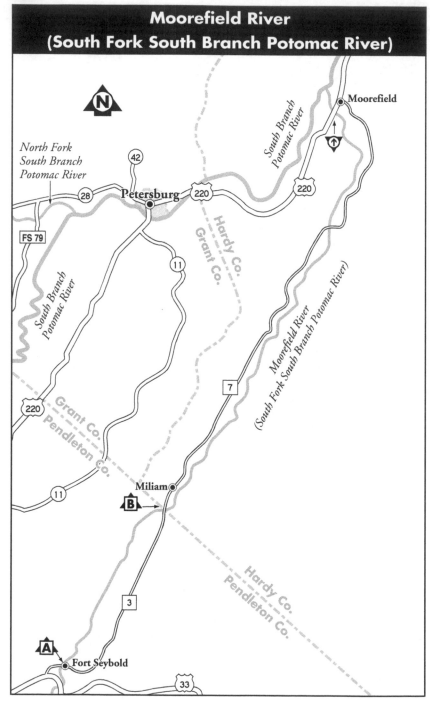

Moorefield River
(South Fork South Branch Potomac River)

SHUTTLE: The take-out is 2 miles south of Milam (upstream) on "7/3" almost at the county line. The put-in is just a few more miles south at the bridge at Fort Seybert on Pendleton "7" (same road). It's one of the easiest shuttles in the state.

GAUGE: There is a yellow gauge on the Milam bridge and another on the US 220 bridge in Moorefield that roughly correlates to it. Optimal levels on these gauges fall between 1–3 feet. Levels between 4.5–6 feet on the Springfield gauge usually indicate runability. Call the Baltimore-Washington office of the National Weather Service, (703) 260-0303, for this reading.

BELOW THE MILAM BRIDGE

CLASS	1–2
LENGTH	25
TIME	8.5
GAUGE	PHONE
LEVEL	2 FT. AT MOOREFIELD
FLOW	FREE FLOWING/DAM
GRADIENT	NA
VOLUME	M
SOLITUDE	A
SCENERY	B

DESCRIPTION: The small river winds placidly through the pastoral scenery with enough short, straightforward rapids to make things interesting. The rapids are more numerous at the upper end but thin out toward Moorefield.

SHUTTLE: Milam can be reached by taking the South Branch River Road "7" south of Moorefield. The bridge is a couple of miles south of Milam. Take out either at the bridge in Moorefield or continue 3 more miles to the Old Fields bridge on the South Branch (US 220). Because the river is never very far from the highway, many shorter trips on this small stream are possible.

GAUGE: The adjusted yellow numbers on the bridge in Milam are still too low. Don't run unless you have at least a foot. You'll need at least 2.7 feet at the USGS Moorefield gauge for a good run. Call the Baltimore-Washington office of the National Weather Service, (703) 260-0303, for this reading.

NORTH FORK OF THE SOUTH BRANCH OF THE POTOMAC RIVER

This is the most famous whitewater in the Eastern panhandle, providing miles of bouncy Class 2–3 whitewater in one of the state's most beautiful mountain valleys. Discovered by canoeists from Washington, DC during the 1950s, it later became the site of the famous Petersburg Whitewater Weekend. For decades this hugely popular event brought hundreds of paddlers together from all over

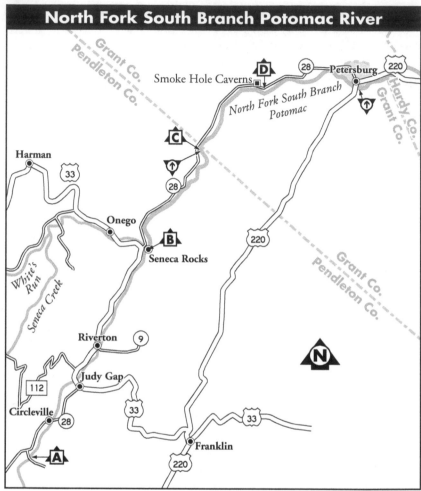

the Eastern US and introduced many of us to the sport of wildwater racing. But eventually it it got too big for its own good. Rowdy
crowds of spectators overwhelmed the resources of the area, the race
was phased out, and only memories remain. But the wonderful
river that drew everyone to the area is still a fabulous intermediate
run.

MAPS: Spruce Knob, Circleville, Onego, Upper Tract,
Hopeville, Petersburg West (USGS); Pendleton, Grant (County); Monongahela National Forest Map

CHERRY GROVE TO THE MOUTH OF SENECA CREEK

CLASS	1−2 (3)
LENGTH	19
TIME	4
GAUGE	PHONE
LEVEL	3−6 FT. AT PETERSBURG
FLOW	FREE FLOWING
GRADIENT	34
VOLUME	S
SOLITUDE	B
SCENERY	A−D

DESCRIPTION: This is a zesty stream that flows straight through the valley, hugging the base of North Fork Mountain. Most of the trip is a cobble bar run with a few large rocks.

DIFFICULTIES: This run is straightforward, but picks up speed at the end. It's a small stream, so watch out for downed trees and other flood debris. About 1 mile above the take-out, you'll begin to find things picking up to Class 3. This is due to a series of small ledges that cut across the river at 30- to 40-degree angles. Watch for a low-water bridge near Riverton.

SHUTTLE: The whole run is never far from highways, so numerous choices can be made for trips of various lengths. Put in at the bridge on Snowy Mountain Road (CR 17). You can take out at bridges at Judy Gap, Riverton, or on the Harper's Gap Road (CR 9) just beside Hedrick's Motel. Take out just past the mouth of Seneca Creek at the Seneca Rocks Recreation Area parking lot.

GAUGE: Call (703) 260-0305 for the Petersburg reading following the recorded weather forecast. The optimal level is between 3–6 feet. The online gauge at Cabins, WV, is probably more accurate, and should read between 6.1–8 feet.

MOUTH OF SENECA TO ABOVE THE FORMER DOLLY CAMPGROUNDS

CLASS	2−3
LENGTH	10
TIME	2−3
GAUGE	PHONE
LEVEL	2.5-5 FT. AT PETERSBURG
FLOW	FREE FLOWING
GRADIENT	22
VOLUME	S−M
SOLITUDE	B
SCENERY	B

DESCRIPTION: Unquestionably this is some of West Virginia's finest canoeing. This river is a solid, continuous Class 2+ run at medium water levels with a touch of Class 3 when the water comes up. Every conceivable type of rapid makes an appearance. There are fast runs with good bouncy waves, cobble bars, small ledges, and plenty of sharp turns. The entire run was seemingly designed to test the beginning to intermediate paddler's repertoire of strokes.

Some of the state's most breathtaking scenery can be seen from this section of the Potomac. Seneca and Champe Rocks are in the immediate vicinity, while the imposing majesties of Allegheny Front and North Fork Mountain loom in the distance on either

side of the river, which provides a splendid backdrop for canoeing. Trout and bass fishing are available on this clear, unpolluted river, but its proximity to the road and numerous vacation cabins place its fragile beauty in a precarious position.

The popularity of this section of the Potomac comes at a price. Some landowners have been victims of abuses by inconsiderate trespassers. Use public access points or ask permission for other areas. This caution applies to all of the rivers described in this book.

DIFFICULTIES: About three-quarters of the way into the trip, the river turns left around a point and goes through a stopper. Just past the stopper there appears to be a flat pool, but actually a very deceptive diagonal ledge lies ahead. This will flip an unwary paddler. The only passage in low or medium water is way over against the left bank.

SHUTTLE: Put in under the bridge over Seneca Creek on WV 28. This stream joins the North Fork in a few hundred yards. Take-out above where Dolly Camp Grounds used to be, near the Grant-Pendleton county line.

GAUGE: Call (703) 260-0305 for the Petersburg reading. The optimal level is between 2.4–5 feet. The online gauge at Cabins, WV should read between 5.4–7 feet.

CLASS	3–3+
LENGTH	5
TIME	4
GAUGE	PHONE
LEVEL	2.3–5 FT. AT PETERSBURG
FLOW	FREE FLOWING
GRADIENT	33
VOLUME	M
SOLITUDE	B
SCENERY	A

FROM THE FORMER DOLLY CAMPGROUND TO SMOKE HOLE CAVERNS

DESCRIPTION: The Hopeville Canyon on the North Fork is a fun run that can get pretty interesting in high water. It is a good river for intermediates to test their capability for moving on to advanced paddling. The rapids are medium sized and require precise maneuvering around boulders. It is more difficult than anything appearing in the upper portions of the river and has considerably more volume than the sections above the Mouth of Seneca.

DIFFICULTIES: There are many rapids in the canyon and a few more near the road before getting to the take-out. The area is prone to rockslides, and new rapids are in the making. Keep your eyes open! Rock Jumble, formed by the flood just above Cave Rapids, is the steepest drop on this run. The last couple of miles between Harman's Pool and Smoke Hole Caverns are mostly straightforward cobble bar rapids.

SHUTTLE: Easily done on WV 28, which parallels the river. Put in above where Dolly Camp Grounds used to be and take-out by the remnants of a primitive bridge near Smoke Hole Caverns. (Note comments on shuttle in previous section.)

GAUGE: Call (703) 260-0305 for the Petersburg reading following the recorded weather forecast. Optimal level is between 2.3–5 feet. Some variation can be expected because the Petersburg gauge also includes the South Branch discharge. The online gauge at Cabins, WV, should read between 5.1–7 feet.

SMOKE HOLE CAVERNS TO PETERSBURG

CLASS	I –3
LENGTH	9
TIME	2+
GAUGE	PHONE
LEVEL	4.5
FLOW	FREE FLOWING
GRADIENT	20
VOLUME	M
SOLITUDE	A
SCENERY	B

DESCRIPTION: The run into Petersburg is not paddled very often, but it contains some nice water. Many of the rapids are visible from the road, but soon the river takes off to join the South Branch, fresh out of Smoke Hole country. It passes through fairly open, well-kept farmland, and although it leaves the mountains behind, there are still some spectacular scenes to come, particularly at the place known as Royal Glen, the site of a broken-out dam.

DIFFICULTIES: The old, broken-out Royal Glen Dam can be run on the left. The reinforcing bars and debris that once made this a tricky spot are gone. Further down toward Petersburg, the paddler will encounter an entertaining staircase of river-wide ledges, some of which produce sticky hydraulics.

SHUTTLE: Put in across from the Smoke Hole Caverns (worth a trip in themselves) on WV 28 and take out on the left bank before the bridge in Petersburg. This is next to the big parking lot and city park adjacent to the Petersburg fire hall.

GAUGE: The optimal level is 4.5 feet at Petersburg. Call the Baltimore-Washington office of the National Weather Service at (703) 260-0305.

Petersburg White Water Weekend

Saturday, April 4th, dawned cold and gray, with a raw wind blowing down the valley of the North Fork. A

light drizzle fell from time to time but scarcely enough to dampen the spirits of the racers who, in any case, were going to get wet. After several years of low and medium-low water levels, the North Fork was running in great style, reportedly at or above the 2-foot level. Contestants in the expert's race emerged from the canyon exhilarated and breathless and spoke respectfully of the size of the waves. Not everyone finished. In at least one instance, a pair of contestants stopped to assist a swamped boat, thereby impairing their own chances of winning. Norm and Barbara Holcombe, running C2M, deserve special mention for their good sportsmanship in coming to the aid of Glenna and King Goodwin. This is part of the tradition of our sport but such actions always make us proud.

The cruising race also encountered unusually rough conditions on the upper part of the course and several boats were swamped. One capsized Grumman resisted all efforts of sweeps, Henry de Marne and John Lentz, to dislodge it. However, considering the number of entrants in both races, casualties were few. An unbelievable 130 boats started in the cruising class: 84 were registered in the expert group. If the popularity of Petersburg Weekend continues to grow, we may have to spread the downriver events over 2 days. (Possibly this would also have the beneficial effect of spreading Sunday spectators over a larger portion of the riverbank. As it is, a tremendous traffic jam occurs in the area of the April Fools' Race).

The Petersburg Slalom, held for the first time on Seneca Creek instead of at Harmon's Store Rapids, was utterly new and different. This narrow stream had fallen considerably during the night and offered contestants both swift water and a guidance system, which bounced them from one rock to another. It was hard to avoid a gate completely; the presence of a gate was indicative of

some water flow and there wasn't much anywhere else. The kayakers, who are noted for their ability to run anything a trout can slide through, had the best time of it. One was heard to exclaim, at the bottom of the course: "Wow, that all happened so fast I can't remember anything about it!" Dick Bridge and Frank Daspit had hung an interesting and well-engineered course; remarkably, not one gate fell down during the race. Bright sunshine warmed the scene, sparkled the river and etched the mountains against a blue sky, bringing another great Petersburg Weekend to a close.

Many thanks to all the willing workers and participants who brought their talents and energies to Petersburg and used them well. We are especially grateful to Race Chairman Joe Monahan and Bob Burrell, Frank Daspit, and Dick Bridge, and to our Awards ceremony speaker, Ramone Eaton. The Petersburg area welcomed us, as always, with hospitable lodgings and great pancake and sausage breakfasts. Everybody come again next year!

Betty Riedel

Reprinted from Canoe Cruisers Association of Washington
Cruiser, April 1970.

UPPER SENECA CREEK

Born high on West Virginia's tallest mountain, Seneca Creek starts as a very small, steep, and difficult run. Upper Seneca Creek is way up in the mountains, hard to catch up, and hard to get to. It passes through some gorgeous country, but getting downriver in one piece requires expert skills and a penchant for running high ledges. The lower section of Seneca Creek is a lively little ripsnorter and is a pure delight when there's enough water. Its course traverses pastoral farmlands around the northern edge of Spruce Mountain, then heads east toward the imposing majesty of Seneca Rocks.

MAPS: USGS: Onego; County: Pendleton; Monongahela National Forest Map

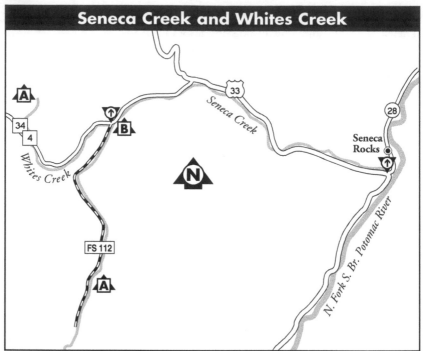

Seneca Creek and Whites Creek

CLASS	4–5+
LENGTH	13
TIME	6+
GAUGE	PHONE, WEB
LEVEL	SEE BELOW
FLOW	FREE FLOWING
GRADIENT	100–350+
VOLUME	VS
SOLITUDE	B
SCENERY	A

JUDY SPRINGS TO FOREST SERVICE CAMPGROUNDS

DESCRIPTION: This run is a mini-expedition for committed teams capable of moving quickly and cautiously through very rough country. A trail parallels the creek for most of the length making portaging and scouting fairly easy. The run generally flows through long sections of continuous Class 3–4 ledges and slides punctuated by big Class 5+ drops. Although the big drops don't come at you as constantly as most other steep creeks, it's a very long run and stamina and judgment are essential. Due to beaver colonies, downed trees are a constant problem. If you don't know your limits, you could get hurt!

DIFFICULTIES: Below Judy Springs the river enters a geological fault, which creates a narrow channel in the bedrock. After a few minor ledges and slides, boaters will confront a couple of 10-foot high falls. Upper Seneca Falls, a 30-foot waterfall with a very deep pool at the bottom, is about 2 miles into the run. It is a beautiful falls and one of the cleanest 30 footers you'll ever see. It is easily

scouted on the right. After a mile or so of small ledges interrupted by a 12-foot falls, you will come to a steep, 20-foot, double ledge drop called Standing Rock Falls. It falls about 12 feet onto a rock shelf and then another 8 feet into a pool. It is by far the sketchiest drop on this creek and is easily carried on the left. Further down, you'll reach Knife's Edge, a ledge combination, culminating in a 10-foot diagonal ledge drop into a steep-walled mini-gorge. The drop creates a 90-degree bend in a narrow channel, followed by a steep slide into an ugly hole. The run picks up for the next mile or so with several ledge and slide drops. One slide has a strange rock at the bottom with a bad recirculating eddy on the left. Lower Seneca Falls, a 20-foot falls into a stiff hole, marks the end of the steep stuff on Seneca Creek. Unfortunately, the creek now enters a scrapy, dredged channel for the last 4 miles of the run. Downed trees require portaging.

SHUTTLE: The put-in is on the north side of Spruce Knob near the Judy Springs trailhead. This is reached by turning onto 33/4 a few miles north of Route 33 above Circleville and following FS 112 over Spruce Knob before turning onto FS 33. The trail is on the Monongahela National Forest Map. Walk along the river until it becomes big enough to boat. Take out at the Forest Service Campground just off of Rt. 33 or, if time permits, continue on to the Mouth of Seneca.

GAUGE: There is a gauge on the North Fork of the South Branch of the Potomac at Cabins. This should read around 2,500 cfs or higher for a good level. Examine at the take-out. Seneca Creek will be pretty high for the upper section to run. A reading of 6+ feet and rising on the Dry Fork at Hendricks, or 7 feet and rising at Parsons is also a good indicator.

LOWER SENECA CREEK—FOREST SERVICE CAMPGROUNDS
TO WV 28 BRIDGE

CLASS	3–4
TIME	3
GAUGE	PHONE
LEVEL	5–8 FEET AT PETERSBURG
FLOW	FREE FLOWING
GRADIENT	70–90
VOLUME	S
SOLITUDE	B
SCENERY	B

DESCRIPTION: This run is essentially a 6-mile-long rapid with one or two very short pools breaking up the waves. The course is extremely narrow, especially in the upper parts, and very fast. Because there are few obstructions, very little maneuvering is required. Just skirt up and go. The creek often runs after early spring thaws or heavy rains.

DIFFICULTIES: Very few at the levels indicated. Just above and below the Onego Bridge are some sloping ledges and some

hydraulics that demand attention. About a half-mile downstream one encounters two pools that run out sharply to the left, then and S-curve to the right. Each of these rapids has a big hole right in the main channel. Within sight of Seneca Rocks a bulldozed, graded cobble section totally bypasses Junkyard Falls (an 8-foot staircase descent).

SHUTTLE: Put in at the small bridge that once led to the USFS Seneca Campgrounds (obliterated by the 1985 flood). Take-out at the left side of the WV 28 bridge, the put-in for the Petersburg Cruiser Race.

GAUGE: There is a paddler's gauge painted on the WV 28 bridge; 2 inches to 1 foot is a good range of levels for paddling. At Petersburg a reading of 4.5 to 8 feet is a good indicator; call the Baltimore-Washington office of the National Weather Service: (703) 260-0305.

WHITE'S CREEK

MAPS: Whitmer (USGS); Pendleton (County); Monongahela National Forest Map

CR 33-3 TO SENECA CREEK

CLASS	4+
TIME	1.8
GAUGE	NONE
LEVEL	NA
FLOW	FREE FLOWING
GRADIENT	200 FPM+
VOLUME	VS
SOLITUDE	A
SCENERY	A

DESCRIPTION: This is one screaming little creek run you can try when Seneca Creek is bank-full. You'll feel like a human pinball as you crash through narrow slots, hurl yourself over slides, and dart around blind curves. Scout this on foot and check for downed trees before proceeding, then put on your elbow pads before you launch!

SHUTTLE: From Seneca Rocks, drive west on US 33, then turn left onto 33/4, which winds along beside Seneca Creek. At the confluence of White's Creek and Seneca Creek, the road curves right and continues up a forest road. Drive up the road until the creek gets too small to paddle, then put on.

GAUGE: None. If Seneca Creek is flooding, inspect on site.

OTHER STREAMS IN THE
SOUTH BRANCH OF THE POTOMAC BASIN

LUNICE CREEK

LUNICE CREEK

MAPS: USGS: Maysville, Rig; County: Grant

DESCRIPTION: This very shallow, small trout stream can occasionally be run from near the vicinity of Maysville all the way into the South Branch at Petersburg near the tannery. It can be run when the water is very high elsewhere and offers fairly continuous Class 1–2 action.

CLASS	1–2
LENGTH	10
TIME	3.5
GAUGE	VISUAL
LEVEL	NA
FLOW	FREE FLOWING
GRADIENT	NA
VOLUME	VS
SOLITUDE	A
SCENERY	B

THORN CREEK

THORN CREEK

MAPS: USGS: Sugar Grove; County: Pendleton; Monongahela National Forest Map

DESCRIPTION: This little headwater tributary of the South Branch has 7.5 miles of Class 2–3 water from near Moyers to the mouth. At a left turn 2.5 miles into the trip there are two intersecting rapids, the second of which is blocked by a log. There's a nasty-looking, 5-foot ledge at the mouth. There is lots of limestone in the area and many caves along the run.

GAUGE: None. It's worth a look when the Petersburg gauge is over 4 feet. Call the Baltimore/Washington Office of the National Weather Service at (703) 260-0305.

CLASS	2–3
LENGTH	7.5
TIME	2.5
GRADIENT	40 FT/MI.
GAUGE	PHONE
LEVEL	4+
FEET AT PETERSBURG	
FLOW	FREE FLOWING
VOLUME	VS
SOLITUDE	A
SCENERY	B

THE MAIN STEM OF THE POTOMAC RIVER

CLASS	1–2
LENGTH	115
TIME	4–5 DAYS
GAUGE	PHONE
LEVEL	2.6+ AT HANCOCK
FLOW	FREE FLOWING/DAM
GRADIENT	NA
VOLUME	L
SOLITUDE	A
SCENERY	B–C

A

GREEN SPRING TO HARPER'S FERRY, WV

MAPS: USGS: Old Town, Paw Paw, Great Cacapon, Artemas, Bellgrove, Hancock, Cherry Run, Big Pool, Hedgesville, Williamsport, Shepardstown, Keedysville, Charles Town, Harper's Ferry. Counties: Hampshire, Morgan, Berkeley, Jefferson; the Maryland and West Virginia State Road Map

DESCRIPTION: From 2 miles below Green Spring, West Virginia (Oldtown, Maryland), where the North and South Branch of the Potomac meet to form the great Potomac River, the beautiful, historic West Virginia-Maryland border river flows majestically for almost 115 miles toward Harper's Ferry. The river is mostly wide, flat water, but there are occasional Class 1–2 riverwide rapids. In most places it's suitable for well-coached beginners in open boats. It gets dangerous in high water for paddlers with marginal skills.

The historic C&O Canal follows the river along the Maryland shore. A well-maintained hiking and cycling trail follows the old canal towpath. The National Park Service manages the Canal as a National Historic Park. There are a number of historic or restored remains are worth visiting. Civil War battlefields and Revolutionary War sites add further interest to canoe runs in this area. There are several developed campsites along the river, to use as a base.

This sort of information could fill a book, so we recommend *The Hiker's Guide to the C&O Canal.* It's crammed with information about historic sites, camping areas, roads, and other points of interest in the area, and canoeists will find it invaluable in planning their trip. It can be purchased from the Mason-Dixon Council of the Boy Scouts, PO Box 2133, 18600 Crestwood Drive, Hagerstown, MD 21742.

Also in Maryland just south of Hagerstown, Fort Frederick State Park is a great location for camping. It's the site of a historic Revolutionary War fort and a particularly impressive portion of the canal. Historic Antietam Battlefield is nearby. The river is beautiful here, with interesting, closely spaced rapids. It is a shame that West Virginia has never developed a state park along this magnificently beautiful and historic river.

DIFFICULTIES: Several of the old C&O Canal dams still remain. Dam No. 6, just above the mouth of the Cacapon, is broken out. About 10 miles below Fort Frederick, Dam No. 5

creates a 5-mile-long lake and must be portaged on the West Virginia side. There is a power-plant dam right below Williamsport, Maryland. Dam No. 4 is a high one, creating a 13-mile-long lake (Big Slackwater), and is located near Falling Waters, West Virginia. The last dam in West Virginia, Dam No. 3, is in ruins. It's very runable, but some passages may have hidden dangers from rebar and other debris.

The 2 miles of the Potomac below Dam No. 3 down to Harper's Ferry, the mouth of the Shenandoah, and 1 mile farther to Sandy Hook, Maryland, below the US 340 bridge, are definitely not for beginners. This beautiful stretch, called the Needles, is wide and powerful with continuous Class 1–2+ rapids. If the river is high, it can be dangerous. Flipped or swamped boats can be difficult to recover; with high water and cold temperatures, a swimmer might not survive. A half-mile below Harper's Ferry, White Horse Rapid appears on the left side of the river. The biggest waves on this section are found here. There are many rock islands here that invite exploration.

SHUTTLE: Because so many different trips can be planned for this long section of river, the best advice seems to be to consult West Virginia and Maryland road maps for major access points or the county maps for more detail.

GAUGE: Most of the river can be run all year; the Hancock, MD, gauge should read 2.6 or more to run the river above that point.

LOST RIVER

MAPS: Lost City, Needmore, Baker (USGS); Hardy (County)

LOST RIVER TO THE WV 55 BRIDGE ABOVE WARDENSVILLE

DESCRIPTION: This is a long, straightforward stretch of river. The first two-thirds of the run follows a long valley with low banks and pleasant rural scenery. The river is clear and unpolluted, flowing through a series of Class 1–2 riffles. Watch out for an occasional barbed-wire fence! Below Baker the river begins cutting through mountains and ridges, creating an almost gorge-like stretch. You'll find lots of nice little rapids: cobble bars, small boulders, and low ledges. There's one carry at a low-water bridge towards the end of the run.

GAUGE: See section B.

CLASS	2
LENGTH	15
TIME	5
GAUGE	PHONE
LEVEL	4–6 FEET AT COOTES STORE
FLOW	FREE FLOWING
GRADIENT	40
VOLUME	S
SOLITUDE	A
SCENERY	B

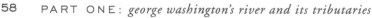

CLASS	2–4
LENGTH	6
TIME	2
GAUGE	PHONE
LEVEL	4–6 FT. AT COOTES STORE
FLOW	FREE FLOWING
GRADIENT	40
VOLUME	S
SOLITUDE	A
SCENERY	B

THE DRY GORGE OF THE LOST RIVER WV 55 BRIDGE ABOVE WAR-
DENSVILLE TO WV 259 BRIDGE BELOW WARDENSVILLE

DESCRIPTION: This section of the Lost River, called the Dry Gorge, is the most unique and best-named river in the state—it doesn't always exist! In low water the river actually disappears into the ground just beyond the bridge above Wardensville, leaving the rest of the riverbed dry for most of the year. The river traverses some unknown Stygian course, only to emerge several miles away, seemingly *de novo*, to form the Cacapon River.

DIFFICULTIES: A run on this section can only be made in high water. When the underground river can't handle all of the flow the river spills into the flood channel cut around the mountain. Fantastic! For the first couple of miles there are frequent Class 2–3 rapids. Two islands mark landslide-choked channels that necessitate a carry. Below the islands there is a series of steep ledges with hydraulics. This is a very steep rapid and can be really mean in high water. Run just to the right of center, then carry the low-water bridge below. There are many chutes and drops through narrow passages that require maneuvering back and forth across the river to find the next passage, and a low-water bridge that must be carried near the end of the flood channel (on the right).

Soon the underwater river miraculously reappears from a series of springs, and the volume of the river doubles. Where the flood channel and the underground river merge, there's another series of steep ledges. It's a heavier rapid than the first series. There are also several more good drops before reaching the take-out bridge. From here, the river, now called the Cacapon, is much tamer. Catching the Dry Gorge wet is well worth the wait.

SHUTTLE: Very simple—use the WV 55 bridge upstream of Wardensville, and take-out at the WV 259 bridge downstream of Wardensville, or to eliminate some flat water, at the low-water bridge off WV 55 above Wardensville.

GAUGE: There is a paddler's gauge at the upper bridge above Wardensville. A reading of 3 inches is enough for Section A; zero on this gauge is enough for Section B. The Cootes Store gauge on the North Fork of the Shenandoah should read between 4–6

Lost River, Trout Run, and Waites Run

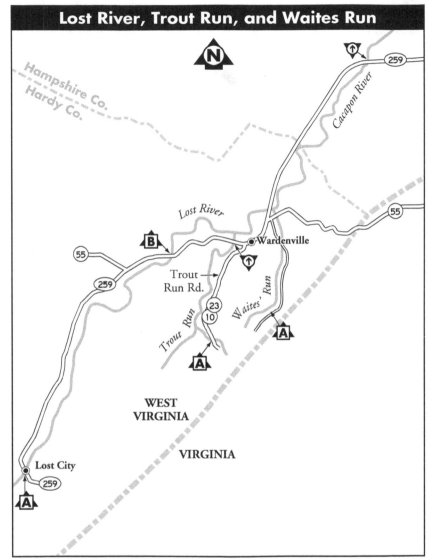

feet and the Great Cacapon gauge should read over 4 feet. Call
the Baltimore-Washington office of the National Weather Service at (703) 260-0305.

TROUT RUN

MAPS: USGS: Baker, Wardensville; County: Hardy

CLASS	3–4
LENGTH	3 MILES
TIME	2
GAUGE	PHONE
LEVEL	5 FT. + AT COOTES STORE
FLOW	FREE FLOWING
GRADIENT	75/1 @100
VOLUME	VS
SOLITUDE	A
SCENERY	A–B

TROUT RUN ROAD TO THE WV 55 BRIDGE

DESCRIPTION: This tiny slalom tributary to the Lost River is one of the best advanced runs in the Eastern Panhandle. It's small and does not come up often, but knowledgeable paddlers keep it in mind during prolonged rainy periods. The first 1.5 miles is an easygoing Class 2–3, a good warm-up for the gorge below.

DIFFICULTIES: The river soon enters a small gorge; the gradient here is 100 fpm, creating several tight, rocky Class-4 rapids. These have all been run, but scouting is advised to check for clearance and debris. Two low-water bridges mark the end of the hardest rapids. From there it's just 3 more miles of easy Class 1–2.

SHUTTLE: Trout Run Road turns south on Route 55 west of Wardensville. Drive upriver about 5.5 miles and put in at the bridge. The take-out is at the Route 55 bridge near Wardensville.

GAUGE: Check the Route 55 gauge on the Lost River near Wardensville. Look for 2.5–5 feet; this is a lot of water, and the creek won't be up often! You'll need about 5 feet at Cootes Store; call the Washington Weather Service at (703) 260-0305.

WAITES RUN

MAPS: USGS: Baker, Wardensville; County: Hardy

A. WILSON COVE TO WV 55 BRIDGE NEAR CONFLUENCE OF LOST RIVER

DESCRIPTION: This tiny tributary of the Lost River comes in at Wardensville. It's Class 3–4 with an 80 ft/mi gradient. It's even smaller than Trout Run and needs a lot of water to become runable. It's a small stream, so scout carefully ahead for strainers!

SHUTTLE: Drive up CR 5-1 take a look! From Wardensville, take Waites Run Rd. (CR 5-1), just off North Mountain Road, and head upstream. Put in where it seems runable.

GAUGE: See Trout Run, above. You'll probably need about 7 feet at Cootes Store. Call the Baltimore-Washington office of the National Weather Service at (703) 260-0305.

CACAPON RIVER

MAPS: Wardensville, Yellow Springs, Capon Springs, Capon Bridge, Largent, Paw Paw, Great Cacapon (USGS); Hardy, Hampshire, Morgan (County)

ABOVE CAPON BRIDGE (US 50)

CLASS	I
LENGTH	30
TIME	2 DAYS
GAUGE	PHONE
LEVEL	4 FT. + AT GREAT CACAPON
FLOW	FREE FLOWING
GRADIENT	NA
VOLUME	MEDIUM
SOLITUDE	B
SCENERY	A–D

DESCRIPTION: The long section of the Cacapon River from Wardensville to US 50 offers little in the way of whitewater except for occasional riffles in medium water. A good secondary road follows the river from Capon Bridge to Yellow Spring. From there to Wardensville, WV 259 is handy. Many short trips are possible. The pools are often long and deep; at least one is behind the remains of an old mill dam. Unfortunately some parts of the river look like a rural slum, thanks to closely-spaced cabins and trailers that line the banks. Sewage from these places, and towns upstream, has caused increased algae growth in recent years.

GAUGE: Check the riffles across the road from the Cacapon Restaurant on US 55 in Wardensville. If this is runable, so is everything else. Call the Baltimore-Washington office of the National Weather Service at (703) 260-0305 and look for a reading at Great Cacapon of over 4 feet.

CAPON BRIDGE TO WV 127 BRIDGE

CLASS	I–3
LENGTH	I 2
GRADIENT	I 4
VOLUME	549
TIME	4
GAUGE	PHONE
LEVEL	2 FT. + AT GREAT CACAPON
FLOW	FREE FLOWING
SOLITUDE	B
SCENERY	A

DESCRIPTION: This is a very popular canoeing stream, with good rapids and exquisite scenery. It's often up in the winter; the snow-covered banks combine with the unusual rock formations for a wonderfully scenic run. It's a great float-fishing stream for canoeists who know how to run whitewater, but be careful—many inexperienced paddlers have drowned here over the years.

The trip begins with flat water and a few riffles flowing through open farmland. After about 3 miles, the river turns left past high rocky cliffs, and things get a little more interesting. There are three small to medium-sized ledges that require skill and possibly scouting for correct passage. Toward the end of the run a spectacular rock formation, Caudy's Castle, may be seen

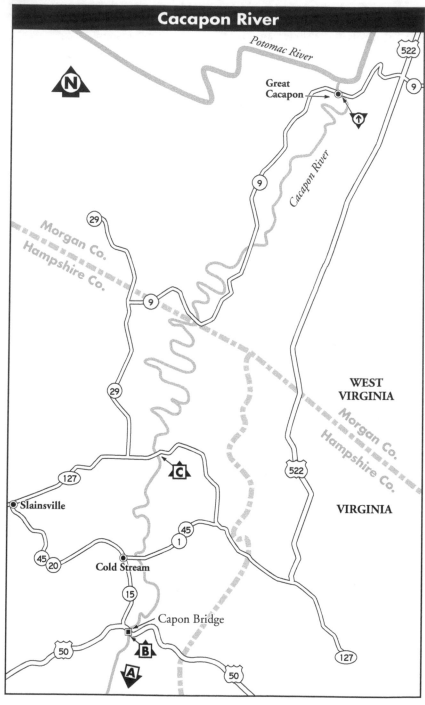

Cacapon River

Potomac River

522

9

Great
Cacapon

9

Cacapon River

29

Morgan Co.
Hampshire Co.

9

WEST
VIRGINIA

29

Morgan Co.
Hampshire Co.

522

C

VIRGINIA

127

Slainsville

45

1

45
20

Cold Stream

15

Capon Bridge

B

50

A

50

127

high on the left. It is well worth an exploratory side trip. From here on to the bridge you'll find a good deal of flat water.

DIFFICULTIES: The first low ledge, at the end of a right-hand turn with a cliff on the left, is best run on the far right in lower water. Right below this is a nice sandy beach suitable for lunch stops. The second ledge is at the end of a spectacular rock formation called "Chapel Rock," which is always runable on the far left. The third ledge is sort of big, and intermediate paddlers may want to scout. In low water the passage is on the right, but at the risk of banging your stern pretty hard. At 9 inches or more, the best passage is just left of center, but it requires more skill in maneuvering.

SHUTTLE: Put in under the US 50 bridge on the left (which is rather steep) or drive down the left side of the river 3 miles to Cold Stream for a riverside put-in that cuts off most of the flat water. Take-out on the right under the WV 127 bridge. It's a difficult climb. To reach this from Cold Stream, simply continue to Slanesville on "15" and "45/20," turn right on WV 29 and drive on to WV 127. Be sure to leave your car at the second bridge. (The first is over the North River.)

GAUGE: Both bridges have canoeing gauges, but we can't improve on Roger Corbett and Louis Matacia's warning not to continue when the first riffle below the US 50 bridge is scrapy. The Cacapon gets pretty slow if the water is too low; at these levels taking a hike is more rewarding. Gauge readings may be obtained from the National Weather Service, (703) 260-0305. The Great Cacapon gauge should be over 4 feet.

WV 127 TO POTOMAC RIVER

DESCRIPTION: The river below the WV 127 bridge has very little gradient all of the way to the mouth of the Potomac at Great Cacapon. It transcribes huge loops through the mountains and ridges with a few mild rapids and many long, flat pools. It is an ideal float-fishing stream and contains some of the best bass fishing water in the state. (*Hint:* use eels, live or artificial, for bait. Catfish minnows are also good.) The river is rich in wildlife; it is not unusual to see beaver, wild turkey, and deer. If you are making a float trip, try to get on the river at daybreak. Eat your breakfast at mid-morning.

CLASS	FLAT WATER
LENGTH	40
TIME	4 DAYS
GAUGE	VISUAL
LEVEL	2 FT. + AT GREAT CACAPON
FLOW	FREE FLOWING
GRADIENT	NA
VOLUME	M
SOLITUDE	A
SCENERY	B

Much of the scenery down to Largent is pretty good, but there are a lot of vacation cabins and summer homes along the way, ranging from expensive whoppers to rangy trailers. New trailer parks and fishing camps are going in every day. (Is this what is to become of all West Virginia rivers?)

DIFFICULTIES: The only difficulty is a high dam about 4 miles above Great Cacapon. Carry on the left. Most landowners are not enthusiastic about having paddlers camp on their lands because of past abuses; always check first.

SHUTTLE: There are many possibilities here. Largent is reached from near the WV 127 bridge by taking WV 29 north to WV 9 and then turning right. Continue straight on WV 9 to Great Cacapon. The state of West Virginia has constructed access areas at WV 9, Great Cacapon, at WV 127, and at Cold Stream.

GAUGE: Call the Baltimore-Washington office of the National Weather Service at (703) 260-0305. Look for a reading at Great Cacapon of over 2 feet.

SHENANDOAH RIVER

MAPS: USGS: Round Hill, Charles Town, Harper's Ferry; County: Jefferson, WV, Clarke, VA, Loudon, VA, Washington County, MD, Frederic County, MD

VA 7 TO BLOOMERY ROAD NEAR WV 9

CLASS	A–1
LENGTH	13
TIME	4.5
GAUGE	PHONE
LEVEL	1.5+ AT MILLVILLE
FLOW	FREE FLOWING
GRADIENT	NA
VOLUME	L
SOLITUDE	B
SCENERY	B

DESCRIPTION: This is a good beginner's run near several canoe liveries that contains easy, smooth water runable even in the driest summer. There are occasional riffles formed by low limestone ledges or old fish-trap weirs. These wash out at moderate water levels (3 feet at the Millville USGS gauge.) The scenery is pleasant though not outstanding, banks are often high and tree-lined, and where they give way to bluffs, look for caves. There are also some views of the Blue Ridge to the east.

SHUTTLE: Put in at the Virginia Game Commission access area at VA 7 bridge, and take-out along Bloomery Road below WV 9. The shuttle routes are also quite scenic.

GAUGE: The minimum level might be 1.5 feet at Millville, although the river is mostly flat and could probably be run much lower.

BLOOMERY ROAD TO MILLVILLE

CLASS	1–2
LENGTH	3.5
TIME	1.5
GAUGE	PHONE
LEVEL	1.7+ FEET AT MILLVILLE
FLOW	FREE FLOWING
GRADIENT	NA
VOLUME	L
SOLITUDE	B
SCENERY	A–B

DESCRIPTION: Put in below WV 9 where Bloomery Road leaves the river. This is at the top of a short, interesting, Class-2 staircase rapid. Enjoy it while you can, because a wide, mile-long pool formed by a 20-foot power dam lies downstream. The dam is a masonry structure that's been extended a few feet higher by a wooden crest. At low levels (2 feet or less at the Millville USGS gauge), the water flows under the crest rather than over it. At these levels paddle to the left edge of the dam and you'll find a wooden ramp down which you can portage. Higher levels mean a tougher portage on the left on power company property. If you can't see the wooden crest before approaching the brink of the dam, the water's high and you can get washed over! Below the dam are more staircase ledges, which end in the pool at Millville.

GAUGE: Minimum level, 1.7 feet on the Millville gauge. Call the National Weather Service at (703) 260-0305.

MILLVILLE, WV TO SANDY HOOK, MD

CLASS	1–2 (3)
LENGTH	7
TIME	2
GAUGE	PHONE
LEVEL	2+ FT. AT MILLVILLE
FLOW	FREE FLOWING
GRADIENT	20–30
VOLUME	2,588
SOLITUDE	C
SCENERY	A–B

DESCRIPTION: This is a tremendously beautiful river no matter how you look at it. The river passes between majestic cliffs; winds through interesting islands; passes along the historic, nineteenth century charm of Harper's Ferry and the site of John Brown's fateful escapade; and finally joins the mighty Potomac through a magnificent gap in the Blue Ridge, the last water to bathe the West Virginia mountains. The river is home to an incredible variety of waterfowl.

The fabled Shenandoah Staircase may be seen just under and upstream from the US 340 bridge in Harper's Ferry. Like many rivers in the Eastern Panhandle, the rapids here are formed by the sharp, upthrusting ends of sedimentary rock. This creates a long, interesting series of ledges that span the entire river diagonally from right to left. This provides boaters with a variety of entertainment under fairly safe conditions. A paddler can find a passage, eddy out, ferry in either direction to find the next passage and so on. When the river is high it is powerful and dangerous, and some very large holes form where the ledges used to be.

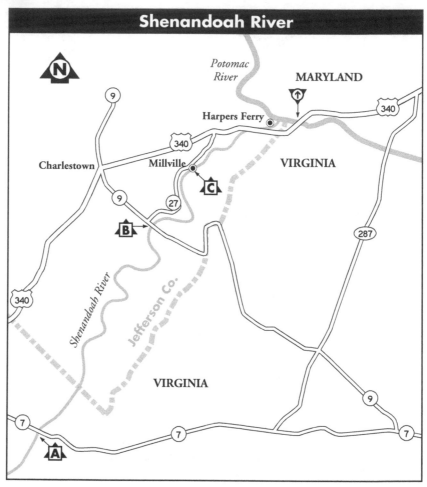

The Harper's Ferry area is a "must-see" for every West Virginian. It's an excellent place for the whole family, regardless of their interests. Some people just like to climb one of the many cliffs in the area, sit on a rock, and watch the river go by all day.

DIFFICULTIES: Not many, aside from getting there. The river begins as flat water, and the first rapid begins against a high cliff as the river turns to the right. The good water is on the left. The river then pools behind a river-wide barrage, Bull Falls. This 3–4-foot ledge has many possible passages. The ones on the left contain the heaviest water, and the ones on the right may not have enough unless the water is high. The novice should scout this first. There

will be at least one hydraulic and a series of haystacks below each passage. Another nice 100-yard descent follows immediately and will be rather turbulent at levels over 1 foot.

The Staircase, already described, is next, with the heaviest water just under and below the bridge. A half-mile down the Potomac, White Horse Rapids has a pretty good set of standing waves. Flips are common and rescues are difficult in high water.

SHUTTLE: Get to the put-in by driving west of Harper's Ferry on US 340 and turning left at the first interchange to Millville (marked by a sign to the right, "Harper's Ferry Caverns"). Put in at the pump house at river level. This whole area is a zoo on weekends, with heavy crowds and traffic. There have been a lot of break-ins here, so don't leave anything of value in the car. Just upstream of the pump house is a campground where secure parking is available for a fee. To alleviate congestion in the old town the National Park Service has forbidden boaters and tubers to land or take out in Harper's Ferry.

The take-out at the Potomac Wayside Area at the Virginia end of the US 340 bridge (over the Potomac)is pretty marginal. It's very crowded, the climb to the road is very steep, and parking is extremely limited. Try to get permission to park in the large lot next to the gas station.

Do not try to take out at Sandy Hook. Getting to the river involves crossing a busy railroad track. The National Park Service, who owns the land around it, will arrest you, fine you, and confiscate boats!

There's a take-out over in Weverton, Maryland. At the yellow light just inside the state, turn downstream near Cindy D's Restaurant and drive to the end of the road. If you block the gate you will be towed, so park on the shoulder.

Consider going down to the boat ramp in Brunswick, MD—a 3-mile flat paddle downstream. Take 340 to the first Brunswick/Knoxville exit, take the first right (Rt. 478), go under an overpass and across the only road going over the tracks. Turn right to the boat ramp. Do not block the ramp!

If you just want to run the Needles of the Potomac (see "The Main Stem of the Potomac," page 57), continue exactly 2 miles up the road from Sandy Hook to a convenient put-in.

GAUGE: Use the Millville reading (don't confuse this with the staff gauge on the pump house at the put-in). You'll want at least 2 feet. If over 4 feet, the Shenandoah is pretty high and Bull Falls will be dangerous. Call the Baltimore-Washington office of the National Weather Service at (703) 260-0305.

OTHER STREAMS IN THE MAIN STEM OF THE POTOMAC BASIN

LITTLE CACAPON RIVER

MAPS: USGS: Levels, Largent, Paw Paw; County Hampshire

FRENCHBURG TO LITTLE CACAPON

CLASS	I
LENGTH	24
GAUGE	PHONE
LEVEL	3.2 FT. + AT COOTES STORE
FLOW	FREE FLOWING/DAM
GRADIENT	NA
VOLUME	M
SOLITUDE	B
SCENERY	B

DESCRIPTION: This is an attractive run through a quiet valley. The first 3 miles are almost continuous riffles over gravel and small ledges. The remainder of the run is slower. The river starts in a fairly narrow rural valley, but the last several miles seem remote and beautiful, with steep wooded slopes creating an almost canyon-like atmosphere. High water is necessary to run from Frenchburg. Enough water at the start means plenty for the run.

GAUGE: Look for a Cootes Store reading over 3.2 feet. Call the Baltimore-Washington office of the National Weather Service at (703) 260-0305.

TEARCOAT CREEK

MAPS: USGS: Hanging Rock; County: Hampshire

TEARCOAT CREEK

CLASS	2+
LENGTH	3
TIME	I
GAUGE	VISUAL
LEVEL	4.6 AT MOOREFIELD
FLOW	FREE FLOWING/DAM
GRADIENT	NA
VOLUME	SMALL
SOLITUDE	A
SCENERY	A

DESCRIPTION: This is a short but extremely beautiful run cutting across the red shale of Hampshire County. It tumbles over an endless series of ledges separated by short pools at the bottom of a shadowy lichen-covered gorge. US 50 is nearby, but completely screened by vegetation. It's a 3-mile run to North River.

GAUGE: None. Look for the Moorefield River to be over 4.6 feet at Moorefield and the Great Cacapon gauge to be over 5 feet.

Call the Baltimore-Washington office of the National Weather Service at (703) 260-0305 for these readings.

NORTH RIVER

MAPS: USGS: Rio, Yellow Spring, Hanging Rock, Capon Bridge, Largent; County: Hampshire

NORTH RIVER

CLASS	I-3
LENGTH	22.5
TIME	7.5
GAUGE	PHONE
LEVEL	4.6 AT MOOREFIELD
FLOW	FREE FLOWING/DAM
GRADIENT	NA
VOLUME	VS
SOLITUDE	A
SCENERY	B

DESCRIPTION: This is a very small tributary of the Cacapon that is occasionally paddled when the water is very high elsewhere. It loops and winds through great meanders for some 21 miles between US 50 and WV 127. There is little gradient so the whitewater isn't very challenging. Be careful at sharp turns and under low branches. There are a few log dams. A few miles above WV 127 there's a 1.5-foot weir with a powerful roller. A large barn with a red silo is on the right.

The most unusual aspect of this run is the access it provides to Ice Mountain, one of the Eastern Panhandle's most incredible wonders. About 13 miles from the put-in, the stream transcribes a sharp left-hand turn and is pinched in by steep rock slides on each side. Find a place to stop and climb up onto this natural refrigerator! Here ice can be found among the rocks and in crevices, even in late summer.

When the river is very high, the North River Gorge is nonstop action over boulders, ledges, and gravel bars with few eddies, from Grassy Lick Run to Rio. Below Rio there are interesting ledges, one of which has a very powerful keeper hydraulic.

GAUGE: Look for the Moorefield gauge on the Moorefield River to read over 4.6 for the river above Rio. You can get by with about 3.3 at Springfield on the Potomac when running the lower river. Call the Baltimore-Washington office of the National Weather Service at (703) 260-0305.

SLEEPY CREEK

MAPS: USGS: Stotlers Cross Roads, Hancock, Cherry Run County: Morgan

CLASS	A–1
LENGTH	19
TIME	6
GAUGE	WEB
LEVEL	OVER 2 AT SIDELING HILL
FLOW	FREE FLOWING/DAM
GRADIENT	NA
VOLUME	S
SOLITUDE	B
SCENERY	A

SMITH CROSSROADS TO POTOMAC RIVER

DESCRIPTION: This is the most beautiful of the four streams in the Eastern Panhandle. It has been run from the Virginia line, but normally paddlers prefer to put in at Smith Crossroads. This stream is at first fairly smooth, but starting about 3 miles above WV 9, it is graced with numerous riffles and small rapids (Class 1). About 2 miles below the start, not far below the low-water bridge at Johnsons Mill, the river turns hard left and plunges 6 feet over a natural dam into a big round pool. The hole at the bottom could be dangerous; novices should carry and others should scout carefully. The scenery from Johnsons Mill to the Potomac is beautiful. The creek flows mostly through woodlands, past pretty bluffs, striking red shale cliffs, and rock formations. Take-out above the Potomac at the village of Sleepy Creek. Access at WV 9 is heavily posted so ask permission. This is strictly a wet-weather run.

GAUGE: None. If the Sideling Hill gauge on Sideling Hill Creek (on the USGS website) reads over 2 feet, you should have enough water. Call the Baltimore-Washington office of the National Weather Service at (703) 260-0305 for a reading.

MEADOW BRANCH OF SLEEPY CREEK

MAPS: USGS: Stotler's Crossroads, Big Pool; County: Morgan

CLASS	2–4+
LENGTH	8.5
TIME	3.5
GAUGE	NONE
LEVEL	NA
FLOW	FREE FLOWING/DAM
GRADIENT	1 @ 160!
VOLUME	VS
SOLITUDE	A
SCENERY	A+

SLEEPY CREEK LAKE TO WV 9

DESCRIPTION: This not-so-sleepy tributary of Sleepy Creek is located just south of Hancock, Maryland. It drops like a rock off of a high plateau in between Sleepy Creek Mountain and Third Hill Mountain. The put-in is at Sleepy Creek Lake. The run starts out pretty flat, and then half way down it drops 200 feet in 1.6 miles through a tight S-turn called the Devil's Nose. It's supposed to be Class 4+! No better description is available, but it sounds pretty interesting. The rest of the run is much easier.

SHUTTLE: To get to Sleepy Creek Lake turn onto CR-7 at Hedgesville, then onto CR 7/8 just past Jones Springs. Follow

signs to the Sleepy Creek Wildlife Management Area. The take-out is on WV 9.

GAUGE: Since the creek up there is very small, the pipe draining the lake needs to be completely full in order for the creek to be up. If Cootes Store is over 7 feet this might be worth a try.

BACK CREEK

MAPS: USGS: Glengary, Tablers Station, Big Pool; County: Berkeley

WV 45 to WV 9

CLASS	A
LENGTH	22
TIME	7.5
GAUGE	VISUAL
LEVEL	NA
FLOW	FREE FLOWING/DAM
GRADIENT	NA
VOLUME	S
SOLITUDE	B
SCENERY	B

DESCRIPTION: This is a pretty run winding up the middle of Berkeley County. It flows through both woodlands and pasture-land with good views of North Mountain to the east. Low-water bridges near Jones Springs and Tomahawk have adequate clearance at moderate levels, but the first one has so much debris jammed against it that it may require a carry. Intermediate access can be made at a ford east of Ganotown, a bridge east of Shanghai, a bridge east of Jones Springs, or two bridges east of Tomahawk.

SHUTTLE: Both access points are on clearly-marked roads.

GAUGE: Look for at least enough water to cleanly run the riffle under WV 45 on the left.

WV 9 to Potomac River

CLASS	I +
LENGTH	9
TIME	3
GAUGE	VISUAL
LEVEL	NA
FLOW	FREE FLOWING/DAM
GRADIENT	NA
VOLUME	VS
SOLITUDE	A
SCENERY	B

DESCRIPTION: After passing a long line of summer homes the creek loses itself in some (mostly) remote woods. There are some fairly long, easy rapids (Class 1+), especially below the first rail-road bridge, and a section with attractive shale cliffs. There is a low-water bridge at Allensville Road, which should be carried. It is scrapy when run at most levels. This is the last take-out on Back Creek. The next take-out in West Virginia is at the upstream end of Little Georgetown, located 4 miles down the Potomac River.

GAUGE: None. Inspect on site. This is a small stream that's only runable during wet periods.

OPEQUON CREEK

MAPS: USGS: Whitehall, Inwood; County: Berkeley

MAPS: USGS: Middle Way, Martinsburg, Hedgesville; County: Berkeley, Jefferson

CLASS	A– I
LENGTH	8
TIME	3
GAUGE	PHONE
LEVEL	2.5
FLOW	FREE FLOWING/DAM
GRADIENT	NA
VOLUME	S
SOLITUDE	A
SCENERY	B

VA 6472 (WADESVILLE) TO WV 51

DESCRIPTION: This is a small stream meandering through a pretty, sparsely populated pastoral valley. Unfortunately, high banks often block much of any view of the scenery, save the many big, wonderful old farmhouses. The stream is mostly flat but swift with many very small riffles formed by fine gravel.

GAUGE: You'll want roughly 2.8 feet at the Opequon Creek, Martinsburg gauge. Call the Baltimore-Washington office of the National Weather Service at (703) 260-0305.

CLASS	A– I
LENGTH	28.8
TIME	9.5
GAUGE	PHONE
LEVEL	2.5
FLOW	FREE FLOWING/DAM
GRADIENT	NA
VOLUME	S
SOLITUDE	A
SCENERY	B–C

WV 51 TO POTOMAC RIVER

DESCRIPTION: This is not as pretty a section as that above. The first few miles have lots of summer homes, and high banks hide the scenery. The noise from roads, railroads, and even an airport is hard to escape. The creek is generally smooth, but there are a few easy riffles and a good current.

SHUTTLE: A secondary road bridge on "12/7" provides an easy take-out about 200 yards above the mouth. The bridge itself is out, but the road dead ends on both sides.

GAUGE: The weather has to be pretty wet to run this creek. If the riffle at Rt. 51 is passable, the river is up. This corresponds roughly to 2.5 feet at Opequon Creek, Martinsburg. Call the Baltimore-Washington office of the National Weather Service at (703) 260-0305.

part**Two**

THE BIG MOUNTAIN RIVER— THE MIGHTY CHEAT

The Cheat watershed is a fantastic resource no matter how you look at it. It is, simply, the largest free-flowing, uncontrolled watershed in the East. All of the water you see high on Bald Knob when riding the Cass Scenic Railroad, or pouring over Spruce Knob through the mountain hamlets of Job and Whitmer, or plunging over Blackwater Falls near Canaan Valley, or forming an enchanting Arnout Hyde photograph in Bruceton Mills, all ends up in the same river—the mighty Cheat. Whitewater paddlers are in a unique position to appreciate all of it.

Most of the Cheat tributaries, and the Lower Cheat itself, have good gradient, lots of action, and spectacular scenery. Because its headwaters are almost entirely in the Monongahela National Forest, water quality is generally excellent. The upper forks are good trout streams, as is Horseshoe Run and the Upper Big Sandy around Bruceton Mills. There is still trout in the Cheat from Parsons to Saint George, and, there, the bass fishing is good until a few miles below Rowlesburg. Here the first of many side streams polluted with acid mine drainage enters.

Mining has been important in the Lower Cheat watershed for generations, but strip mining prior to the passage of federal reclamation laws did tremendous damage. The "Gem of Egypt," the "world's largest shovel," operated in the headwaters of Muddy Creek and Connor Run in the early 1970s. Many other areas were worked by smaller, but no less destructive, machines. Acid mine drainage is a huge problem in the lower Cheat basin; by the time the river enters the Canyon Section below Albright, it is essentially dead. In the spring of 1994 a mine seal in the Muddy Creek headwaters broke, sending millions of gallons of horribly acidic water into Muddy Creek. A rusty "bathtub ring" persisted on the riverbank for months. Friends of Cheat, formed as a response to this disaster, holds an annual river festival on the first weekend of May. They have done a lot to improve water quality in the area. The Lower Big Sandy and the Blackwater also suffer from mine acid problems.

There are many camping areas throughout the watershed. There is primitive camping along Shavers Fork in the Cheat Bridge area (FS 209), where "12" crosses Glady Fork, and at Jenningston on Dry Fork. The Forest Service has an excellent fee campground at Stuart Recreation Area on Shavers Fork, which is rarely open during paddling season. There are more primitive areas at Bear Heaven and Horseshoe Run. Dolly Sods, Laurel Fork, and Otter Creek are Forest Service Wilderness Areas. There are two state parks, Blackwater Falls and Canaan Valley (both have camping), and a National Wildlife Refuge nearby (also called Canaan Valley). There is an effort now to protect the entire Lower Blackwater Canyon from logging and development. You'll find a State Forest and campground at Cooper's Rock near Morgantown and two popular private campgrounds at the entrance to the Cheat Canyon in Albright.

Dam builders are everywhere, but only a few products of their activity exist. Low, but very dangerous dams exist on the Shavers Fork and on The Dry Fork just below Harman. There's also a nasty dam at the Albright Power Station just upstream of the Canyon put-ins. A power company dam near the Pennsylvania State Line created Cheat Lake. The USCOE once had plans for a huge dam at Rowlesburg on the Cheat, but they have never been successful in obtaining funds to build it. Although this could have made summer paddling on the Cheat Canyon and Narrows more reliable, it would have also spoiled the entire Cheat Valley between Rowlesburg and Parsons.

The history of the Cheat watershed could be the subject of an entire book. Buffs of the railroad and early logging days will nod in recognition as they paddle by the sites of the old logging towns along the rivers, like Spruce, Evenwood, Gladwin, Jenningston, Laneville, and many others. Some towns still exist today in the form of "bear camp" towns, like Bemis, while others have crumbled to dust. The wild and woolly Brooklyn Heights, where a dollar would buy you anything, is now known only as "the place across the river from Hendricks." The peaceful, outward calm of the mountain hamlets of Job and Whitmer belies its lawless past when murder, lynching, and robbery were the rule. No town has such interesting history as Saint George. Dating from before the Revolution, it changed sides many times during the Civil War. It had its title of county seat and its records forcibly stolen and removed to Parsons by an outlaw army. But this lovely little town, repeatedly saved by the pluck of its people, still prospers. George Washington passed through the lower Cheat and Big Sandy several times while trying to find a waterway from the Potomac to the

Ohio. Ill-informed locals told George that the Cheat was navigable upstream for miles, and it's headwaters weren't too far from equally navigable Potomac headwaters (the North Branch). It's a good thing that George didn't try it! We often wonder if our present leaders and policy makers get better advice than this today.

Logging is still a principal industry in the Upper Cheat watershed, although the logs are not floated downstream to mills anymore. Agriculture does not flourish in such rugged terrain and is limited to high mountain hay farms and fertile flood plains along the Cheat below Parsons. Preston County was once responsible for producing much of America's buckwheat, a product celebrated annually with a huge festival in Kingwood each September. Mining was a big part of the lower watershed's history, but today only a handful of operations remain open. The watershed has many under-appreciated natural and scenic attractions, and there is vast potential for all kinds of outdoor activities here.

Wildlife flourishes in the Cheat basin, including several black-bear breeding areas and plentiful deer and turkey. Some species, like the Cheat Mountain salamander, are limited entirely to this area. In other places, several closely related species exist together. Twenty-two species of warblers live together on Gaudineer Knob on upper Shavers Fork! The uppermost reaches of the Cheat forks contain native brook trout, although their days may be numbered if strip mining and clearcutting continue at the present rate. Beaver, muskrat, and an occasional otter may be seen. The high country is a botanist's delight, home to the highly aromatic ramp and rare orchids. Balsam fir exists in several stands in the Cheat basin, and American Larch makes its southernmost stand near the head of the Cheat Canyon at Cranesville.

DRY FORK OF THE CHEAT RIVER

This upper portion of this stream is nestled snugly between Rich and Allegheny Mountain, but it has its source high up on Rich. From Gandy Creek confluence on down, this is a tremendously picturesque little stream. It winds through an immense, high mountain valley reminiscent of Switzerland. When viewed from US 33 off Rich Mountain, the panorama is fantastic. As the river approaches and passes Jenningston, the scenery, although beautiful, becomes more pastoral than other Cheat tributaries. Signs of civilization, such as quaint old homesteads, churches, and rural schools are always present.

The Dry Fork is aptly named; water levels get really low in the summer and go up and down faster than the other Cheat tributaries.

MAPS: Whitmer, Harman, Mozark Mountain (USGS); Randolph, Tucker (County); Monongahela National Forest Map

CLASS	I
LENGTH	2+
TIME	I+
GAUGE	WEB
LEVEL	5–7 FT. AT HENDRICKS
FLOW	FREE FLOWING
GRADIENT	80–100 FT/MI.
VOLUME	VS
SOLITUDE	A
SCENERY	B

A

ABOVE GANDY CREEK

DESCRIPTION: This section of river is very small and exceedingly steep and follows Spruce Knob Road very closely. In periods of high run-off following the spring melts, you could run it for some distance above the mouth of Gandy Creek. It would be a continuous Class-2 chute, with only a few carries. The river is very high up and the scenery is magnificent. The weather is always colder than at lower elevations and can be rather severe.

GAUGE: Inspect from the road. The Gauge at Hendricks is found on the USGS web site. 5–7 feet is a good range for Section A. The Parsons gauge should read over 5 feet. Call the Pittsburgh Weather Service tape at (412) 262-5290.

CLASS	I–3
LENGTH	I2
TIME	4
GAUGE	WEB
LEVEL	3.5–7 FT. AT HENDRICKS
FLOW	FREE FLOWING
GRADIENT	40
VOLUME	S
SOLITUDE	A
SCENERY	B

B

GANDY CREEK TO WAYSIDE PARK (WV 32)

DESCRIPTION: The stream tumbles continuously at a Class 1–2 pace from the mouth of Gandy Creek through a series of highland meadow farms down to the US 33 bridge. There are no difficulties in this upper section unless a fallen tree or log temporarily dams the stream; at 2 feet or above, you'll need good boat control to negotiate the waves.

DIFFICULTIES: After passing under the US 33 bridge, there are long sections of channelized cobbles. Watch for a low-water bridge just downstream of the Medical Center and a wooden dam just below Harman. The latter can be run, but scout to avoid the middle piling. From Harman to the take-out, the stream returns to its continuous Class-2 character with two Class-3 rapids in the last half mile.

SHUTTLE: The put-in may be reached from US 33 by taking "29" south just upstream from the bridge. Continue through Job to the next fork. A put-in can be made on either Gandy Creek or Dry Fork at a bridge just upstream from the fork. The take-out

is located 2 miles north of Harman on WV 32 at the Wayside Park.

GAUGE: If you can run the ledges just downstream of the bridge, you'll be fine. The Gauge at Hendricks is on the USGS web site: 3.5–7 feet for Section B. Parsons on the Cheat should be reading over 5 feet. Call the Pittsburgh Weather Service tape at (412) 262-5290.

WV 32 TO JENNINGSTON

CLASS	1–2
LENGTH	7
TIME	2
GAUGE	WEB
LEVEL	3.2–7 FT. AT HENDRICKS
FLOW	FREE FLOWING
GRADIENT	36
VOLUME	S
SOLITUDE	A
SCENERY	A–B

DESCRIPTION: This is a charming run lazily meandering through scenic farmland. The area is rich in history from the boom days of logging. Approaching Jenningston, more isolated parts of the forest can be seen, but there are many remains of old homesteads, schools, churches, and other reminders of more populous times. The river is steady Class 2 with the intervening pools being short, thus providing almost continuous action. At higher water levels, the rapids could easily reach Class 3 in the lower stretches. The mouth of the Laurel Fork, about a half mile above Jenningston bridge, is a beautiful spot, and the stream contains many gentle "playing around" rapids.

DIFFICULTIES: Other than an occasional overhanging branch or low swinging bridge, there are no difficulties. Little maneuvering is involved. Try and catch this one with snow on the ground; it's beautiful.

SHUTTLE: Halfway between the villages of Dry Fork and Harman, a bridge crosses the stream from WV 32. Launch the boats from the small Wayside Park on the opposite side. Take out at the homemade picnic grounds on the left bank below the bridge in Jenningston. Find Jenningston by turning left at the first road past the village of Red Creek when traveling toward Parsons on WV 72. The river is 2 miles from this junction.

GAUGE: WV 32 runs close to the upper river here, so visual inspection is easy. If you can canoe the first 50–100 yards below the put-in you'll have no trouble. The Gauge at Hendricks is on the USGS web site. 3.2–7 feet is a good range for this section. Parsons on the Cheat should be running over 5 feet. Call the Pittsburgh Weather Service tape at (412) 262-5290.

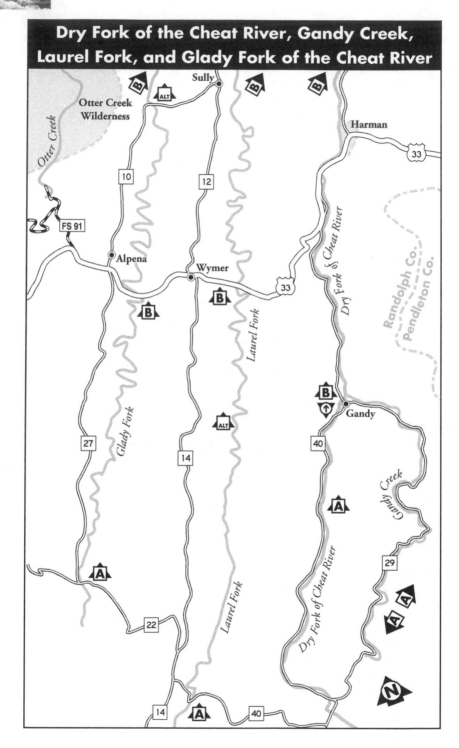

Dry Fork of the Cheat River, Gandy Creek, Laurel Fork, and Glady Fork of the Cheat River

Sully

Otter Creek Wilderness

Otter Creek

Harman

33

10

12

FS 91

Alpena

Wymer

33

Dry Fork of Cheat River

Randolph Co.
Pendleton Co.

Laurel Fork

Glady Fork

Gandy

27

40

14

A

Laurel Fork

29

22

14

A

40

Dry Fork of Cheat River

Gandy Creek

N

Dry Fork of Cheat River, Red Creek, and Otter Creek

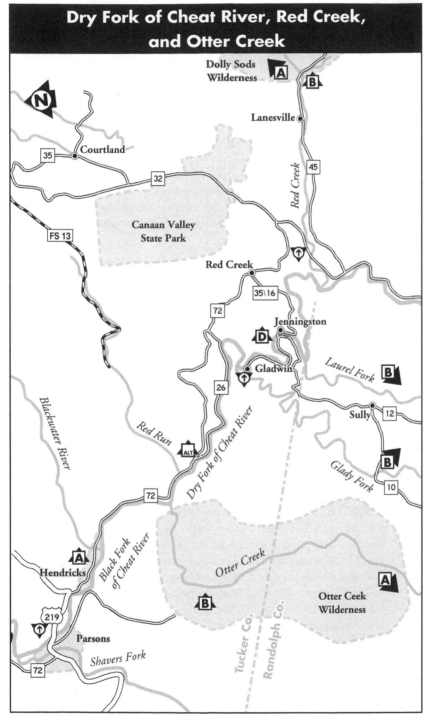

Dolly Sods Wilderness A B

Lanesville

N

Courtland

35

32

Red Creek

45

Canaan Valley State Park

FS 13

Red Creek

35\16

72

Jenningston

D

Gladwin

Laurel Fork B

26

Sully 12

Blackwater River

Red Run

ALT

Dry Fork of Cheat River

Gladly Fork B

10

72

Black Fork of Cheat River

Otter Creek

Hendricks A

B

Otter Ceek Wilderness A

219

Parsons

Shavers Fork

Tucker Co.

Randolph Co.

72

CLASS	2–3 (4)
LENGTH	12
TIME	4
GAUGE	PHONE
LEVEL	3–7 FT. AT HENDRICKS
FLOW	FREE FLOWING
GRADIENT	25
VOLUME	723
SOLITUDE	B
SCENERY	A–B

DESCRIPTION: This section of the Dry Fork does not meander, but flows directly northwest to Parsons through a rather deep trough. It is a classic Class-3 run. The rapids are fairly close together, providing rather continuous excitement. There are a few small ledges, but most rapids are long boulder gardens. The holes and waves get heavy when the water is up, but the worst of it is easily avoided. Flood effects are still evident; one post-flood rapid is created by cobbles, forcing the river into a narrow chute. The river at Gladwin, where the Glady Fork comes in, has a wonderful play spot near the road.

DIFFICULTIES: About 1 mile below the put-in, the river divides. After the forks rejoin, a steep rapid veers off to the right and curves back to the left. Paddlers are pushed to the right, and must either scramble quickly back to the far left or get ready to bust through a big hydraulic at the bottom. There are a couple of wide hydraulics below here that can be avoided by sticking to the far right side of the river.

The two rapids below the mouth of Otter Creek are good Class-4 in high water. The first rapid is a right-hand turn blocked by large rocks, and care is needed to avoid broaching in the turn. The next rapid is probably the most difficult of the entire run. The approach is partly obscured by a bus-sized boulder on the left. You must make an S-turn around this boulder beginning at the right and then immediately going back to the left and then over a drop through some fairly heavy and complicated water.

SHUTTLE: This is exciting! Hendricks is located on WV 72, a narrow, torturous road winding over high mountains and deep hollows. The scenery is superb, but if you want to look around you'd better stop your car. Take out where the river comes close to the road downstream of Otter Creek, or go a mile or two further to the American Whitewater access point. The AW access is located just upstream of the first swinging bridge below the mouth of the Blackwater. It is reached by taking the first turn towards the Dry Fork on the river right side of the WV 72 bridge over the Blackwater.

For a shorter trip with an easier shuttle, put in at Rich Ford on CR 26, which turns south off of WV 72 just east of Red Run. Jenningston is on "35/16," which turns off near the village of Red

Creek. If you reach this village from Parsons, you've passed the turn-off.

GAUGE: The Gauge at Hendricks is found on the USGS website; 3–7 feet is a good range. At high levels (and people run it really high) the playing is fantastic! Look for a reading over 4 feet at the Parsons Gauge. Call the Pittsburgh Weather Service tape at (412) 262-5290.

BLACK FORK OF THE CHEAT RIVER

The Black Fork's name, like its water, is the contraction of the Blackwater and the Dry Fork Rivers. Don't confuse it with its untamed shrew of a mother—the Blackwater, but think of it as a chip off the old block—the Dry Fork.

MAPS: Mozark Mountain, Parsons (USGS); Tucker (County)

MOUTH OF BLACKWATER RIVER TO PARSONS TANNERY

CLASS	2
LENGTH	4
TIME	1
GAUGE	PHONE
LEVEL	4–6 FT. (PARSONS)
FLOW	FREE FLOWING
GRADIENT	25
VOLUME	1,109
SOLITUDE	B
SCENERY	B

DESCRIPTION: This is an end-of-the-day-type of trip, ideally topping off a lower Shavers Fork or Dry Fork trip. The river courses between wooded mountains that are only partially spoiled by traces of civilization. Few maneuvers are necessary, but the volume and gradient combine to provide a rocking-horse ride over 3-foot, uniform standing waves.

SHUTTLE: Put in at American Whitewater's access site in Hendricks, which can be reached by taking the first turn towards the Dry Fork on the river on the right side of the WV 77 bridge over the Blackwater. You can also put in at the bridge and run the Blackwater River to the junction with Dry Fork. You could take out at the Parsons tannery (this is private land, so permission should be secured), or extend the trip 2 miles past the junction with Shavers Fork and on to the Holly Meadows bridge for a more scenic take-out. This spot can be reached from WV 72 below Parsons by turning right on "1." (See maps for the Dry Fork of Cheat River.)

GAUGE: The Parsons gauge on the Cheat should be 4–6 feet; call the Pittsburgh Weather Service at (412) 262-5290. The Hendricks gauge should read over 2.2 feet for this section.

GANDY CREEK

Gandy Creek disappears into a cave in a high meadow on the west side of Spruce Knob. A mile and a half away over the ridge, Gandy emerges as a whitewater stream. During flood periods when there is enough volume for paddling, it's a sporty run.

MAPS: Spruce Knob, Whitmer (USGS); Randolph (County); Monongahela National Forest Map

CLASS	2–3
LENGTH	13
TIME	4
GAUGE	WEB
LEVEL	4.5–8 FT. AT HENDRICKS
FLOW	FREE FLOWING
GRADIENT	37
VOLUME	S
SOLITUDE	A
SCENERY	A

SINKS OF GANDY OUTLET TO DRY FORK

DESCRIPTION: The most significant water on this run is a big diagonal stopper under a footbridge halfway down. It's pretty fast, continuous water, with 3-foot waves and holes along the road above Whitmer.

DIFFICULTIES: Like all small, steep streams there is a constant danger of being pushed into barbed-wire and steel-cable fences, strained under log footbridges, and impaled on sturdy fallen tree branches. The paddler should be able to scramble for small eddies like a pro quarterback buying time for covered receivers.

SHUTTLE: Easy. Pick your section along "29" from Dry Fork to the Sinks exit. (See map on p. 78.)

GAUGE: This run requires 4.5–8 feet at Hendricks, found on the USGS web site. The Gladwin gauge, also found on here, should read over 6.5 feet. Eleven feet on the Cheat at Parsons is also a good indicator; call the Pittsburgh Weather Service at (412) 262-5290.

RED CREEK

This little river drains the Dolly Sods area and is available only in very wet times. The upper section is one of the steepest and most isolated runs in northern West Virginia. The scenery is unspoiled, but the rapids are extremely difficult.

MAPS: Laneville, Hopeville (USGS); Tucker, Randolph (County); Monongahela National Forest Map

BLACKBIRD KNOB TRAIL TO FS 19

CLASS	4–5+(6)
LENGTH	7.2
TIME	5–7
GAUGE	VISUAL
LEVEL	NA
FLOW	FREE FLOWING
GRADIENT	80–280
VOLUME	VS
SOLITUDE	C
SCENERY	A+

DESCRIPTION: The run is long and isolated, and the thought of an injury here is too horrible to contemplate. It should be treated as an expedition for teams of committed experts only. The top half of the run is small and clean, but the lower half was badly scoured by the 1985 floods and has not yet stabilized, which creates trashy rapids and invites trees to fall in and clog things up. The run contains a good mix of slides, falls, and "loose" boulder drops. The boulder drops change frequently, especially after high water periods. After one high-water weekend in the spring of 2000, the hardest boulder drop on the creek was completely washed away! You'll put in on a fork of the creek, which will probably be fairly scrapy. After paddling almost 2 miles of small slides and rapids, you'll reach the junction of another, similar fork. The real descent begins here.

DIFFICULTIES: Below the junction of the two forks the river begins to drop at the frightening rate of 280 fpm for almost 3 miles. The creek goes over more slides than you'll probably ever see anywhere else. The action starts with a 100-plus yard "super slide" that drops a total of about 20 feet. The next drop is a 12–15 foot falls onto a solid rock shelf called The Clapper. This is followed by The Double Clapper, a 10-foot junky falls onto a slide. Some boulder-garden drops and small slides lead to a 15-foot waterfall that's best run left of center. After running a 6-foot ledge onto a small slide, you'll reach a most interesting phenomenon, a 200–300 yard slide that covers several bends in the creek. Although not very steep, it may be the longest slide in the entire state. The very next rapid is another slide that necks down at the bottom where the channel is blocked by a large boulder. You can't duck this, so portage on the left. After one more boulder drop, there's a rapid with another boulder that has fallen over that blocks the channel. This should also be portaged on the left. The next mile contains several good slides mixed with more boulder drops. A few are fairly steep and should be scouted. Soon you will reach the Devil's Cauldron, which is a 75-yard slide ending with a 15-foot falls into a mean hole. About a mile downstream, you will reach Finale Gorge, a series of 3 ledges ranging from 5–12 feet. The final 2.5 miles are anticlimactic, dropping steadily through a wide dredged-out channel.

SHUTTLE: It's about a 2-mile hike from the Blackbird Knob Trailhead to the river. To reach the trailhead, continue on FS 19 past Laneville to Dolly Sods, then make a left on FS 73. Follow this to the Blackbird Knob Trailhead parking lot just past Red Creek Campground. The Blackbird Knob Trail, shown on the Monongahela National Forest map, heads down to the river. Early in the trail, you will come to a fork. Take the left fork. *Note:* FS 73 is closed during the winter and early spring, so Red Creek has a short window of runability. The take-out is reached by taking "45" east of WV 32 for 6 miles to the take-out bridge. An alternative take-out is at the Laneville low-water bridge.

GAUGE: None. Examine the flow at the take-out. You'll need to be able to float this area without scraping to make a run on the upper section. Red Creek runs almost as often as the North Fork of the Blackwater; when the Blackwater River at Davis is over 500 cfs (3.7 feet), there is a good chance that Red creek will be going. Parsons should be at least 7 feet and rising, and Hendricks on the Dry Fork should be over 6 feet. Call the Pittsburgh Weather Service at (412) 262-5290.

NORTH BRANCH BRIDGE TO WV 32

CLASS	3–4
LENGTH	6
TIME	2
GAUGE	VISUAL
LEVEL	NA
FLOW	FREE FLOWING
GRADIENT	75
VOLUME	S
SOLITUDE	A
SCENERY	A

DESCRIPTION: Put in at the bridge on the North Branch just above the confluence with the South Branch and be ready for a heavily bulldozed, channelized run over cobbles. The river falls at a steady rate through the ghost lumber town of Laneville, past the first footbridge and ford, and on to the second footbridge at the ancient Canaan Crossing. This second footbridge marks a section of low ledges and stoppers. The course continues with Mount Porte Crayon towering 2,500 feet on the left and Cabin Mountain on the right. Surprisingly soon, the WV 32 bridge appears. The river continues for 1 mile to join the Dry Fork of the Cheat. The most convenient take-out is a quarter mile upstream from the mouth of the old bridge.

DIFFICULTIES: The upper part of the river may be described as busy, below the low-water bridge at Laneville it consists of bigger drops and waves. Approach the Laneville low-water bridge with caution and carry on the right. The first big ledge comes up fast at the end of an S-turn. *Beware:* downed trees may clog the smaller channels.

SHUTTLE: The put-in is reached by taking "45" east of WV 32 for 6 miles to the put-in bridge. If the water in the upper part appears too low, try an alternative put-in at the Laneville low-water bridge (also reachable via FS 19). The take-out bridge is on WV 32. (See map on p. 79.)

GAUGE: The Parsons gauge should be over 5 feet; call the Pittsburgh Weather Service at (412) 262-5290. Another good indicator is the Petersburg Gauge on the nearby North Fork of the South Branch of the Potomac. It should read 4 feet or higher. Call the Baltimore-Washington Weather Service at (703) 260-0305.

LAUREL FORK OF THE CHEAT RIVER

Both sections of this river carry a paddler back to the eighteenth century. The upper Laurel Fork is an intimate, easy stream flowing through the Laurel Fork-North Wilderness area. The lower section is one of the best runs of the Cheat basin, a long trip through uninhabited and virtually inaccessible country in a high valley between Middle and Rich Mountains.

MAPS: Sinks of Gandy, Glady, Whitmer, Harman (USGS); Tucker, Randolph (County); Monongahela National Forest Map

LAUREL FORK CAMPGROUND TO US 33

CLASS	I
LENGTH	I 6
TIME	5
GAUGE	PHONE
LEVEL	7+ FT.
FLOW	FREE FLOWING
GRADIENT	2 I
VOLUME	S
SOLITUDE	A
SCENERY	A

DESCRIPTION: The river's availability is limited to periods of very high water in the winter and spring. You'll leave civilization behind for a day of chasing deer and beaver along a swift-flowing river through marshy glades. The river has continuous fast water in a shallow, narrow bed.

DIFFICULTIES: Paddlers must be able to control their boats well enough to avoid being pushed into fallen and overhanging trees.

SHUTTLE: From the take-out at the US 33 bridge go west 1 mile, then south along the spine of Middle Mountain, on FS 14, for 12 miles, and then left down to Laurel Fork campground on the road to Spruce Knob.

GAUGE: Do not expect this section to be up unless the Parsons gauge is over 7 feet; call the Pittsburgh Weather Service at (412) 262-5290.

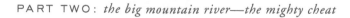

CLASS	3–4
LENGTH	13
TIME	5
GAUGE	PHONE
LEVEL	5+ FT.
FLOW	FREE FLOWING
GRADIENT	9 @ 71
VOLUME	S
SOLITUDE	A
SCENERY	A

US 33 TO JENNINGSTON

DESCRIPTION: The remnants of an early logging railroad play tag with the meandering river for the first 3.6 miles, crossing it 4 times where abandoned bridges remain. At this point, one hour into the trip, you encounter the first series of 2–4-foot ledges. These continue regularly for the next 2 miles until you reach the granddaddy of them all, a 12-foot unrunable waterfall. Portage on the left along the railway bed. After lunch at the foot of the falls, get ready for 7 miles of continuous Class-3 rapids to the mouth of the river. There are a total of eight bridge crossings on the run. Although none of the bridges remain, the abutments are readily spotted as landmarks. Between the seventh and eighth bridges there is a 50-yard tunnel from one limb of a half-mile loop to the other. During the 1985 flood a bridge abutment at the upstream end of the tunnel fell into the river. The resulting rapid is best run on the left. The last few miles are braided, with lots of strainers. Several hydraulics just above the Dry Fork junction create excellent hydraulics for playing, but at the end of such a long run you may not be interested. They get nasty at high water.

DIFFICULTIES: Spotting the falls from upstream should be no problem. It takes about an hour and a half of paddling time to reach the falls. There are six bridge crossings to the falls; the sixth one is about 1 mile above the falls. The falls are just around a right turn, where a ledge in the turn slopes to the outside (left). Under about 1 foot, the right side is shallow, so run the ledge on the left to get to the pool above the falls.

Well below the falls there is a sharp right turn, a slide that drops left to right, which then curls back to the left at the bottom. Run on the tongue above the curl, bearing left but not letting the curler do a job on you. Running on the right will require you to punch a hole at the bottom.

Watch out for strainers, particularly on the lower section, caused by eroding riverbanks.

The only other consideration is the fatigue of 13 miles of wilderness travel that includes 9 miles of continuous maneuvering. The take-out is about a quarter-mile downstream on the Dry Fork at Jenningston. The river is quite notorious for the big holes that develop at higher levels. Watch out!

SHUTTLE: Jenningston can be reached by following CR 45 down the mountain from WV 72 at Red Creek. The take-out will be the first bridge you come to on the Dry Fork below its confluence with the Laurel Fork. To reach the put-in, follow CR 45 up the other side of the valley; it changes to CR 12 at the Randolph County Line. Follow this to CR 10, which reaches US 33 at Wymer. Turn east, and the put-in is just down the hill on WV 33.

GAUGE: None. You'll have to estimate flow from on-site inspection. The Parsons gauge needs to be over 5 feet; Call Pittsburgh Weather Service at (412) 262-5290. Three other good indicators are found on the USGS Web Site: The Glady Fork at Evenwood should be over 4.5 feet, the Shavers Fork at Bemis should be over 5 feet, and the Dry Fork at Hendricks should read over 5500 cfs.

GLADY FORK OF THE CHEAT RIVER

The Glady Fork above US 33 is a milder version of the better-known stretch of river below it. Except for its pastoral start, it's a beautiful wilderness run flowing alongside Spruce Knob, the highest point in West Virginia. There are very few flat pools anywhere on the small, fast-moving lower section.

MAPS: Glady, Bowden, Harman, Mozark Mountain (USGS); Randolph, Tucker (County); Monongahela National Forest Map

GLADY TO THE US 33 BRIDGE

CLASS	1–2
LENGTH	14
TIME	4.5
GAUGE	WEB
LEVEL	OVER 3,000 CFS AT HENDRICKS
FLOW	FREE FLOWING
GRADIENT	20
VOLUME	VS
SOLITUDE	A
SCENERY	A

DESCRIPTION: Unlike the section below US33, this section doesn't gorge up. Rather, it flows through a gentle valley, passing softly through forested and rhododendron-lined banks. Appropriately enough, it passes lots of little patches of meadow or "glades" that gave the river its name. There are many easy riffles and an abundance of smooth water.

SHUTTLE: From the US 33 bridge over the Glady Fork, drive west and turn left onto CR 27. This heads due south to Glady. Turn left again onto CR 22 and put in at the bridge.

GAUGE: Check the USGS web site. Look for Dry Fork at Hendricks to be over 3500 cfs.

CLASS	1–3
LENGTH	16.5
TIME	5–6
GAUGE	WEB
LEVEL	OVER 4.2 FT. AT EVENWOOD
PERMITS	NO
FLOW	FREE FLOWING
GRADIENT	9@33; 7.5@46
VOLUME	S
SOLITUDE	A
SCENERY	A

US 33 BRIDGE TO ITS MOUTH ON DRY FORK (GLADWIN)

DESCRIPTION: The entire run is in unspoiled wilderness; the gradient is gradual but continuous, and the rapids are not particularly difficult. The upper river is quite shallow. It meanders a lot, and the turns can be tight. Fallen trees may block key channels, and all paddlers in your group should be able to make fast eddy turns in Class 2+ water. The lower part of the river is in a deep valley and is much more channelized.

From the US 33 bridge to Sully (mile 9), the current keeps up a steady Class-2 pace at first. Later the gradient begins to pick up and the last 3 or 4 miles have interesting waves and small holes. Do not get too close to the low-water bridge at the take-out because the current moves very powerfully under it.

SHUTTLE: Put in at the US 33 bridge. A take-out for a 9-mile trip may be had by taking "12" north out of Alpena and parking at the bridge. There is excellent camping here and along the road to the left. It is about 7.5 river miles from this bridge to Gladwin. Continue on "12," taking a left at each of the next two forks. At the bottom of the very steep hill, turn left again and cross the low-water bridge, which is the take-out. To extend the trip further, continue on this road over the hill until it dead-ends at the Dry Fork. Paddlers will carry the low-water bridge and continue down to the Dry Fork for 3 miles (see map, page 78).

GAUGE: The faded paddler's gauge at the mid-point Bridge is very hard to find and no longer accurate. The USGS gauge at Evenwood, reported on their web site, should be a minimum of 4.2 feet. The Parsons gauge on the Cheat should be over 5 feet. Call the Pittsburgh Weather Service at (412) 262-5290.

OTTER CREEK

Otter Creek flows out of a roadless wilderness that's home to black bear, turkey, and visiting backpackers. It's little, steep, and hard to catch up. A hiking trail, the remains of an old logging road, parallels the river for most of its length. It's well worth walking this beautiful stream even if you have no intention of running it.

MAPS: Bowden, Parsons, Mozark Mountain (USGS); Randolph, Tucker (County); Monongahela National Forest Map

ALPENA GAP TO BIG SPRINGS GAP TRAIL

CLASS	4–5+
LENGTH	10.5
TIME	5–7
GAUGE	PHONE
LEVEL	5+ FT.
FLOW	FREE FLOWING
GRADIENT	40–240
VOLUME	VS
SOLITUDE	B
SCENERY	A+

DESCRIPTION: Upper Otter Creek is very steep and isolated. It should be considered an expedition, and only the most capable boaters should even consider it. The "hard" drops on the lower section are similar to the "easy" drops on the upper section! There are also a number of steep slides and boulder rapids to contend with, as well as one waterfall. The upper stretch has fewer downed trees than the lower, but you still need to watch out for trapped debris.

DIFFICULTIES: For the first 4 miles, Otter Creek meanders through a marshy area before beginning its 200-fpm descent to the Big Springs Gap Trail. About 6 miles into the trip the river steepens noticeably, entering a 4-mile stretch with a gradient of over 240 fpm. After two slides, a large tributary enters, greatly increasing the flow. Below here, a 15-foot waterfall lands on rocks! This should be run on the right or portaged on the left. Next, there are several nasty slides; one of them has a vicious pinning rock that's especially hard to avoid. Below here the river goes through a series of tight, obstructed boulder rapids broken up by occasional smaller ledges and slides. Some of these are pretty juicy, and fallen logs occasionally cause problems. About 3 miles into the steep section (about 9 miles into the run) you reach the most difficult boulder drops on the run. Several of these are steep, blind, and studded with undercuts. Scouting is always a good idea. Just when you think that the action is over, you're faced with yet another tough drop! Stamina is a major prerequisite to completing a run down Otter! Finally, it "eases up" to Class 4 as it approaches the Big Springs Gap Trail.

SHUTTLE: Most people continue down Lower Otter to the Dry Fork and take out at the Otter Creek Parking Area. The put-in is at the headwaters near Alpena Gap off US 33. Take a service road back into Otter Creek Wilderness. Follow this straight back until the road ends at a trailhead and a small creek called Condon Run. Scrape your way down Condon into a marsh where you'll find a series of limestone-filled tumbling drums and a dam. These are maintained by the West Virginia DNR as an experiment in trying to neutralize this naturally acidic stream to improve its potential for native trout. The dam is a 5-foot drop onto concrete, easily portaged on the left.

GAUGE: This creek is very difficult to catch up, so don't miss an opportunity to run it. The mouth of Otter Creek is accessible via a footbridge, which crosses from a parking area on WV 72. The drop should be "well-padded, with no rocks showing." However, this is a pushy level for lower Otter Creek, so watch out! There is a gauge in the pool above the last rapid before the mouth. This should read 3.3–3.4 for a minimum. Above 3.8 the rapids start to get real juicy! There are also two gauges at Alpena Gap near the drums. The first is located on the left above the dam and should read 0.7 for a minimum. The second is below the dam and should read 1.5 for a minimum. You'll need at least 7 feet and rising on the Cheat gauge in Parsons to complete the run. The Dry Fork at Hendricks should be at least 4,000–5,000 cfs.

BIG SPRINGS GAP TO THE DRY FORK

CLASS	4
LENGTH	2.6
TIME	3
INCLUDING HIKE-IN	
GAUGE	PHONE
LEVEL	4.5– 5.5 FT.
PERMITS	NO
FLOW	FREE FLOWING
GRADIENT	100
VOLUME	S
SOLITUDE	A
SCENERY	A+

DESCRIPTION: From the Big Springs Gap put-in to the Dry Fork a paddler is confronted with a long series of complex boulder rapids. While not as hard as those in the upper stretch, many drops are steep and blind. A few require scouting; most can be boat-scouted by strong parties comfortable with grabbing small eddies. At low water there are few holes of any size, but there's lots of downed timber and numerous potential pinning spots. At high water the river is fast and pushy, something of a wild aquatic bobsled run. It's beautiful and exhilarating, but very tiring.

DIFFICULTIES: Watch out for wood!

SHUTTLE: Set up the take-out at the Hendricks gauge for a fast 2.5-mile finish down the Dry Fork from Otter Creek's mouth. Shuttle back into Parsons and follow signs to Fernow Experimental Forest. Park at Big Springs Gap Trail and carry your boat 20 minutes down the trail to the put-in.

GAUGE: The mouth of Otter Creek is accessible via a footbridge crossing from a parking area off WV 72. If the last drop on the creek looks runable, there's plenty of water to do Section B. You'll need about 6 feet and rising on the Parsons gauge on the Cheat gauge in Parsons to do Section B.

RED RUN

Not to be confused with Red Creek, this steep little stream drains Canaan Valley. Its mouth is just upstream of Otter Creek. The lower section of Red Run is the most difficult run in the Canaan area. It runs through a steep gorge and is very remote. The creek is very small and continuous, with only a few small eddies to stop. An impressive series of gnarly boulder drops starts early in the trip and continues all the way to the end. The rapids are very tight and abusive, with lots of undercuts and sieves. The scenery is breathtaking, but the rapids are so intense that you'll hardly notice.

MAPS: Mozark Mountain (USGS); Tucker (County); Mononga-hela National Forest Map

CONFLUENCE OF NORTH AND SOUTH FORK TO RED RUN FORD

CLASS	4–5
LENGTH	1.5
TIME	1–2
GAUGE	VISUAL
LEVEL	NA
FLOW	FREE FLOWING
GRADIENT	186
VOLUME	VS
SOLITUDE	C
SCENERY	A

DESCRIPTION: This upper part of Red Run is a fast and fun stretch that makes a good add-on to the lower part or a good substitute when the other steep creeks are too high. The scenery is very pretty, flowing through groves of laurels with the occasional side stream cascading in. The action is utterly continuous through slides and rock gardens in a steep creekbed.

DIFFICULTIES: A few of the rapids are fairly steep and you may want to scout. Eddies are at a premium so be careful. Being a small stream, you always need to watch out for strainers.

SHUTTLE: To reach the put-in get on Canaan Heights Road off of WV 32 between Davis and Canaan Valley. This leads back into the woods. Turn right at a fork and pass a gate. Soon you will be in the Red Run drainage. Eventually, you'll cross the North Fork of Red Run, a very small stream that parallels the road on the left side. The confluence of the North and South Fork is not visible from the road but the creek swings close just afterwards, where you'll see a few slides and boulder drops. Put in here. About 1.5 miles further down the road, you'll see a ford on your left. This is the take-out.

GAUGE: See section B. You need more water to run this stretch than section B. Look for a minimum of 1.6 on the gauge at the Red Run Ford to run this.

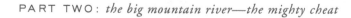

RED RUN FORD TO DRY FORK OF THE CHEAT

CLASS	5–6
LENGTH	4.8
TIME	5+
GAUGE	VISUAL
LEVEL	NA
FLOW	FREE FLOWING
GRADIENT	0.8 @ 150 4 @250
VOLUME	VS
SOLITUDE	C
SCENERY	A+

DESCRIPTION: Lower Red Run should be treated as an expedition by experienced creek-boaters in excellent physical shape. People who go in without the right gear and preparation might not come out! You need the skill to be comfortable on the Upper Blackwater and other high-end runs in the area. Luckily, just in case you get in over your head, there's an old logging road on the right bank high up at the rim of the gorge.

DIFFICULTIES: The creek drops over continuous small rock gardens for almost a mile before getting down to business. After a long slide, you'll come to Goliath, a long, steep, three-part rapid. The first part is a 10-foot ledge onto a twisty slide that pillows off the right bank, then caroms into the left bank and off a 5-foot ledge. A small slide carries you to the second part, which is a steep series of boulder drops that lead into a narrow slot followed by a 7-foot ledge. The third part is immediate as the creek splits around a rock island. The right half drops several feet into a pile of rocks and is unrunable. Run down the left over a series of ledges. The next several boulder drops are pretty steep and one has a very nasty undercut at the bottom.

The run continues through more stretches of steep boulder drops and a few slides until you reach a 20-foot waterfall. It lands in a mess of rocks and boulders with no good landing spot. It has been run but it's definitely not recommended. Portage on the right. *Note:* There is a slide leading into the falls, make sure you don't accidentally start down the slide. Look for a large horizon line.

Immediately below the falls, you want to cut left and paddle back into a huge cave. There is a small rapid in the cave before it empties back into the main channel underneath a beautiful waterfall pouring in from above.

Right below here, the gradient steepens and the creek goes through the toughest boulder drops on the run. There are several narrow 5–8 foot drops with ugly boulders and undercuts waiting at the bottom. At one point, the creek splits on an island (take the right) and goes down a steep series of ledges called S••t Your Pants. The channels converge, then there's a 5-foot ledge. The water on the left (where most of the water goes) drops into a horrible looking sieve. You definitely want to get right but the water pushes real hard left. Portage if there is any doubt.

Red Run, Blackwater River, N. Fork of the Blackwater River, Little Blackwater River, Glade Run, N. Branch of the Blackwater River, and Black Fork of the Cheat River

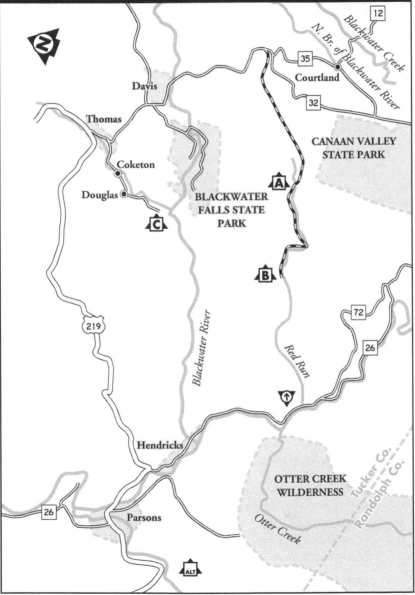

After awhile the gradient begins to let up slightly and you'll see some houses as you approach the end of the run. The slide just above the bridge gives little indication of the craziness upstream.

SHUTTLE: To reach the put-in, get on Canaan Heights Road off of Rt. 32 between Davis and Canaan Valley. This goes back into the woods. Turn right at a fork and pass a gate. Red Run will collect itself for awhile, and you will eventually see a ford on your left. This is the put-in. There's a bridge over Red Run on Rt. 72, but since there's not much parking it's best to continue down the Dry Fork to the Otter Creek parking lot. There is a logging road that goes up the right bank of the creek (it connects with Rt. 72 near the bridge). If you don't have two vehicles, you can hike up this road as far as you are willing to walk and put in.

GAUGE: There's a gauge on river right just above the ford at the put-in. You need a minimum of 1.4 here for a low-water run. The put-in is way back in the woods, so examine at the take-out before deciding to give it a try. If the slide at the Rt. 72 bridge looks runable without being too scrapy, you should have enough water. The Dry Fork at Hendricks (check the USGS web site) needs to be in the 4,000–5,000 cfs range.

THE BLACKWATER RIVER

The Blackwater River has its headwaters in a vast upland swamp in Canaan Valley. Multiple branches funnel the 150-square-mile drainage basin into 2 main forks, which pass through the nineteenth-century logging capitals of Davis and Thomas. Here they leap off the mountain as falls, each 50 feet high. This is the beginning of a relentless rush through a steep canyon to the Dry Fork, 8 miles and 1,000 feet below. Both falls, the one preserved by a state park and the other on the North Fork, are worth seeing.

The waters of the Blackwater are non-silted, brown, and covered with suds, a form of natural pollution noted since the days of Thomas Lewis. This 1746 explorer appropriately called this stream the "River Styx." The dark color is attributed to organic acids from the upland swamps leaching iron oxides from the red shale that lines the riverbed. There have been extensive efforts on the North Fork of the Blackwater to reclaim areas damaged by mining.

MAPS: Blackwater Falls, Davis, Mozark Mountain (USGS); Tucker (County); Monongahela National Forest Map

CANAAN VALLEY SECTION: WV 32
NEAR TIMBERLINE SKI AREA TO DAVIS

CLASS	A–2+
LENGTH	11
TIME	4
GAUGE	PHONE
LEVEL	2.6–3.6 FT.
FLOW	FREE FLOWING
GRADIENT	9
VOLUME	193
SOLITUDE	A
SCENERY	A

DESCRIPTION: In 1994, the US Fish and Wildlife Service purchased land to establish the Canaan Valley National Wildlife Refuge. Their goal was to protect the high altitude wetland and northern forest area drained by this section of the Blackwater River, which is home to hundreds of unique plants and animals. This is a fairly new National Wildlife Area, and there may be restrictions on paddling through this section in the future. The best way to avoid such regulation is to travel quietly and with respect.

The river is flat but swift, with clear brown ("black") water. Beaver-gnawed stumps are found throughout. The character of the river changes when it passes through a gap in Brown Mountain. From here on down, "Delta Road 1" parallels the river. The last few miles contain many enjoyable small ledges. The trip ends in the pool of a 10-foot dam at Davis. There's a mix of flatwater and mild rapids between here and Blackwater falls, but no good take-out below the dam.

SHUTTLE: The put-in is on WV 35 in Cortland, reached from WV 32 south of Davis. take out above the dam in Davis.

GAUGE: See section B.

UPPER BLACKWATER RIVER–
OVERLOOK TRAIL TO NORTH FORK JUNCTION

CLASS	5+ (6)
LENGTH	2.5
TIME	4
GAUGE	PHONE
LEVEL	2.5–3.5
PERMITS	No
FLOW	FREE FLOWING
GRADIENT	250
VOLUME	S
SOLITUDE	B
SCENERY	A+

DESCRIPTION: This is the famous "Upper B." Joe Monahan and his group ran this incredibly steep, congested run in 1971, but they made a lot of carries. It wasn't until the 1990s that people started to run it regularly. Although short, it's extremely steep, technical, and isolated. Every rapid has a runable path through it, but some of the channels in the major rapids end in undercuts and sieves so you'll want to scout when in doubt. Rhododendron hells and giant boulder piles will make this a strenuous activity. Although elite experts familiar with the run can move through it with surprising speed, first timers running without guides will find the going slow and arduous. High water is pushy, but opens up the big drops. Low water slows the pace, but increases pinning

possibilities even in the "easier" rapids. The run keeps coming at you from the moment that you put on to the moment you reach the North Fork, so endurance as well as skill comes into play.

The streambed is fairly loose in spots and changes slightly after each high-water period. The run generally has done a good job reconstructing its rapids and seems to still be in the act of "cleaning itself up." Many small rocks that used to mess with paddlers have been moved out of the way by the forces of nature. There still are some small underwater rocks to watch out for but their numbers decline with each passing year.

DIFFICULTIES: The put-in is about 100 yards below Blackwater Falls and directly below a rapid called Puke. A few paddlers have run Puke, but it is quite an ugly drop and is not recommended. The first rapid is called Phil's or 100 Yard Dash and will let you know real quickly if you belong on the run or not. It is a long series of ledges with juicy holes that gives you a good indication of what to expect for the rest of the run.

About a half mile into the run, you'll reach Z-Falls, a steep series of ledges. After several more steep boulder drops, you'll come to Tomko Falls, which signals the start of the steepest section on the run. Here noted hair boater Dean Tomko lost a boat for the first time in his life. It contains two, closely spaced, 8-foot ledges, the second of which needs to be boofed in the correct place to avoid a nasty pin. After a small slide, you reach Shock To The System, a constricted 8-foot drop into a bad hole. You'll definitely want to look at the next rapid, known as Sticky Fingers. It contains a horrible sieve that has been the scene of one fatality and several other close calls. Most people walk this on the right. Immediately below lies Pinball, a steep, shallow series of drops run far left. Avoid the temptation to go down the right (where most of the water goes) because it drops onto a deadly sieve. Boof left or Piton is next. It's a narrow 8-foot drop into a juicy hole that you boof angling left. This leads right into Flatliner Falls, a 6-foot drop off a slab of rock run in the center.

Things start to calm down slightly as you pass Pendleton Falls cascading in on the right, but it isn't over yet. Soon you're faced with blind boulder drops. When the river character changes to slides, look out for My Nerves Are Shot and I Can't Take It Anymore! This is a 200-yard long series of slides with some bad holes to avoid. The run finishes with a junky 5-foot ledge best boofed right of center angling right into a narrow slot called Tightness.

SHUTTLE: State Park management does not permit paddlers access to the Upper Blackwater via their river-right stairway to the base of the falls. This cuts out "the gap": two steep, demanding drops featured on the cover of several Wildwater Designs

catalogues. In a negotiated settlement, the park agreed to allow access via a steep trail departing from the river-left overlook on 29/1. They ask that kayakers park across the street and avoid filling up the limited parking spaces at the overlook. You could take out at North Fork Junction, but the climb is pretty strenuous. Many paddlers combine this run with the lower Blackwater and take out at Hendricks.

GAUGE: Use the Davis gauge. This run is extremely channelized and can be run quite low: 200 cfs (2.5 feet) should be considered a minimum (although it can be run a little lower). The maximum varies depending on the skill of the party involved. Most paddlers run this between 200–320 cfs (2.5–3 feet). The run is rarely attempted above 500 cfs (3.7 feet).

Blackwater Falls to the Junction with the North Fork— April 15, 1982

Lured by warm weather, decent water levels, and the slow pace of spring business, I decided to head down to West Virginia. After a 6-hour drive from Philly I crashed in the parking lot of Eastern River Expeditions in Albright. At 7 a.m. I was awakened by two guides asking if I wanted to run the Upper Yough. I declined; it was my first time out, and I wanted something easier. Hah!

As the warmth of the morning sun revived me, I decided it was time to go inside and wake up John Connelly, and with Bill Dallam, we discussed the possibilities. The Tygart was at 4.5; the Cheat at 3 and as we were trying to decide between the two, somebody mentioned the Blackwater—the Upper Blackwater, above the normal run. Now let it be said that I had been looking at that little gem since 1972, when I hiked it one cold February day.

Three things were necessary; the right people, perfect weather, and good water. We had the first two. Bill called Transmontain in Davis and found sufficient water. Despite a low Cheat, the late spring snows must have lingered on the Plateau. When Kinsey, one of John's guides, agreed to run shuttle, that was it.

After several hours of errands and general fiddling, we arrived at Blackwater Falls. The river is channeled between huge boulders, and the first three drops ranged from marginal to impossible. After a short hike downstream we found easier water, and despite the advanced hour of 1 p.m., we put in. The plan was for our shuttle driver to proceed to North Fork Junction and wait. Bill felt that the length of the run would be about 3 miles; if we got lucky, Kinsey could join us for the run out to Hendricks. We pulled together the essentials, just in case: first-aid kit, throw rope, extra food, and water. Stuffing our boats, we carried down the tourist path to the base of the falls, put in, and ran 100 yards to the first portage.

The river is incredibly steep, and for a while the ratio of boating to hiking was about 50:50. We were nervous, because we knew that if the topography was wrong, we could be stopped dead a long way from help. A pattern developed. I'd get out ahead and sneak down as far as I could. Once I'd found a cul-de-sac, Bill would scout, then run the drop. John and I would watch to see what happened to Bill, then run or carry. Many of the drops, though quite fierce looking at the top, were reasonably straightforward once we got into them.

There was one delightful stretch in which one steep, complex drop followed another, all runable, and none particularly dangerous. Many of the ledges had rocks at the bottom, demanding good control and fast turns to avoid trouble just as you dropped over the lip. John Connelly pinned nose first once, but was held for only a second. Standing on the rocks you could feel the river tilting downstream. A wild and exciting place to be, as long as you made no mistakes!

Then the bottom fell out: four utterly unrunable drops blocked our path. Only this time the portage was really bad; we'd left the trail behind, and huge rocks and laurel hells lined the banks. The drops were too obstructed for lining, so we had to "carry"—push, lift, drag,

curse, etc. I needed help in muscling my overweight, soon-to-be-retired Hahn C-1 through the brush. As we emerged at the river's edge the sun was starting to sink behind a ridge. We knew time was running out and that we were tiring. Not wishing to contemplate a night out, we pushed on.

The rapids continued to be quite demanding, only now none of us felt quite as frisky as before. I began to wonder if I had the strength to make some of the moves, and we were running some pretty stout stuff with minimal scouting. There was not much margin for error. As the sun winked from behind a tree-covered ridge, I missed an eddy at the top of a long, obscure drop. Fortunately, it was all runable, but this isn't exactly my style. I dipped into an eddy above a blind drop to contemplate my folly, only to have Bill and John follow me in. They figured I knew what I was doing. Carrying a drop, we came upon a major tributary. Was this the junction? We would soon find out.

The canyon opened up tremendously here and the rapids were now much saner. The sun shone on us again, creating reflections, which would have been beautiful had they not made it so difficult to see where we were going. I was tired enough to resolve to carry anything that looked the least bit demanding, since I could drag my boat along the high-water channel without much trouble. No more laurel hells, anyway. The canyon here is quite attractive, much more intimate than it is below. On one of my portages, I spied the railroad trestle, perched high on a ridge. But the junction was still a long way downhill. A few brisk runs and a carry later, we arrived at our take-out. Three cairns showed that Kinsey had been there. We shook hands, stashed boats, and headed up the hill in the gathering twilight.

The climb was incredibly steep, and tired as we were, it seemed interminable. It was dusk by the time we got onto the tracks, and as we headed out, we ran into

Kinsey, his pack loaded with clothing and rescue gear. A local man had provided easy access to the tracks; we chatted for a while, then headed for civilization and food in the van.

The next day we ran our boats out to Hendricks. The same local man we met yesterday offered us parking, and delighted us with a demonstration of how he had trained his dog to retrieve golf balls in the rugged country in which he lived. He warned us that the lower section had been reported impassable by an earlier party, but after the preceding day's experience we weren't too worried. The first mile below the junction was reminiscent of the upper stretch, but we carried twice because of low water. The great slide was also too low, and the waterfall below was bounced and slid down by Dallam as John and I gestured derisively from shore. The gauge at Hendricks read minus-3 inches, a bit thin, but a better option than trying to drag the boats up the hill to the tracks.

Charlie Walbridge

Reprinted from Canoe Cruisers Association of Washington,
Cruiser, July 1982.

CLASS	4 (5)
LENGTH	7
TIME	4
GAUGE	PHONE
LEVEL	1−2.5 FT.
FLOW	FREE FLOWING
GRADIENT	5@112
VOLUME	193
SOLITUDE	B
SCENERY	A

LOWER BLACKWATER RIVER—NORTH FORK JUNCTION TO HENDRICKS

DESCRIPTION: The Blackwater and the North Fork converge about a mile below their initial drops. The gradient below here is more realistic for padding, but this section still has a reputation for continuous difficulty. The challenge lies in reading and negotiating chutes over staircase ledges randomly strewn with large boulders. There are no pools of any size. Constant maneuvering in a pushy current is required, and moving side eddies provide the only rest or rescue spots. The first 5 miles are the steepest, and several of the drops are quite complex. The steep banks are unstable, and trees frequently fall into the river and clog the chutes. By the time you get to the easier last 2 miles you'll be ready to relax.

DIFFICULTIES: This is a strenuous trip. The carry in is exhausting, especially for open boaters. The rapids are mostly Class 4, but a lack of pools and the fatigue of constant maneuvering make it seem harder. Another complication is that the river runs in a southwesterly direction, into the afternoon sun. Sunglasses are recommended for afternoon paddling.

About 200 yards downstream from the put-in are two, closely-spaced drops that are Class 5 at most water levels. The first, Krakatoa, is a two-part ledge drop. Two aggressive holes must be dealt with. At the second drop, called the Ledge, the whole river falls 6 feet into a very powerful hole. The next few drops are blind and have inconsiderately placed rocks at the bottom. Scout if you can't see the route from your boat.

Below here is Rock and Roll (Class 5), a rapid created by the 1985 flood. It's long and complex, and should be scouted on the right. At the bottom the river narrows to about 6 feet wide between undercut rocks and drops into a juicy hole. At about 1.5 miles a unique rapid serves as a landmark. The water races 75 yards over a flat, sloping, red shale floor. The current reaches horrendous speeds before abruptly dropping into a giant washing machine at the bottom. Shortly below here Tub Run comes in on the right. About halfway through the trip, a trashy 10-foot falls will be encountered. Carry or scrape over on the left. Paddle across the pool and look at the next rapid below, where the river falls into a large hole. This can be scouted, or carried easily on the left.

SHUTTLE: The shuttle is pretty straightforward, but the put-in is horrendous! From the take-out under the WV 72 bridge in Hendricks, follow US 219 to Thomas. Turn right on "27" towards Coketon and Douglas. Where an abandoned railroad bed crosses the river, turn left, and proceed down what is now a rough gravel road along the North Fork. Park somewhere near the gate but don't block it! Walk about 1 mile to the point where 2 forks converge then lower your boat carefully to the river. The grade averages about 45 degrees and some parts are quite unstable. Pick a safe route, go slowly, and don't let go of your boat! The railroad bed follows the river all the way to Hendricks and provides a way back to civilization in emergencies.

GAUGE: The gauge at Davis is on the Pittsburgh Weather Service flow phone Call the Pittsburgh Weather Service flow phone at (412) 262-5290. Look for levels between 2.6–3.6 feet (225–475 cfs). To minimize scraping and boat abuse, try for 350 cfs or more. The Parsons gauge on Cheat needs to be over 5 feet.

NORTH BRANCH OF THE BLACKWATER RIVER

The North Branch at Cortland also travels through the Canaan Valley National Wildlife Refuge. This area was set aside for the protection of the region's unique plant and animal species. It is possible that paddling may become regulated in the future. All those traveling through here should exercise extra caution to minimize impact.

MAPS: Blackwater Falls, Davis (USGS); Tucker (County); Monongahela National Forest Map

CLASS	A
LENGTH	9
TIME	4
GAUGE	VISUAL
LEVEL	NA
FLOW	FREE FLOWING
GRADIENT	3
VOLUME	NA
SOLITUDE	A
SCENERY	A

A

CORTLAND TO CAMP 70

DESCRIPTION: Surprisingly, the North Branch is runable even when the nearby Blackwater is only a trickle over the shale. Don't be discouraged by the unrunable riffle at the bridge and the narrowness of the stream; it is deep enough and gradually widens. About three-quarters of a mile from the start, alders crowd the stream for a quarter mile, but beyond, the depth increases and the only obstacles are occasional beaver dams. The last mile before the Blackwater, the North Branch snakes across broad beaver meadows. After 3.5 miles on the North Branch, the first take-out is 5.5 miles down the Blackwater at Camp 70.

SHUTTLE: Take "35" south from WV 32 to Cortland for the put-in, 700 feet east, below the fence and bridge. For the take-out, go north on WV 32 to Davis, cross the Blackwater, and make the first right. Go across Beaver Creek on an old railroad bridge at Yellow Creek and follow the dirt road 4 miles to Camp 70. If the Blackwater is up, a take-out at this bridge eliminates the roughest part of the road. Whitewater paddlers could continue to Davis for a 19-mile trip.

Some no-shuttle options: Paddling back up the North Branch is quite easy. You could also paddle down the Blackwater from Cortland and return up the North Branch for a 7-mile circuit.

GAUGE: None. If the first half-mile is even marginally runable, there's plenty of water for the rest of the trip. In a normal year, the river is normally runable all spring and occasionally in other seasons. This is due not only to the low gradient and the bogs, but also to the geologic structure. About 1.5 miles below Freeland Run, the Blackwater leaves the Greenbrier limestone to enter a shale ridge. Just over a mile north in the same limestone layer is the North Branch, 40 feet lower. Some of the mainstream's water is pirated underground to Cortland.

NORTH FORK OF THE BLACKWATER RIVER

The North Fork makes its way through the logging towns of Thomas, Coketon, and Douglas. It flows along lazily for several miles before it drops off the edge of the earth near Douglas. This section is comprised of small rock gardens and sloping ledges. Though the scenery isn't much to look at, this is a nice, relaxing warm-up for the chaos that follows in the next section.

MAPS: Blackwater Falls, Davis (USGS); Tucker (County); Monongahela National Forest Map

THOMAS TO DOUGLAS FALLS

CLASS	2–4
LENGTH	2.5
TIME	2
GAUGE	PHONE
LEVEL	4 AND UP
FLOW	FREE FLOWING
GRADIENT	40
VOLUME	VS
SOLITUDE	B
SCENERY	C

DIFFICULTIES: There is an 8-foot ledge under a bridge about 0.5 miles into the run. About a half mile above Douglas Falls you'll find a 10-foot falls called Barber Shop Falls which should be run on the right. After Long Run (a sizeable tributary) dumps in on the right, you should be looking to get out. The horizon line of Douglas Falls is fairly easy to see, but you should be careful nonetheless.

SHUTTLE: Put in below the dam in Thomas off WV 32. To reach the take-out, follow "27" to where the railroad bed crosses the road (at a bridge over the North Fork). Head downstream until you reach the gate.

GAUGE: The Blackwater at Davis should read 4 feet (600 cfs) or more to run the upper part. If the gauge stick 100 yards above Douglas Falls is under or close to it, you should have good water.

DOUGLAS FALLS TO NORTH FORK JUNCTION

CLASS	5+
LENGTH	5.2
TIME	2.5
GAUGE	VISUAL
LEVEL	-5 IN. & ABOVE
PERMITS	NO
FLOW	FREE FLOWING
GRADIENT	27
VOLUME	VS
SOLITUDE	B
SCENERY	A–B

DESCRIPTION: For years paddlers looked at the North Fork on the way to the Lower Blackwater and shook their heads. It's now run on a regular basis, but it approaches the limits of tight, vertical, obstructed drops. There have been serious injuries here, and "rock rash" from impacts with sharp-edged boulders is a common memento of the run. Nonetheless, today's creek boating has risen to new levels of insanity. If you want to see what's happening, this is a good place. Expect to spend a lot of time scouting, a time-consuming matter in this rugged terrain. Even scrambling back up to the tracks without your boat is a serious matter.

Jason Thomas

North Fork of the Blackwater, below Douglas Falls

DIFFICULTIES: Douglas Falls is a 40-foot waterfall into a very shallow landing pool with a tricky slide approach. It's only been run twice and is not recommended for obvious reasons. The run below here is truly spectacular and will satisfy even the most hard-core creek-boater. Here, boaters can test themselves against an astonishing sequence of slides, waterfalls, and obstructed boulder drops with nasty undercuts. Stay out of the "notches" of steep drops and beware of vertical pins.

The first rapid is a very steep and complex series of boulder drops. Right after, there is a long cascade that drops about 30 feet. After 2, 10-foot falls and some rock gardens, you'll reach Glutial Mash, a 30-foot falls with a deceptively shallow landing pool. The shallow approach slide will make it hard to get speed and a good launch if the river is below 1.5 on the gauge above the put-in. There have been several ankle fractures from pitoning and injured vertebrae from landing flat. The carry is on the right.

After a boulder drop, you'll reach the World's Ugliest Rapid, a double boof on the left to avoid an undercut wall on the right. Cow Pissing On A Flat Rock, a 12-foot falls onto a padded rock, follows. The next several rapids feature slides into drops with

wicked undercut rocks to avoid at the bottom. Soon you'll arrive at Double Indemnity, a long slide that ends in an 8-foot sloping ledge right above an 18-foot waterfall. Run this down the right all the way. Next, there is a sieve-ridden boulder drop called the Double Boof or Rainbow Room. Boof right into a small room then ferry out under a spray and over a small drop. Slides and small drops carry you the rest of the way to the Blackwater.

SHUTTLE: An abandoned railroad bed crosses "27" at Douglas. Most people drive down the abandoned railroad track to the gate, carry, and put in at the base of Douglas Falls. The carry out at North Fork Junction is only for people who thrive on high-intensity aerobic activity! Most paddlers continue downstream, making a high-water run down the Lower Blackwater to Hendricks.

GAUGE: The Davis gauge is on the Pittsburgh Weather Service flow phone, call (412) 644-6562. Look for a reading of 500 cfs (3.7 feet) or more. There's a metal gauge sticking out about 100 yards above Douglas Falls on the right bank, just above a 4-foot ledge. This should read 1.3 for a minimum. The gauge is broken off at 1.6 so, if it is under the water, it will be a juicy run! The Parsons gauge usually needs to be over 5 feet.

LITTLE BLACKWATER RIVER

The Little Blackwater winds down the center of the wildest part of Canaan Valley. Treeless and windswept, the dark river offers panoramic vistas of vast bogs, island meadows, and the encircling mountains that make the valley unique. The stream meanders incessantly, dropping over many little beaver dams, but has only one tree across it.

MAPS: Mount Storm Lake, Davis (USGS); Tucker (County); Monongahela National Forest Map

CAMP 72 TO CAMP 70 (BLACKWATER RIVER)

CLASS	A
LENGTH	6
TIME	3+
GAUGE	VISUAL
LEVEL	NA
FLOW	FREE FLOWING
GRADIENT	5
VOLUME	VS
SOLITUDE	A
SCENERY	A

SHUTTLE: None. Your best approach is to paddle up the Little Blackwater from its junction with the Blackwater. The nearest start is Camp 70. The low gradient and lack of rapids make for easy upriver travel. Turn left on the Little Blackwater after 1.7 miles. For those determined to never go upriver, a rough jeep road leads down to Camp 72 from another jeep road along Cabin Mountain.

GAUGE: None. This stream is normally runable to Camp 72 throughout the spring and for 1.5 miles above the Forks in June. The river is still runable above Camp 72, but no one has yet ascended so far.

GLADE RUN

MAPS: Mount Storm Lake, Davis (USGS); Tucker (County); Monongahela National Forest Map

GLADE RUN

CLASS	A
LENGTH	VARIABLE
TIME	VARIABLE
GAUGE	VISUAL
LEVEL	NA
FLOW	FREE FLOWING
GRADIENT	5
VOLUME	NA
SOLITUDE	A
SCENERY	A

DESCRIPTION: Tiny and shallow, Glade Run is the most scenic of all Canaan Valley streams. This tributary of the Little Blackwater River begins where a narrow logging railroad once bridged the stream. Bumping against the base of Cabin Mountain, it wanders north across beaver meadows within the Canaan Valley National Wildlife Refuge. The area supports many unique species of plants and animals, so do what you can to minimize impact. Glade Run is narrow, deep, and drinkable. Soon it swings northwest across the valley along the end of a low shale ridge. There's a beaver dam made of small, flat plates of shale stacked up and topped with a bit of brush.

SHUTTLE: None. This is definitely an upriver trip. Go up as far as you care to and coast back down. Put in at Camp 70, paddle up the Blackwater 1.7 miles, turn left on the Little Blackwater, and after 1 mile, go right onto Glade Run.

GAUGE: None. Runable within several days of rain or snow melt in April and May. The midsection on shale is the limiting factor.

SHAVERS FORK OF THE CHEAT RIVER

MAPS: Cass, Snyder Knob, Durbin, Wildell, Mill Creek, Beverly East, Glady, Bowden, Parsons (USGS); Pocahontas, Randolph, Tucker (County); Monongahela National Forest Map

Shavers Fork of the Cheat River

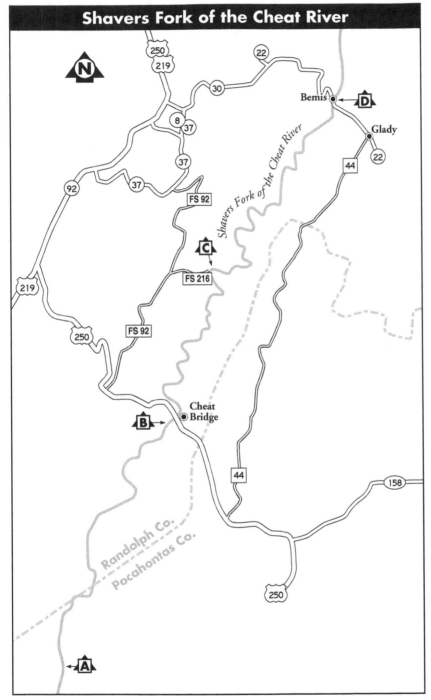

CLASS	1–2
LENGTH	17
TIME	6
GAUGE	VISUAL
LEVEL	NA
FLOW	FREE FLOWING
GRADIENT	18 (5@32)
VOLUME	S
SOLITUDE	A
SCENERY	A

SPRUCE TO CHEAT BRIDGE

DESCRIPTION: The put-in for this run is at 3,900 feet, making it probably the highest run in the East. Here the river is very narrow and fast with mostly Class-2 rapids. There are many easy (Class-1 and -2) rapids and many pools. Your first landmarks are two railroad trestles a few hundred yards apart (Twin Bridges). In another half mile, Rocky Run, or "Rocky Ridge Run," enters from the left. In another 2 miles, you will pass under a third trestle and then be joined by the Second Fork of Shavers from the right (known as Big Run among the locals). The bridge marks the end of the best action—the first 5 miles have a 32 fpm gradient. The river then broadens out a bit but still moves pretty fast. The rapids are Class 1–2, with the Class 2s occurring at sharp bends. We did not see any particularly hazardous or difficult spots anywhere.

Other significant tributaries enter the stream from the left at roughly miles 8 (Beaver Creek), 9 (Buck Run), and 10 (Black Run). The road comes very close to the river at several points between these latter two runs, making access from Cheat Bridge easy. This part would make a splendid open-boat fishing trip. The gradient averages 14–18 fpm and finally drops to only 10. The fourth bridge marks mile 12. From here down to Cheat bridge, the river is very wide and shallow with very few riffles, which are Class 1 and occur at constrictions and bends in the river. The entire run is a 17-mile trip through exquisite scenery. The regenerating spruce forest, the bogs, and mountain meadows are reminiscent of Canada.

SHUTTLE: Your first problem in setting up the shuttle and getting to Spruce. Two private roads (Mower Lumber Co.) exist, but experience has shown that they might be snowbound when you want to paddle. When the roads are clear, the water might be too low. (There is a potential access from Snowshoe Ski Area, but management has refused so far to give permission to paddlers.) Start your shuttle at Cheat Bridge near US 250. Turn right on Red Run Road just east of the river and continue upriver through the extinct town of Cheat Bridge. Don't cross the iron bridge, but stay upstream left all the way.

A permit must be obtained in advance to use the Mower Lumber Co. road. Write to: Mower Lumber Co., PO Box 27, Durbin, WV 26264, and state when you will want to use the road. There is a small daily fee.

GAUGE: The only known run of the entire section was made at a level of exactly nine stones down from the top on the left abutment of the iron bridge above US 250. This was adequate but occasionally scrapy on the first miles.

US 250 TO McGEE RUN

CLASS	1–2 (3)
LENGTH	10.5
TIME	3
GAUGE	VISUAL
LEVEL	1.5+ FT.
PERMITS	NO
FLOW	FREE FLOWING
GRADIENT	21 (2@32)
VOLUME	S
SOLITUDE	A
SCENERY	A

DESCRIPTION: This is a very pleasant run on a beautiful river, one of the finest fishing rivers in the state. No stream in the state receives as many individual fish (or as big) from the state's trout stocking program. Indeed, the last 5.5-mile section has been designated a Fish-for-Fun stream, where angling is limited to barbless hooks and all trout must be returned. This is where you find the best fishermen in the state! The river is flanked by spruce, hemlock, and even balsam. The wildlife is fantastic, especially the birds. The run is very easy down to Water Tank Run, which enters from the right through large culverts. (If you want to keep track, the names of the runs that you will pass in order from the put-in are Red Run, Stonecoal, Whitmeadow from the left, Glade and John's Camp from the right, Crouch from the left, then Water Tank, and finally Yokum and McGee from the left.)

DIFFICULTIES: At Water Tank, the river becomes steeper and the rapids more or less continuous, although only Class 2. There are three nice drops—one just below Glade Run, one right at Yokum and one more before the take-out. Just upstream from the mouth of Yokum, the paddler passes under the bridge and coal conveyor of the controversial Linan Mines. There has been considerable question about whether an industrial development like this can coexist with a beautiful, near-wilderness trout stream. If not, anglers and whitewater paddlers will be the first to know.

SHUTTLE: Put in at the US 250 bridge. To reach the take-out, head back west along this highway and take the second road to the right, FS 92. From this forest service road there are many side roads that lead down to Shavers Fork along some of the runs named above. Not all of these roads are passable. Continue on FS 92 to the end and turn right down the hollow of McGee Run (FS 210). There is a primitive campground at the end of the Fish-for-Fun section.

GAUGE: See Section C. If you can paddle around the put-in bridge without scraping, you'll be OK.

CLASS	3–4
LENGTH	13
TIME	6
GAUGE	PHONE
LEVEL	1.5-2 FT. (CR 33/8 GAUGE)
FLOW	FREE FLOWING
GRADIENT	58
VOLUME	VS
SOLITUDE	A
SCENERY	A

McGee Run to Bemis

DESCRIPTION: After the longest shuttle and access paddle in the state and carrying the most spectacular falls in the state, you'll test your paddling skill against 4 miles of hard whitewater. The river drops over six more falls, one of which approaches Class 5, with no slack water between the drops.

The first part is wide and shallow at reasonable water levels, but it soon picks up speed. A landmark at 5 miles is a railroad marker visible from the river, "C-7"; a mile later, "C-6"; and at 7.5 miles, "R/S" is marked in green. Other than these signs, little else characterizes the first 3 hours of the trip except isolated wilderness.

Shortly after the last railroad marker, there is a blind rapid on a sharp right turn, but it is safe to run. High Falls of the Cheat waits at mile 9. It's a river-wide abrupt drop of 15 feet, one of the most spectacular sights in West Virginia. It is a clean drop for those who enjoy running waterfalls. There is a beautiful primitive campsite on the right used by backpackers. This is located at the mouth of Fall Run on the county map or Red Run on the topo.

DIFFICULTIES: High Falls has been run down the center and snuck on the right, but it's rocky and dangerous, so most people will carry. Below High Falls the river becomes narrow, steep, and obstructed. The next few rapids are solid Class 4—powerful and dangerous at high water. Most are technical runs over broken ledges and down narrow chutes. The river then eases up a bit until the second railroad bridge is reached. Beneath the tracks a 10-foot-high broken ledge terminates in a thundering 6-foot-high slide. There's a large boulder in the center of the run-out. At low levels it is difficult to avoid; at high water, a bad hole forms. The river continues through some interesting Class 3+ drops for 1 mile past the second railroad bridge. The 6-foot-high broken ledge you'll encounter here is always challenging and creates a very nasty hydraulic at high water. The approach is very fast and slick, with few good eddies and a number of stopper-sized holes. Once past here, it's only a mile to the bridge at Bemis.

SHUTTLE: The shuttle, like the run, is rather long. Bring your county road maps or atlas! Start driving to Bemis no later than 8:30 a.m. and leave enough vehicles in Bemis so you can shuttle everyone and their boats back to the put-in at the end of the day. Take CR 27 (the road directly across from the Alpine Motel) to Glady and cross the intersection in Glady onto CR 22. Then

drive to the put-in by continuing on CR 22 through Bemis. After the road turns left, it crosses railroad tracks, then shortly turns to dirt as it starts up the mountain. There are several switchbacks on the way up and several on the other side, heading down. There are a number of roads that fork off from the main road left and right, but not at 90-degree angles. DO NOT take any of these. There is an especially deceiving one marked with a Private Road sign that forks off to the left shortly after you start up the mountain. Stay on the main road as it goes to the right and continues up the mountain. After you come down the other side of the mountain, reach an intersection. Go left onto CR 30. The dirt road soon turns to paved. This road eventually ends at an intersection with another paved road and there is a gas plant on your left. Turn left here onto CR 37/8. You will pass an Izaak Walton League building on your left. Soon, the paved road ends and turns to dirt and gravel. Continue and then take a left fork where you see a Forest Service Route 92 road sign. Drive along 92, passing one intersection and several roads off to the left. Eventually, one of these roads to the left has a Forest Service road sign for 210. This is McGee Run Road. Take it to the put-in. This is the shortest route and takes about 1 hour. 4WD is not needed unless snow is present. Going via Elkins doubles the time required for the trip.

GAUGE: Refers to the CR 33/8 gauge described in Section E; a good range for this section is 2–3 feet. The Parsons gauge can be used as a rule of thumb by subtracting 2.5 and halving the remainder. Call the Pittsburgh Weather Service at (412) 262-5290. On the USGS web site, look for a range of 5.5–6.5 feet at Cheat Bridge, 3.3–4.4 feet at Bemis. At higher levels the rapids become very aggressive in the section below the falls.

D
BEMIS TO CR 33/8 BRIDGE

CLASS	2–3
LENGTH	14
TIME	2
GAUGE	PHONE
LEVEL	1.5–2.5 FT.
FLOW	FREE FLOWING
GRADIENT	3@65 (6@30)
VOLUME	544
SOLITUDE	A
SCENERY	A–B

DESCRIPTION: The ledges at Bemis were bulldozed and filled in after the 1985 flood, breaking the long rapids into short pieces. The current run is still a solid Class 3. The last few miles are broad and full of strainers . . . a pain at low water. Nonetheless, the scenery is magnificent!

DIFFICULTIES: This section of Shavers Fork is for solid intermediates only. It's pretty far out in the woods, although the railroad right-of-way is available for walking out. Below the filled-in ledges there is a series of short rapids followed by pools, which used to be one long rapid. A right turn at the railroad bridge

signals a neat series of runable holes. The river tames considerably after this, but paddlers still need to pay attention. There's a dam at the former site of Bowden Bridge. Below here is a 5-mile stretch that follows the highway until the CR 33/8 bridge is reached. There are only a few riffles and many fishing cabins and trailer camps along the banks here, so most paddlers will take out at Bowden Bridge for a 9-mile trip. The Bowden National Fish Hatchery is nearby and is worth a visit.

SHUTTLE: For the shorter trip, take out just upstream of the washed-out Bowden Bridge, which can be seen from US 33. Bemis is reached by turning south from Alpena and taking "27" up to Glady. Turn right in Glady and travel 2 miles into Bemis. Put in under the bridge.

GAUGE: See section E.

CLASS	1–2
LENGTH	2 2
TIME	7
GAUGE	PHONE
LEVEL	1–2.5 FT.
(CR 33/8 GAUGE)	
FLOW	FREE FLOWING
GRADIENT	1 9
VOLUME	5 4 4
SOLITUDE	A
SCENERY	A–B

CR 33/8 BRIDGE TO PARSONS

DESCRIPTION: This part of Shavers Fork (and the section of the Cheat it flows into) is a pleasant interlude between its raucous birthplace high on Bald Knob and its furious descent through the Cheat Canyon. The water volume in this section is fairly large, but soon doubles when it joins with the Black Fork in Parsons. This river, one of the state's most scenic, appeals to the novice as well as to the expert. There are many ideal camping places and several vigorous rapids for playing around. The action and current are almost continuous, with very little quiet water. The scenery through the deep hollows is spectacular. Many rocky bluffs and waterfalls line the river, while the shores are studded with magnificent growths of hemlock. Some of the rapids approach Class 3 at higher water levels, but a novice can always find an easy passage if so desired.

SHUTTLE: This section can be run in smaller segments. From CR 33/8 to the steel bridge near Clifton Run is 6 miles by car, 8 by boat. From here on, the road on the right side of the river is rough. It comes close to the river at several points. If you want to do the whole thing, drive to Elkins and take US 219 to Parsons.

GAUGE: Located on the west bridge support on the upstream side of the CR 33/8 put-in. *Note:* this is the *old* US 33 bridge now bypassed by the new US 33 higher on the mountain, near the Stuart Recreation Area. CR 33/8, which may also be marked only as

Shavers Fork of the Cheat River

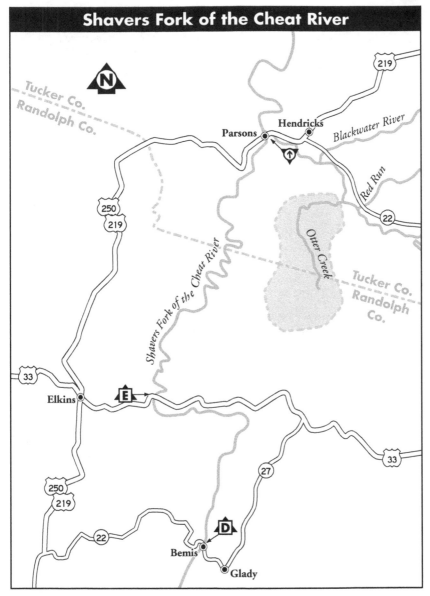

CR 33, can be accessed at Bowden if you are traveling west, or at the top of the mountain when leaving Elkins if you are traveling east. On the USGS web site, look for a minimum of 500 cfs at Bowden for Section D and E.

For an approximate reading for either section you can subtract 2.5 from the Parsons government gauge on the Cheat and halve the remainder. Call (412) 262-5290.

CHEAT RIVER

The Cheat begins in the real mountains of the state as four big forks: Shavers, Glady, Laurel, and Dry, each separated from its neighbors by high mountain ridges. Shavers Fork actually flows on top of one of these ridges for miles. In this country, the shuttles are as fascinating as the rivers. Although Shavers Fork is generally considered the main source of the Cheat, the Dry Fork has the most interesting tributaries. These include fascinating Gandy Creek, a stream that goes through a mountain; Red Creek, draining the unique Dolly Sods Wilderness Area; Laurel and Glady Forks, isolated and beautiful; the fabulous Otter Creek, which runs entirely within a wilderness area; and finally the wild and raucous Blackwater. The latter joins the Dry Fork with such volume that the river is called Black Fork until it joins the Shavers Fork in Parsons to form the Cheat.

Two other significant paddling tributaries enter the lower part of the Cheat: Horseshoe Run near historic Saint George and the Big Sandy in the middle of Cheat Canyon near Masontown. The Cheat officially ends when it joins the Monongahela at Point Marion, Pennsylvania.

MAPS: Parsons, Saint George, Rowlesburg, Kingwood, Valley Point, Masontown, Lake Lynn (USGS); Tucker, Preston, Monongalia (County); Monongahela National Forest Map

CLASS	B–1
LENGTH	36
TIME	1-2 DAYS
GAUGE	PHONE
LEVEL	3–4.5 FT.
FLOW	FREE FLOWING
GRADIENT	7
VOLUME	VS
SOLITUDE	A–B
SCENERY	B

PARSONS TO ROWLESBURG

DESCRIPTION: This is a lazy, beautiful river meandering alternately through well-kept farmland and spectacular bluffs. There are occasional Class-1 rapids that will offer no problems unless the water is very high. One of the better rapids is just before the Holly Meadows Bridge (3 miles from Parsons). The next bridge, 8 miles downstream, leads to the historic village of Saint George. About 2 miles below Saint George the river leaves the highway and enters a beautiful gorge. Some nice easy rapids occur here.

Below Hannahsville you'll find the area known as Seven Islands. It is particularly scenic. The highway does not approach this section, but there's a dirt road along the left side of the river. There are many deep pools suitable for swimming and fishing. Bass may be taken all along the river, while trout are caught in the riffles of the upper stretches. Many primitive camping sites exist, and the river is ideal for open-boat touring.

SHUTTLE: Due to the nearness of roads, shuttles can be set up most anywhere for shorter runs, particularly along WV 72.

GAUGE: See section D.

THE CHEAT NARROWS: ROWLESBURG TO ALBRIGHT POWER DAM

CLASS	2–4
LENGTH	14
TIME	4–5
GAUGE	PHONE
LEVEL	0–7+ FT.
FLOW	FREE FLOWING
GRADIENT	5@20
VOLUME	2,207
SOLITUDE	B
SCENERY	C

DESCRIPTION: Leaving Rowlesburg quietly and broadly, the river soon becomes narrower and starts to pick up speed. Approximately 3 miles below Rowlesburg, after passing several Class 1–2 riffles, you encounter the first big waves, which are opposite a worked-out limestone mine (Cave Rapids). For the next 5 miles the rapids become increasingly difficult. There are good rescue spots after each rapid, but in high water (4–5 feet) it's not so easy. After passing several Class-3 rapids, the river narrows and the paddler enters a long series of rapids called the "Narrows." The entire river is necked down by the presence of an automobile-sized boulder (Calamity Rock) in midstream, making passage at any level difficult. This boulder is largely out of the water at 1 foot on the Albright gauge and becomes completely submerged at just over 2 feet. Run the boulder on the right, whether in your boat or afoot. There are two problems: entering the passage correctly, which is not always easy due to the combination of waves immediately above it, and managing the powerful drop at the end of the chute. This drop will flip a raft instantly in high water.

There are three major rapids below this boulder that also pass through narrow confines. This creates a tremendous turbulence and results in powerful crosscurrents and eddies. In high water you simply blast through 5-foot standing waves and try to maintain stability, while at lower levels you must be more precise in maneuvering around the exposed boulders. Paddlers inexperienced with big water might be fooled into thinking that they can "sneak" down the sides of these narrow rapids in relatively calm water, but usually they get sucked over into the big stuff by the high velocity of the main channel.

The first of these major rapids (Wind Rapids) is the most difficult in high water and consists of a wide hydraulic before it reaches the chute. The hydraulic is best taken on the far left. There is also a strong hydraulic about halfway down the chute on the left, always an interesting scene. The second rapid (Rocking Horse) is the longest narrow passage—100 yards of turbulence. The last rapid is easier but still interesting. Then paddlers must concentrate on dodging boulders and catching the best chutes all the way to the railroad bridge. By now, strip-mine pollution has seriously affected the river. The scenery at Preston is depressing,

and the river widens out leaving few places for rapids to form. Two miles below the WV 7 bridge there is a short Class-2 rapid, but nothing except the scenery improves very much. WV 72 parallels the river on the left as far as the bridge, while a local road continues on the right below it, giving plenty of opportunity for scouting and/or setting up shorter trips. The Albright Power Dam has a dangerous hole and should be portaged before paddling down to the WV 26 bridge.

SHUTTLE: Rowlesburg City park is a good put-in, while the right side of the river 200–300 yards above the Albright Power Station provides a take-out. Paddlers interested in the best rapids put in opposite the limestone caves and take out at the mouth of Lick Run for a 5-mile trip.

GAUGE: See section D.

The Last Trip Report: Cheat River 1984

After being in Europe so many years and away from whitewater paddling, I thought that since I was settled back in West Virginia, it would be nice to get out on the river again. Memorial Day was coming up and I thought there would be a fair number of paddlers there. I might even run into some of the old gang. Doren and I retrieved our boats from storage and found them to be still in good shape. He hadn't paddled since junior high and was somewhat skeptical about being able to handle the Cheat Canyon. I reassured him with a "So what? Remember how warm the water always used to be?", more for my confidence than his.

The road over to Albright was as we had remembered it, but we were not prepared for the sight that greeted us at the old ball field. A huge black-topped parking lot filled with hundreds of cars stood where we used to camp. A surly attendant charged us $2 to park and we went over to the river. All of the trees had been cut down and in their place were several gift shops and rafting firms in front of which were mountains of rafts and many people hustling back and forth yelling at each other.

Guides were helping large parties of people board the huge rafts. The gift shops were crammed with souvenir hunters. The most popular item seemed to be a small 8-inch raft made out of black foam rubber in Japan.

I noticed that practically every person boarding a raft carried his own 6-pack of beer. They didn't look like rafters—these people were dressed "fit to kill" and bringing along all sorts of weird stuff like transistor radios (the Pirates were in a double header today), badminton rackets, huge coolers of food, and beach blankets. The raft design had also changed a good bit. They were all rigged with large sponsons and screens sticking up on all sides of the raft about 3 feet. I asked a guide what they were for and he gave me a how-stupid-can-you-be look. "To keep the rafters from getting splashed, of course."

At the far end of the parking lot was a bar and next to it an amusement park complete with Ferris wheel, merry-go-round, and dodge'em cars. We headed back to the car to get our boats and gear, but upon returning had a good deal of difficulty finding a put-in. Each 100 yards was reserved for the exclusive use of one of the many rafting concessions and each made it quite clear we were unwelcome to put in at their part. I noticed we were receiving a lot of stares. I guess my cut-off-at-the-knees paddling britches and Doren's faded blue jeans weren't in style any more. We finally managed to find a spot way upstream, so we were skirting up when this officious looking fellow with Ws and Vs all over his jacket came up to us and said, "Just where do you think you're going?"

"Just paddling down to Jenkinsburg," I said.

"Not in those heaps you're not! Your life jackets aren't approved, your helmets aren't thick enough, you don't have safety spring releases on your skirts, your boats aren't licensed, and they're made out of obsolete materials."

"Obsolete materials?"

"Yeah. The only boats allowed on this river have to be made out of hexapolymethaurethene. It's absolutely indestructible. Only approved companies make them and your homemade pigs are illegal. Besides you have to be rated to run this river."

"By whom?" I asked.

"By our organization" and he quickly flashed the emblem on his jacket at me.

I ventured that I had safely run this river in boats such as this as far back as 1966 and he responded by saying that those were the days before really serious paddling had begun and for us to get the hell out or he would call the sheriff.

Rather than create a scene, we took our boats back to the car, but we still wanted to see the river again, even from a raft. After being told repeatedly that you had to be booked at least 3 months in advance, we finally found an outfit that had a couple of cancellations. "That will be 30 bucks," said the man. Well, there's one thing that hadn't changed, $15 a head was the price it used to be, I thought.

"What about the other guy? Ain't he gonna ride?" spoke the petulant guide. I should have known better by now and we forked over another $30. As we got into the raft, I picked up a paddle and sat in the bow as I wanted to be up where the action was. I was immediately scolded and told to get back in the center where it was safer and that only the guides did the paddling. Four guides per raft, no wonder it's so expensive.

At last we were on our way. I looked forward to Decision Rapid with keen anticipation and with fond nostalgia, but we were through it before I knew it. The rafts were so large and bombproof, that there was no sensation of thrill at all. The fellow next to me had his radio turned up and all were into their second beer. The piles of beer cans in the trash eddies told me what happened

to all of the empties from those 6-packs. As we went through the next rapids, a huge billboard was seen on the right bank extolling the virtues of Red Cap ale while another on the left exhorted all to join the thousands of members in a West Virginia whitewater club. I was looking forward to seeing Big Nasty again feeling that it might be exciting even in this big tub, but it was also disappointing. I made some comment to the guide about Big Nasty and he replied that such names were frowned upon because they tended to scare the customers. He called it "Angel Foam Slide" as was the long vacation cabin development that lined both shores. Most of the cabins and trailers were perched on top of old strip-mine benches. Four customers began playing bridge to relieve the boredom while a fifth was taking a snooze.

At this point I was wondering how the big raft would make it through the narrow squeeze in Even Nastier. As we approached, my question was answered—all of the boulders had been blasted away to clear a channel. The rafts made a lunch stop below High Falls, getting there by going down a blasted channel on the right. The good stuff on the left was off limits to everybody and was reserved for the exclusive use of the Albright Kayak Club who had a trailer perched on top of the high ledge. At the lunch stop there was a bar, hamburger stand, and Dairy Queen.

And so it went. I was glad when we reached the Jenkinsburg Bridge, the fifth we had gone under. The buses were waiting for us in a big asphalt-covered parking lot at riverside. The trip back to Albright via the Preston Scenic 4-lane expressway only took 10 minutes. I cried most of the way back, this Memorial Day, 1984.

Bob Burrell

Reprinted from West Virginia Wildwater Association
Splashes, February 1973.

Cheat River

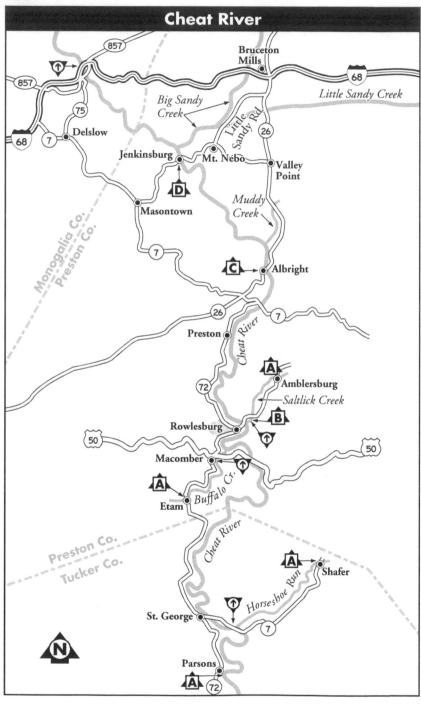

Cheat Canyon : Albright WV 26 Bridge to
Jenkinsburg Bridge

CLASS	3–4 (5)
LENGTH	11
TIME	4
GAUGE	Phone
LEVEL	1–7 ft.
FLOW	Free Flowing
GRADIENT	25
VOLUME	2,207
SOLITUDE	B
SCENERY	A

DESCRIPTION: John Berry led the first descent of the Cheat Canyon in the spring of 1957, camping overnight at High Falls. In the 1960s, the Cheat Canyon was considered the most difficult river in the East. It has moved down a few notches as paddling skills have improved, but it hasn't gotten any easier and should not be taken lightly. At low water, it's a notorious boat buster. At high levels it's pushy and turbulent, and big holes wait to catch paddlers who miss their lines. Massive boulders litter the riverbed, blocking the view through many rapids and contributing to the complexity of the run.

The Cheat will rise quickly following normal spring rains and can go up several feet during a run. In November of 1985 it set records. After receiving 6 inches of rain during a 3-day period, the Cheat headwaters took 14 inches of rain, 8 inches in just 12 hours. The river rose from 3 feet the day before to crest at 28 feet (an estimated 250,000 cfs) at 7:30 a.m. on November 5th. This "thousand-year flood" washed lives, homes, and businesses downstream. It destroyed half of Albright and forever changed the Cheat.

Many chutes in the canyon are pretty narrow, but the river gauge at Albright Bridge is located in a wide, shallow spot. A 2-inch difference on the gauge changes the rapids downstream a lot. The run is rather long and far from any roads. A problem will leave you miles from any help in very rough country. Walking out of the canyon takes a full 2 hours, and you still may be miles from the nearest farmhouse. The Allegheny Trail runs on the right side of the river, high up on the canyon wall.

A detailed description of all the difficult rapids in the Cheat Canyon is impractical due to their number and complexity (there are more than 38 that are Class 3 or better). Although there are few long, flat pools, each set of rapids is separated from the next by a quiet section.

DIFFICULTIES: 1.5 miles below Albright is Decision Rapid (Class 4), beginning as a long, wide rock garden and narrowing to drop over a series of eroded ledges. There are major hydraulics here and complex countercurrents. If this is too much, take out on the right, because this is your last chance and the rapids don't

get any easier. After a mile of pools and small drops you'll encounter Beech Run (Class 4). Run this one from right to left. At
levels below 2.5 feet, be careful to avoid the rocks that clog the
channel about two-thirds of the way down.

1.5 miles downstream is Big Nasty (Class 4), marked by a large
pool preceding a bend to the right. Enter left-center, and haul
yourself quickly left to miss the hole. At 2 feet neither the run nor
the consequences are very serious. At 3 feet, the line is a more difficult to hold, and a mistake will allow Mr. Nasty to invite you to
stay for lunch—his. Between 3 and 5 feet he just gets hungrier!
He's been known to juggle several rafts or decked boats simultaneously at these levels. Typewriter, a really great surfing wave, is
just downstream.

Even Nastier (Class 4) is two rapids below here. Start right
of center (or left at high water), then watch out for some nasty
midstream pinning rocks. The stretch below here is known as
the "Doldrums." There are several miles of easy Class-3 drops separated by long pools. The river is pretty slow here at low water,
but at 3 feet or more there's lots of good playing. The last rapid of
the Doldrums, "No Balls," is a wonderful surfing spot at 2–2.5
feet on the gauge.

Now the river picks up significantly. Soon a loud roar and a
spectacularly beautiful sheer cliff on river right warns paddlers
that something special is waiting downstream. High Falls Rapids
(Class 4 at lower levels, 4+ at higher water) was named for a 60-
foot waterfall dropping into the river from the cliff. It consists of
a wide, shallow reef dropping steeply into a natural amphitheater.
Finding a good passage through the reef, starting center or right of
center, is not easy. It's best to follow someone familiar with the
route or to scout carefully. Next is Maze Rapids, where you'll
work left to right to pick a line through a complex puzzle of boulders strewn randomly in the riverbed.

Below Maze, eddy out right and scout Upper Coliseum Rapids
(Class 4 at low levels, Class 5 above 3 feet). This rapid has
changed a little bit each year since 1985. At the top of the rapid is
Recyclotron, a huge, horribly ugly hole with a nasty backwash.
Skirt this on the left, then cut towards the center. The river now
washes quickly into Lower Coliseum Rapid. All but the most daring will want to run right, avoiding the huge holes to the left of
Coliseum Rock. The next drop, Pete Morgan Rapid (Class 4), was
named for a resident of Albright who for years read the bridge
gauge for paddlers who called his gas station at the Rt. 26 Bridge.
It's best to run it on the left. The cliff on the right bank, below the
drop, is very undercut in places, so stay away from it!

Jeff Simco

Cheat River (Decision)

Below you'll find a few Class 3s, then the river calms down over the last 2 miles to Jenkinsburg. take out below the bridge, at the mouth of the Big Sandy.

SHUTTLE: Put in at the Albright Bridge or, to avoid some flat water, use Cheat Canyon Campground (fee) or the Friends of Cheat access (behind Teter's Campground). The river-left access road from Masontown to the Jenkinsburg bridge (Locals now call it "Bull Run Bridge") still works, but the preferred route is through Valley Point. From WV 26, turn left on CR 15 towards Hudson. At the Mount Nebo intersection, take the more gradual of two left turns, and go to the right of a large A-frame house. It's 4 more miles to the river. The shuttle takes about 45 minutes each way. You can save time and vehicle wear by arranging for a pickup from Glen Miller's Shuttle Service at (304) 379-3404. Call early; he books up fast for popular times on prime late spring weekends.

GAUGE: See section D.

JENKINSBURG BRIDGE TO CHEAT LAKE

CLASS	3, B, A
LENGTH	8
TIME	3
GAUGE	PHONE
LEVEL	0–7 FT.
FLOW	FREE FLOWING
GRADIENT	4@16
VOLUME	2,632
SOLITUDE	A
SCENERY	A

DESCRIPTION: This interesting run is seldom paddled. There are only 4 miles of rapids followed by a long, flat paddle. It is a good indication of what some of the easier rapids in the upper canyon are like. The first rapid is encountered about 50 yards below the mouth of the Big Sandy, with the best passage toward the right in low water. If this is too low, forget it. You will encounter 4 good rapids (Class 3) and several riffles in the first 4 miles. The last rapid is divided by a gravel bar called Grassy Island. High above this island on the right is the Coopers Rock State Forest overlook. In our experience, the only danger on the trip is the risk of being run over by powerboat cowboys and, on at least one occasion, a damned seaplane! The long flat paddle to the take-out is beautiful but wearisome, and there is no easy access there. You'll have to pay to take out at the marina, so you may as well paddle on down another mile to the "857" bridge.

SHUTTLE: Long! Jenkinsburg is described in section C. To reach the take-out, go back out to WV 26, turn left, and head for I-68. Exit at Cheat Lake and drive towards the lake. Leave a car on the east side of the Ices Ferry bridge. There's a very long, rough jeep road on River Left from Pisgah down to the Beaver Hole, at the end of the last whitewater. Check your topo maps to find this one.

GAUGE: The lower parts of the Cheat (sections B, C, D, and E) are usually up through mid-June, and rise quickly in the early summer and late fall following heavy rains. A paddler's gauge is painted on the downstream side of the river-right piling on the Route 26 Bridge in Albright. It must be read on site. What these readings mean has changed every year since the 1985 flood, but here are some recent guidelines: The Narrows is good fun down to about 1 foot, but care is needed over 4 feet as a couple of rapids develop nasty holes. Most canyon runs are made between 2–5 feet. Levels under 2 feet are fine for advanced beginners (led by experts), but it's a rather long day. Intermediates who are comfortable on the Lower Yough at over 3 feet will do fine on the Cheat Canyon at 2–3 feet. At levels over 4 feet, the big rapids on the Cheat Canyon become huge and violent. They require solid big-water boating skills. Experts who know the river well go down regularly at 7–8 feet. The section below Jenkinsburg is a lot like the Narrows in difficulty, but more open.

The Albright Power station reading is on the Pittsburgh Weather Service tape; call (412) 262-5290. Unfortunately, there's

no straightforward correlation between this number and the Albright Bridge gauge. The author's best guess: multiply the power station reading by 1.8 to get a rough approximation of the bridge gauge; add 0.1 if the power station is reading 1 foot or less,

Local outfitters usually know what the Albright gauge is doing. If the river is rising, don't put on if the levels are approaching your personal cut-off. The mighty Cheat can rise a foot an hour all day!

HORSESHOE RUN

This is a simple, clear stream draining the northernmost portion of the Monongahela National Forest. It flows past Forest Service and YMCA camps bearing the same name. The stream is named after a huge loop in the Cheat just upstream from its mouth.

MAPS: Lead Mine, Saint George (USGS); Tucker (County)

SHAFER TO BRIDGE ABOVE SAINT GEORGE

CLASS	1–3
LENGTH	9
TIME	3
GAUGE	PHONE
LEVEL	6 FT.
FLOW	FREE FLOWING
GRADIENT	41
VOLUME	VS
SOLITUDE	A
SCENERY	B

DESCRIPTION: After 2.6 miles of uncomplicated moving water, the paddler negotiates a series of low ledges near Lead Mine. One mile downstream, the river passes under the bridge going up Hile Run. Between here and the YMCA camp is the most interesting section. The run channels and drops over easy gravel bars towards the end with half the gradient of the upper stream.

DIFFICULTIES: The real difficulty is catching this tiny trout stream when it is high enough to run. While it is suitable for novices, it is not a bore to the intermediate or advanced paddler because of its continuous drop and scenic surroundings. *Caution:* If you happen to run it in the summer, each of the camps may not have had the time to take down temporary dams made out of pipes and planks. These could be dangerous.

SHUTTLE: The put-in is reached from WV 72 by driving through Saint George and out "1" to Camp Horseshoe, on to Lead Mine, and then on "7" to Shafer where several small streams join to form Horseshoe Run. The first bridge you cross on your way from Saint George is the take-out.

GAUGE: None. The level refers to the Parsons gauge, which is only a general guide. It needs to be over 6 feet. The bridge on the side road up Hile Run should not be showing more than 7 stones on the right-side abutment for the creek to be up.

BUFFALO CREEK

A ride on Buffalo Creek is better than any mechanical bull. It's steep, narrow and fun! The only difficulty occurs just below the second bridge, where a blind bend hides three medium-sized ledges. You might want to scout here.

MAPS: Rowlesburg (USGS); Preston (County)

WV 72 TO MACOMBER

CLASS	3
LENGTH	4.5
TIME	1.5
GAUGE	VISUAL
LEVEL	1.6– 2.2 FT.
FLOW	FREE FLOWING
GRADIENT	86
VOLUME	S
SOLITUDE	A
SCENERY	B

SHUTTLE: Put in a mile below Etam at the WV 72 bridge. Shuttle on WV 72 and take out at the US 50 bridge.

GAUGE: There's a gauge on the left below the second bridge encountered. The Cheat River at Albright needs to be at 7 feet or more.

SALTLICK CREEK

MAPS: Kingwood, Rowlesburg (USGS); Preston (County)

AMBLERSBURG TO ROWLESBURG

CLASS	3
LENGTH	4
TIME	1
GAUGE	VISUAL
LEVEL	NA
FLOW	FREE FLOWING
GRADIENT	52
VOLUME	S
SOLITUDE	A
SCENERY	B

DESCRIPTION: This is a good thing to try when the Cheat is too high and it has been raining steadily for a day. The run parallels the main line of the B&O as it descends Briery Mountain from Terra Alta. With good water the river is continuous Class 3 with some stoppers and haystacks. There is a 5-foot dam at the B&O switching yards that can be run but is usually carried.

DIFFICULTIES: Higher on this little tributary, logs and trees are a significant hazard, and in this section they are still a potential threat. Look out for the dam.

SHUTTLE: CR 51 parallels the full length of the creek.

GAUGE: None. When Calamity Rock on the Cheat is buried, the Parsons gauge is 6 feet, and there isn't time to get to the upstream tributaries of the Cheat, go for it.

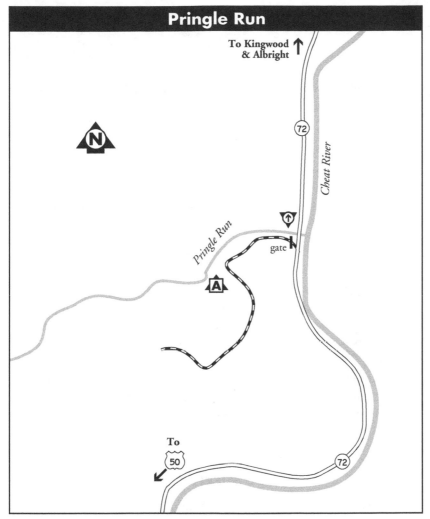

PRINGLE RUN

Pringle Run is short but very steep. It contains several challenging boulder drops, some steep slides, and a waterfall. Although it's not that long, you'll need expert creeking skills to get down in one piece. The scenery could be very pretty, but trash along the banks ruins this aspect. Your eyes will be glued to the rapids anyway. As with all small steep creeks, scout when in doubt and be on the lookout for downed trees. This creek can be run several times or combined with one of the many other creeks in the area.

MAPS: Rowlesburg, Kingwood (USGS); Preston (County)

CLASS	4–5+
LENGTH	O.6
TIME	1–2
GAUGE	VISUAL
LEVEL	NA
FLOW	FREE FLOWING
GRADIENT	4OO
VOLUME	VS
SOLITUDE	B
SCENERY	B

ABOVE FALLS TO CHEAT RIVER

DIFFICULTIES: After a few boulder drops, you'll come to the big falls on the run. A shallow approach slide splits into two channels. The left side falls 25 feet onto a rock; the right side cascades down a little further before leaping off a 20-footer into a deep pocket. The shallow approach may make it difficult to get to the right channel, so be careful. Portage on the right if in doubt.

Immediately below the falls, there's a long, fast slide that is about 75 yards long. From here to the Cheat, you'll be faced with a continuous series of tight boulder drops 4–8 feet in height. Several of these drops are close together and require a paddler to make several intense maneuvers before reaching an eddy to rest. The drops are tight; there are a few undercuts to avoid, so watch out.

SHUTTLE: Pringle Run dumps into the Cheat near the end of the Cheat Narrows. There's a dirt road that goes up along the creek. If it is gated (and it usually is), park at the bottom and carry up. Keep walking past the falls until you see the creek flatten out. put in here.

GAUGE: There is no accurate gauge for this creek. If the Big Sandy is over 6.5 feet and rising and if the Blackwater is over 500 cfs and rising, Pringle Run should be running. If the creek looks runable at the bottom, then you'll have a good level.

DOUGHERTY CREEK

MAPS: Kingwood, Terre Alta (USGS); Preston (County)

CLASS	4
LENGTH	2+
TIME	1
GAUGE	VISUAL
LEVEL	NA
FLOW	FREE FLOWING
GRADIENT	25O FT./MI.
VOLUME	VS
SOLITUDE	B

DOUGHERTY CREEK

DESCRIPTION: This is about as small and steep as the creeks get around here. There are no really big drops, but it's very fast and blind with lots of long sliding ledges. It's a slam-bang run that demands lightning reflexes and coolness under fire. There are some very tight turns against rock outcrops, and elbow pads are recommended. There are not many eddies, so a downed tree could cause lots of problems. Scout ahead carefully before you

get in your boat or go down with someone who has been there recently.

DIFFICULTIES: The usual small creek stuff times 2. Watch out for trees! This creek will take your head off if it catches you napping! Several people have gotten eye injuries from low-hanging branches.

GAUGE: None. Inspect from the bridge on CR 7-12. The water should look boney but passable; watch out if it appears at all phat! This creek is only up for short periods following very heavy rains.

ROARING CREEK

MAPS: Kingwood, Terre Alta (USGS); Preston (County)

BRANDONVILLE PIKE TO RUTHBELLE

CLASS	4
LENGTH	5
TIME	2
GAUGE	VISUAL
LEVEL	NA
FLOW	FREE FLOWING
GRADIENT	100
VOLUME	VS
SOLITUDE	A

DESCRIPTION: Roaring Creek might be pretty tiny at the take-out by Appalachian Wildwaters in Ruthbelle, but it's even tinier up by Brandonville Pike. It's no more than a boat-length wide at the put-in. The first mile is steep, obstructed, low-volume creek boating. Then a tributary comes in and makes the river a bit more passable. There are a number of moderately-steep sliding ledges below, with easier going in between. The lower river has a broken, 6-foot-high ledge that you'll want to scout to find a clean line. From here it's fast-moving boulder rapids all the way to the Cheat.

SHUTTLE: Drive up CR 22 from Ruthbelle, then turn right on Brandonville Pike (CR 3). The put-in is a few miles down the road. There's also a gated side road part way up (close the gate after you) that allows access to a bench above the creek at the mid-point.

GAUGE: None. Inspect from the bridge in Ruthbelle. This creek is up for short periods following heavy rains.

MUDDY CREEK

MAPS: Cuzzart, Valley Point (USGS); Preston (County)

CLASS	3 (4)
LENGTH	8.5
TIME	3
GAUGE	VISUAL
LEVEL	OVER 9 FT. AT ROCKVILLE
FLOW	FREE FLOWING
GRADIENT	60 (1 @ 120)
VOLUME	S
SOLITUDE	A–B
SCENERY	B

UPPER MUDDY CREEK

DESCRIPTION: When everything else is much too high for comfort, Upper Muddy Creek offers paddlers some good options. To start, there's a mile-long stretch of steep, fast moving Class 4 up by Cuzzart. Put in on CR 28 for a wild run down to CR 5. (This stretch is often run on the same day as Beaver Creek, the Little Sandy tributary) Below here there's many, many miles of easy Class-3 water. The rapids are busy but straightforward, with the usual small-stream tree and brush hazards. The upper 3.5 miles are very satisfying, running through isolated forests and past farms. The last 4 miles parallel CR 17 as it runs downhill to meet WV 26.

SHUTTLE: Get out those county road maps! There are a number of possible access points depending on your skill and daring.

GAUGE: None, but the river is easily inspected at the access points. What you see is what you get. You'll want the Rockville gauge on the Big Sandy to be at least 8 feet and rising.

CLASS	4 (5)
LENGTH	4
TIME	2.5
GAUGE	VISUAL
LEVEL	5+ FT.
FLOW	FREE FLOWING
GRADIENT	75
VOLUME	S
SOLITUDE	A
SCENERY	B

WV 26 BRIDGE TO CHEAT RIVER

DESCRIPTION: Before World War II this was a clean stream with trout. But extensive mining in the headwaters has killed everything in it, and today the river runs reddish brown with mine waste. The T&T Mine Spill, which occurred on its headwaters, spurred the formation of Friends of Cheat. It will be a long time before this damage can be repaired. The creek runs along WV 26; there's a roadside rest and an old iron furnace halfway down that's sometimes used for camping.

It's an interesting whitewater run despite the pollution. There are rocks, rocks, and more rocks! The rapids are first-rate when there's enough water. Below the put-in the river goes through a series of boulder gardens. At low levels it's rocky and abusive, but at high water it's a real screamer. Be sure you know where the big drops are!

DIFFICULTIES: Below the put-in is Little Muddy Rift, a narrow, twisting drop of 10 feet, within 20 feet, with undercut rocks. A mile later the river drops over Big Muddy Rift, a wide, slanting

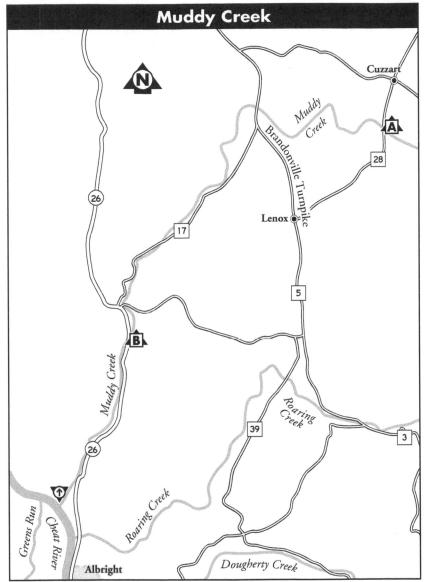

shelf about 20 feet high and 100 yards long. Stop and visit the antique iron furnace along WV 26 to get a good look at this one. Both are easily portaged on the right. This is a very steep stream with few eddies and lots of sharp rocks. Because of extensive logging in the area, there are plenty of downed trees and other debris.

SHUTTLE: Put in at WV 26 bridge; take out at the Friends of Cheat access located behind Teter's Campground.

GAUGE: This reading refers to a painted gauge located on the upstream side of a bridge abutment on Beech Run Road (near Teter's Campground). The gauge is getting worn and hard to read, but suffice it to say it takes more water than you'd think to make this run good. A reading of 5 feet is a nice, moderate level; less would be scrapy and abusive. If Rockville is running over 7 feet it might be worth checking this one out.

GREENS RUN

MAPS: Kingwood, Valley Point (USGS); Preston (County)

GREENS RUN ROAD TO CHEAT RIVER

CLASS	2–4+
LENGTH	2.5
TIME	NA
GAUGE	VISUAL
LEVEL	NA
FLOW	FREE FLOWING
GRADIENT	100
VOLUME	VS
SOLITUDE	C
SCENERY	B-

DESCRIPTION: Greens is a short run with a split personality. It starts off fast and furious for the first half mile, then calms down. The rest of the run is mostly continuous Class-2 rapids, with a few downed trees. Every now and then, there's a slide or a ledge that gives hope of more action. But it goes back to Class 2. The scenery is fairly pretty in spots but there are signs of mining as you get closer to the Cheat. The rocks on the run have an orange color to them, which also detracts from their beauty. This would be an ideal run for paddlers who are beginning to run creeks, but experienced creekers will probably skip this one and look for something with more consistent action.

DIFFICULTIES: The first half mile contains several long slides and ledges that drop continuously. There is an 8–10 foot falls that marks the end of the good action. About halfway through the run, there is a long slide that wraps around a bend in the creek. As you get close to the Cheat, there is a 6-foot ledge run on the left.

SHUTTLE: Put in on Greens Run Road off Rt. 26 heading towards Kingwood from Albright. The take-out is at the Friends of Cheat put-in for the Cheat Canyon at the mouth of Muddy Creek. You'll need to ferry across the Cheat and walk up the right bank to where Muddy Creek comes in.

GAUGE: Like most small streams in the area, there's no good gauge. If it looks like there's enough water at the put-in, you're set to go. When the Big Sandy gauge at Rockville is reading 7 feet and rising there's a good chance that Greens will be up.

THE BIG SANDY CREEK OF PRESTON COUNTY

MAPS: Brandonville, Bruceton, Valley Point (USGS); Preston (County)

Pennsylvania State Line to Bruceton Mills

CLASS	I
LENGTH	5
TIME	2–3
GAUGE	Visual
LEVEL	NA
FLOW	Free Flowing
GRADIENT	3
VOLUME	VS
SOLITUDE	B
SCENERY	B

DESCRIPTION: The Big Sandy Creek in Preston County, from the Pennsylvania State line to Bruceton Mills, a very small, intimate stream with a 3-fpm gradient flowing through rhododendron thickets and small farms. The bed is sandy to muddy, but there is good fishing for trout and bass. There are some easy rapids at Clifton Mills and flat water from there to the dam in Bruceton Mills.

SHUTTLE: Put in at the steel bridge on the road north of Brandonville, West Virginia. The put-in is actually on a tributary of the Big Sandy, Little Sandy Creek. (This should not be confused with another Little Sandy Creek.) The take-out is on the right above the dam, so be careful in high water.

GAUGE: Runable all summer, although the riffles get scrapy.

Upper Big Sandy: May 1969

The 1969 Big Sandy Creek weekend of the WVWA was either a successful catastrophe or a disastrous mess. On May 10 and 11, 17 paddlers started at Bruceton Mills, 7 finished at Rockville, 6 walked out as soon as possible into the roadless area, and 3 boats were eaten up by the raging waters.

After two days of rain the diminutive watershed of this usually small stream was saturated. The level was 2 feet higher than that previously run by the trip leader. This level at the deceptively sluggish looking put-in should have been enough to deter all but experts if we had been wise enough to know what lay ahead. The trip was billed as one for intermediates, a term that once again proved to have infinite breadth. Apparently if one

has wet a paddle thrice the beginner label washes off and extensive experience with white water instills humility that one can never get to the self-declared expert class.

Saturday's trip participants were Bill Hollowell and Fred Leverett, Bob Putnam and Byron Babcock, and Duane and Terry Rings of Parkersburg in aluminum canoes and Drew Hunter, Todd Martin, and Jack Sargent of Bellwood, Pennsylvania, Karen Oglebay, Gib Lancaster, and Joe Monahan of Cumberland, Maryland, and yours truly in C-1s.

Seven hours, 20 flips, 2 expended boats, and innumerable scoutings and linings later, this group arrived at the nineteenth-century bridge at Rockville. We were a tired, chilled, wet, elated, bruised, and unfortunately sometimes shaken crew. We had seen, felt, and occasionally paddled through some very memorable Class-4 water.

To describe the river in detail would be difficult. It will suffice to say there were 2 pools—the 2 miles below Bruceton and halfway down above the "runable" 6-foot falls. The rest is rapid after rapid after rapid, interrupted by stoppers, hydraulic jumps, roller eddies, and standing waves. If that still sounds boring try turning three boats over simultaneously while six are pulled out of the water for scouting and then watch the remaining one scramble for paddles, boats, and bodies. As Joe Monahan says, "It was like a Chinese fire drill."

On Sunday, only two of Saturday's paddlers appeared at the put-in, Monahan and myself. Also paddling were Fred Walburn, chairman of the Appalachian River Runners, and Andy Goff of Cumberland. The second day's water was still higher—2.6 feet at Bruceton and 5.9 feet at Rockville. The trip was quick and pleasant without scouting and with only two flips until the last mile. At that Fred and Joe broached on the same rock in rapid succession. The force of the water at this

particular calamity rock resulted in a functioning trap door in the bottom of Joe's boat and ended his trip.

This was in all the kind of memorable trip weekend for which we all look. It was a chance to test a paddler's skill and courage against a worthy opponent. That it cost some boats is part of the game, but even then, they all are salvageable. Undoubtedly, the trip was too much for the skills of some of us, but it will probably serve as a humbling stimulus to learn more of the ways of boats and moving water and will be the subject of stories for years. Unfortunately there were only three WVWA members supporting this club-sponsored trip—Monahan, Hollowell, and myself.

Paul Davidson

Reprinted from West Virginia Wildwater Association
Splashes, June 1969.

UPPER BIG SANDY: BRUCETON MILLS TO ROCKVILLE

CLASS	1–4
LENGTH	6
TIME	2
GAUGE	PHONE
LEVEL	5.8–8 FT.
PERMITS	No
FLOW	FREE FLOWING
GRADIENT	4@9 (2@45)
VOLUME	425
SOLITUDE	B
SCENERY	A

DESCRIPTION: The Upper Sandy run tips down beside Chestnut Ridge and slides into the Cheat Canyon, providing 6 miles of progressive slalom training while working up to low Class 4. Camping is available at nearby Cooper's Rock State Park and in Albright.

DIFFICULTIES: Hazel Run Rapids is the first problem and appears as an impassable barricade of boulders. Try the second passage from the right. Just below the mouth of the Little Sandy (on the left), there's a long slide rapid where the water zips quickly over sliding ledges terminating in playful holes. Then you'll encounter a 6–8-foot falls (Falkenstein Falls) that is recognized easily by a large shelf rock jutting out from the left. Land and scout from this rock. The first shelf is run by cutting hard left below the ledge, then working back towards the center for second drop. At higher levels you can run straight over the far left or right.

There's a series of excellent Class-3+ rapids just below the falls, continuing until the take-out. This is where the best action is. Several steep drops over ledges around blind bends require quick decisions and paddle responses. This is good Class 4 at high water.

The approach to the Rockville Bridge is tricky. At normal water levels, it's easiest to start in the center and then cut sharply to the right. At high levels the far left and far right are no problem.

SHUTTLE: Put in below the dam at Bruceton Mills. Rockville can be reached by taking Little Sandy Road, turning right off WV 26 just after crossing the Little Sandy. Take a right at the first fork, go over a short, steep hill with a wonderful vista, and look for a dirt road bearing right several miles later. take out under the Rockville Bridge on the left. This place gets very popular. Parking is limited on busy days, so be careful not to block access to private property.

GAUGE: See section C.

CLASS	4–5 (6)
LENGTH	5.5
TIME	3
GAUGE	VISUAL
LEVEL	5.4–7.2 FT.
PERMITS	NO
FLOW	FREE FLOWING
GRADIENT	(4@80)
VOLUME	415
SOLITUDE	B
SCENERY	A+

LOWER BIG SANDY: ROCKVILLE TO THE CHEAT RIVER

DESCRIPTION: The Lower Big Sandy is an exciting, beautiful, piquant mistress who shows occasional flares of bad temper to even the most experienced paddlers. This is some of the most remote, scenic, and challenging whitewater in northern West Virginia. The two falls are spectacular, and the boulder rapids and ledge drops have a uniquely wonderful character. If a walkout is necessary, you can follow the old railroad bed on river right back up to Rockville. Don't go downstream; the railroad bed ends about a mile above Jenkinsburg on the wrong side of the river.

DIFFICULTIES: Plenty! Several rapids require scouting and carrying. At 1.5 miles there is a rather difficult sequence terminating in 18-foot Wonder Falls. It ends with a turbulent three-part drop into the pool just above the falls. Scout and carry the falls on either side, or run it down the center. The next series of rapids is very busy for a quarter mile, followed by a broad ledge split by a large rock in midstream. The passage on the right ends in a curler, which throws a paddler towards an undercut rock. Run just left of center. The next big one is Zoom Flume (Class 4+), a sloping 8–10-foot drop that lots of people find intimidating. Scouting on the right is recommended; the cheese-grater rock shelf below has taken its share of skin. Then get out of your boat (if you are still in it) and scout the next rapid, Little Splat (Class 5). It's steep and complex, with a hidden rock in the final diagonal ledge. Routes vary with water levels, but at moderate flows, you'll want to run down the far left. Below here the second falls, Big Splat (Class 6)

drops a total of 25 feet. Hardcore experts often run it, but every-one else carries on the left or right. Below here is an outstanding series of three, tricky Class-4+ rapids that can get nasty at high flows. Then the river calms down before dropping over several more hard drops. The rapid on the right side of First Island (Class 5) is one of the toughest on the river. It is hardest at low flows when the rock in the center of the bottom drop is virtually un-avoidable. Carry on the left over the island, or sneak down the left side. Second Island (Class 4) is also tricky and is best run on the right. Three and a half miles and 272 feet of drop later, the pad-dler, who may well be hiking by now, will reach the Cheat River near Jenkinsburg.

SHUTTLE: Put in at Rockville (see Section A). The take-out is on the left at the mouth of Big Sandy on the Cheat. Take the steep trail up through the Laurel thicket to the parking area. Jenkins-burg is reached by continuing on the road from Rockville (from the left side of the river). Turn right at the top of the hill, then take a left at the next crossing and proceed to Mount Nebo School. At Mount Nebo bear hard right to Jenkinsburg. The road is usually passable by conventional vehicles.

GAUGE: The readings refer to a government gauge at the bridge at Rockville. Call the Pittsburgh Weather Service at (412) 262-5290, or read it on site. There's also a paddler's gauge under the Bruceton Mills Bridge. The recommended range is 0–2 feet.

The First Run of Big Splat: April 1982

After running the Upper Blackwater I hooked up with Dean Tomko, Wick Walker, Jim Hammil, and Jesse Whittemore for a run down the lower Big Sandy. At 5.5 feet it was a bit low, but still enough for a good run. Our passage was uneventful (except for Jim Hammil's swim at Undercut Rock rapids) until we got to Big Splat.

As we were carrying, Jesse took a look at the rapid and decided that today was his day to try it, because, after years of looking, he finally found the line. As he scouted the drop, Wick Walker, Jim Hammil, and I set up for rescue. Hammil sat in his boat; I belayed myself on the top of the "flake" of rock at the base of the drop; Wick stood by in his swimming harness while I held the

rope, Dean studied the drop, too, waiting to see what happened to Jesse.

Although the entry to the drop is steep and complex, the crux is the last bit: a 12-foot drop with a huge flake of rock jutting out on river right. To miss the flake, the ledge must be run from right to left with speed and precision, and because of the difficulties involved, I had never contemplated running it.

Jesse eddied out above the drop and hit his line perfectly. It looked easy. To our surprise, Jesse got up and ran it again. He was less sharp, but still clean. Watching this, Dean Tomko began to get psyched. His run was shaky, but the purity of Jesse's line saved him. He was wet, but safe. We proceeded on, excited by that memorable display of skill in a true Class-6 drop.

Charlie Walbridge

Reprinted from Canoe Cruisers Association of Washington
Cruiser, July 1982.

SOVERN RUN

MAPS: Bruceton Mills, Valley Point (USGS); Preston (County)

CR 14-3 to Big Sandy

CLASS	4–5
LENGTH	0.9
TIME	1–2
GAUGE	Visual
LEVEL	NA
FLOW	Free Flowing
GRADIENT	300
VOLUME	VS
SOLITUDE	C
SCENERY	A

DESCRIPTION: This creek is really tiny and very uninterrupted. It has a lot of steep slides and some steep boulder drops. It's fun if you're ready for it! The road to Rockville runs right along the creek but it's hardly noticeable. Eddies are at a premium. It is very difficult to stop in some places. There are always a few downed trees to watch for, so be careful. This creek is one of the smallest runable streams in the state, so feel lucky if you catch it up.

DIFFICULTIES: Right near the beginning, there are two pretty-steep slides that are very close together. Further down, you'll come to some pretty tight boulder drops. At the end there's a long, smooth slide that carries you into a steep 20-foot falls near a cabin

Big Sandy Creek, Laurel Run, and Little Sandy Creek

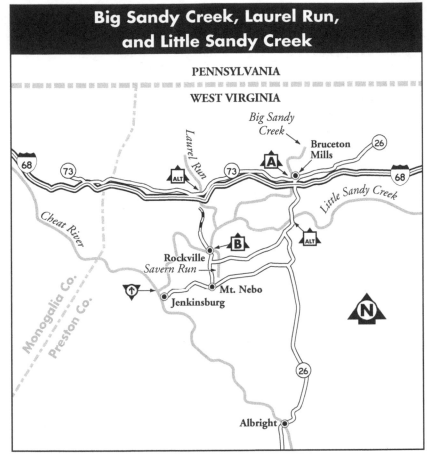

that's visible from the road bridge. The Big Sandy is about 200 yards below here.

SHUTTLE: The put-in is at the top of the hill just before turn down to Rockville. You can take out at Rockville or continue down the Big Sandy for a high water run.

GAUGE: Sovern Run is really hard to catch up. It is tiny and runs off quickly. The Rockville gauge on the Big Sandy needs to be at least 7 feet and rising. If Sovern looks runable at the put-in, you should have enough to get down it.

LITTLE SANDY CREEK

MAPS: Bruceton Mills, Brandonville, Valley Point (USGS); Preston (County)

CR 5-15 BRIDGE TO WV 26

CLASS	1–3
LENGTH	8
TIME	3
GAUGE	PHONE
LEVEL	OVER 8 FT. (ROCKVILLE)
PERMITS	NO
FLOW	FREE FLOWING
GRADIENT	30 (1 @60)
VOLUME	S
SOLITUDE	B
SCENERY	A–B

DESCRIPTION: This is a good place for Class-3 boaters when the area gets hammered by rain and the Rockville gauge is reading 8 feet and rising! The river has been run from the Hazelton Exit of Interstate 68, but it's mostly flat water from here to the CR 5/15 bridge. From here there's about 5 miles of good Class 2–3 white-water down to the CR 3 (Brandonville Pike) bridge, with the hardest (3+) drops coming just above the take-out. The last 3 miles from CR 3 to Rt. 26 is mostly flat water.

SHUTTLE: Get out your county road maps! The put-in and take-out can both be reached from WV 26 by a variety of routes.

GAUGE: You'll need around 8 feet at Rockville to make this run. Call Pittsburgh Weather Service (412) 262-5290

WV 26 TO ROCKVILLE

CLASS	3–4
LENGTH	5
TIME	2
GAUGE	PHONE
LEVEL	6–8.5 FT. (ROCKVILLE)
FLOW	FREE FLOWING
GRADIENT	41 (1 @70)
VOLUME	S
SOLITUDE	B
SCENERY	A

DESCRIPTION: This section has tougher whitewater than the Bruceton-to-Rockville section of the Big Sandy and is a very popular alternative. At low water it's picky and technical; at high levels it's very fast and continuous. After a 20-minute paddle on flat water, you'll reach the first of several ledges. Below here there are many fast, tight Class 3–4 rapids, dropping 70 feet in a mile. The last 2 miles of this trip are on the hard part of a swollen Upper Big Sandy! If you're up to it, the run from WV 26 to Jenkinsburg, down Section B of the Big Sandy, is a fabulous whitewater trip.

DIFFICULTIES: There's a beaver dam just below the put-in that creates a nasty hole in high water. Below here, many sloping ledges twist and turn unpredictably around boulders and logs. You must be quick to avoid getting pinned! The last half-mile is a very bouncy, continuous rapid called Kiss The Bride. It's named for a paddler who flipped and hit her head hard a few weeks before her wedding. She had to grow bangs to hide the scar. The whole run is very pushy and turbulent at high flows!

SHUTTLE: Put in at WV 26 bridge 2 miles south of Bruceton Mills. The shuttle to Rockville is rough but direct. Take "26/16," (Little Sandy Road) right at the fork on "14/3," then right again

on "14" (Rockville Road) to the bridge over Big Sandy. NEVER EVER use the parking lot at the Little Sandy Church of the Nazarene on Sundays!

GAUGE: Look at the rapid below the bridge; if it looks runable, you're good to go. You'll need around 6.5 feet at Rockville to make this run, but if this gauge is over 8.5 feet, watch out! Call Pittsburgh Weather Service at (412) 262-5290.

LAUREL CREEK

MAPS: Bruceton Mills (USGS); Presto (County)

CR 73 To ROCKVILLE

CLASS	2 (4)
LENGTH	3
TIME	1
GAUGE	PHONE
LEVEL	OVER 7 FT. AT ROCKVILLE
FLOW	FREE FLOWING
GRADIENT	30
VOLUME	VS
SOLITUDE	A
SCENERY	A

DESCRIPTION: The boaters who discovered the Little Sandy turned their attention here, but its short length and wildly varying difficulty have kept it from becoming popular. On the plus side, it's a short run passing through some nice forested country. It's also a wonderful trout stream! Most of the run is fast Class 2, picking up as you paddle downstream. The last drop into the Big Sandy is a serious Class-4 ledge! Now the paddler is confronted with the Class-4 rapids of the Upper Big Sandy at high water.

Laurel Creek has been run for some distance upstream, with one intrepid party putting in at the Lake O' Woods dam! The whitewater here is not too difficult, but strainer hazards will make most boaters uncomfortable. The stretch to the CR 2 bridge is very small, with lots of downed trees. Below here the channel becomes braided, and the river flows through the tangled brushy floodplain and low-lying islands with unnerving frequency.

SHUTTLE: Turn off of WV 26 into Bruceton Mills and drive through town. Main Street is CR 73, and you'll reach the bridge over Laurel Creek in a few miles. Don't be tempted to run your shuttle down CR 14 to Rockville without a 4WD with plenty of clearance. The last few miles into the gorge are virtually abandoned and very rough! Instead, drive south on WV 26 from Bruceton, turn left on CR 26-16 (Little Sandy Road), bear right at the first intersection, and turn right onto CR 14 (Rockville Road). The Rockville bridge, just down the hill, is your take-out.

GAUGE: None, but if it looks good at the CR 73 bridge, you're good to go. Rockville on the Big Sandy needs to be over 7 feet.

BEAVER CREEK

MAPS: Brandonville (USGS); Preston (County)

CR 3-16 TO BRANDONVILLE PIKE

CLASS	4
LENGTH	1
TIME	30 MIN.
GAUGE	PHONE
LEVEL	8.5 FT. + FT. (ROCKVILLE)
PERMITS	NO
FLOW	FREE FLOWING
GRADIENT	100
VOLUME	VS
SOLITUDE	A
SCENERY	A

DESCRIPTION: This feisty tributary of the Little Sandy is only 1 mile long and extremely small, but it runs fast and furious when the water comes up. None of its drops are really serious by themselves, but they are pretty relentless and somewhat blind. A downed tree could cause real problems, so watch out! The last mile is over the best part of the Little Sandy. There's a Class-3 rapid at an island just above the bridge on Brandonville Pike.

SHUTTLE: The take-out is at the Brandonville Pike (CR 3) bridge over the Little Sandy. Drive south on Brandonville Pike, then turn left on CR 3/16 (Spiker Road). It looks like a private road and wanders past high fields into the woods. Eventually it comes to the Beaver Creek bridge. Put in here.

GAUGE: None. If the water looks good at the put-in, go to it! Rockville needs to be over 8.5 feet, and even then you'll want recent rains.

FIKES CREEK

MAPS: Brandonville (USGS); Fayette, PA (County)

FORBES STATE FOREST TO GIBBON GLADE

CLASS	4–5
LENGTH	3
TIME	1
GAUGE	VISUAL
LEVEL	7+ FT. (ROCKVILLE)
FLOW	FREE FLOWING
GRADIENT	80–200+
VOLUME	VS
SOLITUDE	B
SCENERY	A

DESCRIPTION: This tiny tributary of the Big Sandy is a feisty version of its big sister. Starting off small and steep, it careens down the valley at 200 feet per mile! Rocky, technical Class-4 rapids rule. Eddies are at a premium, especially at high water, and small groups are recommended. There are several Class-5 drops where choosing the wrong route could be fatal. Portaging through the thick rhododendron and greenbriar is a real workout. Dozens of other rapids require special care and good boat control.

About halfway down, Fikes merges with a "Little Sandy Creek" (not the one in Preston County), doubling its size. Below

Bull Run

the junction there are two especially memorable drops: a long sloping ledge that you run down the right and then cut towards the center at the bottom and a long technical boulder field with many blind drops and tight moves in quick succession. It doesn't let up until just above the road in Gibbon Glade. Watch out! Below the bridge at the take-out there's a very low-hanging pipe stretching across the river. There's a couple of more miles of Class-3 action below here past several bridges before the flat section of the Big Sandy is reached at the Pennsylvania State Line.

DIFFICULTIES: Three, steep, blind drops are encountered early in the trip. A rock shelf coming in from the left warns of the first. "Hubbard's Cupboard" is not runable; a pinning rock that nearly killed a paddler is hidden in the big drop. Two other big drops, marked by clusters of enormous boulders, have dangerous chutes and must be scouted. This is a very small stream, so keep an eye out for strainers and debris!

SHUTTLE: Find Gibbon Glade, which lies just across the Pennsylvania line (off Rt. 381) on Canaan Church Road. Head south

from the bridge and take the first left just before Canaan Church. Turn left again on Maust Road (signed), a rough dirt road leading into the woods. Look for a grassy, gated lane on the left, just past the Forbes State Forest boundary sign. Carry your boats down the road, then work downhill to the creek. It's about a 15-minute walk if you take a direct route and don't get lost.

GAUGE: None, but a medium-sized flat rock on river-right just upstream of the bridge is a good guide. It should be barely under water; if it's buried this little creek gets very nasty! The Rockville Gauge on the Big Sandy should be over 7 feet. Call the Pittsburgh Weather Service at (412) 262-5290. Also remember that the water in Fikes Creek is a half-day away from here. Depending on whether the crest is downstream or upstream of the gauge, you could be in for a big disappointment or a nasty surprise.

BULL RUN

MAPS: Kingwood, Valley Point (USGS); Preston (County)

CLASS	5–6
LENGTH	1
TIME	3
GAUGE	PHONE
LEVEL	NA
FLOW	FREE FLOWING
GRADIENT	400
VOLUME	VS
SOLITUDE	C
SCENERY	B

BULL RUN TO CHEAT RIVER

DESCRIPTION: Bull Run flows along timidly for a few miles before making an abrupt plunge into the Cheat Canyon. Once a clean stream, it has been badly polluted with acid runoff since the early 1970s. The run starts off furiously with some drops approaching the limits of runability before it calms down to a continuous series of small but blind boulder drops. Trees are a constant threat, but the run has been cleaned up considerably by some dedicated WVU paddlers. Undercuts and sieves are also a problem in many of the rapids, so be careful.

DIFFICULTIES: The first rapid is a tilted slide that wants to send you into an ugly cave on the left. Start left and drive right with right angle. After an 8-foot drop run on the left, you will reach Brutus, a steep mess of boulder drops and undercuts leading into a 10-foot cascade. This should be scouted on the right. After Brutus, be ready to get out and look at one of the most impressive series of drops in this guidebook, the Matador.

The Matador is a complex sequence of ledges leading into a sheer 25–30 foot waterfall with a junky launch lip and a shallow landing pool (the rapid drops between 50–60 feet overall). As of

Jim Warlick

Bull Run (Matador)

this writing, the Matador has been run once (by Bobby Miller) and walked by several hardcore creek boaters.

Below the Matador are two steep rapids: a 12-foot cascade run on the right and a constricted double drop on the left. The rest of the creek is less steep, but with many blind, continuous drops. One particular rapid heads left, then falls off a 6–8 foot right-hand drop into a very narrow slot.

As you near the Cheat, you'll come to the "Horn of the Bull," a slide ending with an ugly 20-foot drop into a shallow pool. This is a recommended portage due to a shallow approach and a strange shelf jutting out halfway down the falls. The rapid above this is a narrow 10-foot high cascade that shoves you into "the Horn," so make sure to catch the eddy. Just below here there's a slide into a severe undercut rock. Carry this one, too.

SHUTTLE: Bull Run enters the Cheat a mile below the Jenkins-burg bridge. There is an old road running along the left bank of the Cheat almost the whole way. Carry your boat up this road or,

if you have 4WD, drive as far down as you can. The put-in is reached by heading up Bull Run Road towards Masontown until the creek rises to meet the road. Put in at the first good slide that you see.

GAUGES: There are no solid gauges that tell if Bull Run is up. Like all the Lower Cheat creeks, you have to go and check them out. Generally, if the Big Sandy is 6.5 feet and rising quickly, the Bull should be runable.

part**Three**

FASTEST WATER TO THE NORTH—
THE TYGART SUB-BASIN

Of the rivers that flow out of the mountain heartland toward the Ohio River, the Tygart ranks among the mightiest. The water quality is only fair, however. Much of the watershed suffers from acid pollution and siltation from mining operations. Some municipalities lack secondary sewage treatment facilities and this, coupled with the industrial wastes of the lower valley, causes serious problems in the lower watershed. But most of the Tygart's upper tributaries are good trout streams. Near Huttonsville the river offers superb bass fishing as well. The Buckhannon has suffered many devastating fish kills from abandoned mine runoff. There are new mines on both the Buckhannon and Lower Tygart.

State parks exist at Audra on the Middle Fork, at Tygart Lake, and at the spectacular Valley Falls on the Lower Tygart. In 1934, in the depths of the depression, The USCOE dammed the Tygart just above Grafton. The project was the salvation of this town, which prospered during the construction. Releases are designed to improve downstream navigation on the Monongahela and Ohio, subsidizing barge traffic on these rivers. Stonewall Jackson Reservoir, located on the West Fork near Weston, produces recognized benefits for the state. In addition to flood control between Weston and Clarksburg, well-planned recreational facilities were built in conjunction with state agencies.

Points of interest on the Tygart include the area around Valley Head and Mingo Flats, historic sites of American Indian travel and encampment. In the mid-to-late 1700s this area was on the outer fringes of white settlement. It was populated by a rough, self-reliant group of settlers known as "bordermen." One of them, Jesse Hughes, could outrun a pursuer while reloading his flintlock. Once the gun was loaded, his surprised enemy was as good as dead! At the beginning of the Civil War, after Virginia withdrew from the Union, West Virginia seceded from Virginia and rejoined the North. Robert E. Lee was sent over the Allegheny Mountains to straighten out the upstart mountaineers, but poor roads and bad weather caused him more trouble than the opposition. The trenches built at his headquarters near Huttonsville

Jason Thomas

Tygart Valley River

remain. Philippi was the site of the first major land battle of the Civil War, and the unusual double-laned covered bridge that was the focus of that battle still stands.

Near Philippi the Tygart picks up two major tributaries, the Middle Fork and the Buckhannon. This latter river is named for Buckongahlas, the daring and determined chief of the Delaware Indians who terrorized area settlers during this time. His ghost is said to stalk lonely river crossings throughout the area. The Tygart meets its sister river, the West Fork, in Fairmont to form the Monongahela.

The West Fork is fairly flat and winds gently through largely settled areas, but the Middle Fork, most of the Buckhannon, and parts of the Tygart pass through some wild country. A minor tributary of the Tygart, Three Fork Creek, has its mouth in Grafton below the Tygart Reservoir. A nearby trout stream, Whiteday Creek, joins the Monongahela not many miles away.

Ghost towns are common along the Buckhannon, where mills once stood harnessing its power. Beverly, located on the Tygart above Elkins, was once the largest town around and the seat of

Randolph County. Now Elkins is the county seat, and bitter animosities still remain between Beverly and Elkins because of this. Hammond, below Valley Falls, was the site of the largest brickyard in the East. Once it was a large community with trainloads of bricks leaving everyday. In the early 1940s a disastrous fire, followed by some hanky-panky with the till, destroyed the industry. The remains of the kilns exist today, and the distinctive bricks made by the firm are found everywhere in the vicinity.

Although the Tygart Valley in Randolph County has some nice farms in the rich bottoms and a few mines in the nearby mountains, its main industry is timber production. Elkins is the headquarters of the Monongahela National Forest and the host of the Mountain State Forest Festival held each year in early October. Elkins is a major cultural center, too. Each summer the world-renowned Augusta Festival is held at Davis and Elkins College, featuring folk music, dance, and crafts. Down the road, Snow Shoe—West Virginia's biggest ski resort—draws skiers from all over the South. It's an ideal place for whitewater paddlers to live due to the proximity of many superb rivers.

Barbour and Upshur counties do not have much supportive industry. Their county seats, Philippi and Buckhannon, are small college towns. Although these counties are not usually thought of as mountainous, they are quite rugged and underlain with vast coal deposits. Because of their weak economic base, they are a prime target for the strippers' bulldozers. Taylor and Marion counties are small, but underlain with rich natural gas fields. This, along with glassmaking, is the major business activity. Grafton was once an important railroad center. It declined but is now returning economically. Fairmont, located downstream on the Tygart, is both a small college town and a busy industrial city.

TYGART VALLEY RIVER

The Tygart begins high in the mountains of Randolph County, not too far from the headwaters of the Elk, and flows through a wide, beautiful valley to Elkins. The river here is known as "Tygart's Valley River." It was named for David Tygart, the first white man who settled there. Unlike his neighbors, he was able to leave before being killed by native inhabitants.

MAPS: Valley Head, Adolph, Mill Creek, Beverly West, Beverly East, Elkins, Junior, Belington, Audra, Philippi, Nestorville, Fairmont East, Fairmont West (USGS); Randolph, Barbour, Marion (County); Monongahela National Forest Map

CLASS	I
LENGTH	32+
TIME	2 DAYS
GAUGE	VISUAL
LEVEL	NA
FLOW	FREE FLOWING
GRADIENT	3
VOLUME	S
SOLITUDE	B
SCENERY	B

ABOVE ELKINS

DESCRIPTION: From Mill Creek to the bridge at the western edge of Elkins is a distance of 32 miles. The river drops only 100 feet in this distance and rarely exceeds a Class-1 rating. It is a small river most of the way, getting larger near Elkins. The Tygart Valley is a broad, picturesque valley studded with prosperous farms and walled off in the distance by the mountains. The river, which meanders lazily through this scenic country, is only canoeable during the spring or wet periods. The river has been run as high as Valley Head, and there is some Class-2 water between there and Huttonsville. Watch for fences and a 2-foot weir. The changing scenery is wonderful, and a tremendous amount of wildlife can be seen. This part of the Tygart could be broken up into several shorter runs.

CLASS	3
LENGTH	5
TIME	2
GAUGE	PHONE (BELINGTON)
LEVEL	4–6 FT.
FLOW	FREE FLOWING
GRADIENT	25
VOLUME	790
SOLITUDE	A
SCENERY	C–D

THE TYGART LOOP—NORTON TO BEAVER CREEK

DESCRIPTION: The river from Elkins to Norton is rather slow and dreary, containing a few riffles and a 3-foot ledge. At Harding the river leaves the highway and picks up speed, providing Class-3 entertainment for intermediates not yet up to other sections of the Tygart. Earlier editions of the book described the "Twin Giants" as a major Class-5 rapid. This drop, a sharp left turn in powerful current part way down, is not that difficult. Be aware that, as with most of the Tygart, many rocks are undercut. The pinning potential is often greater than it looks.

SHUTTLE: Put in under the WV 151 bridge, located just south of the US 33 bridge at Norton reached from US 250 just north of its junction with US 33. Turn west and swing down and around the hill to the left. The take-out is 3 miles north of US 250, south of Junior where the highway bridges Beaver Creek. The river from here into Belington is flat and unattractive.

GAUGE: Call the Pittsburgh National Weather Service, (412) 262-5290, and check the Belington gauge reading. You'll want 3.5–8 feet.

Martin

Towards the end of the Tygart Gorge just above the mouth of the Buckhannon there's a huge block of sandstone rising up in mid-stream. And on top of this rock, almost 20 feet up, grows a small hemlock tree. The river is calm here, giving rise to quiet thought. And every time I go by this place I think of Martin.

Back in the early 1970s I began what was to be a series of pilgrimages to the Cumberland Plateau of East Tennessee. And it was here I met Martin. He was 20 years old and a fine C-1 paddler: strong, quick, and incredibly brave. He led us and an assortment of local paddlers down a number of steep creeks, including a wild, high-water run of the Piney. Despite his skill, his manner was quiet and low-key. I liked that.

For the next couple of years our paths would cross at the usual places: Savage Races, Gauley releases, and the sweet Southern creeks near Oak Ridge, his home town. We'd paddle together every few months, enjoying each other's company, then saying goodbye until the next time. In the winter of 1973 I was trying to run a struggling business and he was working as a forester in the Tennessee mountains. He, like me, was unhappy with his job and depressed about the difficulty of getting a career started. When I wrote him about my plans to work at the newly created Nantahala Outdoor Center. He knew Payson Kennedy and liked the idea of working there. It would be a chance to get his head together and for us to run some rivers. Me and Martin, working at the Center together! Hot Damn!

On my way down to North Carolina I made a detour to the popular Petersburg Races. Pulling into the slalom site I saw the Oak Ridge gang: Mark, Kenny, Monte, and the rest. After exchanging greetings I asked

about Martin. It was then that they told me that he'd killed himself the previous week.

Stunned and speechless, I ran the race in a haze. The next day we crossed the mountains to run the Tygart Gorge. It was a beautiful, sparkling spring day and a perfect water level. As the rock came into view, I noticed the tree for the first time. My eyes misted as I thought of how the tree had to struggle to survive and how it persevered despite all odds. I felt sorry that Martin would miss this beautiful river, and that I would miss his company as well.

Time passed and I learned more. That summer I met one of the many young women who had had a crush on Martin during his brief life. She told me about the night when she sat talking with him by a campfire. He described his life as like being in a long tunnel, with the light at the end receding and the walls moving in. This glimpse of his dark side spooked her, but she thought nothing of it until she heard he was dead. Much later his mother, responding to a condolence letter I mailed 2 years earlier, told me that there had been no sign of anything unusual during his last visit the week before he died. His depression, they thought, must have been sudden and overwhelming.

That little tree is long gone; the high waters of the 1985 flood washed it away. But its memory, like that of Martin, stays with me. Each time I pass that huge rock, I look back over what seems like an impossibly long time to the days when I traveled vast distances with a few friends and we ran rivers together. And I wish, more than anything else, that I could have shared more of it with him.

Charlie Walbridge

Tygart River, Roaring Creek

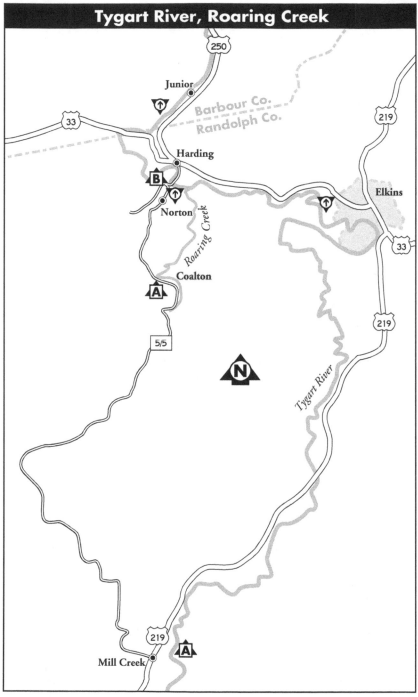

CLASS	3–5
LENGTH	11
TIME	3–4
GAUGE	PHONE
LEVEL	3.5–7 (BELINGTON)
FLOW	FREE FLOWING
GRADIENT	37
VOLUME	790
SOLITUDE	B
SCENERY	A

THE TYGART GORGE:
BELINGTON TO THE MOUTH OF THE BUCKHANNON

DESCRIPTION: This is the most rugged portion of the Tygart. The rapids are continuous, complex, and bodacious. The river tumbles through an attractive gorge, civilized only by railroad tracks on the right bank. The water is clean but acid-polluted.

The trip starts out with a literal bang—three large ledges! Then it's one narrow, steep rapid after another for several miles. Huge boulders in most of the rapids limit your ability to see downstream. The river then broadens, and the rapids gentle down to Class-2 or -3 before joining the Middle Fork. In about 2 miles the river necks down and drops 80 feet in about 1.25 miles, which is terrific for a river of its size, followed by many rapids with absolutely sinister counter-currents, boils, and holes. Finally the river broadens and welcomes its sister, the Buckhannon.

DIFFICULTIES: About 3.7 miles below Belington (or just below Papa Weese's camp), the river begins tumbling over 6–8-foot ledges between boxcar-sized boulders separated by 3–4-foot sluiceways. The first of these is Keyhole, which is a high ledge with several distinct chutes. The chute on the far right is safest, but is very tight with a sharp left turn against a large rock. Always scout since debris can lodge here. The next two ledges are blind and need to be scouted as well. Some will want to carry the fourth drop, Hard Tongue Falls, which roars over the ledge and caroms off a boulder on the left before dropping into an incredible boiling cauldron. Named for "Crazy Dave" Hartung, the first to run it, it *will* put a knot in your stomach! Below here watch out for Lets Make A Deal, a row of boulders across the river forming three slots. Choose the middle slot; the left is undercut and the right is full of rubble. Then there's "The Room"—a left-hand chute into a seeming dead-end. Eddy right and fight your way out the back door. Soon the Middle Fork River enters on the left, flowing through an impressive group of huge gray boulders.

Two miles below here the river pools against a river-wide boulder barrage that pushes it to the left. Here it drops 25 feet through a 75-yard-long S-shaped chute. This is S-Turn Rapid. In general, run this by starting center, move left, then move right to avoid a left-side hole and, finally, finish left. (At high levels, you can sneak S-Turn by paddling down the right side to the bottom of the S and dropping over a boulder pile) The next drop is Shoulder Snapper Falls, an 8-foot high sloping ledge. A well-known racer

popped his shoulder here many years ago. At water levels under 4.5 feet, the run-out is surprisingly rocky and several injuries have occurred here. Portaging might be a good idea. The right center is a straight shot at higher levels. In either event, scouting is advised.

A half-mile below, look out for Hook, the second rapid turning sharply left below Shoulder Snapper. This rapid requires a boater to hold a narrow line between some very bad holes before cutting hard left to make the turn. It's harder than it looks and worth scouting. Below is Instant Ender, so save time for playing when the river is between 4–4.2 feet!

SHUTTLE: Put in at the Highway 11 bridge in Belington. The take-out is reached from US 119, taking "36" to Carrollton. At the mouth of the Buckhannon, paddle upstream about 100 yards and take out at a rocky ledge on the left, then hike out 1 mile up the active railroad tracks! Watch out for trains! At high water (6 feet+) it's probably faster to travel the remaining 5.3 miles down to Philippi, especially when paddling a heavy open boat.

There's another takeout about 1.5 miles below the mouth of Buckhannon on river right, reached from Route 250 by following county road "250/6" and "30/6" all the way to the river. It's hard to find, but worth it.

To avoid 3 miles of uninteresting flat water, take US 250 east of Philippi, turning right at Mt. Pleasant Road, then left for 0.7 miles, and right 1 mile down over something imitating a road to the riverbank (Papa Weese's Paradise, a fishing camp).

GAUGE: Call the Pittsburgh National Weather Service at (412) 262-5290. The Belington gauge is located on the left bank below the bridge; most people want between 3.5–7 feet. It's been run at higher levels, and the rapids get really huge.

MOUTH OF BUCKHANNON TO PHILIPPI

DESCRIPTION: This is a pleasant short trip close to Philippi consisting of several rapids curving gently around large boulders. At low-to-medium–water levels (3.5–4.5 feet), the rapids are formed at narrow spots on the river and are of Class 1–2 difficulty. The scenery begins in a nice woodsy setting but soon breaks down when an extremely long strip mine appears on the left bank. This gives way to pastoral hillsides above the small college town of Philippi. The first half of the trip contains most of the action while the latter is mostly flat. Contrary to what the Philippi topo map shows, there are no "falls" on this section and it is an

CLASS	1–2(3)
LENGTH	5.3
TIME	1.5
GAUGE	PHONE
LEVEL	3–6 (PHILIPPI)
FLOW	FREE FLOWING
GRADIENT	7
VOLUME	1,782
SOLITUDE	A
SCENERY	B–C

excellent open boat run. There is one river-wide ledge (2 feet in low water) just above the historic, double-lane covered bridge. Alderson-Broaddus College is high on the hill in the background. Run in the center. Below the bridge is a 5.5-mile flat-water paddle through mostly depressing scenery until the first rapids of the Arden Run are encountered. At high water it's faster and less strenuous to paddle out to Phillipi than to carry out the tracks.

SHUTTLE: With rare covered bridges found both at the put-in and the take-out, this is a uniquely historic run. Put in at Carrollton on the Buckhannon River and run about three-quarters of a Class 2–3 rapids down to the Tygart. The put-in at a covered bridge in Carrollton is reached by turning onto CR 36 from US 119 south of Philippi.

GAUGE: Call the Pittsburgh National Weather Service, (412) 262-5290, to check the Belington gauge. You'll want between 4–8 feet for good water levels in both rivers.

CLASS	3–5
LENGTH	8
TIME	3
GAUGE	WEB
LEVEL	400+
	CFS (PHILIPPI)
FLOW	FREE FLOWING
GRADIENT	27
VOLUME	1,782
SOLITUDE	B
SCENERY	B

TWO MILES ABOVE ARDEN TO BIG COVE RUN

DESCRIPTION: The Tygart runs big and flat river for 5.5 miles below Philippi, gathering courage for the 170-foot jump to the reservoir behind the Grafton dam. All but the last 3 miles of the run below Arden may be scouted from a secondary road, which runs from Philippi to the ancient concrete bridge at Teter Creek. Some of the best water is in the remaining run to the reservoir. The river drops over big rock ledges and reefs and is strewn with huge boulders. As you approach the reservoir during drawdown season ugly mud slopes detract from the otherwise unspoiled nature of the area.

DIFFICULTIES: About a mile below Arden there's a ledge channeled on the left. The current continues down the left side 50 feet, dropping over a boulder and ending in two stoppers. The larger upstream wave must be skirted to the right if one is to maintain alignment and speed for running a ledge and the second stopper. In the second rapid downstream from Laurel Creek (which enters from the right under a steel bridge), the river narrows and piles over a rapid succession of three ledges with unavoidable 5-foot standing waves. Three hundred yards below this rapid, the river funnels over a ledge to the left that undercuts a shelf rock with minimal clearance. This can be negotiated, but it is dangerous.

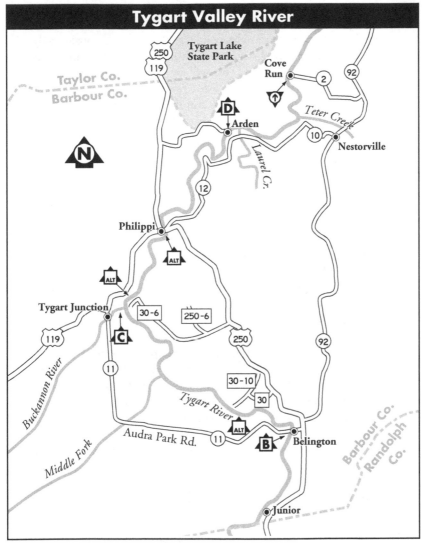

Tygart Valley River

Taylor Co.
Barbour Co.

250
119
Tygart Lake
State Park

Cove
Run

92
2

D
Arden

Teter Creek

10
Nestorville

N

Laurel Cr.

12

Philippi

ALT

ALT

Tygart Junction

30-6   250-6

119

C

250

92

11

30-10

30

Buckannon River

Middle Fork

Audra Park Rd.   11   ALT   B   Belington

Barbour Co.
Randolph Co.

Junior

Five hundred yards from here the river spills over Moats Falls, a complex, 15- to 20-foot river-wide falls. Some people run it on the right at low water after sneaking under the natural bridge. More recently paddlers have run this falls right over the middle: a 15-foot drop into the suds. For the squeamish and/or less advanced boater, it's easy to carry along the road on the right. One mile below is Classic Rapid, where the river is narrowed and split by a partially submerged, house-sized boulder. This is a powerful drop that's worth scouting. It's fairly flat from here to the Teter Creek Bridge.

Impressive Wells Falls is about 2 miles below Teter Creek Bridge. Here the river pools up behind a natural rock dam, turns to the left, then runs right, while necking down considerably. There are big diagonal stoppers pushing to the right in this turn. As you regain alignment, you will be riding a huge tongue of water dropping 10 feet over a slide towards a formidable hole. You can miss it if you hold your line, but if you slide off the tongue to the right, you will be stopped dead. This may be the most powerful runable rapid in the entire Monongahela Basin and should be scouted. The next rapid is a mean one: a sheer drop into a nasty hole. Both this and Wells Falls are easily carried on the right. The other rapids below Teter Creek are nice Class 3 and offer no special problems. The entire Arden section is worthy of respect during high water; the drops are huge, the holes powerful, and the water gets pretty squirrely.

SHUTTLE: From Arden use the dirt road on the right side of the river for the shuttle. Drive about 2 miles upstream to the first rapids for an easy put-in. Beginners should take out at the Arden Bridge. Intermediates can take out at Laurel Creek. Experts may proceed with caution and scout the falls. Take out at Teter Creek for a short roadside run. To reach the Cove Run take-out, turn right at Teter Creek and go out to the main highway, WV 92, and turn left. Take Cove Run Road "2" to the left, then a right, another right and then a left at the succeeding forks. The last part takes you down a very steep unimproved road to the river. Be sure you can recognize this point from the water. You will not find any rapids on the lower part until around the first of October. Peak drawdown is generally reached at the end of February. Then you'll find another 1.8 miles of rapids dropping at 30 fpm. Afterwards you'd have to paddle another 2 miles of flat water across Tygart Lake to reach the first take-out: the Wildcat Hollow Boat Club on river left.

GAUGE: The Philippi gauge on the Tygart is the best one for this section, but there are ongoing problems with it. The City of Philippi has a rubble dam and a water supply intake near the gauge, and they periodically deepen the pool during low flow periods. So the old readings in feet are unreliable. But since the USCOE uses this gauge to manage Tygart Lake, the USGS checks and re-rates it often. Go to the USGS web site and check the cfs rating. The minimum level for Section D is 400 cfs. For those who are interested, the ledge at Moats Falls is runable at levels over 3,000 cfs. You can also call the Pittsburgh office of the National Weather Service, (412) 262-5290, and check The Belington gauge. A reading of 3.5 feet or more should provide plenty of water for this run.

Valley Falls Dropping,1977

Remember the western chase scene where the natives are eluded by the hero when he jumped his horse off the cliff into the river and swam across the impassable canyon? Want to try the same thing without bringing the Humane Society down on your head? Make the jump in your boat.

Cal "The Animal" Smith did it on July 20 over the brink of 16-foot Valley Falls. He dropped over the edge, disappeared entirely—the full length of his kayak—and then popped-up the same track he went down, stern first, halfway back up the waterfall. He then turned broadside in the plunge, flipped, and came out. He was able to push off the cliff base rocks and wash downstream with his boat. It was such fun he tried it again with similar results except that this time boat and paddler parted company and the more valuable of the two became a drum for the waterfall.

After the kayak was cleared from the base of the falls I tried the leap in a C-1—into the drink, reverse pop, flipped, and ejected in the falls. Frank Jernejcic was next. Attempting to avoid our repeated failures to clear the base of the cataract, Frank blasted down the approach at full tilt, shot out beyond the vertical current, nosed into the backwash and was flipped-in head first. It was an unbelievable downstream end-over-end. Frank rolled up and back paddled to safety.

Not to be outdone and since no one had yet run the falls remaining upright, I climbed back to the top once more. This time full speed over the abyss, into the foam on a low brace, and paddled hard to escape the counter current. Success!

During the hour that this drama played, tourists seemed to come out of the woods in droves. Cameras clicking and whirring, adulation, charges of mental

illness, applause, tributes of beer, kisses for the heroes, official pictures by the State Park photographer, and the satisfaction of knowing we had done our best.

Since photos of the late Martin Begun running 15-foot Potter's Falls appeared in Whitewater last summer, American paddlers have been seeking safe falls to run. In May, Bob Obst from Wisconsin tried to run Valley Falls with frightening results. He reportedly was temporarily pinned on the bottom by the current and then shot up from the deep, clearing the water upside-down before he was carried back into the falls. He was shook enough that no one else followed him at that time.

In late June, six Ohiopyle guides dropped the Big Sandy Falls with one accident. The first paddler smashed his bow on a base rock. All others dropped without mishap. The flow at that time was about 500 cfs. Big Sandy Falls is a height similar to Valley Falls. The flow at Valley Falls on July 20 was about 250 cfs.

Given a falls with a clean approach, a vertical drop, and a 15-foot deep, rock-free pool, dropping seems to be safe for paddler and equipment. In my experience it is much less traumatic than jumping into water from a similar height. The danger is, obviously, in being able to get away from the plunge at the bottom of the falls. This must relate to the volume of water in the river, the breadth of the curtain of water over the lip, and, to a lesser extent, the topography of the pool.

At this point I can only say falls dropping was fun and was reasonably safe at Valley Falls on July 20. Any other place or any other level I would approach with trepidation. For any paddler looking for a falls to drop, West Virginia now has two that are proven to be runable. Proceed at your own risk with caution and good sense.

Paul Davidson

Reprinted from West Virginia Wildwater Association *Splashes*, July 1977.

Jason Thomas

Tygart Valley River (Hamburger)

VALLEY FALLS TO HAMMOND

CLASS	3—5
LENGTH	1.5
TIME	1
GAUGE	PHONE
LEVEL	0—1 FT. (COLFAX)
FLOW	FREE FLOWING
GRADIENT	60
VOLUME	2,259
SOLITUDE	B—C
SCENERY	A

DESCRIPTION: This section of the Tygart requires a cavalier attitude. In addition to the gradient, the river necks down 80% as it enters the rapids. The first ledge, Valley Falls is a river-wide ledge about 12 feet high with 3 distinct chutes. Two are runable, but scouting is essential. The next ledge is about 12 feet high and appears unrunable, but at low water can be run on the left of the right half. The third ledge, Punk Rock, is a Class-3 rapid with two runable channels, both requiring right-angle turns to the left after running tight along the right bank. The fourth ledge, Hamburger Helper, is clearly Class 5. Here the river narrows to a single channel and drops 8 feet over a boulder. There's a thin flow at center and a boiling flume to each side. The fifth rapid, Twist and Shout, is a series of 3, rapid drops in a 20-foot channel. The bottom two have huge holes up against the undercut right shore. The remaining three ledges (This, That, and It) are straightforward, the last of which can be reached from the take-out.

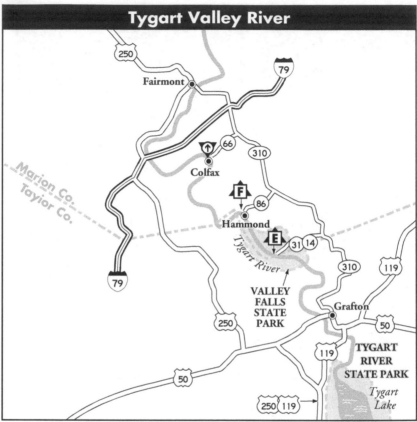

Due to the discharge of Grafton Dam, this section can be "run" anytime, but if several gates are open, the whole valley is a nightmare of explosive, moving, 12- to 15-foot waves and terrible holes. An interesting sight, but no place for anyone's boat.

Access Note: This section was closed for a while until American Whitewater and the West Virginia Rivers Coalition negotiated to keep it open. The terms are that paddlers must stop at park headquarters and provide names, addresses, and phone numbers of all party members. From the parking lot it's a 200-yard portage via a bridge over the railroad tracks to the pool above the first drop. Boaters are permitted to re-run the drops, but intentional swimming, with or without a PFD, is not allowed. Please cooperate!

SHUTTLE: Reach Valley Falls State Park by following signs from Fairmont or Grafton along WV 310 to CR 31/14. Reach Hammond on the yellow brick road (honest!), known as CR 86, just off of WV 310. The road is rough, and you'll have to walk the last bit or hike up the railbed instead. The shuttle can also be run on a rough dirt road on river left, reachable from Route 50 or

250. A county road map is needed to find this road.

GAUGE: Run Valley Falls only after making an on-site observation. Most runs are made at low summer flows. River outfitters use 750 cfs as a high-water cutoff point, but expert paddlers can go down at higher levels by exercising great caution at the big drops. Call Grafton Dam at (304) 265-1760 to find out what they are releasing. The Pittsburgh office of the National Weather Service, (412) 262-5290, lists the Colfax gauge. 0–1 foot is a good range.

HAMMOND TO COLFAX

CLASS	1–2, B
LENGTH	5
TIME	1.5
GAUGE	VISUAL
LEVEL	0–3 FT.
FLOW	FREE FLOWING
GRADIENT	4 (1@20)
VOLUME	2,547
SOLITUDE	A
SCENERY	A–C

DESCRIPTION: Unless there are several gates open at the Grafton Dam, this is a pleasant Class 1–2 run for 1 mile below the brickyard. Take the first island to the left and the rest on the right for the best rapids. The remaining 4 miles are flat through attractive scenery. Take out at Colfax on the left just past the bridge or paddle 4.5 more miles of flat water to Fairmont.

SHUTTLE: To get to Hammond, see section E. Colfax is on CR 66 west from WV 310 and north from Hammond.

GAUGE: A homemade gauge is located on bridge support at Colfax. This section has been run at 8 feet.

MIDDLE FORK RIVER

MAPS: Adolph, Cassity, Ellamore, Audra (USGS); Randolph, Upshur, Barbour (County)

ADOLPH TO US 33

CLASS	2
LENGTH	16
TIME	5.5
GAUGE	VISUAL
LEVEL	NA
FLOW	FREE FLOWING
GRADIENT	30 (3@50)
VOLUME	VS
SOLITUDE	A
SCENERY	A–C

DESCRIPTION: Not yet a river, this creek rushes along in a fairly continuous Class-2 style. There is one short bouldery stretch below Cassity before the river gradually flattens. The scenery includes a pretty wooded valley above Cassity, some unattractive mines at Cassity, and an interesting little canyon from Cassity to US 33. From US 33 to the Laurel Fork, the river is totally flat.

GAUGE: None. Inspect from shore.

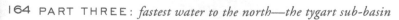

CLASS	1–3
LENGTH	5
TIME	2
GAUGE	VISUAL
LEVEL	3.2–6 FT.
FLOW	FREE FLOWING
GRADIENT	26 FPM
VOLUME	330
SOLITUDE	A
SCENERY	A–B

B

LAUREL FORK TO AUDRA STATE PARK

DESCRIPTION: This interesting and lively little trout stream starts off quite tranquilly over Class-1 riffles past delightful little islands and then gradually changes character. The rapids become more numerous, more continuous, and more complicated. Passing the halfway mark, the paddler's view is obscured by numerous boulders and rock gardens, making it a thrilling Class-3 challenge for the intermediate paddler. As the State Park is reached, the intensity, but not the continuity, of the rapids lets up.

The river is quite attractive, but the "Middle Fork Resort" halfway through the trip on the river's left is quite developed, with a number of riverside buildings. There are a few gas wells and small, well-kept cabins throughout the run.

DIFFICULTIES: There are no difficulties other than the possibility of broaching on the numerous boulders. One rapid at about halfway may appear choked, and locating the correct passage in lower water may be difficult. There are many 2–3-foot ledges and a vigorous 8-foot drop just below the resort, but most are straightforward and easily run. This run could be mean in very high water (over 6 feet). In general, the best passages, including around the islands, are to the left. Do not run the rapid under the bridge unless you plan to run section C because the area below is fenced in, and you'd have to paddle a good piece downstream before carrying back up. By the way, this rapid is much more difficult than anything above.

SHUTTLE: The take-out is immediately above the CR 11 bridge. A parking lot is located on the right. To reach the put-in, take the road "10/6" upstream that leaves the park on the left side of the river. This hard-surface road soon makes a sharp right toward Buckhannon, but a dirt road continues straight (to Mount Nebo) and should be taken. Soon this dirt road forks again. Take the left fork down the steep hillside to a clearing and another fork. Bear to the left; just past a vacation cabin there is a spot to park and easily launch boats (known by locals as Finnegan's Ford). This road continues upstream a considerable distance. A fast Class-1 run in high water could be made by putting in at a Boy Scout camp 5 miles above.

GAUGE: See Section C.

AUDRA STATE PARK TO TYGART JUNCTION

CLASS	4
LENGTH	6
TIME	3
GAUGE	PHONE
LEVEL	3.2–5 FT.
FLOW	FREE FLOWING
GRADIENT	(2.5@79)
VOLUME	330
SOLITUDE	B–C
SCENERY	A

DESCRIPTION: Look at the rapid under the bridge at Audra State Park and admire the lush sylvan surroundings. Subtract the road, bridge, and bathhouse, and you'll know what to expect for the first 2.6 miles of this run. It's a beautiful, busy, boat buster. The rapids under the bridge can be run on the right side: head straight for the retaining wall of the swimming area and then slip to the left down into the pool when the water is low. In the warm months, watch out for the buoy line demarcating the swimming area! It's more entertaining to fandango down through the center when the water's high. Beyond the pool you'll have to carefully pick channels for the next hour to the first of three major rapids above the mouth of the Middle Fork.

The river empties into the Tygart Gorge at about its midpoint. The only way out is to paddle the remaining 4 miles to the mouth of the Buckhannon. The result: two trips for the price of one. First there is the steep, rocky, technical paddling of the lower Middle Fork, and then the much heavier, pushy Tygart with its tripled volume.

DIFFICULTIES: About an hour into the trip a hemlock-bedecked isle looms midstream. It cannot be run on the left except in high water. The right side is an interesting slide rapid with a stopper that tends to shunt the unwary into a left-side whirlpool. Several cycles may be required before breaking out. The big three rapids in the last half-mile of the Middle Fork are next and will require scouting. The first is long and goes around a corner to the right after about 100 yards. The worst drop is before the turn. Enter in the middle and then cut left. The next big rapid, recognized by a giant boulder on the bottom left is very obstructed. Run down the right over high, clean ledges. The third and last rapid before the Tygart is called the Wall. It can be run on the left where the water smashes into a cliff, or you can pick your way down the other side. Below, a short, rocky rapid empties into the Tygart.

SHUTTLE: Audra State Park is reached via CR 11 from either US 119 or 250. Follow signs to Audra State Park. For the take-out, see the Tygart, section B. The beautifully laid out campgrounds at Audra provide the finest riverside camping to be found anywhere in West Virginia.

GAUGE: There is a USGS gauge on river right, just upstream of the bridge at Audra State Park. Call Pittsburgh office of the National Weather Service, (412) 262-5290, and listen for the Audra reading. There is a staff gauge on the opposite shore on the downstream face of a large boulder. This gauge corresponds to the government gauge and can be read directly. The minimum level is 3.2 feet; 6 feet is a real handful. A reading of 4 feet or more on the Tygart at Belington is also a good indicator.

BUCKHANNON RIVER

MAPS: Alton, Buckhannon, Century, Audra (USGS); Upshur, Barbour (County)

ALEXANDER TO TENMILE

CLASS	I–3
LENGTH	9
TIME	3
GAUGE	PHONE
LEVEL	7–10
(BUCKHANNON)	
FLOW	FREE FLOWING
GRADIENT	27
VOLUME	584
SOLITUDE	A
SCENERY	A–B

DESCRIPTION: This deceptive river is extremely sluggish below Buckhannon and its small size in the headwaters area near Alexander belie what is in store for paddlers between Alton (pronounced Elton by the locals) and Sago. The river begins at a very small scenic stream where the right and left forks meet at Alexander. There is hardly anything more than straightforward riffles for 5 miles until well below Alton. Here the gradient picks up to 40 fpm, and the rapids become complicated and closely spaced. Each drop is fairly steep and, in low water, a good deal of tight maneuvering is necessary. The gradient and the many bends in the river limit your downstream vision. All but advanced paddlers should arrange a take out at Tenmile because the river's character changes drastically from there on. Because the best action is below Alton, most will not want to bother with the Alexander to Alton stretch.

DIFFICULTIES: None. Most of the rapids below Alton are 50- to 100-yard descents through rock gardens.

SHUTTLE: From Alexander take CR 11 west to WV 20, then right through Adrian to CR 22, then again right to Sago. Continue on CR 22 to CR 9 at Tallmansville. Turn right on "9" and proceed south to CR 9/8 and turn right to Tenmile. Alton may be reached via CR 11/15 and 32/14 from Alexander. See shuttle for section B.

GAUGE: See section B.

Buckhannon River and the Middle Fork River

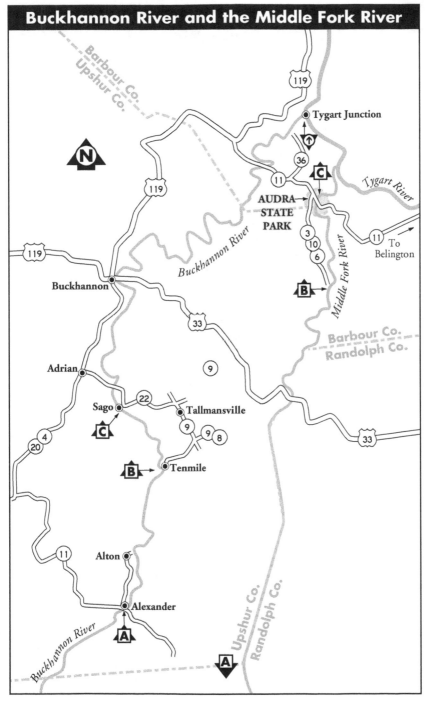

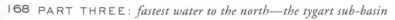

CLASS	3–4
LENGTH	4
TIME	2
GAUGE	PHONE
LEVEL	7–10
	(BUCKHANNON)
FLOW	FREE FLOWING
GRADIENT	53
VOLUME	M
SOLITUDE	A
SCENERY	B

TENMILE TO SAGO

DESCRIPTION: This is an isolated stretch of Class 3–4 water on a river running through nineteenth-century Appalachia. It's one of those crude nuggets that good paddlers love to find. The first 3 miles are very difficult and some scouting is required. The last mile into Sago is fairly flat with comparatively minor rapids. New mining operations have marred a lot of nice scenery and more is planned for the area.

DIFFICULTIES: Shortly below Tenmile the river pools behind a boulder-choked natural dam. The water flows primarily to the right side and seemingly sluices in a boulder-studded, 15-foot channel at a right angle across to the left side; however, most of this sluice leaks out under 8-foot boulders from the downstream side, creating a very dangerous trap. A paddler was washed under and between the big boulders in 1970. Avoid this gnarly channel entirely and sneak your boat down the secondary channel on the left side of this obstruction.

The river slides along over interesting rapids for a mile below the sieve to the second bad rapid. This is a long boulder-strewn slide complicated by an S-shaped entrance, which frequently results involuntarily in eddy turns. If this happens, the paddler should back down the rest of the rapids rather than chance broaching on a rapid-dividing wet boulder halfway down.

The third rapid is nasty, and should be inspected from the right side. The river drops 3 feet through narrow passages at the top and then races over irregular rocks on a left slant to batter against an ugly shelf. It is sometimes run as far left as possible, sneaking out between two entrance boulders.

Beyond this the river slides and drops over innumerable ledges and around large boulders. The rotted bridge piers of the ghost town of Ours Mills indicate the end of the action.

SHUTTLE: This is a dandy place to get lost. Sago, Alton, and Alexander are all connected with WV 20 by good roads. Difficult, unmarked roads connect Sago with Tenmile, Alton, and Alexander. All are very time-consuming. Finding Sago and Alton is no problem. Tenmile can be reached from Sago via Tallmansville by following our directions. If you try one of the "shortcuts," take plenty of gas, maps, and a flashlight. Read the shuttle for section A, and have a copy of the Upshur County map handy.

GAUGE: This run is good between 7–10 feet at Buckhannon; call the Pittsburgh Weather Service at (412) 262-5290 for a reading. About ten stones showing on the right abutment of the Alton Bridge ensures adequate water.

BELOW SAGO TO TYGART RIVER

CLASS	I
LENGTH	36
TIME	2 DAYS
GAUGE	PHONE
LEVEL	NA
FLOW	FREE FLOWING
GRADIENT	3
VOLUME	MEDIUM
SOLITUDE	A
SCENERY	B

DESCRIPTION: From Sago the river winds placidly for 36 miles to Carrollton, dropping only 2 to 3 fpm in the process. This would make an excellent canoe-camping-fishing trip. The scenery gets pretty in one wild section near the confluence with Sand Run. The good whitewater section starts about a half mile above the covered bridge at Carrollton. This has been described under section C of the Tygart.

GAUGE: See section B.

OTHER TYGART TRIBUTARIES

ROARING CREEK

MAPS: Junior (USGS); Randolph (County)

ROARING CREEK: COALTON TO THE TYGART

CLASS	I–4
LENGTH	5
TIME	2
GAUGE	NONE
LEVEL	NA
PERMITS	NO
FLOW	FREE FLOWING
GRADIENT	85 (I @ I 35; I @ I 60)
VOLUME	VS
SOLITUDE	A
SCENERY	B

DESCRIPTION: This is a very small creek with lots of action and a very nasty log-filled drop at the end. The river runs south of Norton along CR 5/5 to Coalton. The first mile is flat, ending with a three-foot ledge. The next 4 miles increase gradually from Class 2 to 4, becoming increasingly technical. Halfway down is "Bad to the Bone," a very steep ledge drop studded with trees. You may have to walk this one.

SHUTTLE: Take CR 5/5 south of WV 33 near Norton.

GAUGE: None; this is a flood run. Inspect on site.

LAUREL CREEK

MAPS: Nestorville (USGS); Barbour (County); Monongahela National Forest Map

WV 38 TO TYGART RIVER

CLASS	2–5 (6)
LENGTH	5.5
TIME	2
GAUGE	VISUAL
LEVEL	NA
PERMITS	No
FLOW	FREE FLOWING
GRADIENT	50 (1 @ 100)
VOLUME	VS
SOLITUDE	A
SCENERY	A

DESCRIPTION: This cleverly named torrent affords a 5.5-mile run that evolves from placid to thrilling. The cruise starts with a relaxing 2.5-mile float through a mostly wooded, gorge-like valley marred only by a few mining scars. There are many riffles and uncomplicated rapids. After passing the first bridge, the gradient increases, and rounded sandstone boulders form long, complex rapids. This is great fun and quite exciting, but it can only be considered a warm-up exercise if the final mile from the second bridge down to the Tygart is on your itinerary. Rapids become steeper and more complex, climaxing in a memorable stretch that begins with a steep boulder rapid in which the water piles into a big, nightmarish "floating" boulder with about half the river flowing underneath it (Class 6). Next are two huge sloping ledges, which are, in turn, followed by a ten-foot falls runable on the extreme right and two short but intense and exacting boulder piles. If you survive all this and make it to the Tygart, congratulate yourself.

SHUTTLE: Take WV 38 east to WV 92. Turn left and go 3 miles to CR 10 and left to Moatsville. Follow the road up the Tygart 2.7 miles to Laurel Creek.

GAUGE: None. Check visually. The Tygart probably needs to be over 8 feet at Philippi.

TETER CREEK

Tiny Teter Creek tumbles into the Tygart near Moatsville in Barbour County, West Virginia. This is only a 1.5-mile run from WV 92; you can start at WV 32 near Nestorville for a good warm-up.

MAPS: Nestorville (USGS); Barbour (County)

Laurel, Sandy, and Teter Creek

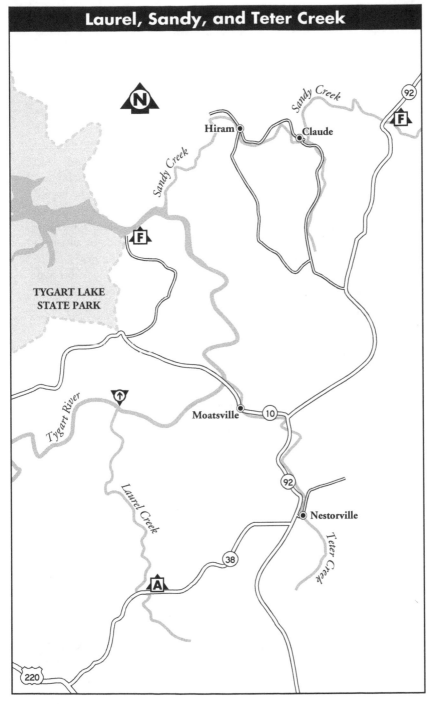

CLASS	1–4+
LENGTH	4
TIME	1.5
GAUGE	NONE
LEVEL	NA
PERMITS	No
FLOW	FREE FLOWING
GRADIENT	(2.5@ 120)
VOLUME	VS
SOLITUDE	A
SCENERY	A

NESTORVILLE TO TYGART RIVER

DESCRIPTION: The first mile is an easy float over Class 2–3 boulder gardens and ledges. Just above the bridge in Moatsville is a long, broken ledge that can be negotiable via a complex route on the right. If this bothers you, take out here. Below here the river drops 120 fpm through narrow slots, around blind bends, and down a 100-yard long slide. The current rushes into menacing undercuts in an exquisite boulder-filled environment. The rapids look nasty from the top, but most can be eddy scouted by skilled boaters. Occasional stray logs will keep your party alert. The steepest drop, The Three Amigos, runs along the left side of an island towards the end of the run. After punching two stout holes, negotiate a narrow sluice into a final horseshoe-shaped ledge. You may want to carry this one. There are more juicy drops below here!

SHUTTLE: WV 92 and CR 10-1 parallel the creek.

GAUGE: None. If the big ledge above the bridge looks runable, you'll be okay. The Tygart gauge at Philippi should be over 7 feet.

SANDY CREEK

Sandy Creek is the least popular of the three lower Tygart tributaries, but contains some great whitewater in an isolated setting.

MAPS: Thornton (USGS); Barbour, Taylor, Preston (County)

CLASS	1–4+
LENGTH	8
TIME	2.5
GAUGE	NONE
LEVEL	NA
PERMITS	No
FLOW	FREE FLOWING
GRADIENT	50 (1@100)
VOLUME	VS
SOLITUDE	A
SCENERY	A

WV 92 TO TYGART LAKE

DESCRIPTION: This river is 2–3 times larger than Teter or Laurel Creek. There are two sections; one recommended for novices and another for advanced paddlers. The creek from WV 92 to the second bridge at Hiram is mostly flat with a swift current and occasional riffles. It twists through an attractive gorge-like valley past wooded slopes, fields, and an occasional house. By the time it gets to Claude it is 2–3 times larger than at the 92 bridge.

There is one solid Class-3+ rapid just above Hiram. Below here roads and civilization depart and the stream roars downhill to

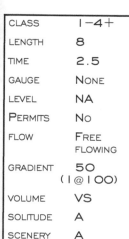

the Tygart. The whitewater varies from easy boulder patches to formidable ledges and steep boulder dams. A huge rock in the center of the stream covered with lush growth marks the beginning of the good stuff! There are some very obstructed drops below here, which deserve careful scouting. They resemble the easier rapids on the Upper Yough. When you get to the lake, paddle out of the Sandy Gorge and turn right. A dirt road, CR 8, reaches Tygart Lake about a mile downstream.

SHUTTLE: Follow CR 10-1 down to the Tygart at the mouth of Teter Creek, cross the old concrete bridge, and continue to the second right. This is CR 8; follow it all the way to Tygart Lake. The last mile or so is rough and may require 4WD when wet or icy. The river can be run from WV 92, but those seeking the best whitewater should use the bridge at Claude. To get there, turn left from WV 92 onto Claude Road (CR 1) and follow it to the first bridge, at Claude. You can continue down the road another mile or so to Hiram, where a second bridge crosses the river.

GAUGE: None. Check visually. This is a much bigger river than Teter or Laurel Creek and should hold its water a while longer. A Tygart reading of over 7 feet at Philippi is a good indicator.

THE FORKS OF THE BUCKHANNON RIVER

These small headwater streams are well off the beaten track, but provide entertainment for solid intermediates looking to explore new country.

RIGHT FORK OF THE BUCKHANNON RIVER

This is a marginal run, even at high water. The first 3 miles to Silica are tiny and scrapy with occasional tree hazards. A decent-sized tributary makes boating reasonable from there on down. Not far past Silica is a small island, below which is an imposing, tilting, double ledge (3 feet and 6 feet). Afterward, there are a few other small ledges, then nonstop whitewater (Class 3) to Selbyville. There is a six-foot dam at a camp in Selbyville; carry on the left. The river is much slower below here to Alexander on the Buckhannon.

MAPS: Pickens, Goshen, Alton (USGS); Randolph, Upshur (County)

CLASS	3
LENGTH	12
TIME	4
GAUGE	VISUAL
LEVEL	NA
FLOW	FREE FLOWING
GRADIENT	2@110
VOLUME	VS
SOLITUDE	A
SCENERY	B

PICKENS TO SELBYVILLE

GAUGE: None. Runable during wet periods. Inspect on site.

LEFT FORK OF THE RIGHT FORK OF THE BUCKHANNON RIVER

MAPS: Pickens, Alton (USGS); Randolph, Upshur (County)

CLASS	1–3
LENGTH	7
TIME	2.5
GAUGE	NONE
LEVEL	NA
FLOW	FREE FLOWING
GRADIENT	2@75
VOLUME	VS
SOLITUDE	A
SCENERY	A

HELVETIA TO SELBYVILLE

DESCRIPTION: This is a lovely run. At first the river follows the road, but after Czar it flows through a narrow, uninhabited valley. The whitewater is continuous and builds to a bouncy Class-3 run over submerged boulders.

GAUGE: None. Runable during wet periods. Inspect on site.

LEFT FORK OF THE BUCKHANNON RIVER

MAPS: Pickens, Alton (USGS); Randolph, Upshur (County)

CLASS	2–3
LENGTH	8
TIME	3
GAUGE	NONE
LEVEL	NA
FLOW	FREE FLOWING
GRADIENT	5@60
VOLUME	VS
SOLITUDE	A
SCENERY	B

HELVETIA-ADOLPH ROAD TO ALEXANDER

DESCRIPTION: This run is nonstop, easy Class 2–3 whitewater with an even gradient. The river travels through a pretty, wooded canyon marred by some road scars, a few cabins, and a mine vent. There are two low-water railroad bridges requiring carries and a midpoint road crossing at Palace Valley. The lower part of the run is a less steep, but still interesting. The Left Fork joins the Right Fork at Alexander to form the main Buckhannon

GAUGE: None. Runable during wet periods. Inspect on site.

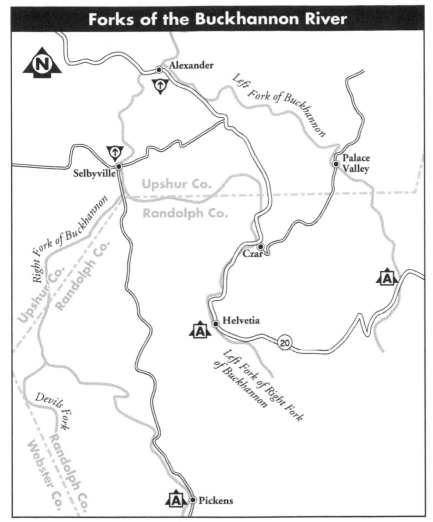

Forks of the Buckhannon River

MISCELLANEOUS
MONONGAHELA TRIBUTARIES

THREE FORK CREEK

This is a very small stream that needs a lot of rain to paddle. The water is very acidic and the rocks are orange. The scenery is mostly attractive, and there is a short stretch with very interesting rapids.

MAPS: Newburg, Gladesville, Thornton (USGS); Preston, Taylor (County)

CLASS	I–4
LENGTH	I 2
TIME	7.5
GAUGE	THREE FORK CREEK NEAR GRAFTON (WEB)
LEVEL	4-7 FT.
FLOW	FREE FLOWING
GRADIENT	(2@ 30/I.5@60)
VOLUME	S
SOLITUDE	A
SCENERY	B–C

A

NEAR WV 92 TO THORNTON

DESCRIPTION: The first 4 miles from WV 92 to CR 33 (Gladesville-Independence Road) are small and can only be run when the water is very high. Most runs usually start at the CR 33 bridge. Here laurel and hemlock crowd in on the stream, and the water is flat with only occasional riffles. Later the river begins picking up speed and complexity. The CR 33-9 bridge marks a distinct change from easy whitewater to action-packed Class 3–4.

Before the water tapers off to a Class 2 for another 3 miles, there are 3 "falls" in a 3-mile, Class-4 section below. You might consider taking out at the second bridge (CR 7) beyond the last falls. The lower part of the river from here to Grafton moves along steadily through attractive country, with occasional Class 1–2 riffles.

DIFFICULTIES: Just before, under, and beyond the second bridge from the put-in is Victoria Falls, which drops over a steep slide into very turbulent water, then over a 2–4-foot ledge into a powerful hydraulic. The rapids after this are all closely spaced, steep, and complex. The second and third falls are near the end of this 1.5-mile course. The first of these, Yosemite, is a steep staircase descent taken on the right, and the next rapid, the third falls (Niagara), is a river-wide shelf with several passages. Scouting is recommended for the first and third falls. The falls have been given these grand names not only for the power they connote, but also to bring a suggestion of beauty to this otherwise forlorn land.

SHUTTLE: Put in at the first bridge below WV 92 on the Three Fork Creek Road "35," or at the bridge next to the tavern on "33," 2.5 miles south of Gladesville. Take outs can be made at the CR 7 bridge, the next bridge downstream at Irontown, or under the US 50 bridge at Thornton. For nothing but action, put in at the Victoria Falls bridge reached by taking the road next to the cemetery from Gladesville. There are many take-outs between here and Grafton.

GAUGE: There is an online gauge for Three Fork Creek on the USGS web site. Paddleable levels range from 4–7 feet.

Three Fork Creek

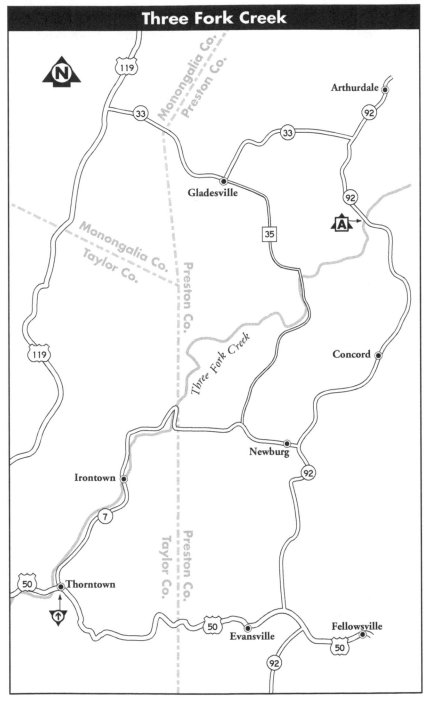

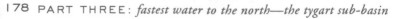

WHITEDAY CREEK

This anxious little screamer forms the Monongalia-Marion county line. The lower section has good playing at high water and is run regularly by local paddlers. The steep section above the put-in has been run, during very high water, but it's full of trees.

MAPS: Rivesville (USGS); Monongahela, Marion (County)

CLASS	1–3
LENGTH	9
TIME	3
GAUGE	VISUAL
LEVEL	1–3
FLOW	FREE FLOWING
GRADIENT	3@55/ 6@23
VOLUME	S
SOLITUDE	A
SCENERY	B

A

CAMP CALICO TO THE MONONGAHELA RIVER

DESCRIPTION: The first 2 miles are continuous Class 3+ with no pools and few eddies. A road runs alongside for an abbreviated run. The stream here is only 20 to 40 feet wide. The second or middle part down to WV 73 consists of more open Class-2 water, while the final 3 miles consist of mainly Class 2–3 waves and ledges.

DIFFICULTIES: In the first quarter mile there is a left-hand bend against an auto-sized boulder. Stay to the right of center to avoid another partially submerged rock in the bend. You can eddy out immediately to pick up paddlers and gear. Several islands and fallen trees invigorate the next 2 miles. The dam below the WV 73 bridge strangely enough no longer exists; it washed out.

SHUTTLE: Take CR 79 east from CR 73 at the golf course and turn right at a sign identifying Camp Calico. Put in at the pool above the bridge. Alternatively, all of the roads turning right from CR 79 reach Whiteday Creek or CR 73/1, which parallels the creek. From CR 73/1 you can drive upstream or downstream to find a put-in as water level permits. To reach the take-out, take CR 36 from CR 73 at Smithtown and proceed to the third bridge over these troubled waters, a half-mile short of the Opekiska Locks.

GAUGE: There are gauges on the WV 73 bridge on a right-side rock just below and on the first bridge downstream along CR 36. All are similar in the paddling range. The lower river will likely be up after a heavy winter or early spring rain. A 0.5 reading is adequate for playing on the 3 miles below WV 73.

Whiteday Creek

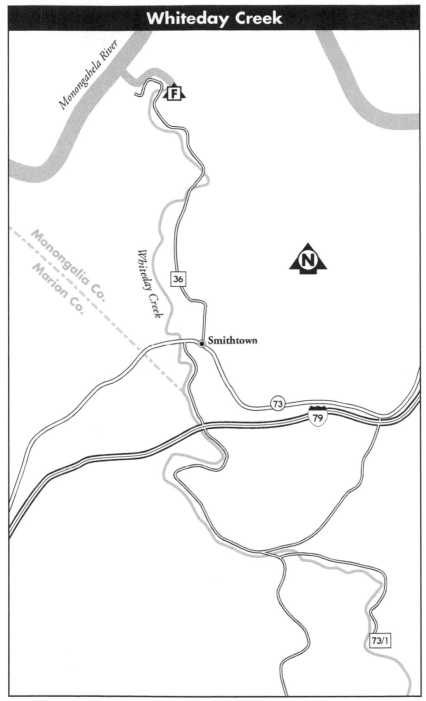

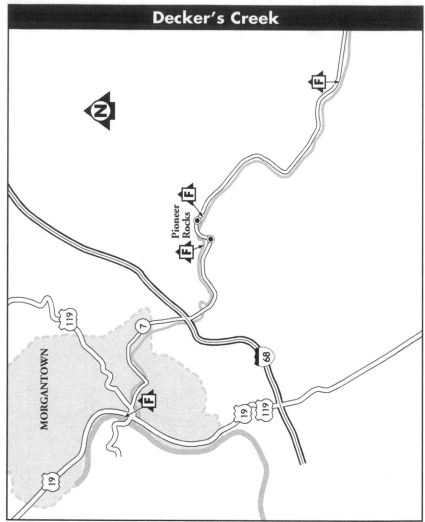

DECKER'S CREEK

This is the only whitewater stream that Monongalia County owns all by itself, and it's a humdinger. The upper section moves right along at a fast, small-stream, Class 2–3 pace through dense laurel thickets, ledges, fallen logs, and low-hanging branches. The infamous Class-6 Pioneer Rocks section is next, followed by a Class 1–3 section as it flows through Morganton.

MAPS: Masontown, Morgantown South, Morgantown North (USGS); Monongalia (County)

UPPER SECTION—PRESTON-MONONGALIA COUNTY LINE TO
WV 7 BRIDGE

CLASS	2–3 (5+)
LENGTH	5
TIME	1
GAUGE	VISUAL
LEVEL	1 + FT.
FLOW	FREE FLOWING
GRADIENT	40
VOLUME	99
SOLITUDE	B
SCENERY	A–C

DESCRIPTION: This very rocky stream follows WV 7 very closely. The scenery is pleasing until it passes through the Greer Limestone Quarry. You actually paddle through culverts here! On the other hand, the limestone quarry neutralizes the water's acidity and improves the creek's water quality! Most people take out above the infamous last mile.

DIFFICULTIES: Right above the Lions Club picnic area there's a rather impressive Class-5+ double drop. Most people running this stretch will want to carry it, but steep banks will make portaging difficult. Watch out for downed trees, trapped debris, and a possible blocked culvert at the quarry. Three low-water bridges here must be carried. At high water, mark the takeout so you don't get sucked into the infamous, 200 fpm Pioneer Rocks section.

SHUTTLE: Park near the county line on WV 7 for a reasonable put-in, or pick up the creek in Masontown. Take out somewhere above the highway sign that reads "HILL." It should really say "HELL," since this marks the start of some outrageous Class-6 water.

GAUGE: Refer to the Dellslow Bridge gauge. See Section B.

PIONEER ROCK SECTION—HIGHWAY SIGN "HILL" TO RT. 7 BRIDGE

CLASS	6
LENGTH	1
TIME	3+
GAUGE	VISUAL
LEVEL	1 + FT.
FLOW	FREE FLOWING
GRADIENT	200
VOLUME	99
SOLITUDE	C
SCENERY	B

DESCRIPTION: The Pioneer Rocks section consists of one outrageous drop after another for an unbelievable mile to the WV 7 bridge. There are an alarming number of deadly sieves, caves, and undercuts throughout the run, making this one of the most dangerous runs in the state. Although a few local experts run it fairly regularly, lots of very good boaters try it once and never go back. You could get hurt or killed if you mess up. Anyone who wants to try this stretch should examine it (and their sanity) very carefully.

DIFFICULTIES: The whole run is extremely difficult and dangerous. The first drop, called Hercules, is a 6-foot ledge into a

nasty hole backed by a rock just under the surface. Deduction is next and is a series of drops leading into an 8-foot ledge backed by a horrible sieve. Some locals have partly filled this sieve in with concrete, but it's still very dangerous. Several steep drops lead into the most difficult section on the run. Top Hat marks the start of the toughest part and is a straightforward 10-foot boof. The next drop, Hairline, is extremely dangerous with at least half of the flow going into a horrible cave on the right. It requires paddlers to ferry in front of this cave, then negotiate a few ledges. Carry on the right. Eyes is next, an ugly 10-foot drop run to the far left under an overhanging rock. This is followed by a slide between two undercut rocks called Teeth. Edge of the World marks the end of the toughest section and is probably the most difficult rapid on the run. A sketchy boulder drop approach leads to an 8-foot drop onto a rock with a horrible sieve on the right. The run calms down below here with several nice boulder drops and slides that carry you to the take-out.

SHUTTLE: Takeout at the bridge in Dellslow on Rt.7. Put-in at the top of the hill where the road and the creek start to flatten out.

GAUGE: There is a gauge painted on the takeout bridge. It reads in the number of bars showing. Five bars is a medium flow. Seven bars should be considered a minimum.

CLASS	1–3
LENGTH	6
TIME	2
GAUGE	VISUAL
LEVEL	0–2 FT.
FLOW	FREE FLOWING
GRADIENT	28 (2@50)
VOLUME	99
SOLITUDE	B
SCENERY	D

(THE TOWN SECTION) WV 7 BRIDGE AT DELLSLOW TO THE MONONGAHELA RIVER

DESCRIPTION: This once beautiful creek is now polluted with strip mine acids, crushed limestone, and other pollutants. The scenery is terrible—the river literally runs through the bowels of Morgantown—but there's good action for intermediate paddlers. On a more positive note, the railroad bed along Deckers Creek from Morgantown to Masontown and along the Monongahela has been turned into a paved bike path. The waterfront area of Morgantown is being revitalized, and there are several rather nice restaurants in the "Wharf District" near the end of this run.

DIFFICULTIES: Within 25 yards of the put-in there is a 4-foot, S-turn ledge that is Class 3 at medium water. The first 2 miles drop 104 feet with most of that occurring in the first mile. Numerous hazards line the way. At mile 1 the broken-down bridge at

Richard may be choked with debris. Later, after turning the corner below the bridge at Rock Forge, you enter a long, sterile channel built by the Department of Highways to replace the river they bulldozed aside. Below I-68 there is a dangerous falls consisting of very sharp boulders left behind by the construction. Scout for the best passage because you don't want to hit these sharp rocks. You may need to carry the low-water bridge at Marilla Park if the water is high. At mile 5 the river drops sharply over a series of ledges and heads under a high overpass. The water gets up to Class 3 and turns sharply to the right through standing waves. The left-hand "bank" is a concrete wall. Just below this there is another ledge. Run on the far left down a tight passage between the bank and a fallen tree. The final ledge is a few hundred yards below this and should be scouted to find the best passage.

SHUTTLE: Put in just above the WV 7 bridge at Dellslow. There's a pay parking lot at the mouth of Deckers Creek in the "Wharf District" just off University Avenue. Turn right at the bottom of the access road and drive all the way to the end. An alternate (free) take-out can be reached by paddling down the Monongahela under the Westover Bridge and taking out at the foot of Walnut Street on river right one block beyond the bridge. You could park your car behind the Brew Pub restaurant.

GAUGE: None. The top of the right footing of the Dellslow Bridge can be considered zero.

DUNKARD CREEK

MAPS: USGS: Blacksville, Osage; County: Monongalia

A

DUNKARD CREEK

CLASS	I
LENGTH	30
TIME	2–3 DAYS
GAUGE	NONE
LEVEL	NA
FLOW	FREE FLOWING
GRADIENT	NA
VOLUME	VS
SOLITUDE	B
SCENERY	B

DESCRIPTION: This is a long, winding stream that parallels the Mason-Dixon Line through northern Monongalia County. Its mouth is on the Monongahela north of Point Marion, Pennsylvania. Float fishing is popular, and in high water there are a few Class-1 rifles. The stream is rich in waterfowl and the bass and muskie fishing outstanding. It can be run from as far west as Blacksville and on through Mt. Morris, Pennsylvania! Although the road distance between bridges is short, the river distance may be twice as far due to its wide meanders.

partFour

THE NORTHWEST QUADRANT—
THE OHIO BASIN

Although this section of the state is hilly, the rivers here don't have enough gradient to create good whitewater. The land is sparsely populated and rural in character. Much of the scenery is farms and second-growth timber. The rivers are lined by mud banks and sand beaches with rare outcroppings of rocks. Some huge sycamores and other hardwoods can be found along the river bottoms.

Fishing is a popular pastime here, and bass, catfish, and some muskies can be caught. Some of the largest muskies in the state are caught from Little Kanawha and Middle Island Creek.

Historically this area was the birthplace of the chemical and petroleum industries in this country. Many old, abandoned, shallow oil wells dot the countryside while the associated structures and access roads have almost been reclaimed by nature. Brine wells in the Ohio River Valley spawned Semet-Solveys (FMC), Union Carbide, and other industrial concerns, which are now prominent in the Ohio-Kanawha River area.

The most famous resident of this area was pioneer hero Lewis Wetzel, who, among other things, used to run between Morgantown and Wheeling (all the way), and would think nothing of swimming over to Ohio in the winter. He's West Virginia's answer to Davy Crockett.

LITTLE KANAWHA RIVER

The Little Kanawha starts as a small trout stream in the mountains of southern Upshur County. Here, below Route 20, is where the only real whitewater in the watershed is found. The Little Kanawha headwaters are pinched between the Holly and Buckhannon Rivers, and they come "up" when the Buckhannon is "really high." Between Arlington and Wildcat it's a small creek with a steep gradient. Then it crosses a corner of Lewis County, getting big enough to be a river before entering Braxton County. Except for one ledge at Falls Mill, the journey across Braxton, Gilmer, Calhoun, Wirt, and Wood Counties is rather uneventful. The scenery is generally pastoral, and the river is

slow flowing between mud banks. This seems to be the poison-ivy capital of the world! Remnants of several turn-of-the-century locks exist, one of which, Well's Locks below Elizabeth, must be carried.

Many of the small- to medium-sized tributaries of the Little Kanawha are runable in periods of high runoff. These all have similar characteristics: mud banks, shallow riffles, long pools, and fallen trees. The five largest tributaries are the Hughes River, the West Fork of the Little Kanawha, Steer Creek, Leading Creek, and Reedy Creek. The Hughes River and several of its tributaries are described below. The West Fork starts in Calhoun County and joins with the Henry's Fork at the Wirt/Calhoun County line. Steer Creek joins the Little Kanawha near Russett in Calhoun County. Leading Creek drains a sizeable portion off Gilmer and Lewis Counties to join the Little Kanawha below Glenville. Reedy Creek and its many forks join the Little Kanawha upstream of Elizabeth.

MAPS: Rock Cave, Walkerville, Hacker Valley, Newville, Orlando, Burnsville, Gilmer, Glenville, Tanner, Grantsville, Annamoriah, Burning Springs, Girta, Elizabeth, Kanawha, South Petersburg, Parkersburg (USGS); Upshur, Lewis, Braxton, Gilmer, Calhoun, Wirt, Wood (County)

ARLINGTON TO WILDCAT

CLASS	3–5
LENGTH	10
TIME	3–4
GAUGE	USGS WEB
LEVEL	@ 1500 CFS
FLOW	FREE FLOWING
GRADIENT	75 (1 @ 150)
VOLUME	VS
SOLITUDE	A
SCENERY	A–B

DESCRIPTION: This is a small, steep run through the rugged mountains of southern Upshur County. Isolated and seldom visited, it's small and hard to catch up. At the put-in, there's a 10-foot-long shallow sloping ledge. It will be scrapy even at good boatable flows. (Consider the Tygart or Buckhannon as alternatives.) This drop is not typical of the rest of the run, and the stream becomes increasingly tight and technical, blocked with many constricting boulders. Since these rocks are not large enough to obstruct a paddler's visibility most of the way, most rapids can be found by boat scouting. But there are several that deserve a good look from the bank.

DIFFICULTIES: One memorable spot consists of a midstream chute over a 6-foot ledge with a large boulder sitting just below the drop. Towards the end of the run, you'll encounter a rapid similar to Keyhole in the Tygart Gorge: a high ledge with three nasty-looking chutes. The center slot has been run successfully for whatever that's worth. The gradient ends quickly and you should start watching for your take-out at the Little Panther Fork junction. The remaining 5 miles to Wildcat are flat.

SHUTTLE: You'll need your county road maps for this one! The run is south of WV 4, an east/west road crossing I-79 south of Buckhannon and Weston. The Little Panther Fork take-out can be reached by turning south on WV 4 near Boyd on CR 35/3. Don't get lured onto any road in poorer condition. At the first three-way intersection turn right, and right again at the next three-way intersection. This is CR 46/1. It is a rough road; 4WD is unnecessary, but high clearance helps avoid scraping. At the bottom of the hill, turn left and cross the Little Panther Fork. There's an open field less than 100 yards away, on the left. Walk across the field to a sandy beach. It's hard to spot from the river, so it should be flagged.

To get to the put-in, drive upstream on CR 46/1; this turns into CR 20/15 and ends up in Arlington on WV 20. Put in behind the small church just above the WV 20 bridge.

GAUGE: The Wildcat reading is found on the USGS website. The actual gauge is located below where the Right Fork comes in; 5.5–7 feet is a good range, but this stream is flashy and you won't know what you have until you get there. It's worth trying whenever the Buckhannon is around 12–14 feet.

CLASS	C–1 (4)
LENGTH	13
TIME	4
GAUGE	WEB
LEVEL	5.5–7 FT.
FLOW	FREE FLOWING
GRADIENT	10
VOLUME	274
SOLITUDE	A
SCENERY	A–B

WILDCAT TO FALLS MILL

DESCRIPTION: This run is good for novices in winter and early spring when the water is up. The entire trip is remote and scenic. Don't expect much in the way of rapids, especially in high water. The gradient allows no more than Class-1 riffles. There is a lot of flat water, but it moves along at a good flow. The pool below the falls has been a popular fishing and swimming hole for generations.

DIFFICULTIES: There is only one and it's a kicker—the falls that gave the hamlet at the take-out its name. Novices can easily take out above the falls, while more experienced paddlers may want to run it. There's nothing to it, actually, just paddle down over the steep drop and into a big hole.

SHUTTLE: Use WV 4 from Falls Mill east to Ireland and turn right on WV 50 to Wildcat.

GAUGE: The Wildcat reading is found on the USGS website; 5.5–7 feet is a good range.

Little Kanawha River and Right Fork of the Little Kanawha River

BURNSVILLE TO PARKERSBURG

CLASS	A–B
LENGTH	108
TIME	9 DAYS
GAUGE	VISUAL
LEVEL	NA
FLOW	FREE FLOWING
GRADIENT	NA
VOLUME	VS
SOLITUDE	A–B
SCENERY	A–C

DESCRIPTION: Now the Little Kanawha begins a long, placid journey to meet the Ohio in Parkersburg. Start from the pool of the Burnsville Dam, just below the take-out of the Falls Mill run. The trip to Grantsville is pretty bland, with minimal current, passing through rolling woods and pasture marred by a few mining operations. But the stretch from Grantsville to the WV 5 Bridge below Bigbend is a very popular fishing trip. The river leaves civilization behind for 5 miles, when it leaves the road 2 miles below Grantsville. Fishermen often reach the take-out with impressive stringers of bass on board!

The Annamoriah to Creston run is the most remote and scenic run on the Little Kanawha. Most people launch along CR 1 near Industry, about 1.2 miles east of the WV 5 bridge. From Industry to Creston is 8 miles, from WV 5 to Creston, 14. Choose the distance you like, then settle back for pleasant paddle. The shuttle is

easy; just follow WV 5 across the mountain between Annamoriah and Creston. The river forms a large bend here, so the shuttle is only 4 miles.

Sanoma, located on CR 36, 4 miles west of Creston, is the put-in for the remote, 5-mile trip to Burning Springs. *Beware:* The low-water bridge at Sanoma forms a very bad hydraulic at high water. A ferry operated here until the mid 1950s. In the summer, when the Little Kanawha dropped down to a trickle, the operator left his ferryboat in the center of the river, dropped a ramp to each bank, and charged a fee to drive across his boat! The Burning Springs take-out is along WV 5 where the river returns to the road.

The river is flat, with little current from Burning Springs to Parkersburg on the Ohio River. Eight miles below Elizabeth the Hughes River joins in but the river remains the same. The last 12 miles are in the backwaters of the Ohio River.

RIGHT FORK OF THE LITTLE KANAWHA RIVER

MAPS: Hacker Valley (USGS); Webster, Upshur, Lewis, Braxton (County)

CLEVELAND TO WILDCAT

CLASS	2–3
LENGTH	8
TIME	3
GAUGE	WEB
LEVEL	6–8.5 FT.
FLOW	FREE FLOWING
GRADIENT	60 (1 @ 80)
VOLUME	S
SCENERY	A
SOLITUDE	A

DESCRIPTION: This run has plenty of rapids and enough gradient to test an intermediate paddler. The initial mile is pretty quiet, but once the river turns away from WV 20 things start to happen. Most rapids are straightforward, formed by low ledges. Occasionally a rock garden is thrown in to offer added technical challenge. The run is isolated and attractive, with minimal signs of human activity.

DIFFICULTIES: Part of the way through the run and just beyond an attractive cabin on river right, there's a steep stair-step drop that hugs the right channel. Those not familiar with it should scout from river left or boat scout from a tiny eddy near the top. The river right rock shelf is slightly undercut, and it may collect wood.

SHUTTLE: From the WV 20 bridge in Cleveland, go north to Rock Cave, then south on WV 4 to Ireland. Turn onto the Wildcat-Ireland road (CR 50) and head towards Wildcat. Turn downstream before crossing the Wildcat bridge and go 1.3 miles

downstream to a river ford just below the confluence of the right fork and the main stem. Do not try to shuttle along the Right Fork; this requires a stream crossing that's impassible when the river is up.

GAUGE: The Wildcat Gauge on the Little Kanawha is listed on the USGS website; 6–8.5 feet is a good range. At levels over 7 feet the rapids are quite continuous; over 8 feet there are 3 miles of Class-3 whitewater.

HUGHES RIVER

The Hughes River drainage is made up of three main watersheds— its North Fork, South Fork, and Goose Creek. In general, there are highways and summer camps close by. At Cairo the scenery takes a step down, but after a mile or so it returns to peaceful surroundings. Scenery is pastoral, lightly populated, but slightly trashy, with frequent high mud banks, which prevent seeing much of anything anyway.

The North and South Forks join together in Cairo, forming the Hughes River proper, which then flows 12.5 miles to its confluence with the Little Kanawha. Goose Creek comes in from the right halfway down, adding significant flow. The South Fork has been paddled 55 miles from Smithville, and the North Fork is runable for 45 miles from the town of Toll Gate on US 50. The river has been flooded by a dam at North Bend State Park below Harrisville.

BONDS CREEK

MAPS: Ellenboro, Harrisville (USGS); Ritchie (County)

PIKE TO CORNWALLIS

DESCRIPTION: The first half of this run has good current carrying the boater over gravel bars and past boulder-studded banks, small cliffs, and interesting side ravines. Remains of the area's oil and gas boom are sometimes visible, but the river is in a thick hemlock forest, and the scenery is well above average. The second part becomes broader and slower moving. The North Bend Rail-Trail goes through two tunnels, but paddlers must cross a long pool as the creek makes a loop approaching Cornwallis. At the mouth of the tunnel there is a small playable hydraulic.

CLASS	A–1
LENGTH	8
TIME	3
GAUGE	VISUAL
LEVEL	NA
FLOW	FREE FLOWING
GRADIENT	12
VOLUME	VS
SOLITUDE	B
SCENERY	B

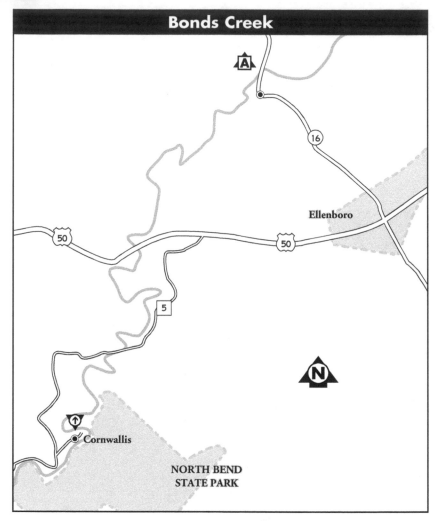

SHUTTLE: Take out at the North Bend Rail-Trail at Cornwallis. From here take CR 5 to US 50, then go east to WV 16 at Ellenboro. Continue north to Pike and put in at the bridge. There is another access at CR 8 downstream for a shorter run.

GAUGE: None. On the middle pier at the take-out bridge, there should be 8.5 concrete sections above water.

GOOSE CREEK

This is a pleasant flatwater creek with attractive scenery. Numerous rock walls and ledges are encountered, along with some very small side

Goose Creek

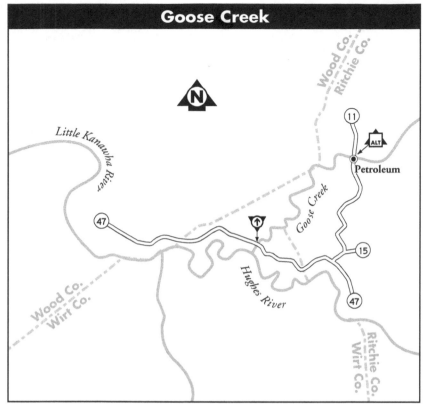

streams with attractive waterfalls. The current is fast and the waves are small. The North Bend Rail-Trail crosses the creek four times in the first couple of miles below Petroleum.

MAPS: Petroleum (USGS); Ritchie, Wirt (County)

A

PETROLEUM TO FREEPORT

SHUTTLE: The take-out is below the WV 47 bridge in Freeport where Goose Creek joins the Hughes. The shuttle from Freeport to Petroleum is 9 miles via WV 47, CR 15, and CR 11. Go east from Freeport to Cisco, where you turn left on CR 15. There is an arrow pointing toward Hughes River Public Hunting Area and a sign "To Cairo." CR 11 is the second left, 1.4 miles from WV 47. The put-in can be made at Petroleum, or turn right on CR 18 toward Nutter Farm and put in at Myers Fork, 1.6 miles upstream.

CLASS	I
LENGTH	10
TIME	3.5
GAUGE	VISUAL
LEVEL	NONE
FLOW	FREE FLOWING
GRADIENT	20
VOLUME	S
SOLITUDE	A
SCENERY	A

MILL CREEK

Mill Creek drains the red clay hills of Jackson and Roan Counties. It and its tributaries offer many miles of pleasant small-creek flatwater paddling. When I-77 was built through Ripley, it occupied part of Mill Creek's flood plain. When the creek came up, it flooded parts of I-77! Highway engineers have designed a system of 6 to 8 small flood-control dams. These structures ruined some of the tributaries for canoeing but gradually release excess water, keeping the main river up for longer periods.

MAPS: Ripley, Cottageville, Ravenswood (USGS); Jackson (County)

FROZENCAMP TO THE OHIO RIVER

CLASS	A–B
LENGTH	38
TIME	3 DAYS
GAUGE	VISUAL
LEVEL	NA
FLOW	FREE FLOWING
GRADIENT	NA
VOLUME	S
SOLITUDE	A
SCENERY	A

DESCRIPTION: Put in near Frozencamp at the confluence with Little Mill Creek. From here it's 13 miles to Cedar Lake. The first few miles follow US 33 closely, picking up Frozencamp Creek, Elk Fork, and Tug Fork. The prettiest part of the river are the 6 miles between Elk Fork and the CR 26 bridge. The Staats Mill covered bridge was relocated here when O'Brien Lake flooded most of the Tug Fork.

The 8 miles from Cedar Lakes to Ripley give paddlers a chance to paddle through small-town West Virginia. You'll be floating a block away from the Jackson County courthouse and could even take a lunch break at the Dairy Queen. But you're quite likely to see wildlife in the less developed part of the run. There's a 3-foot-high dam just below the city water plant in Ripley that can be run on the far right with caution. It creates a nice surfing wave at high levels. Look for a foot of water over the dam to run downstream; 2 feet to run the part above town.

From Ripley it's 17 miles to the Ohio River. The scenery is civilized, but attractive. The broad valley around Evans and Cottageville is actually quite pretty. Parchment Creek enters on river left just above state-owned Rollins Lake. The last 8 miles are on the backwater from the Racine lock and dam on the Ohio River. Take out at the CR 5 bridge near Angerona to miss this stretch. Below here a massive logjam blocks the entrance to the lake. It's 100 yards wide and infested with snakes when the weather is warm. Next, look for a Great Blue Heron rookery high in the sycamores lining the bank. There's public access at the state fairgrounds in Cottageville and 100 yards up

Lick Creek near Millwood. If you would like to continue the last 1.5 miles to the Ohio, just paddle a short distance to the mouth of Mill Creek (that's right, another one!) for an easy take out.

OTHER STREAMS OF THE NORTHWEST QUADRANT

WHEELING AND LITTLE WHEELING CREEKS

These streams, which flow through beautiful downtown Wheeling, aren't much to look at. They are capable of coming up quickly, causing property damage and loss of life. They definitely have whitewater (actually brown). Wheeling Creek is rafted occasionally by college students. Low-water bridges and interstate construction added formidable hazards to the run.

MAPS: Wheeling (USGS); Ohio (County)

MIDDLE ISLAND CREEK

This is northern West Virginia's most popular float-fishing stream, yielding lunker-sized muskies. It winds for miles through Doddridge, Tyler, and Pleasants Counties to its mouth at Saint Marys.

MAPS: West Union, Shirley, Middlebourne, Paden City, Bens Run, Raven Rock (USGS); Doddridge, Tyler, Pleasants (County)

SHERWOOD TO OHIO RIVE

Description: One really unique feature that makes Middle Island Creek stand out among West Virginia streams is "The Jug," a combination of natural and manufactured phenomena where the creek traverses a 4-mile loop to return 100 feet from the put-in. This is made possible by a 9-foot-high low-water bridge (possibly a record), which spans and dams a very narrow notch through an equally narrow ridge. The creek is forced around a balloon-shaped peninsula only to return to the original bed just a few boat lengths downstream. The circuitous route is densely vegetated and some tree dodging must be done. The take-out is at the put-in. (Or is

CLASS	A
LENGTH	73+
TIME	6 DAYS
GAUGE	NONE
LEVEL	NA
FLOW	FREE FLOWING
GRADIENT	NA
VOLUME	M
	(612 CFS)
SOLITUDE	B
SCENERY	B

the put-in at the take-out?) The Jug is located just east of Middle-bourne on WV 18. Look for a beer joint called The Jug on a bend in the road. The real "Jug" is directly behind it.

The "Jug" of Middle Island Creek or I Got There Before Ed Gertler Did

As co-perpetrator of *A Canoeing and Kayaking Guide to West Virginia* I am used to getting letters and phone calls from paddlers seeking specific trip information in West Virginia. Many of the requests are a bit wacky like the chap from New York City who told me he was just getting into whitewater and could I suggest a few begin-ner trips in West Virginia, preferably those that started and began at the same spot!

I had written a tongue-in-cheek article one April Fool's day about a mythical Reversing Creek that car-ried a paddler down to the Ohio. Then, when the USCOE filled the interlock pool, it would carry the paddler back upstream to the put in, but I didn't think this fellow was ready for it. Then there are the Maine paddlers who spend Sunday afternoon running short rapids to the sea, waiting for the tide to come in and then riding the waves back in the direction they had come.

But none of these was really satisfactory so I contin-ued my search and am glad to report I found just the perfect place for the person who does not want to fool with a shuttle. It is located in Tyler County near the me-tropolis of Middlebourne on Middle Island Creek. Well actually you don't really canoe the Creek either. What you do is paddle a large oxbow that leads off and re-enters the main Creek. It is 3 miles long and transcribes a large island of about 1.5 square miles complete with farm, houses, etc. But what is absolutely fantastic about the Jug is that the entry point and take-out point are lit-erally no more than two canoe lengths apart! Between the two channels is a high point that quickly broadens

out so that the outline of the Jug looks like an enormous teardrop.

I was a bit dubious about running the thing because the two channels looked very narrow and cluttered with shrubs, but as I entered I was whisked along on a nice current and the channel immediately broadened out. It resembled paddling in the Okeefenokee because so many trees were standing in the water due to several days of rain. Sycamore, green ash, and black willow trees presented the main obstacles, but the paddling was usually straightforward. The channel is deep and I never hit bottom once. Paddling in and out amongst the trees was fun, and I played tag with flocks of wood ducks all morning—and so on until I was back to where I had parked the truck for the easiest run I had ever made. I could just as easily have paddled around the Jug again. It is another unique geologic wonder in a state that has so many.

Bob Burrell

Reprinted from Canoe Cruisers Association of Washington
Cruiser, October 1976

POCATALICO RIVER

MAPS: Walton, Kettle, Romance, Sissonville, Pocatalico, Saint Albans (USGS); Roane, Kanawha, Putnam (County)

POCATALICO RIVER

CLASS	I
LENGTH	50
TIME	4 DAYS
GAUGE	NONE
LEVEL	NA
FLOW	FREE FLOWING
GRADIENT	NA
VOLUME	S
SOLITUDE	B
SCENERY	B

DESCRIPTION: The Pocatalico River, known locally as the Poca, is a small, meandering, flatwater stream that is generally characterized by long pools alternating with short riffles. In high water it can be run from the vicinity of Walton in Roane County to its junction with the Kanawha River at Poca (a 50-mile run). There is almost always a road near the river, although the section below Walton to Cicerone is admittedly a pretty low-grade road. Fishing is good for bass and muskie, although this stream does not seem a particularly popular spot.

If you wish to paddle a section of the river, consult a set of county road maps. Often the road along the river is not well marked, particularly near the headwaters where the best scenery and fishing are to be found.

part**Five**

THE BEAUTIFUL VALLEY RIVER— THE GREENBRIER

There are many special places in West Virginia, but many find the broad and lovely Greenbrier Valley to be the most enchanting of all. From its headwaters high on Shaver's Mountain to its junction with the New River above Hinton, it passes through long stretches of attractive rural scenery and offers miles of moderate whitewater. There are no major dams in the Greenbrier Watershed, and the river below Marlinton, along with its tributary, Anthony Creek, are protected by legislation. But all is not as peaceful as it looks. Local watershed groups report continued threats to the trout fishery on Knapp Creek, most recently from a quarry that threatens to release fish-killing metals and sediments into this pristine stream. However, many people who live in the area care deeply about the river, and this has made a big difference.

The late Warren Blackhurst immortalized the history of the Upper Greenbrier in novels depicting life there in the early logging days. Knapp's Creek, Deer Creek, and the Greenbrier were all used to float out logs during spring high water. If you are ever bouncing down the Greenbrier at high water in your PFD and wetsuit, enjoying the swollen river in the safety of your canoe, consider what it must have been like for the old-time rivermen. Loggers rode the river for miles on huge white pine logs, holding on to the wet bark with heavy caulked boots and cumbersome peaveys. The state has wisely captured the romance and history of this era by developing the Cass Scenic Railroad as a prime tourist attraction.

The area offers possibilities for extended bike trips along the river, too. The Greenbrier River Trail, a rail-to-trail conversion, runs downstream for 78 miles to Caldwell. Upstream, the West Fork Trail follows the bed of an old logging railway for 26 miles between Durbin and Glady. Both provide alternate shuttle routes and new ways to enjoy these rivers. For more information contact the West Virginia Rails to Trails Council at (304) 722-6558.

The Greenbrier flows through many quiet and beautiful towns such as Ronceverte (French for Greenbrier) and Alderson. All of these towns developed as important stops along the C&O Railroad, which was the only means of transportation in the area aside from the rivers. Remains of old sawmill towns like Seebert and

Watoga still exist. As the railroad construction approached the big loop of river below Talcott, builders saved time and money by drilling a tunnel through the mountain to Hilldale rather than following the river. This was the famous Big Bend Tunnel where big John Henry, of folk-music fame, met his well-known demise trying to compete against the steam drill. This same region has produced many songs familiar to the folk music and railroad fan. John Hardy, a C&O employee, who "killed him a man on the West Virginia line," sprang out of the folk idiom here. One of the most celebrated train wrecks in history and song, that of the No. 143, the FFV, took place just east of Bellepoint near the tunnel.

In addition to agriculture and cattle production, the entire region is also well known for timber production, especially in the Durbin and Bartow area. Due to the wealth of scenic attractions and the fishing in the Greenbrier, tourism and recreation is a primary industry. In addition to the native brook trout mentioned above, the forks are heavily stocked with hatchery trout. The river is also well known for bass, catfish, and walleyes below Marlinton.

The paddle or drive from Durbin to Hinton is very scenic and offers many possibilities for historical side trips. In addition to the Cass Scenic Railroad, the river also flows by Seneca and Calvin Price State Forests and Watoga State Park. The latter has a campground away from the river. The Forest Service has two excellent campgrounds on Anthony Creek (Blue Bend and Blue Meadow), and there is a private campground at the mouth of this same stream. The Forest Service also maintains an interesting campground on an island in the middle of the East Fork above Bartow. Other than that, primitive campsites must be found on private land and permission to camp there secured. The USCOE permits camping in trailers below Bluestone Dam.

Canoeing has been popular on the Greenbrier for decades. Marlinton, Lewisburg, or Hinton would make excellent bases of paddling operations. Touring the entire length of the river and taking in all of the attractions in this area would make an outstanding vacation. Most of the trip, with the few exceptions noted in the descriptions, lends itself quite well to traditional open-boat camping and is perfect for youth groups.

GREENBRIER RIVER

From its source the Greenbrier winds its way for 150 miles through some of the most beautiful and productive land in the state to meet the New River in Hinton. It begins high in the mountains at the "Birthplace of Rivers," a region that also gives rise to the Tygart, Cheat, and Potomac Rivers.

The West Fork of the Greenbrier is an extremely popular, tiny trout stream beginning very near the source of Glady Fork of the Cheat. The Greenbrier and Shavers Fork parallel each other, but the former flows southwest in the valley while the latter flows northeast on top of the mountain. The East Fork is also a very small trout stream that drains the western slopes of Spruce Knob. The two forks join in Durbin and head for scenic Cass and busy Marlinton.

Below Marlinton the valley broadens. As the river moves from Pocahontas County into Greenbrier County, it drains some of the richest, most productive farms in the state. This portion of the Monongahela National Forest is particularly well kept, the roads are good, and there is an abundance of scenic attractions. The river has one final fling of wildness below Talcott before merging with the New River at Bellepoint below the Bluestone Dam.

MAPS: Wildell, Durbin, Thornwood, Greenbank, Cass Clover Lick, Edray, Marlinton, Hillsboro, Denmar, Droop, Anthony, White Sulphur Springs, Lewisburg, Ronceverte, Fort Spring, Asbury, Alderson, Talcot, Monroe, Forest Hill, Hinton (USGS); Pocahontas, Greenbrier, Monroe, Summers (County); Monongahela National Forest Map

THE GREENBRIER FORKS AND LITTLE RIVER

CLASS	2
LENGTH	16
TIME	5.5
GAUGE	PHONE
LEVEL	5+ AT BUCKEYE
FLOW	FREE FLOWING
GRADIENT	VARIES
VOLUME	258
SOLITUDE	A–B
SCENERY	A

DESCRIPTION: The West Fork is runable from Wildell or, more reasonably, from the mouth of Little River along FS 44 to Durbin. It is a fast-paced Class 1–2 stream with a few low, angled ledges. The best rapid may be seen from the US 250 bridge. The take-out is a half mile below US 250 at a bridge west of Durbin. This stream passes through the Monongahela National Forest.

The Little River can be paddled from the first road bridge 3 miles above its mouth to the West Fork of Greenbrier. It's a beautiful run down a tiny stream, through dense forests and some glades. It's busy but easy, with only a few small-stream problems.

The East Fork is runable from the Island Campground or from Camp Pocahontas, located at the junction of WV 28 and FS 14, to Durbin. This is a busier stream than the West Fork, passing through pastoral settings along the highway. Low-hanging branches and barbed wire present the greatest hazards. You can take out at the US 250 bridge at Bartow near the motel or 2 miles downstream at an iron bridge to the east of Durbin.

SHUTTLE: Roads parallel these sections along their entire length. Just pick a section and go for it!

GAUGE: There is a paddler's gauge on the Camp Pocahontas Bridge. You will need at least 2 feet on the Marlinton gauge or 5 feet on the Buckeye government gauge. For a reading on the Buckeye gauge, call the USCOE in Huntington at (304) 529-5127.

DURBIN TO CASS

CLASS	1–2
LENGTH	17
TIME	5.5
GAUGE	VISUAL
LEVEL	4.5+
	FT AT BUCKEYE
FLOW	FREE
	FLOWING
GRADIENT	18
VOLUME	258
SOLITUDE	A–B
SCENERY	A

DESCRIPTION: This is a small trout stream that pours easily but steadily through rock gardens and eroded ledges. Stay in the middle about a half mile from the junction of the East and West Forks in order to avoid the concrete pier on the right side of a bridge. For 3 miles below this, the water is fairly calm, but soon the river narrows as the mountains squeeze in. Now the river moves fast through wilderness country. The bed remains narrow and 3-foot haystacks are common at the ends of the rapids, but there are no boulders or souse holes to complicate the passage.

SHUTTLE: Put in on the West Fork at the US 250 bridge near the edge of Durbin. There are two ways to drive to Cass. CR 1 enters US 250 about a mile above the West Fork Bridge and proceeds directly to Cass. For a shorter (8-mile) run, turn onto CR 1/24 and take out in the small hamlet of Hosterman. A longer route over somewhat better roads is US 250 to WV 28 through Green Bank, turning right on secondary WV 7 to Cass.

GAUGE: See section C.

CASS TO MARLINTON

CLASS	1–2
LENGTH	27
TIME	9
GAUGE	VISUAL
LEVEL	4.5+ FT.
	AT BUCKEYE
FLOW	FREE
	FLOWING
GRADIENT	11
VOLUME	428
SOLITUDE	B
SCENERY	B+

DESCRIPTION: The river below Cass has more volume but moves more slowly through uncomplicated rapids with no obstructions. The scenery remains beautiful, although some signs of civilization appear. Many wilderness campsites along the way make the whole trip from Durbin to Marlinton an ideal overnight camping trip in open canoes. In the spring numerous small mountain streams supply fresh water, and trout or bass fishing may be done almost anywhere.

SHUTTLE: Put in at Cass and take out at the WV 39 bridge in Marlinton.

Greenbrier River

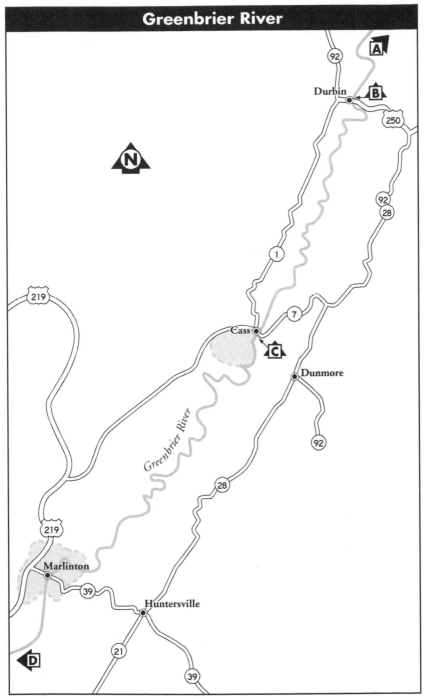

GAUGE: There is a canoeing gauge on the Marlinton Bridge, which should read at least 2 feet for these upper runs. The level of 4.5+ feet refers to the Buckeye gauge; for a reading call the USCOE in Huntington at (304) 529-5604.

CLASS	I
LENGTH	I 6
TIME	5.5
GAUGE	VISUAL
LEVEL	4–6.5 FT.
FLOW	FREE FLOWING
GRADIENT	7
VOLUME	700
SOLITUDE	B
SCENERY	B

MARLINTON TO DENMAR

DESCRIPTION: Below Marlinton the Greenbrier begins to take on the characteristics of a big river. With the flows contributed by streams such as Knapp Creek and Deer Creek, it becomes quite wide and powerful in many places. The rapids are usually formed at narrow places in the river or in its curves. There are many long, flat stretches between the rapids, and the gradient seldom exceeds 7 fpm. This section can be floated most of the year but becomes unrunable in dry summers.

With few exposed rocks, the Marlinton-to-Denmar section is an easy run at all levels. The rapids are mostly Class-1 riffles. Seebert is at the second bridge from Marlinton.

DIFFICULTIES: There is a low-water bridge just below a new high one, which can be run in the middle. For this section, as well as any of the lower Greenbrier, novices should make decisions well before approaching any rapids, as the water may be very swift. If in doubt, always stick to the inside bend of any curving rapid on this river (although this is not always a good rule to follow elsewhere).

SHUTTLE: Set up shuttle from US 219 and take "27" into Seebert (the road to Watoga State Park) or "31" into Denmar. A new riverside campground exists on the left at Watoga State Forest.

GAUGE: The river can be run down to 0.5 feet on the Marlinton gauge located on the WV 39 bridge in Marlinton, the lower right-bank bridge pier. Readings may be obtained from Brill's Exxon Station, (304) 799-8229. An ideal level is about 1.5–2 feet, although runs over 3 feet have been made. At 2 feet or greater the current is swift, and long fields of large haystacks appear. At 3 feet the flat water is moving fast and powerfully, most of the boulders have been covered, and the waves, particularly on the outside of the curves, may reach 5 to 6 feet. At this level it's no place for inexperienced whitewater paddlers. In the Marlinton area, you need about 4 feet on the government gauge at Buckeye. To be consistent, this is the reading we have listed.

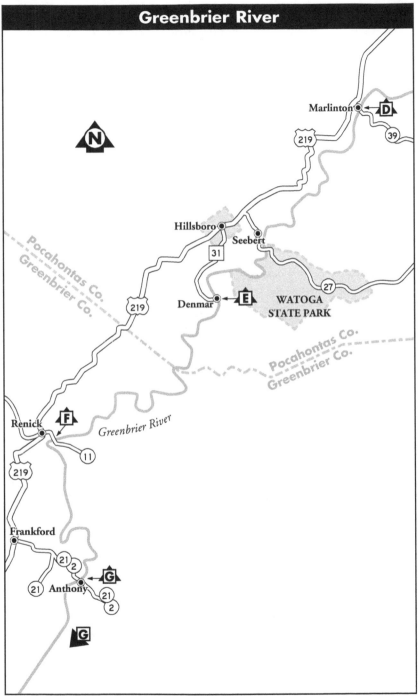

Greenbrier River

Marlinton **D**

219

39

N

Hillsboro

Seebert

31

Pocahontas Co.
Greenbrier Co.

219

Denmar **E**

WATOGA
STATE PARK

27

Pocahontas Co.
Greenbrier Co.

Renick **F**

Greenbrier River

11

219

Frankford

21
2

21

Anthony **G**

21
2

G

DENMAR TO RENICK

CLASS	I
LENGTH	17.5
TIME	6
GAUGE	PHONE
LEVEL	4–6.5
FLOW	FREE FLOWING
GRADIENT	6
VOLUME	1,090
SOLITUDE	*
SCENERY	B

DESCRIPTION: The river continues winding its way into Greenbrier County, picking up volume from numerous side streams. Summer cloudbursts can bring up the river fast! Don't try to take out at Spice Run Station, located about 4.5 miles from Denmar. Apparently boaters aren't welcome here. About a mile below Spice Run, after the river bends to the left, there are some big waves along the right bank. These can get to over 5 feet at high levels.

SHUTTLE: From US 219, get on WV 31 to reach Denmar; to reach Renick, exit from US 219 onto WV 11.

GAUGE: The Buckeye gauge should read between 4–6.5 feet. For a reading call the USCOE in Huntington at (304) 529-5604.

RENICK TO ANTHONY

CLASS	I (3)
LENGTH	10
TIME	4
GAUGE	PHONE
LEVEL	3.5+
FLOW	FREE FLOWING
GRADIENT	10
VOLUME	1,300
SOLITUDE	B
SCENERY	B

DESCRIPTION: The Greenbrier has a much larger volume here, being very broad and powerful in places. Rapids are usually formed at narrow places in the river with long, flat pools between. It can be floated most of the year, but it is fun to catch it in high water when the current is swift and large haystacks appear for long stretches.

There are no danger spots on this section, but there is one rapid 3 miles above Anthony that open-boat paddlers should scout. Before the rapid begins, the river curves slightly to the right, toward the railroad track. There is a concrete post beside the tracks with a "W" on it. The rapid parallels the track for 100 yards and piles up against car-sized boulders before it curves to the left.

The mouth of Anthony Creek is on the left near the take-out.

SHUTTLE: Put in on the right side of the river in Renick below the US 219 bridge. Take out on the right bank below the bridge at Anthony Station. This is also a good camping spot. Take "21" from Frankford to reach Anthony.

GAUGE: The Buckeye gauge should read over 3.5 feet. Call the USCOE in Huntington at (304) 529-5604 for this reading.

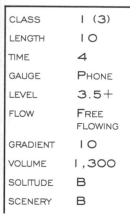

ANTHONY TO RONCEVERTE

CLASS	I
LENGTH	18
TIME	7
GAUGE	PHONE
LEVEL	3.5 FT. +
FLOW	FREE FLOWING
GRADIENT	4
VOLUME	1,420
SOLITUDE	B
SCENERY	B

DESCRIPTION: The river moves rather slowly through occasional rapids. There is a rock dam at Ronceverte that sticks its head up every summer during the dry season. High water washes over it so there may be a passage. Scout if appropriate.

SHUTTLE: Put in on the right bank below the "21" bridge at Anthony and take out on the right bank at Ronceverte City Park just before going under the bridge.

GAUGE: See section I.

RONCEVERTE TO ALDERSON

CLASS	1–2+ (4)
LENGTH	15
TIME	5
GAUGE	VISUAL
LEVEL	3.5 FT. +
FLOW	FREE FLOWING
GRADIENT	10
VOLUME	1,830
SOLITUDE	B
SCENERY	B

DESCRIPTION: The current is more powerful here, and the rapids below Fort Spring become more numerous and interesting, consisting of nice runable ledges up to 2 feet and boulder patches with waves up to 3 feet. Catching this section in high water will be exciting.

SHUTTLE: Put in at Ronceverte City Park and take out on the right bank near the bridge in Alderson. This is rather steep. For a shorter 6-mile trip that contains most of the good rapids, put in at Fort Spring near the junction of WV 63 and CR 43.

GAUGE: See section I.

ALDERSON TO TALCOTT

CLASS	A–1
LENGTH	14
TIME	5
GAUGE	PHONE
LEVEL	3 FT. +
FLOW	FREE FLOWING
GRADIENT	3
VOLUME	1,998
SOLITUDE	*
SCENERY	B

DESCRIPTION: The river is fairly flat most of the way in this section and offers few rapids. This part of the river is excellent for float-fishing. You can catch bass or just relax in a beautiful place.

SHUTTLE: Made from WV 3. Put in wherever you can at Alderson and if you find a good spot, tell us. take out at Talcott at the "17" bridge.

GAUGE: The levels shown are recommended minimums on the

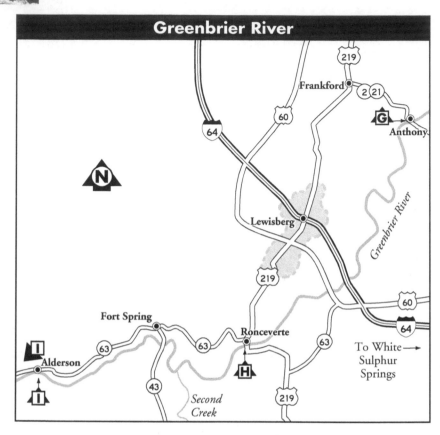

Greenbrier River

Frankford

Anthony

G

Lewisberg

Fort Spring

Ronceverte

I Alderson

H

Second Creek

To White → Sulphur Springs

Alderson gauge; call the Bluestone Dam at (304) 466-0156 for a reading. These readings correspond fairly well with readings from the Buckeye gauge.

TALCOTT TO BELLEPOINT

CLASS	2 (4)
LENGTH	16
TIME	6
GAUGE	PHONE
LEVEL	1.5+ FEET AT HILLDALE
FLOW	FREE FLOWING
GRADIENT	5
VOLUME	2,400
SOLITUDE	B
SCENERY	B+

DESCRIPTION: The river is fairly flat for 2.5 miles below Talcott before it begins to transcribe a big loop—the famed Big Bend. The sheer rock cliff on river right creates one of the most impressive river vistas in West Virginia. Novice whitewater paddlers should approach Bacon Falls with caution when the Hilldale gauge is over 4 feet! Shortly below Bacon Falls is a shallow, tilted ledge called the Lindsey Slide (Class 2+). There are several fun Class-2 rapids from here to Bellepoint separated by long pools.

DIFFICULTIES: Bacon Falls, the first rapid below Talcott, is easily recognized upstream by the sheer rock cliff on river right. It's

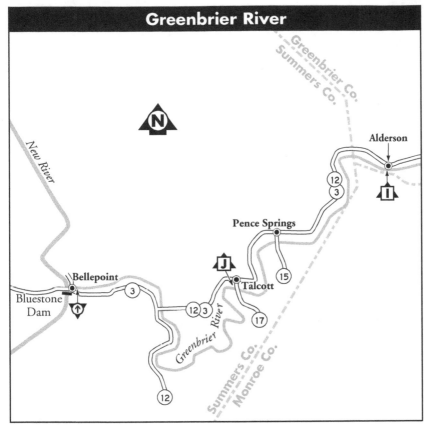

Greenbrier River

a sloping, river-wide ledge that's eroded on the far right. Approach on the left side and scout from here. At low levels the river channels on river right. There are several steep, stair-step drops next to the cliffs, followed by tight maneuvers around large boulders. When the Hilldale Gauge is between 2 and 3 feet some straightforward passages open up that are obvious when you are scouting. At levels over 4 feet the scouting points start to go underwater and large holes develop in the rapid. This rapid gets up to Class 4 in difficulty, depending on the level.

SHUTTLE: Put in at the public access at the CR 17 bridge in Talcott. Take out on river right at the WV 107 bridge in Bellepointe, just above the confluence with the New River. Or take out at Willowood Bridge on SR 3 for an 11-mile trip.

GAUGE: Refer to the Alderson gauge; the levels shown are recommended minimums. These readings correspond fairly well to the Buckeye gauge. Call the Bluestone Dam at (304) 466-0156 for a reading.

GREENBRIER RIVER TRIBUTARIES

ANTHONY CREEK

This small stream tumbles through beautiful, sparsely settled country. It's a key tributary of the Greenbrier and one of the few in the state protected by legislation. The river from Neola to Blue Bend Recreation Area is a small trout stream that descends gently over gravel bars, generally following CR 15 and CR 16. The rapids do not exceed Class-2, but many sharp turns and fallen-limb hazards exist.

From Blue Bend to its mouth on the Greenbrier, Anthony Creek passes through wilderness and drops more steeply as it cuts beside Gunpowder Ridge. The rapids for the first 3 or 4 miles are easily negotiated Class-2 drops over minor ledges.

MAPS: Alvon, Anthony (USGS); Greenbrier (County); Monongahela National Forest Map

NEOLA TO THE GREENBRIER RIVER

CLASS	1–2+
LENGTH	15
TIME	4
GAUGE	VISUAL
LEVEL	1 FT.
FLOW	FREE FLOWING
GRADIENT	10@15, 5@30
VOLUME	S
SOLITUDE	A
SCENERY	A

DESCRIPTION: After a long flat stretch, an island splits the river with the most difficult passage to the left. The next rapid consists of a ledge that runs almost parallel to the banks of the stream. Run perpendicular to the ledge to avoid broaching. Soon enter a pool and then turn sharp right (this is as near as any river can make a 90-degree bend) to the first in a series of intricate Class-2 boulder rapids—easily Class 3 in high water. After a mile of this, the gorge opens up and enters the wide Greenbrier Valley.

SHUTTLE: Put in at a bridge in Neola, or for a 5-mile trip, at a bridge immediately above Blue Bend Park. A dirt road just downstream from this latter bridge leads directly under it. Take out a quarter mile above the mouth on the right. Reach this site from a dirt road along the east bank of the Greenbrier, marked "Camp Anthony." To take out on the Greenbrier River, paddle upstream 100 yards and ferry across to river right. There's public access to the Greenbrier River Trail at the CR 21/2 bridge in Anthony.

GAUGE: There is no gauge at present, so examine the water at each put-in. More water (at least 1.5 feet under the bridge) is needed for the section beginning at Neola. If you scrape when leaving the swimming area of Blue Bend itself, do not proceed. Enough water to carry you over this little ledge without scraping is regard-

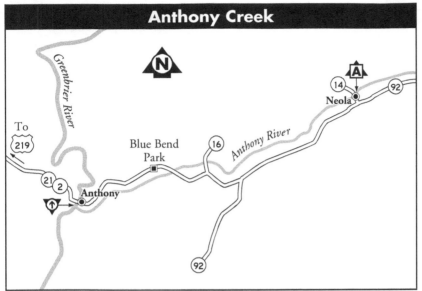

ed as zero. In general, this is an early spring runoff stream, but it has been caught at high levels at later times, even in summer following prolonged rains. During one summer run a lucky canoeist just happened to find the stream at a runable level. It dropped 6 inches in the hour it took to run from Blue Bend to the take-out.

SECOND CREEK

MAPS: Gap Mills, Ronceverte, Fort Spring (USGS); Monroe, Greenbrier (County)

A

HOLLYWOOD TO US 219

DESCRIPTION: This remote trout stream passes through a beautiful hemlock gorge. Rapids are formed by low ledges and are fairly continuous. Three medium-high ledges are encountered, the third being about 4 feet high. Run near the center. Expect to find at least one fallen tree on this stretch.

SHUTTLE: From US 219 bridge, take CR 219/1 through Second Creek and then continue 3.1 miles uphill to CR 16, where you will turn left. Proceed for 1.4 miles and then go left on CR 18 for 0.8 miles to Hollywood.

CLASS	1–3
LENGTH	8
TIME	3
GAUGE	VISUAL
LEVEL	2–2.8 FT.
FLOW	FREE FLOWING
GRADIENT	45
VOLUME	S
SOLITUDE	A
SCENERY	A

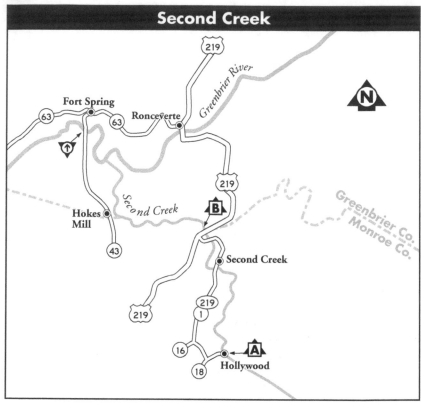

GAUGE: See section B.

US 219 TO THE GREENBRIER RIVER AT FORT SPRING

CLASS	1–2
LENGTH	9
TIME	3
GAUGE	VISUAL
LEVEL	1.8–2.8 FT
FLOW	FREE FLOWING
GRADIENT	25
VOLUME	S
SOLITUDE	B
SCENERY	B+

DESCRIPTION: Below the US 219 bridge, the scenery is pastoral with wooded hillsides and limestone cliffs. Easy, straightforward rapids offer a bouncy ride. Many caves and a covered bridge enhance this section. Below the covered bridge is a low-water bridge forming a sharp 3-foot drop. A second low-water bridge exists near the mouth at the Greenbrier.

SHUTTLE: Probably the best take-out is Fort Spring on the Greenbrier 3 miles below the mouth of Second Creek. Take US 219 to Ronceverte and WV 63 to Fort Spring. Alternatively, take CR 48 south, before crossing Greenbrier at Ronceverte, to Hokes Mill.

GAUGE: The levels indicated above refer to a USGS gauge upstream of the US 219 bridge. The gauge has been a victim of budget cuts, but the staff at the site can still be read.

DEER CREEK

MAPS: Green Bank, Cass (USGS); Pocahontas (County)

CONFLUENCE WITH NORTH FORK OF DEER CREEK TO CASS

CLASS	1–2
LENGTH	5
TIME	2
GAUGE	NONE
LEVEL	NA
FLOW	FREE FLOWING
GRADIENT	21 (1@27)
VOLUME	S
SOLITUDE	B
SCENERY	B+

DESCRIPTION: The stream winds around a pretty mountain cove for a short while, then turns northwest into a nice wooded canyon. There are plenty of riffles and the water is swift. Near the end of the canyon is a loop away from the road, which is decorated with interesting rock formations. It has almost continuous, easy, rock-studded Class 1–2 rapids. A take out may be made at Peters Mt. Trail crossing (a ford).

SHUTTLE: WV 68 out of Cass runs along the river for some distance. Put in where convenient; take out at Cass.

GAUGE: None. Inspect on site.

KNAPP CREEK

MAPS: Marlinton (USGS); Pocahontas (County)

HUNTERSVILLE TO MARLINTON

CLASS	1
LENGTH	6
TIME	2
GAUGE	NONE
LEVEL	NA
FLOW	FREE FLOWING
GRADIENT	15
VOLUME	S
SOLITUDE	B
SCENERY	B+

DESCRIPTION: This is a small, clean, shallow, locally-famous trout stream. It runs parallel to WV 39 from Huntersville to Marlinton, except for the last couple of miles where it detours through suburban Marlinton. The scenery is generally quite good considering the close proximity of the road and houses. Although the rapids never exceed Class 1, there is good current all the way.

SHUTTLE: Put in at the bridge at Huntersville or at any other wide spot in the road for the next several miles downstream. Take

out at the ball field behind the Marlinton grade school. The trip should not take more than a couple of hours even if you drift most of the time.

GAUGE: None. Inspect on site.

MUDDY CREEK

MAPS: Asbury, Dawson, Fort Spring, Alderson (USGS); Greenbrier (County)

CLASS	A–2
LENGTH	11.5
TIME	4
GAUGE	NONE
LEVEL	NA
FLOW	FREE FLOWING
GRADIENT	19
VOLUME	S
SOLITUDE	B
SCENERY	B+

ASBURY-BLUE SULPHUR SPRINGS ROAD (CR 31)
TO WV 63 BELOW ALDERSON

DESCRIPTION: Most of the river is flat and sluggish, winding through an attractive pastoral valley. When it meets WV 12 above Palestine, long, bouncy Class-2 rapids appear. A 4-foot-high breached dam at Palestine can be run on the right side of the chute. Below the dam the rapids disappear, and the last few miles are through a pretty flatwater gorge.

SHUTTLE: Take WV 12 out of Alderson and turn left onto CR 31. CR 25 crosses Muddy Creek at the mid-point and offers an opportunity for planning shorter trips.

GAUGE: None. Inspect on site.

part**Six**

WILDEST WATER FROM THE CENTRAL HEARTLAND

This section covers two distinct watersheds—the Elk and the Gauley. Most of the action is in Webster and Nicholas Counties, both very rugged and isolated. Nicholas County alone probably has more whitewater than any other county in West Virginia. The headwaters are in the Monongahela National Forest, specifically the rich Gauley Ranger District. There's a great variety of whitewater here, including some of the most difficult rivers in the state.

The Elk Basin is one of the few in the state that has been studied extensively by the State Department of Natural Resources. It has few major tributaries but many small creeks. The Back Fork of the Elk, which has its mouth in Webster Springs, has been designated by the state as a Fish-For-Fun stream. Unfortunately, this watershed is not in the Monongahela National Forest, and silt from strip-mining and logging has impacted this noble activity. Other important tributaries include the Birch and Little Birch Rivers and both forks of the Holly. The headwaters of the Elk are very close to those of the Tygart, but they flow in the opposite direction. The Elk's mouth in Charleston, on the Kanawha, was the winter camp of the famous pioneer Simon Kenton.

Webster and Nicholas Counties are rich in natural resources, but there is little significant industry here. The land is too rugged for agriculture, and the recovery of its two main resources, coal and timber, are environmentally destructive. Webster Springs was once an important tourist center featuring fine hotels, and Richwood was a booming lumber center, but the glory days of both are long gone. Today Route 19 is a major commercial corridor. There's a large shopping complex in Summersville, with the usual chain restaurants and comfortable places to stay. Tourism has blossomed here, and the Gauley River above and below the dam is its focal point. Powerboating, fishing, and diving are extremely popular uses of the lake in summer. The Summersville Police Department enforces local speed limits with a vengeance, and the stretch of Route 19 through town is ranked as the nation's number-one speed trap. Unless you want to contribute heavily to the local economy, watch your speedometer!

The Monongahela National Forest affords superb recreational opportunities near the rivers. There are many primitive camping sites along the upper Williams River and two Forest Service campgrounds along the Cranberry. There is an additional campground at Summit Lake, between the North Fork of the Cherry and the Cranberry. The Williams and the Cranberry together drain a wild area known as the Cranberry Back Country, which is now protected under the National Wilderness Act. The area contains a magnificent natural wonder, the Cranberry Glades. This high altitude swamp creates a life zone containing plants and animals normally found in northern Canada. Naturalists gather to see wild orchids and other rare plants in profusion, and many garden clubs sponsor wildflower tours here.

The USCOE hasn't ignored the region. There's a large reservoir at Sutton on the Elk, one of the oldest in the state, and a newer one at Summersville on the Gauley. Both are popular for water recreation and have developed campgrounds useful to paddlers. Summersville Dam releases water in the fall, creating the famous Gauley Season. Once limited to a handful of decked boaters, the river is now a major tourist attraction. Tens of thousands of commercial rafters and hard-boat paddlers make the run on fall weekends, bringing millions of dollars into the local economy. In the late 1970s a potent combination of recreational and business interests joined forces to protect the Gauley as a National River and guarantee these releases. It's now administered jointly by the State of West Virginia and the National Park Service.

As the river's name suggests, American Indians used the Lower Elk as a hunting ground for centuries. A significant Civil War battle was fought high over the Gauley at Carnifex Ferry, now the site of a state historical park. Confederate General John B. Floyd, realizing that he was outnumbered, withdrew his entire force across the Gauley in the dead of night. This battle, along with several others, helped West Virginia break away from the Old Dominion and become a separate state.

Nicholas County was the scene of considerable early logging, especially hardwoods. Many old logging towns have disappeared, as have the early regional railroads. West Virginia Midland, Stroud's Creek and Muddlety, and Erbacon and Summersville, to name a few, no longer exist. One of the most recent railroads to disappear was the Buffalo Creek and Gauley (BC&G) near Clay, the largest coal-fired operation east of the Mississippi. It hauled coal, timber and, oddly enough, milk as recently as the mid-1960s. Sawmills come and go, but the most impressive was a steam-operated facility in nearby Swandale. It was dismantled when the BC&G shut down.

Richwood and Webster Springs are both located near excellent whitewater, although there are few motels and restaurants in these areas. Summersville and the Route 19 strip offer many types of accommodations, along good access to the Gauley and the Meadow Rivers.

GAULEY RIVER

The Gauley has an amazing number of tributaries. It begins high in the recesses of Webster County as a wild little creek, then settles down for a long, placid cruise near the border of the national forest. Then it picks up the "fruit basket" rivers of the Monongahela National Forest, the Cherry, the Cranberry, and the Williams. These whitewater gems offer great action and wonderful scenery. By now the Gauley is a large river, and it becomes active again as it carves its way through Nicholas County. Caught in the backwaters of Summersville Reservoir, it re-awakens below the dam to create some of the most famous whitewater rapids in the country. Picking up the nasty Meadow River partway down, it doesn't rest until it meets the New at Gauley

Whitewater Photography, Fayetteville, WV

Gauley River (Pillow Rock)

Bridge to form the Kanawha. These streams offer a wide range of whitewater difficulty, including some of the most memorable rapids in West Virginia.

MAPS: Sharp Knob, Bergoo, Webster Springs, Cowen, Camden on Gauley, Craigsville, Summersville Dam, Ansted, Gauley Bridge (USGS); Webster, Nicholas, Fayette (County); Monongahela National Forest Map

CLASS	3–4
LENGTH	5
TIME	2
GAUGE	PHONE
LEVEL	13–15 FT. (CRAIGSVILLE)
FLOW	FREE FLOWING
GRADIENT	70
VOLUME	S
SOLITUDE	A
SCENERY	A–C

A

ABOVE JERRYVILLE

DESCRIPTION: These headwaters of the Gauley are pretty small and rocky, but when everything is flooded it might be worth a look. Paddlers have reported 5 miles of Class 3–4 whitewater above Jerryville, tight and steep in the upper reaches. Unfortunately, the riverside shuttle road has been gated off, so you'll have to hoof it.

SHUTTLE: None

GAUGE: Use the gauge described in section C. The gauge is 35 miles downstream, so there may be many local variables.

CLASS	1–2
LENGTH	40
TIME	14
GAUGE	PHONE
LEVEL	11–13 FEET (AT CRAIGSVILLE)
FLOW	FREE FLOWING
GRADIENT	15
VOLUME	572
SOLITUDE	B
SCENERY	A–B

B

JERRYVILLE TO CURTIN

DESCRIPTION: The first portion of this run is the smallest and steepest (257 cfs, 18 fpm). The course is obvious and easily scouted from the road. For several miles around Bolair the river is lined with ramshackle homes. It is a 12-mile trip to Bolair where the river runs back to WV 20. The highway then parallels the river for the next 6 miles, and 1 mile later the Williams doubles the river's discharge.

Below the mouth of the Williams the river is much larger. Here it leaves civilization to meander through the national forest for 9 miles. The course has low ledges, calm pools, and boulder rapids with medium-sized standing waves. The trip can be ended when the river flows out of the forest at Camden on the Gauley. Above and below Camden for about 3 miles the river is flat before the next 11-mile segment again leaves the road. There are some easy rapids to be found here, too. The Cranberry enters the Gauley 2 miles above the take-out.

Gauley River

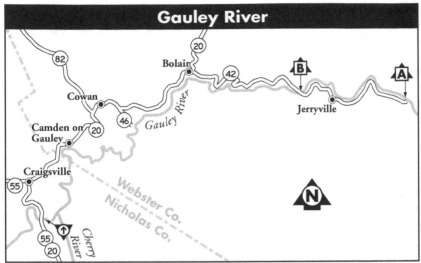

DIFFICULTIES: The only major problem on this scenic excursion is a 6-foot slanting ledge in the section between the mouth of the Williams and Camden. The lower portions of the river can get awfully big in the spring, and there is enough gradient to make swims very uncomfortable and long.

SHUTTLE: There is access to the river at Jerryville and Bolair. The next suggested put-in is at the CR 46 bridge just above the mouth of the Williams; there is also easy access in Camden. The final take-out is on the right side just beyond the WV 20 and 55 bridge at Curtin.

GAUGE: See section C, below.

C

CRUPPERNECK BEND SECTION: CURTIN
TO THE CONFLUENCE WITH BIG BEAVER CREEK

CLASS	2–3 (4)
LENGTH	8.5
TIME	2.5
GAUGE	PHONE
LEVEL	10–13 FT. (CRAIGSVILLE)
FLOW	FREE FLOWING
GRADIENT	20 (1 @ 40)
VOLUME	1,202
SOLITUDE	B
SCENERY	A

DESCRIPTION: This part of the river is known as the Top Gauley or the Crupperneck section. It's a big river, very scenic and great for kayaking. Above 11.5 feet the river is powerful and deserves additional caution. It usually has boatable flows into late spring or early summer and comes up often after thunderstorms. Below the put-in, the river transcribes a huge hook called Crupperneck Bend. There's a great view of this from WV 20.

DIFFICULTIES: The 2-mile section below Panther Creek has the most gradient and five or six Class-3 boulder drops. Some

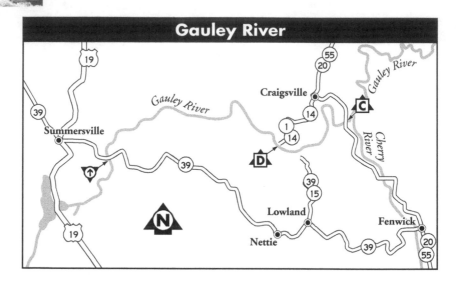

may require scouting by inexperienced parties. The last one, known as "Ships Prow," is the hardest one; it's a tough carry so scout carefully on the right. Enter at top center, follow the main current to the right, and scramble for one of three chutes that will take you to the bottom.

Note: There is 1–7 miles of flatwater to WV 39, the nearest take-out on Summersville Lake. When the lake is very low, more rapids are exposed. The flatwater, along with the silt-covered banks, will discourage most paddlers from attempting this last bit.

SHUTTLE: Put in under the Curtin Bridge (WV 20/55) near the mouth of the Cherry. To reach the take-out, drive up the Cherry River to Fenwick and turn onto WV 39/15 towards Nettie. At Lowland, turn onto CR 39/15 which dead ends on the Gauley at the Peter's Creek confluence, 4.6 miles into the trip. To run the harder rapids downstream, go west from the Curtin Bridge to the top of the hill and turn left onto CR 14, Crupperneck Road. The road runs along the top of a ridge until it deadends at CR 14/1, which soon descends steeply towards the river. At a large flat the public road ends and private roads continue downhill. These roads may or may not be gated. At 5.6 miles some concrete pylons mark a river-right take-out that requires a short, brushy scramble up a bank. At 6.6 miles there is a well-hidden trail on river right. A mile further there is a sandy beach on the right and a short distance beyond that there's another trail at the mouth of Big Beaver Creek. If the private roads are gated, the pylons require a 0.25-mile carry, the hidden trail requires a 0.5-mile carry, and the sandy beach needs a 1.5-mile carry, and Big Beaver

Creek requires a 2-mile carry (or a steep 0.5-mile carry to CR 5). From there it's 8 miles of flatwater to the WV 39 bridge.

GAUGE: The Craigsville gauge on the Gauley is located near the put-in and provides an inflow reading for Summersville Lake. Call Summersville Dam at (304) 872-5809. The best levels are between 10 to 15 feet, or 425–4,920 cfs. If you can get through the riffle under the Curtin Bridge, you've got enough water.

First Hard-Boat Run of the Gauley River— September 1, 1968

"The traditional Labor Day trip on the New River was run as always, but was disappointingly low (1,600 cfs). Our dampened enthusiasms were getting the better of us when John Sweet, decidedly enfrenzied about something, just bubbled out the horrifying news that the Gauley River would be running 1,200 cfs out of the dam on the next day. (This is a river two-thirds the size of the Yough).

"Gol-ley!!!"—Our terrifying stupor soon turned into a gleam of insanity. The parting of the paddlers thus ensued, leaving six of us to pioneer the river.

To those of you who are not familiar with the May 1961 trip report, see the August 1965 *Cruiser*. The rafters who ran the Gauley left it with a few impressions—mental ones and probably physical ones, too. They told tales of 10-man rafts sucked asunder, people swimming through caves, having curlers crash over their heads, and other trivial niceties.

We—John Sweet (C-1), Norm Holcombe (C-1), Miha Tomczech–from Yugoslavia (C-1), Jimmy Holcombe (C-1), Jack Wright (MITWWC K-1), and myself, Jim Stuart (K-1)—camped above the Summersville Dam, ate breakfast, and set up the shuttle. What ho!— John Sweet brings a story of a man in Summersville who had run the whole river in his rowboat??? Ha!!! Some kind of nut. We put in below the feedout tubes of the immense Summersville dam and embarked on our 24-

mile sojourn. We were the first whitewater boats to do so as far as we know.

The river plunged through Class-3, 4 (and possibly a 5) rapids for the next 4 miles where it passes through a West Virginia state park. Just past the park overlook we encountered Evan, Ann, and Ami Shuster (PSOC), the latter papoose style. They had hiked in to watch and take pictures.

In the next rapid the river ran about 30 yards down and smacked into an immense rock wall. The channel was quite narrow so you had no choice but to run at the wall and bounce off the pillow sideways. John made it look simple. Norm, Miha, Jack, and I made it OK, but with a little more fun. Jimmy, however, picked up just a little too much speed. He rammed the wall, broke through his knee braces, flipped, and flushed downstream. Much to his credit, he ran the rest of the river with one strap over both knees. Eric got some good pictures.

On down to the junction of the Meadow river and Carnifex ferry. Here a railroad grade joins the river. After here the bottom drops out of the river. Whooosh!!!
The nature of the river is somewhat different than any other rivers in the area. After every rapid (or set of rapids) the river turns to flatwater. Often very long stretches of flatwater. This makes the run doubly grueling.

The rapids themselves were nearly all class 4, 5, and sometimes 6. Except for a few stinkers, the rapids were exciting roller coasters. There were big waves, big drops, big holes, and some moderate turbulence.

John thrilled us at two exciting drops. The first was a double drop totaling 13 feet (Iron Ring) and the second was a single 10-foot fall. (Sweet'd Falls) He ran both successfully, but classed them as sixes. The rest of us scouted carefully, but talked ourselves into carrying. What a pity.

What's this but a couple of rowboats stashed along the side? Heh heh—gulp!

The rapids continue to within 3 miles of the end. Speaking of the end—it's a long way from the start. It's an extremely exhausting trip. As Jack Wright aptly put it "12 + 12 = 24".

About 7 hours into the trip we met some fishermen.

"How far is it to Swiss?" (the take-out), we asked.

"Oh, 'bout elebin mile."

"Oh, really—gee—thanks!!"

Luckily it was only about 4–5 miles which we ground out despite "fanny fatigue."

Dinner that night consisted of a Vienna Sausage Mulligan stew to which we all contributed (yuk).

After this we headed for the Yough—quite satisfied."

Jim Stuart

Reprinted from Canoe Cruisers Association of Washington
Cruiser, October 1968.

SUMMERSVILLE DAM TO MASON'S BRANCH

CLASS	4–5
LENGTH	9
TIME	3
GAUGE	PHONE
LEVEL	250–4,500 CFS
FLOW	DAM
GRADIENT	28
VOLUME	2,605
SOLITUDE	C
SCENERY	A

DESCRIPTION: Pull out all the stops to describe this run. It's the absolute swirling, pounding, crashing end! First rafted in 1961, it was paddled in 1968 by a group of top-ranked American slalom racers. The word spread quickly, a legend was born, and private use and commercial rafting grew quickly. While not the wilderness experience of decades ago, the rapids remain unchanged. They're big, wild, tough, dangerous, and intoxicating. The popularity of this whitewater led to the establishment of the Gauley River National Recreation Area, administered by the National Park Service.

In the Gauley canyon, the river runs with alternating rapids and pools. The rapids are impressive, and the pools give paddlers an opportunity to marvel at the grandeur of this vernal, steep-walled canyon. No river in this part of the world picked up so many named rapids as quickly. This is the best evidence of their power, complexity, and variety.

A rundown of the named rapids in the order they appear follows: Initiation (Class 4)—The drop starts below the far end of

the dam outflow parking area and ends with a big crashing wave at the base of the final drop. Two kayakers have died and several others have been trapped in a crack hidden underwater on the right, so run to the left. There's a great play hole called Hungry Mother and several other unnamed spots where hundreds of rodeo paddlers hang out. Insignificant (Class 5) is anything but! A high sandstone wall appears in the distance about 45 minutes into the trip. Below it is a long, open rapid with a bad hole in the center, often marked by inverted boats and bobbing helmets. Iron Curtain (Class 4) is named for the iron oxide stains on the high sandstone wall on the right. Six Pack Rock, in the middle of the runout, is undercut. Just downstream Pillow Rock (Class 5) drops 25 feet stretched over 50 yards of holes and then crashes into a terminal megachunk of Guyandotte sandstone. The Pillow is where the river hits the wall that extends out from the left. Volkswagen Rock, in the center of the biggest turbulence, is a pourover with an attitude. Many paddlers start their swims here. The rapid is visible from the Carnifex Ferry overlooks. Scout or carry on either side; most people use the right.

Lost Paddle (Class 5) is the first rapid below the mouth of the Meadow River and the pool at Carnifex Ferry. Nicholas County natives know it as Mile Long Shoals. It's generally divided into three drops, the first is 200 yards of rocks and holes after which the river channels to the right side and drops steeply over the second drop. Catch the eddy on the right to scout. The second drop is big water with big crashing waves; the right side is more gradual. Run the third drop on the left to avoid large holes. The last drop, Tumblehome, is an ugly place to swim. The left side, where an expert paddler died in the 1970s, is badly undercut. There is a run down the far right through several large holes; another line cuts from a left-hand eddy into a center chute. Below here the water is powerful and confused all the way to the end. A narrow final chute creates a popular ender spot. Ship Rock (Class 3+) is where a huge, undercut, flat rock, 10 feet high and 50 feet long, blocks the center of the Gauley. Running far right all the way is probably safest, although most people run left and cut right. Drifting towards Ship Rock takes the paddler into an underwater sieve capable of trapping and holding bodies. There have been two fatalities and several narrow escapes here.

Two rapids below Ship Rock the river bends to the right and the current is compressed along the right shore by a rocky point. This is Iron Ring (Class 5) named for a huge iron ring set in the rocks. The ring was sawed off and stolen by vandals in the 1980s and only the stub remains. Loggers attempted to blast a passage through this spot, creating an irregular mid-channel obstruction.

The river drops down a 6-foot-high slide into a massive hole a few feet above a giant boulder. There's a pourover behind here that's nasty all the time and potentially lethal around 1,500 cfs. The line is clean, but you'd better do it right. Carry on the left if you've got a weak stomach. One mile and six rapids below Iron Ring, the Welch sandstone, shale, and thin strata of Sewell coal rise straight up from the right side of the water. Just around the bend, the river drops over a cliff of this sandstone as a heavy, steep, 10-foot falls. Sweets Falls (Class 5) was named for John Sweet, who ran it on the initial Gauley exploratory trip in 1968. Many others have followed, and many have flipped and swum at the bottom. During Gauley Season hundreds of rafting guests will watch your antics from lunch spots developed along the shore. You can sneak the falls via a rocky left-side channel, but watch out for The Box, a very nasty channel up against the left shore just downstream.

DIFFICULTIES: See the Description! This is no place for a sometimes roller. Don't try it without first developing the skill and confidence that makes the Cheat or New River Gorges seem comfortable. Even then, it's best to make your first trip with someone who has previously experienced the Gauley.

SHUTTLE: The put-in is easy: it's at the base of the Summersville Dam just off WV 129. But except for the dam and the State Park, all downstream take-outs are on private land. Their use by private paddlers is through informal arrangements with river outfitters, which can change at any time. Large trucks and busses as well as local people traverse the roads, and the right-of-way must be kept open. Do not block the road, even for a few minutes, when changing or unloading. Crowds are normal during Gauley Season and this popularity, while frustrating at times, is the reason that the river has been protected. Please be patient!

Rafting outfitters have turned this formerly "inaccessible canyon" into one with many take-out options. At Carnifex Ferry Battlefield State Park the Fisherman's Trail, a steep, washed-out goat path, arrives on the river right above Pillow Rock Rapid. Next, a rough jeep road follows the route of the Confederate retreat from the canyon rim to Carnifex Ferry, opposite the mouth of the Meadow River just above Lost Paddle Rapid. There's a rough private road that runs along the river right bank of Sweet Falls. A few miles below here, also on the right, is a sandy beach. Two outfitters own the Mason's Branch access, and the road to it is closed during Gauley season. From here a rough trail runs along Mason's Branch, past an attractive waterfall, and winds its slippery way up Panther Mountain Road. Carrying a boat up this path is a

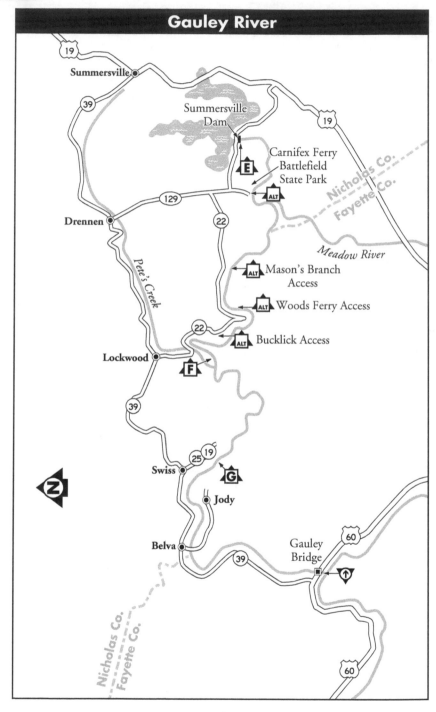

Gauley River

Summersville

Summersville
Dam

Carnifex Ferry
Battlefield
State Park

E

ALT

Nicholas Co.
Fayette Co.

Drennen

Meadow River

Pete's Creek

ALT Mason's Branch
Access

ALT Woods Ferry Access

ALT Bucklick Access

Lockwood

F

Swiss

G

Jody

Z

Belva

Gauley
Bridge

Nicholas Co.
Fayette Co.

strenuous, but popular option. During Gauley Season the West Virginia Rivers Coalition operates a boat shuttle here.

To get to the Mason's Branch trailhead, drive west on WV 129 through the town of Poe. Turn left on a dirt road just past a Methodist church with three crosses in front. This is CR 22, Panther Mountain Road. The trailhead is in a wooded area just beyond the first road coming in from the left; the outfitter access road is a mile or so beyond. American Whitewater rents a field nearby for parking during Gauley Season. At other times, park carefully to avoid blocking the road. An abandoned railroad grade runs along the river-right shore below the mouth of the Meadow. It can be used for scouting or walking out.

GAUGE: The outflow from Summersville Dam, the inflow from the Meadow River, and the total flow of the river at Belva are available from the Charleston District USCOE tape recording at (304) 529-5127 or the Summersville Dam recording at (304) 872-5809. These readings are updated daily. The Gauley above Mason's Branch has been run as low as 250 cfs and as high as 12,000 cfs. Both flows are extreme; the description is for the usual fall releases of 2,300–2,800 cfs. On the Upper Gauley, flows under 1,500 cfs offer less current and greater pinning possibilities. Levels over 3,500 cfs are pushy, with large holes and waves to challenge elite experts. Always take the Meadow River inflow into account on the Upper Gauley, since it comes in right above Lost Paddle.

THE MIDDLE GAULEY: MASON BRANCH TO BUCKLICK BRANCH

CLASS	2–4
LENGTH	5
TIME	1.5
GAUGE	PHONE
LEVEL	500–7,000 CFS
FLOW	DAM + NATURAL FLOW
GRADIENT	21
VOLUME	2,605
SOLITUDE	C
SCENERY	A

DESCRIPTION: The river is very laid back for the next 3 miles, alternating between long pools and easy Class-3 rapids with great playing. The last of these, Guide's Revenge, has a big hole on the left side of a right-hand bend. What a great place to flip a raft! Little Insignificant (Class 4) is a heavy, long rapid with a large hole in the river in left center. You move right to avoid the hole only to be confronted by Julie's Juicer, a rock shelf jutting out from the right that creates a wicked pourover. The Wood's Ferry take-out is in the pool just below here. Ender Waves (Class 3), a series of 6-foot waves, beckons below. There's several miles of easy rapids between here and Backender (Class 4). This drop starts right, and then straightens out and heads for a large hole at

the bottom. Skirt it on the far right. The Bucklick access is just downstream on a right-hand rock shelf.

DIFFICULTIES: Woods Ferry Rapid and Backender—See the description.

SHUTTLE: There are several possibilities. A few people carry down from Panther Mountain Road (CR-22) to the Mason's Branch put in; others enjoy a relaxing float after a high-stress Upper Gauley run. At Woods Ferry a steep private road descends from Saturday Road near Leander to the left side of the river. Another road, also outfitter-owned, comes in from CR-22 (Panther Mountain Road) on river right. It can be reached by continuing down CR 22 past the Mason's Branch access and going straight where the main road turns hard right. The Park Service is attempting to purchase this fantastic road, which reaches the river halfway between Summersville Dam and Swiss, for public access. For now, it's private.

Below Wood's Ferry the railroad runs through a mile-long tunnel through a ridge while the river goes around the ridge to create Koontz's Bend. Downstream, just below Backender, an outfitter access road at Bucklick makes a steep descent from CR 22. Access is permitted here, but during Gauley season boaters must walk and carry their gear a half-mile down the road. The Middle Gauley Campground, a nice alternative to the area's more developed areas, is located between Woods Ferry and Mason's Branch. The facilities are very basic, but the place is quiet and the owners are very friendly.

Panther Mountain Road (CR 22) continues on past Bucklick. Most people get to Bucklick from WV 39 by turning onto CR 22 near Lockwood. Where the blacktop ends, cross the creek and follow the dirt road uphill. Take the left fork and continue upstream along the edge of the canyon for some distance. Enjoy the great upstream views! Incidentally, the right fork takes you down a very tough dirt road to a clearing by the railroad tracks. A 1.5-mile hike along the tracks brings you to the high railroad bridge at Peter's Creek, the old mid-point access, and the downstream end of the Koontz Bend Tunnel.

Expect, in addition to hundreds of kayakers, heavy outfitter truck and bus traffic on CR 22 during Gauley Season. Drive nice and park completely off the road. Anyone blocking the road will probably be towed!

GAUGE: See section F.

THE LOWER GAULEY: BUCKLICK TO SWISS

CLASS	3-4+
LENGTH	10-11.8
TIME	3.5-4
GAUGE	PHONE
LEVEL	500-7,000 CFS
FLOW	DAM + NATURAL FLOW
GRADIENT	26
VOLUME	2,605
SOLITUDE	C
SCENERY	A

DESCRIPTION: This Gauley section is less strenuous than the upper section, but no less challenging! It has the biggest waves and holes, the best scenery, and the best play spots. There are many Class-3 rapids, but you'd better be prepared for Class 4.

The run begins with the best rapids of Koontz Bend. Koontz's Flume (Class 4) is within sight of the Bucklick access. As you head downstream an enormous rock appears on river right. This rock is undercut, and a paddler died here. You can run right-center, avoiding a large hole at the top, or sneak down the far left. Five Boat Hole, at the bottom, is a neat play spot. The sheer cliffs on the right mark the start of the next rapid—Canyon Doors (Class 3+). This is the most beautiful place on the Gauley! It features a series of chutes, waves, and a rodeo hole on bottom left. The next rapid is Junkyard (Class 3+). There's several miles of enjoyable Class 2+ rapids between here and the high railroad bridge at the mouth of Peter's Creek, and several more below it. The last easy rapid, Twisted Sister, has great surfing and a wild mystery move spot for squirt boaters.

Now the river starts to pick up. At Mash (Class 4), a long boulder rapid carries into a powerful chute containing a huge stopper. Diagonal Ledges (Class 3+), the best play spot on the river, is just downstream. Then the river rushes through a long approach into a 10-foot-wide chute (Heaven Help You) with the Pearly Gate at the bottom. Sneak far left at high flows. Next, Rocky Top, a boulder rapid with many entry chutes, runs out past Chicken Ender, a good pop-up spot. River-wide Stopper, a long rapid, is next. At 1,000 cfs the river bends left, then drops into a hole. But at fall release levels, it's a huge, bouncy wave train. Don't miss the fun by running right of the island. Rattlesnake is a long rapid with big waves at the end; run it on the right. After floating through a deep, green pool lined with enormous rocks, the river heads into Pure Screaming Hell (Class 4+), the hardest drop on the lower run. It involves a long, curving approach down the left-center, missing some large holes. Don't get pushed to the outside of the turn where there are dangerous sieves between giant rocks. Stay center and work your way left at the bottom to avoid the biggest hole on the river. From here it's a pleasant float to the take-out.

DIFFICULTIES: Koontz Flume, Mash and Pure Screaming Hell. Check the description and paddle safe!

SHUTTLE: There are a number of access areas at Swiss which is where CR 19/25 diverges from WV 39. For years this area was plagued with break-ins and traffic jams. Today several landowners permit parking for a fee on their property, relieving the congestion. The best spot is 1.8 miles upstream on the right. Go across the railroad tracks just before the road turns away from the river. There's another spot at the big outfitter access downstream. Please remember that people live here, so be respectful when changing clothes in view of their homes. Stay out of the church parking lot, and don't even think of blocking the tracks.

GAUGE: The outflow from Summersville Dam, the inflow from the Meadow River, and the total flow of the river at Belva are available from the Charleston District USCOE tape recording at (304) 529-5127 or the Summersville Dam recording at (304) 872-5809. These readings are updated daily. The Gauley above Mason's Branch has been run as low as 250 cfs and over 12,000 cfs. Both flows are extreme; the description is for the usual fall release level of 2,300–2,800 cfs. On the Upper Gauley, flows under 1,500 offer less current and enhanced pinning possibilities. Levels over 3,500 are pushy, with large holes and waves to challenge elite experts. Always take the Meadow River inflow into account on the Upper Gauley, since it comes in right above Lost Paddle. Below Mason's Branch the river is easier; flows of around 800 cfs are similar to a summer Yough or low Cheat; anything over 7,000 cfs gets big and pushy. The Belva gauge, found on the USGS web site, tells you what the lower river is flowing. You can also add the Summersville dam release and the Meadow River outflow.

CLASS	B–I
LENGTH	10
TIME	3
GAUGE	PHONE
LEVEL	1.8–4 AT BELVA
FLOW	DAM + NATURAL FLOW
GRADIENT	5
VOLUME	2,605
SOLITUDE	B
SCENERY	B

SWISS TO GAULEY BRIDGE

DESCRIPTION: After venting its spleen for 23 miles in the gorge, the Gauley travels quietly for the last 10 miles to its junction with the New at Gauley Bridge. It's a gentle river with pleasant scenery and makes a great beginner run during the fall release.

SHUTTLE: Put in and take out along WV 39 or paddle on down the Kanawha to a hotel right above Kanawha Falls.

GAUGE: The Belva gauge is found on the USGS web site; anything over 1,500 cfs should be enough. If there's enough water spilling over the low ledge a third of a mile above the mouth, you're on.

WILLIAMS RIVER

The Williams begins as a trout stream smothered with branches high in the mountains of Pocahontas County. Eventually it opens, reaching a smooth section, then picks up to Class 2–3 water as it nears Sugar Creek. Below Tea Creek Bridge the Williams is picturesque and remote. It's a little river with very big ideas. At moderate levels it's a great play river with lots of good eddies, waves, and surfing holes. The last section of the Williams is considerably tamer but no less interesting. There is good wave action where the river turns corners, cuts through islands, or encounters the occasional large boulder.

MAPS: Woodrow, Webster Springs, Webster Springs SW, Cowen (USGS); Pocahontas, Webster (County); Monongahela National Forest Map

A

THE WILLIAMS ABOVE TEA CREEK

DESCRIPTION: Where CR 17 crosses the Williams, the river leaves the road. When it reappears, it is flat. It then begins picking up to a Class 2–3 near Sugar Creek and continues for a half-mile to the Tea Creek Bridge.

SHUTTLE: FS 86 follows the Williams from the flat water down to Three Forks; many primitive camping sites are along the way.

GAUGE: See section B.

CLASS	1–3
LENGTH	3.5
TIME	2
GAUGE	VISUAL
LEVEL	NA
FLOW	FREE FLOWING
GRADIENT	NA
VOLUME	S
SOLITUDE	A
SCENERY	A

B

TEA CREEK TO THREE FORKS OF WILLIAMS BRIDGE

DESCRIPTION: The fun is continuous, with lots of rocks to avoid. The river never drops below Class 3, and parts push the limits of that class. All the pools tilt downhill. This is a popular trout-fishing area in the Monongahela National Forest, so show the fishermen proper respect.

DIFFICULTIES: After an easy Class-2 warm-up, you get right into the Class-3 action. County Line Rapid is a steep double drop between boulders best run down the center. The top hole tends to slow you and throw you off line, while the bottom hole is big enough to surf anyone who isn't paddling hard. Bannock

CLASS	3–3+
LENGTH	11
TIME	2
GAUGE	VISUAL
LEVEL	0–3 FT.
FLOW	FREE FLOWING
GRADIENT	53
VOLUME	317
SOLITUDE	A
SCENERY	A

Shoals is a steep, uneven drop—a series of tight, offset chutes through a jumble of boulders. You have to pay attention here!

Three miles above the Three Forks Bridge is Twin Branch Falls, a three-part rapid consisting of a sloping river-wide ledge off to the right, a double hydraulic that must be blasted, and a sheer 4-foot falls studded with bottom-sized boulders and bordered with a holding wave. The third part can be avoided by crossing the river and bumping down a rock pile at the far left. Depending on what has happened to them in the first 8 miles, marginal paddlers may not even want to try this one. Strong boaters will be high enough to walk on water down this rapid.

SHUTTLE: Both ends of the run can be reached from WV 20, 2 miles east of Cowen via CR 46 or from US 219 north of Marlinton via CR 17. These roads meet as FS 86 along the Williams. WV 150, the Highland Scenic Highway, affords easy access to FS 86 just above Tea Creek. There are many access points along the road.

GAUGE: See Section C.

THREE FORKS OF WILLIAMS RIVER TO GAULEY RIVER

CLASS	1–3
LENGTH	10
TIME	3
GAUGE	VISUAL
LEVEL	0–2 FT.
FLOW	FREE FLOWING
GRADIENT	20
VOLUME	317
SOLITUDE	B
SCENERY	B–C

DESCRIPTION: The river here is wider and shallower than above Three Forks. Due to the many tributaries, it picks up volume in the first 2 miles. Nearing the Gauley, the river gradually widens and flattens. The best action is in the first half of the run.

DIFFICULTIES: About 2 miles below the put-in, the river often branches around small islands. Many of these passages may be choked with debris or fallen trees.

SHUTTLE: See section B. Take outs can be arranged at many places along "46."

GAUGE: The USGS gauge is on the left from the Dyer Bridge; 3 feet is a minimum for sections A and B; 2 feet for section C. The Craigsville gauge can be used to estimate levels; it should read over 11.5 feet. Call the Summersville Dam recording at (304) 872-5809 for this reading.

CRANBERRY RIVER

The Cranberry River drains a fabulous area known as the Cranberry Wilderness, then flows through spectacularly wild country until it

Williams River, Cranberry River, Laurel Creek, N. Fork Cherry River, and S. Fork Cherry River

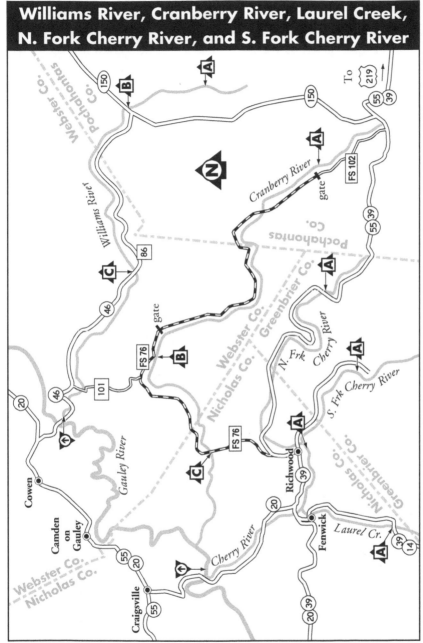

reaches the Gauley River. Hikers in this area should obtain the West Virginia Highlands Conservancy guide.

MAPS: USGS: Lobelia, Webster Springs SE, Webster Springs SW, Camden on Gauley; Webster & Pocahontas (County); Monongahela National Forest Map

CLASS	2–4
LENGTH	15
TIME	6
GAUGE	VISUAL
LEVEL	4.6 FT.
FLOW	FREE FLOWING
GRADIENT	58
VOLUME	S
SOLITUDE	B
SCENERY	A+

ABOVE THE CRANBERRY RECREATION AREA

DESCRIPTION: The South Fork of the Cranberry drains the famous Glades and is accessible from FS 102, a good gravel road but one that is, unfortunately for us, closed to motorized travel. Park near the locked gate at the end of the lower Cranberry Glades parking lot and carry about a half-mile until a small stream appears on the right. This is the South Fork. Initially the river meanders through a dense swamp. After a few miles, the stream begins to drop and does not stop until reaching the recreation area. Most rapids are rather straightforward with no tree problems, but because this is such a small stream you'd better stay alert. Below Dogway Fork you'll encounter some Class-4 boulder rapids called The Roughs by fishermen. Afterwards, the river calms down and travels to the take-out over Class 2–3 rapids.

SHUTTLE: Follow FS 76 back to Richwood and turn east on WV 39 & 55. Turn onto FS 102 and follow signs to the cranberry Glades.

GAUGE: See below. This section has been run successfully at 4.6 feet.

CLASS	3–4
LENGTH	6
TIME	2
GAUGE	VISUAL
LEVEL	3.5–5 FT.
FLOW	FREE FLOWING
GRADIENT	80
VOLUME	215
SOLITUDE	B
SCENERY	A

CRANBERRY RECREATION AREA TO THE WEBSTER COUNTY LINE

DESCRIPTION: It's very steep and very busy. That pretty well describes this section of the Cranberry. Although a forest service road follows the river, it is an unspoiled stretch with great action and impressive scenery. It's a good stream for maneuvering, and countless ledges and boulders complicate the descent. The action is fairly continuous after passing the first mile of fairly flat water. Below the county line the gradient eases, but it is still a steep slalom descent. At low levels the maneuvering is intense, but high water covers up a lot of the boulders and makes the rapids more straightforward and turbulent. With good water it's comparable to Maryland's Famous Upper Yough.

DIFFICULTIES: There is a low, nearly washed-out bridge about a mile below the campground, which may need to be carried. Another carry may be necessary at an eroded ledge, which

sits a boat-length upstream from a channel-blocking boulder. This cannot be run in low water. Below, 1 mile above the county line, is a huge, blind rapid that needs scouting. This is S-Turn Rapid (Class 4+). There is a huge boulder blocking the view on the left at a point where a steep drop begins. The left chute looks easy, but once you turn the corner there's no stopping! The water carries you into a second turn and into a narrow chute between huge boulders. It's tight and nasty, so you may want to scout this one!

SHUTTLE: Set up easily from FS 76 between the Cranberry and Big Rock Campgrounds. Campsite No. 7 is a good put-in.

GAUGE: See section C.

WEBSTER COUNTY LINE TO THE GAULEY RIVER

CLASS	2–3 (4)
LENGTH	7
TIME	2.5
GAUGE	VISUAL
LEVEL	3.5–5 FT.
FLOW	FREE FLOWING
GRADIENT	40
VOLUME	215
SOLITUDE	A
SCENERY	A

DESCRIPTION: This is a delightful stream pouring noisily through some of the state's most beautiful scenery. A put-in can be made anywhere along FS 76 from the Woodbine Recreation Area to the Cranberry Recreation Area. There are many boulder rapids of Class 2–3 difficulty here. A mile above the county line is a nifty S-Turn rapid called the Cranberry Twist. The entrance rapid to the Snake Hole immediately above the FS 76 bridge is also impressive. The descent tapers off slightly at Woodbine. The 2 miles downstream from Woodbine are delightful with straightforward Class 2–3 rapids. The river then broadens out, and there are few boulders and ledges for a short stretch. Then, almost imperceptibly, the river picks up speed and begins to narrow down. The paddler's attention is drawn away from the scenery and turned to dodging boulders and negotiating tight chutes.

DIFFICULTIES: About 3 miles below Woodbine, paddlers enter a 300-yard-long, Class-3 rapid that occupies their attention so much that they may fail to see what's coming. The main part of the river begins to turn right and then makes an S to the left and then out of sight. At the point where the main river turns to the right there is a large brushy island. The action is fast and furious, but you'd better start looking for a Class-3+ drop known as the Cranberry Split. Here the river necks down to about 10 yards wide. A boulder sitting in mid-stream was pushed to one side since the first edition of this book. While the drop is no longer Class 5, it's still a scramble to slip by on the right. The tricky rapids downstream are trivial by comparison.

Two miles below the Split, you enter the Gauley, a wide river whose volume is considerably greater. Caution is urged. There are long stretches of Class 2–3 water with hidden boulders and souse holes. Proceed downriver for 2 miles to Curtin for an easy take out under the WV 20 and 55 bridge. These 2 miles of the Gauley have a 31-fpm gradient. Due to the westerly course of both the rivers, the glare of the sun on the water is considered a hazard and sunglasses are recommended for afternoon paddling.

SHUTTLE: FS 76 leads from the outskirts of Richwood to the recreation areas. The take-out is reached via WV 20 and 55 west of Richwood where there is a bridge over the Gauley.

GAUGE: The USGS gauge is located on river-left just downstream of the FS 76 bridge crossing of the Cranberry near the Woodbine Recreation Area. The gauge is reported to the USGS website and can be read directly. Between 3.5 and 5 feet is ideal; anything over 5 feet is high and pushy. The Gauley River gauge near Craigsville can be used to estimate these levels. You want over 12 feet for section A, over 11.5 feet for section B, and over 11 feet for section C. Call the Summersville Dam recording at (304) 872-5809 for this reading.

NORTH FORK OF THE CHERRY RIVER

This is a small, technical little creek with lots of action. It's the last stream in the area to come up, but when it does, expect lots of tight maneuvers and an occasional strainer.

MAPS: Fork Mountain, Webster Springs SW, Camden on Gauley, Richwood (USGS); Greenbrier, Nicholas (County); Monongahela National Forest Map

CLASS	3–4
LENGTH	13
TIME	3.5
GAUGE	VISUAL
LEVEL	13–14 FT. (CRAIGSVILLE)
FLOW	FREE FLOWING
GRADIENT	66
VOLUME	S
SOLITUDE	B
SCENERY	B–C

THIRD WV 39 AND 55 BRIDGE TO RICHWOOD

DESCRIPTION: This little branch of the Cherry parallels WV 39 and 55 and can be surveyed for water level from the road. But the really good stuff occurs when the road bends away from the river, so watch out!

DIFFICULTIES: About a mile above the Big Bend Picnic Area is a very trashy, dangerous section where the river is trying to reestablish its channel among some islands. You'll find many dangerous downed trees in this braided channel, which changes from

year to year. Most folks will want to put in below this. At the east end of Richwood there's a dam behind the motel which can be run with care. The best Class-4 rapid on the run is just downstream. The second dam has also been run on the left.

SHUTTLE: The usual run is from the second WV 39/55 bridge, where the river crosses from the south to the north side of the road to the Richwood School Bridge. Another 8 miles can be added by going to the third bridge.

GAUGE: None, so inspect from the road. It's worth a look whenever the Craigsville gauge is over 13 feet. Call the Summersville Dam recording at (304) 872-5809 for this reading.

North Fork Cherry River—October 8, 1976

As is usually customary whenever I decide to take a non-paddling, family vacation, the weather usually turns for the worse, and we end up sitting in a campground during hurricane-type weather. This weekend was to be no different. We left for Watoga State Park on Wednesday evening. It began raining early on Thursday morning and continued nonstop for 24 hours.

Everything was up on Friday morning so I headed out by myself to the North Fork of the Cherry. I've been trying to catch this gem with adequate water for a number of years but had only been able to run the lower section from the first bridge above Richwood into town back in a blizzard during the winter of 1974–75. Today the river was out of sight—hopelessly flooded by any definition; there wasn't a single rock visible *"anywhere"* in the river, and it really looked like an exciting trip.

I debated with myself for better than an hour as to whether or not to attempt a run by myself, and, as you might guess, I won. The third section is between the second and third bridges and is the really fun section; it is 8 miles in length by road, and the gradient is between 75 and 100 feet per mile. This is the section I decided to run.

I put in beneath the third bridge, hung a brace, and flushed out. I took out hours later at the second bridge. Some of the river became quite pushy, but I was able to run the entire stretch broadside except for minor

exceptions. This broadside approach enabled me to maneuver quickly right or left if something ahead necessitated such action. Since many of the turns were quite blind, I wanted to be able to get to a bank eddy in case the river was obstructed by a tree or some other flotsam.

There was only one place where the river was completely blocked by a fallen tree, and in this instance the carry (or sneak depending on the water level) is on the left. Other than this carry, the trip was exciting but uneventful. One word of caution; at this level, eddies are scarce or nonexistent, and, if they do exist, are along the bank only.

I hitched a ride back to my car and was lucky enough to get a ride for both me and my boat within a couple of minutes. I headed back to the campground to spend another 24 hours in nonstop rain. We were so disgusted with the weather by Saturday morning, we packed up to leave but couldn't get out. The Greenbrier River was in flood and had the road blocked at Seebert at the west entrance to Watoga State Park and also at Marlinton. I called the Lewisburg State Police to see if we could get home via White Sulphur Springs and Route 60, but even that was impossible; Route 60 at Crawley was blocked. We had no choice but to stay; this was the first time I've ever been blocked from paddling by water.

Bob Taylor

Reprinted from West Virginia Whitewater Association
Splashes, November 1976.

SOUTH FORK OF THE CHERRY RIVER

The river looks like a runt-sized cross between the Williams and Cranberry. It's a small, steep, rocky stream with short pools, and continuous action. The rapids are rock strewn and passages are often intricate. The most obvious choice at the head of a rapid may get you into trouble.

MAPS: Fork Mountain, Richwood (USGS); Greenbrier, Nicholas (County)

BEECH LICK RUN TO RICHWOOD

CLASS	2–3
LENGTH	6
TIME	2
GAUGE	VISUAL
LEVEL	NA
FLOW	FREE FLOWING
GRADIENT	52
VOLUME	S
SOLITUDE	A
SCENERY	B–C

DESCRIPTION: Nearly halfway through the run is a light Class-3 rapid. The 4–5-foot drop is not too bad, provided you hit the narrow chute in the middle—too far right and you pile into a rock . . . too far left and you drop into a deep hole. But the real difficulty is a winding approach that makes it tough to get into good position for the chute. Below here are a few more tangled passages, but the gradient eases up. At high water the river becomes rather pushy, increasing to Class 3–4 difficulty. Watch out!

SHUTTLE: Put in about a half mile above Beech Lick Run where the South Fork road ends at the washed-out bridge. Take out a quarter mile below the junction of the North and South Forks of Cherry at the bridge in front of the Richwood School.

GAUGE: None, so inspect from the road. The Craigsville gauge should be at least 13 feet. Call the Summersville Dam recording at (304) 872-5809 for this reading.

CHERRY RIVER

Boiling eddies, big haystacks, and hidden hydraulics keep paddlers focused on the river instead of the dreary scenery. Due to its narrow, steep, banks, it's a small river with big water. It lacks the tight boulder rapids of the Cranberry and rises and falls quicker, too.

MAPS: Richwood, Camden on Gauley, Craigsville (USGS); Nicholas (County)

WATERGATE INN TO MOUTH ON THE GAULEY

CLASS	2–3
LENGTH	9
TIME	3
GAUGE	VISUAL
LEVEL	0–6 FT.
FLOW	FREE FLOWING
GRADIENT	30
VOLUME	406
SOLITUDE	B
SCENERY	C–D

DESCRIPTION: The action is fairly continuous with little quiet water. Always pass to the left as the river splits at least three times below Fenwick. This river changes drastically with different water levels and offers outstanding surfing at high water.

DIFFICULTIES: About 200 yards above and in sight of the Fenwick Bridge is a steep U-shaped ledge or small falls. Suitable passages exist on both sides. At high water skilled paddlers can run the center, but the route's easily missed from upstream scouting. Below Fenwick after a long quiet stretch, there's a long slide rapid (Riley's) that terminates in two large stopper-waves. There's good surfing here at higher levels. About 2 miles below Holcomb, are three major rapids. The third, Trough Drop, can be a challenge in high water. It consists of two very sharp river-wide drops in heavy water. At lower levels it presents as a series of staggered ledges. There's an easy take-out on the other side of the Gauley.

SHUTTLE: Put in by the Watergate Inn on the west side of Richwood. The Fenwick Bridge is also a popular access point. Take out under the WV 20 and 55 bridge on the Gauley.

GAUGE: A paddler's gauge is found on an old bridge abutment on river left below the new Fenwick Bridge. From 0–1 foot the river is suitable for advanced beginners; the river is well padded at over 2 feet and the water becomes heavy at over 3 feet. A Craigsville reading of 11 feet usually corresponds to a 0 reading at the Fenwick Bridge. Call the Summersville Dam recording at (304) 872-5809 for this reading.

LAUREL CREEK

MAPS: Richwood (USGS); Nicholas (County); Monongahela National Forest Map

JETSVILLE TO FENWICK

CLASS	3+
LENGTH	4
TIME	I
GAUGE	PHONE
LEVEL	I 3–24 FT. (CRAIGSVILLE)
FLOW	FREE FLOWING
GRADIENT	75
VOLUME	S
SOLITUDE	B
SCENERY	B

DESCRIPTION: This is a small mountain stream. The meat of the run occurs in three rocky sections known as Rock Pile no. 1, no. 2, and no. 3. At low water this is a plastic-boat run that requires tight maneuvering and precise boat control. At the old bridge at the confluence of Laurel Creek and Cherry River there may be log jams. Usually the left side is clear, but be careful.

SHUTTLE: From Fenwick Bridge go south off WV 39 on "39/14" paralleling the creek and railroad. Put in at the railroad bridge 4 miles upstream from Fenwick.

GAUGE: A Craigsville gauge reading of 13–24 feet is a good sign. Call the Summersville Dam recording at (304) 872-5809.

BIG BEAVER CREEK

MAPS: Craigsville (USGS); Nicholas (County)

CRAIGSVILLE TO THE GAULEY

CLASS	4 (6)
LENGTH	4.5
TIME	1.5
GAUGE	VISUAL
LEVEL	NA
FLOW	FREE FLOWING
GRADIENT	75
VOLUME	VS
SOLITUDE	A
SCENERY	A

DESCRIPTION: This small creek starts as an intermediate run for about a mile and then changes into one of the strangest creeks you will ever encounter. The many hydraulics are all diagonal and very powerful. All of the exposed rocks are shaped to form huge holes in high water. A Class-6 rapid is formed where the creek funnels down to about 8 feet and then sweeps down a steep white slide into an undercut rock that you can avoid only by pitoning. After this, a fallen tree is waiting. As long as you're out of your boat, you may as well carry the next rapid too—a hairy run around the left side of an island with an unrunable right side. Technical rapids followed by about a mile of hydraulics finish the run to the Gauley.

SHUTTLE: Find CR 5 out of Craigsville. Drive west to the stone bridge crossing Big Beaver Creek. Follow "5," Nile Road, to a 4WD road down to the Gauley.

GAUGE: None. When the water barely washes over the flat rocks at the put-in, the river is up. It's worth a look when the Craigsville gauge is over 12.5 feet. Call the Summersville Dam recording at (304) 872-5809 for this reading.

HOMINY CREEK

MAPS: Nettie, Mount Nebo (USGS); Nicholas (County)

HOMINY FALLS TO MOUNT NEBO

CLASS	2–4
LENGTH	12
TIME	5
GAUGE	VISUAL
LEVEL	NA
FLOW	FREE FLOWING
GRADIENT	54 (6@88)
VOLUME	S
SOLITUDE	B
SCENERY	A

DESCRIPTION: 6 miles white, then 6 miles flat. That about sums it up. You start off by dropping 10 feet over Hominy Falls. Don't continue if there's not enough water to run the falls easily! Below the falls is a long stretch of Class-2+ rapids before you reach the big anticlimax, the flat, bottom section and the pool of Summersville Lake. When the lake is drawn down, a fun Class-4 rapid emerges.

SHUTTLE: CR 13 runs between Mount Nebo and Hominy Falls. Take US 19 from Mount Nebo across the Gauley to the boat ramps and camp area below the bridge. This is the easiest

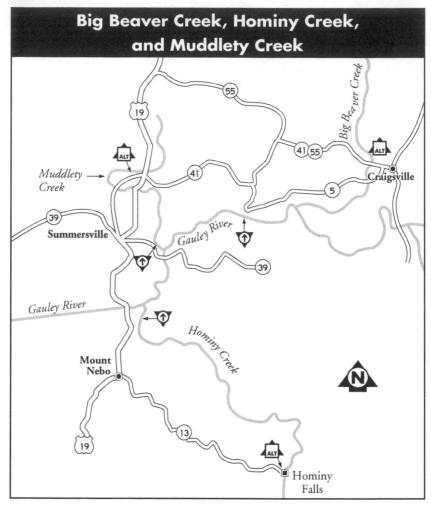

Big Beaver Creek, Hominy Creek, and Muddlety Creek

shuttle but adds the paddle across the lake. Shorten by taking the first left (going south) from the US 19 bridge across the Gauley. Then immediately turn left again down a low-grade dirt road to Hominy Creek. This whole section is less than a half mile, so you may choose to simply carry it.

GAUGE: None. Judge by observing the falls at the put-in.

MUDDLETY CREEK

MAPS: Summersville (USGS); Nicholas (County)

WV 41 TO SUMMERSVILLE LAKE

CLASS	3–4
LENGTH	4.5
TIME	4.5
GAUGE	VISUAL
LEVEL	NA
FLOW	FREE FLOWING
GRADIENT	50
VOLUME	VS
SOLITUDE	A
SCENERY	A

DESCRIPTION: This creek leaves US 19 and civilization, meandering off toward the Gauley River and Summersville Lake in a deceptively lazy manner. Rounding the first curve the gradient picks up, and the drops get very constricted. Several excellent pinning situations exist with trees and rocks so don't spend your time gazing at the scenery. This short, exciting trip comes to an end too soon when you reach the backwater of Summersville Lake.

SHUTTLE: The easiest put-in is at the original streambed before relocation alongside new US 19. The Comfort Inn on the east side of US 19 is a better starting point. A paved hiking trail runs along the river. Take out on Old WV 39 at Summersville Lake.

GAUGE: None. This run requires very high water.

MEADOW RIVER

This lengthy tributary to the Gauley contains a variety of whitewater in isolated, unspoiled sections. The upper section is a great whitewater run. The middle contains the "Miracle Mile" stretch popular with locals. The lower section is one of the toughest runs in the state.

MAPS: Rainelle, Corliss, Winona, Summersville Dam (USGS); Greenbrier, Nicholas, Fayette (County)

EAST RAINELLE TO RUSSELLVILLE

CLASS	3–4+
LENGTH	15
TIME	5
GAUGE	PHONE (MT LOOKOUT)
LEVEL	600–2,000 CFS
FLOW	FREE FLOWING
GRADIENT	32 (4@64)
VOLUME	526
SOLITUDE	A
SCENERY	A

DESCRIPTION: The first 8 miles to the railroad bridge at Burdette Creek are flat, with a fast current broken occasionally by shoals and riffles. The bridge marks the transition point between an easy, gentle river and a furious, exciting course through a canyon.

The whitewater consists of a long, continuous rapid called The Rapids. It begins with a zesty Class-3 run under the bridge and quickly turns into to a Class-4, boulder-strewn descent. It remains that way for almost 4 miles! Diagonal ledges, ledges up to 5 feet

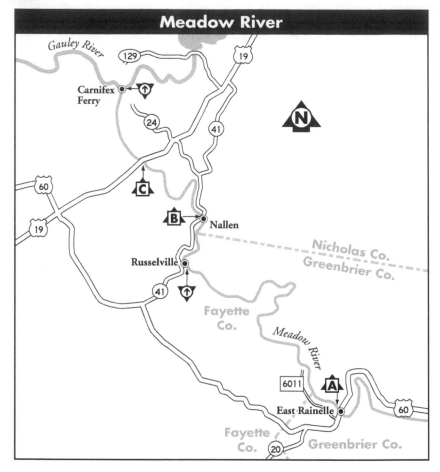

high, holes, stoppers, and tortuous channels characterize the run. There are only two small pools in the entire length of The Rapids, but plenty of eddies offer temporary sanctuary to pooped paddlers.

The banks are choked with rhododendron and mountain laurel, so most scouting is done from eddies. This requires experience, good boat control, and careful spacing between party members. The railroad on river right is available for walking out. Then, as suddenly as The Rapids begin, they end. The remaining 3 miles to the take-out are a fast run with occasional Class 2–3 rapids.

DIFFICULTIES: Two large features deserve special attention. The first is 1.5 miles from the start of The Rapids. The river appears to be completely blocked, but there are two passages on the right. About 1 mile farther, below the second pool in The Rapids, you'll want to get out to scout Natural Weir on the left. The water

plunges over a ledge into a small cauldron, followed by an S-shaped run out over several 2–3-foot ledges. All three chutes present problems, but a particular concern is a badly undercut rock on the far right.

The Middle Meadow gets pretty serious at high water! The rapids get very continuous, and big holes push the rating towards Class 5. Back in the 1980s, one strong group of big-water kayakers lost 2 boats and suffered a dislocated shoulder in the first mile at 3,000 cfs!

SHUTTLE: The put-in is reached from US 60 by driving north on Snake Island Road (CR 60/1) in East Rainelle and continuing for 3 miles. The river runs parallel to the road but it's rather flat and uninteresting. It is easy, but unpleasant, to put in at the city dump. There are other possible access points further downstream, but the roads to them open and close without warning. Ask local paddlers for advice. The take-out is on Nutterwood Road, just off of WV 41.

GAUGE: See section B.

THE MIDDLE MEADOW, NALLEN TO US 19 BRIDGE

CLASS	3–4
LENGTH	5
TIME	3
GAUGE	PHONE (MT. LOOKOUT)
LEVEL	400– 2,000 CFS
FLOW	FREE FLOWING
GRADIENT	39
VOLUME	646
SOLITUDE	B
SCENERY	A

DESCRIPTION: The Meadow is flat from above Russellville to Nallen and for a mile downstream along WV 41. The river is fittingly named here. A mile below Nallen the river begins dropping through boulder gardens between rocky, forested banks. Interesting rapids alternate with short pools all the way to the take-out. It's an ideal intermediate run, with beautiful scenery and an easy shuttle. It's also nice to hang out along the river at any level.

The roadside section from here to the water plant, known as the "Miracle Mile," is very popular with locals. The best rapids are just above and just below the water plant. As Route 41 swings away from the river the gorge gets progressively deeper. Some say the high sandstone cliffs fringed with hemlock are more beautiful than those found on the Gauley. Don't argue, just enjoy. The take-out is at the spectacular Route 19 Bridge.

DIFFICULTIES: The paddler's biggest concern is that many of the large rocks are undercut. The first big drop past the water plant is harder than the rest and is a real handful at high water. Then there's the terrible climb up Hernia Hill to US 19 at the take-out. It's bound to reveal any hidden cardiac problems.

SHUTTLE: Put in about a mile below Nallen to catch the first rapids. The take-out is on the downstream side of the US 19 bridge; carry your gear 200 feet up a steep dirt road to the road.

GAUGE: Readings are from the Mount Lookout gauge at the mouth of the Meadow; call the Summersville Dam at (304) 872-5809 for a reading. Section A and B are runable at 800 cfs, but most paddlers want 1,000–1,200 cfs. Anything over 2,000 cfs is high and makes these sections rather pushy.

CLASS	4–6
LENGTH	5
TIME	3
GAUGE	PHONE (MT LOOKOUT)
LEVEL	500–1200
FLOW	FREE FLOWING
GRADIENT	94 (2@125)
VOLUME	646
SOLITUDE	A–B
SCENERY	A

THE LOWER MEADOW, US 19 BRIDGE TO CARNIFEX FERRY

DESCRIPTION: The Lower Meadow is one of the most dangerous stretches of whitewater in West Virginia. While the gradient is not severe, the river has a drop-pool character and many of its rapids flow around and under giant undercut rocks and dangerous rock sieves. Even the easy drops may contain dangerous traps. There have been three fatalities on this section and many close calls. The last victim was a veteran guide with over 100 successful runs. But the unique challenge and spectacular beauty of the river continues to draw paddlers to the run despite the risks. Jack Wright, Tom Irwin, Frank and Bonnie Birdsong, and Donna Berglund first ran the Lower Meadow in the 1971. Although local experts make the trip in about an hour without problems, it's still a very serious undertaking for first-timers. You should be in top form and ready for anything. Portaging on an old railroad grade on river right is not difficult. The newer grade on the left is higher and ideal for walking out. Go down with someone who knows the river, and wear good shoes to facilitate your carries.

DIFFICULTIES: The first rapid, Rites of Passage (Class 5) can be seen from the US 19 bridge. A hole at the bottom of a 4-foot ledge wants to shove you under a large left-hand undercut! The second drop, Hells Gate (Class 5+), trapped a paddler in the deep drain on the left side. A short distance below are three tough, closely-spaced drops. In the first, Brink of Disaster (Class 5), a messy approach between gnarly pourovers launches you over a 10-foot ledge. The run-out crashes angrily into the left bank and rushes towards Coming Home Sweet Jesus (Class 6). After a tricky approach, the river drops 7 feet into a hole. The hole breaks right and pushes you into "the box," a huge drain under a giant boulder. It was here that a fine Southern paddler met death during a high-water run and another paddler was swept through the drain described above. Sieve City (Class 5+) is

just below here. At low flows there is a tight line above horrible sieves; at levels over 650 a "saner" right-hand channel opens up. All three rapids can be easily portaged on the right.

The river lets up for a half-mile above Gateway to Heaven (Class 5). After a tough set of slots the river narrows into a big slide that should be scouted. There are some easy rapids between here and Lets Make A Deal (Class 4+). Here the river tilts down through a long Class-3 approach into a strong hole. Below here are three doors. The middle door is the best choice, a tight but runable slot. There's a nice pool below to collect yourself in.

Soon a huge bluff marks the beginning of the Islands section. At the first island, run right down a long stretch of Class 3–4 water. At the second island, the center slot is blocked. A top expert from Washington, DC, died here, so finish down the left. Just downstream is a sliding ledge that tends to carry a paddler under a nasty undercut. There are some straightforward Class 4s between here and Double Undercut (Class 5+). Scouted and carried on the left, the rapid is a 6–7-foot, horseshoe-shaped ledge into a bad hole. The right-side undercut is very hard to avoid! Now enjoy the last stretch of Class 3–4 water down to the Gauley.

SHUTTLE: The take-out at Carnifex Ferry follows the route of General Floyd's retreat from Camp Gauley on September 10, 1861. (Coincidentally, it was on the 110th anniversary of the Civil War battle that this river was first paddled.) Your retreat will be the same: on foot, carrying all equipment. Most people prefer a climb to the end of CR 24 (Mt. Lookout Road) on the right-hand shore of the Meadow, which leaves US 19 4 miles north of the put-in. Another option is to continue down the Gauley, but watch out! If the Meadow is running, the Gauley will be booming and Lost Paddle Rapid waits just downstream. It's about 5 miles down to Mason's Branch from here.

GAUGE: Use the Mount Lookout gauge at the mouth of the Meadow; call the Summersville Dam at (304) 872-5809. Section C is now run between 450 and 1,500 cfs with some regularity. Experience says that levels around 750 cfs are ideal, but all readings are dangerous. The river has been run much higher, but the folks who can do that don't need this book!

ELK RIVER

MAPS: Mingo, Sharp Knob, Samp, Skelt, Bergoo, Skelt, Webster Springs, Diana, Erbacon, Newville, Sutton, Gassaway, Herold, Strange Creek, Wydale, Clay, Elkhurst, Newton, Clio, Blue Creek, Big Chimney, Charleston East, Charleston West

(USGS); Pocahontas, Randolph, Webster, Braxton, Clay, Kanawha (County); West Virginia State Road Map.

CLASS	2–3 (4)
LENGTH	20.5
TIME	7
GAUGE	PHONE
LEVEL	6.2–7.5 FT. (WEBSTER SPRINGS)
FLOW	FREE FLOWING
GRADIENT	40
VOLUME	S
SOLITUDE	A
SCENERY	A–B

SLATYFORK TO BERGOO

DESCRIPTION: The Elk starts easily at Slatyfork, but a few miles below changes to a subterranean course similar to Lost River. When there's enough water to fill the normally dry riverbed, Class-3 Falling Spring Run starts with boulder-type rapids, later changing to ledges. Watch for a 3.5-foot, jagged drop and trees in the riverbed. Below Falling Spring Run the river normalizes with miles of easy gravel bars broken occasionally by ledges. One especially interesting set culminates in 6-foot Whitaker Falls.

DIFFICULTIES: Whitaker Falls may be runable on the right or right center, but be careful: at low water it's rocky; at high water there's a nasty hydraulic. Scout/portage via the road on the right.

SHUTTLE: Shuttle may be made by following US 219 north from the Slatyfork put-in to "219/2," which you can follow to Bergoo if you don't mind Class-5 shuttle roads. Entering Randolph County "219/2" changes to "60," which then merges with "49" after 5.7 miles, and then changes again to "26/1" in Webster County. A much longer shuttle may be made on mostly paved road by continuing to Valley Head on US 219, taking a left on WV 15 to the outskirts of Webster Springs and then left again on "26" to Bergoo or upstream on "26/1," which follows the river.

GAUGE: See section C.

CLASS	1–3 (4)
LENGTH	11
TIME	4
GAUGE	PHONE
LEVEL	5–7 FT. (WEBSTER SPRINGS)
FLOW	FREE FLOWING
GRADIENT	31
VOLUME	639
SOLITUDE	B
SCENERY	B

BERGOO TO WEBSTER SPRINGS

DESCRIPTION: This interesting run has a lot of variety. It begins as a small, hell-bent-for-leather, steep ripsnorter with hardly any quiet water. These rapids are all straightforward over rock gardens or shallow ledges. Soon the gradient lets up, but the rapids become heavier and interspersed with some longer pools. Then it finishes up by bouncing downhill over a wild staircase to the outskirts of Webster Springs. The rapids continue all the way through town.

DIFFICULTIES: No real difficulties are reached until you start hitting the ledges below Curtin. At Parcoal one encounters what is essentially a falls, but it acts like a long slide rapids terminating in big stoppers and/or hydraulics at high water levels. At lower water paddlers cannot maneuver in the shallow slide. At right center there is a shallow notch that traps debris and boaters. The best run is on the right, and scouting is always a good idea. The area known as Cherry Falls is a most interesting series of four rather high ledges (2–4 feet) that are very close together. None of this is easily read from upstream. If the water is high enough, it won't make too much difference where you go, but some semblance of alignment between each drop is essential.

SHUTTLE: To reach the put-in, take WV 15 east out of Webster Springs. Turn right at the third road toward Bergoo. The roads are well marked. Take out at the bridge on either side of the island in Webster Springs, although the left side is a shade less difficult.

GAUGE: Call (404) 847-5532 to get the Webster Springs reading on the Elk. Consider 5 feet the minimum for this section. There's a gauge located on the upstream side of a bridge pier on the CR 15-4 at Cherry Falls. Add 4 feet to convert to the USGS gauge at Webster Springs.

WEBSTER SPRINGS TO THE CR 7 BRIDGE

CLASS	2–3
LENGTH	17
TIME	6
GAUGE	PHONE
LEVEL	4.5–7 FT. (WEBSTER SPRINGS)
FLOW	FREE FLOWING
GRADIENT	25 (7@30)
VOLUME	639
SOLITUDE	B
SCENERY	B+

DESCRIPTION: This is the best intermediate run in central West Virginia. The Elk is a big river, and the rapids are mostly straightforward runs through standing and breaking waves. The Class-3 drops occur where the river necks down in a curve or goes around an island. If the water is up, you'll travel fast! The scenery is wonderful: remote, rugged mountains with few signs of civilization. There is some litter and a reclaimed strip mine, but few other distractions. The size of the river keeps strainers to a minimum, but watch out for them near islands and on the outside of bends. A popular downriver race is run here annually in April.

DIFFICULTIES: One of the harder rapids is shortly below Webster Springs. The river bends left to leave a pool, drops sharply, and heads back to the right. There's a mid-stream boulder at low water and a good-sized hole when the river comes up.

SHUTTLE: Put in at the city park on Baker's Island in Webster Springs. To reach the take-out, leave Webster Springs via WV 20 North, then make an immediate left after crossing the Back Fork onto CR 7. The river will run high above the river for 8 miles, then returns to river level. Most paddlers take out at a sandy beach a half-mile past this point, just upstream of a footbridge.

Below here the river is mostly flatwater with occasional riffles. It's 2.7 miles to the CR 7 Bridge at Clifton Ford and 1.8 miles to the backwater of Sutton Reservoir. From here it's a long flat paddle to the nearest access, which explains why this part of the river isn't paddled much.

GAUGE: Call (404) 847-5532 to get the Webster Springs reading on the Elk. 4.5 feet should be considered minimum for this section. Between 5–6 feet, the rapids offer unobstructed descents through moderate waves. At levels over 6 feet the waves get pretty big. As the levels approach 7 feet, Class-4 conditions may be encountered.

SUTTON DAM TO KANAWHA RIVER

CLASS	A–1
LENGTH	97
TIME	NA
GAUGE	VISUAL
LEVEL	NA
FLOW	FREE FLOWING
GRADIENT	3
VOLUME	M
SOLITUDE	B–C
SCENERY	B–D

DESCRIPTION: The gradient between Sutton Dam and the Kanawha River is minimal, so the Elk is a rather peaceful and at times meandering river. There are many riffles, but they seldom exceed a Class-1 rating except during times of heavy runoff, when the river becomes wide and powerful, demanding extra caution. In general, WV 4/US 119 parallels the river almost the entire way, except for a section between Clay Junction and Procious, allowing paddlers to set up many different trips easily. Due to its proximity to Charleston, easy rapids, and good fishing, it is popular with casual canoeists. The river from Ivydale to Procious is fairly well known and scenic except at Clay. Two roadside parks (Mary Chilton and Evans) and Coonskin Park at the edge of Charleston are located near wide rapids that are great for instructional sessions. Below Clendenin the scenery begins to get junky. Major shipping and dredging operations will be seen near Charleston.

GAUGE: The Lower Elk can be run any time except when frozen or during extreme droughts. Float-fishermen enjoy excellent fishing for bass and muskie.

Back Fork Elk River and Elk River

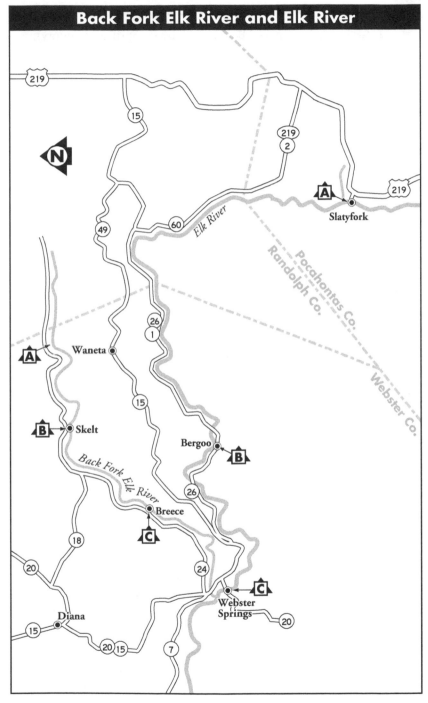

BACK FORK OF THE ELK RIVER

MAPS: Skelt, Samp, Bergoo, Webster Springs (County); Nicholas, Webster (County)

CLASS	2–4
LENGTH	ABOUT 5.5
TIME	4+
GAUGE	PHONE
LEVEL	NA
(WEBSTER SPRINGS)	
FLOW	FREE FLOWING
GRADIENT	60–75
VOLUME	S
SOLITUDE	A
SCENERY	A

BACK FORK OF THE ELK ABOVE SUGAR CREEK

DESCRIPTION: The Back Fork above Sugar Creek is a pretty good run, but getting to the put-in is very difficult. It starts with a 1-mile, 1,000-foot downhill carry from the scenic overlook on WV 15 west of Waneta! This section is nonstop whitewater all the way, with waves, small holes, and a few big runable ledges toward the end. Take out at Sugar Creek or continue farther downstream.

GAUGE: Webster Springs will need to be on the high side, but we don't have an exact reading.

CLASS	2–4
LENGTH	6.4
TIME	4
GAUGE	PHONE
LEVEL	6.2 FT.+
FEET (WEBSTER SPRINGS)	
FLOW	FREE FLOWING
GRADIENT	64
VOLUME	S
SOLITUDE	A
SCENERY	A

SUGAR CREEK TO BREECE

DESCRIPTION: The action starts right away with a series of sloping ledges leading to an 8-foot falls. Sugar Creek is tight and interesting for the half mile to its junction with the main Back Fork. The river then meanders along at a Class-2 pace until the start of the "Three Falls" section.

DIFFICULTIES: The "Three Falls" section contains 6 ledges (Class 3–4) that are 4–12 feet high. The vertical ones have deep plunge pools and provide a good introduction to running small waterfalls. The first ledge is generally run right of center, the others left of center. Scout them before you run! The best carries are on the right via an old logging road that's hidden by rhododendron. Bring a rope to lower your boat to the river 25 feet below. The last big drop, Leo's Ledge, is a sliding ledge that should be scouted.

SHUTTLE: From Webster Springs city park on Baker's Island take WV 20 north across the Back Fork. Bear right on CR 24 and drive at least as far as the giant sycamore tree, reportedly the

biggest in the state. This is the take-out. With 4WD you can continue upstream to Leo's Ledge. To reach the put-in, go back to WV 20 and travel north to CR 18 to Jumbo and Skelt. The road runs along the Right Fork of the Holly for several miles, then crosses a ridge to Sugar Creek. Put in where the road parallels the creek, or a mile upstream to the confluence of Little Sugar Creek.

GAUGE: Use the Webster Springs gauge for reference; call (304) 847-5532. The level should be over 6.2 feet. 6.6 feet means plenty of water and good play spots between the drops. If Webster Springs is reading less than 5.8, Sugar Creek is too low to paddle, but you can drive downstream on a gravel road to the Back Fork. The big ledges below will be scrapy, but passable.

BREECE TO THE WEBSTER SPRINGS BRIDGE

CLASS	2
LENGTH	5.8
TIME	1.5
GAUGE	PHONE
LEVEL	5–7 FT.
(WEBSTER SPRINGS)	
FLOW	FREE FLOWING
GRADIENT	44
VOLUME	S
SOLITUDE	A
SCENERY	A–B

DESCRIPTION: This is a lively stream and a popular trout-fishing area that still suffers occasional damage from silt coming from strip mining and logging. Treated water now discharges from a facility 1.5 miles from town. For the first 3 miles the scenery is wild and hemlocks line the banks. The action is fairly continuous with very few pools. Soon the river reaches Webster Springs. It's a short run when you're in the area running the Elk.

DIFFICULTIES: None, but a riverside home with elaborate landscaping may distract a paddler at one of the more complex rapids in this section.

SHUTTLE: From Webster Springs city park on Baker's Island, take WV 20 north across the Back Fork. Bear right on CR 24 and drive up at least as far as a partly collapsed swinging bridge. A giant sycamore tree, reportedly the biggest in the state, can be found on the other side. With 4WD you could continue upstream to Leo's Ledge.

GAUGE: The Webster Springs gauge should be about 5.8 feet. Call (304) 847-5532 for the reading.

LAUREL CREEK OF THE ELK RIVER

MAPS: Erbacon (USGS); Webster, Braxton (County)

ERBACON TO CENTRALIA

CLASS	3–4
LENGTH	9.5
TIME	3.5
GAUGE	PHONE
LEVEL	6–8 FT.
(WEBSTER SPRINGS)	
FLOW	FREE FLOWING
GRADIENT	55
VOLUME	S
SOLITUDE	A
SCENERY	A

DESCRIPTION: Laurel Creek follows CR 9 out of Cowen for about 15 miles, gathering tributaries as it goes. Six miles above Erbacon it becomes large enough to paddle and it looks like Class 2+ from the road. Erbacon is about as remote a town as you'll find in West Virginia! The stream here is flat, but then the road goes over the mountain and the creek heads toward a narrowing gap at the end of the valley.

Things start to happen suddenly at the end of the flat water and don't let up until Sutton Lake is reached. Three 8-foot ledges in a row should be scouted. The first has a shallow runable chute in the middle. The second has a shallow right-side chute and a nasty middle chute, and the third is a sloping river-wide ledge ending in a 3-foot drop that can be run almost anywhere with enough water. Several hundred yards past here you'll find one of the nastier rapids on the river, two offset holes leading into a midstream rock. One passage had a tree and the other a railroad tie blocking it. Reportedly these have flushed out, but it's worth checking out!

From here the river alternates between Class 2–3 boulder rapids and Class 4 drops. Many are too steep to scout from the boat and require inspection from shore. About halfway through there's a particularly nasty rapid called Headache. The rapid starts right, curves left, then runs right again through a clever assortment of holes and weird currents. A flip here results in a lot of head banging, so wear a good helmet. Things let up only slightly from here, and this creek keeps throwing stuff at you all the way to the end. The last 2 miles to Centralia are on the calm waters of Sutton Lake.

DIFFICULTIES: Plan to spend lots of time on shore scouting. In the lower part we saw trees in the 8–10-inch diameter range that beavers had felled into the stream. These might not wash out in a stream as small as this and could be a real hazard. All blind drops must be scouted. Expect difficult and continuous whitewater for 7.5 miles and prepare accordingly.

Elk River

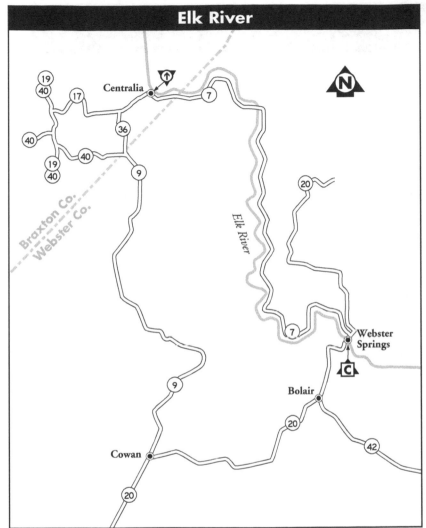

SHUTTLE: This may be the worst shuttle in the state. CR 17 leads off CR 19/40 to Centralia. The camp area on Sutton Lake is your take-out; it's a good place to spend the night so you get an early start on the shuttle. Coming back out from Centralia to CR 19/40, turn left and follow the road through Tesla and Little Birch. Then turn left again on CR 40 up Little Birch River and over the mountain to the town of Rebellion. All of these are

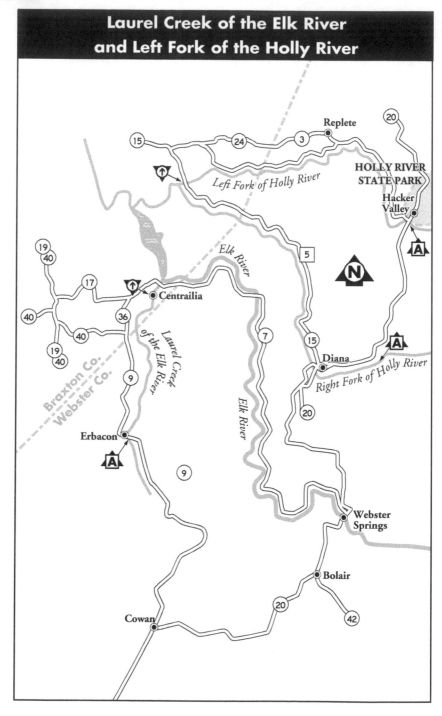

Laurel Creek of the Elk River
and Left Fork of the Holly River

winding and sometimes marginal roads. Fortunately, all are well marked. If you set your shuttle and get on the river in less than 2 hours you are doing well.

GAUGE: The Webster Springs gauge on the Elk provides a reasonable estimate; call (304) 847-5532 for a reading. It should be between 6–8 feet. There is no gauge at Erbacon, and the flatwater here makes estimating river levels difficult. Drive downstream on CR 32 from Erbacon to inspect the first riffle. This is an excellent put-in spot.

LEFT FORK OF THE HOLLY RIVER

MAPS: Hacker Valley, Newville (USGS); Webster, Braxton (County)

HACKER VALLEY TO CONFLUENCE

CLASS	2–3
LENGTH	15.2
TIME	5
GAUGE	PHONE
LEVEL	5.8–8 FT.
FLOW	FREE FLOWING
GRADIENT	45
VOLUME	S
SOLITUDE	A
SCENERY	B

DESCRIPTION: In addition to the exciting and continuous whitewater, the pastoral scenery blends well with the rural development. For the first 7 miles on this small river with continuous, tight rapids, the water is Class 2–3. After dropping over a 3-foot ledge, things pick up to Class 3 for several miles. Then you'll encounter a pool formed by a mill dam built on a natural ledge. This is runable on the far right. Nothing below here is over Class 1.

SHUTTLE: Put in under the "3" bridge near Hacker Valley. To reach the take-out, take "3" from Hacker Valley to Replete. Follow this dirt road for 10 miles through Replete to Kanawha Run. The take-out at the campground can also be reached on a better road from Diana.

GAUGE: Use the right abutment of the concrete bridge at the put-in as a marker. The water should be halfway up the 2-foot abutment for an enjoyable run. The Elk River gauge at Webster Springs should be between 5.8–8 feet; call (304) 847-5532.

RIGHT FORK OF THE HOLLY RIVER

MAPS: Hacker Valley, Newville (USGS); Webster, Braxton (County)

CLASS	1–2
LENGTH	16.9
TIME	5.5
GAUGE	PHONE
LEVEL	5.8–8 FT. AT WEBSTER SPRINGS
FLOW	FREE FLOWING
GRADIENT	35–50
VOLUME	S
SOLITUDE	A
SCENERY	B–C

MUD LICK ROAD TO CONFLUENCE

DESCRIPTION: Above WV 20 the Right Fork is small and tight, with many Class 2–3 ledges and tight spots. The scenery is below average, with many run-down homes. Below WV 20 the river parallels CR 5 most of the way. The rapids are Class 1 and 2, and the river gets pretty flat as it approaches its junction with the Left Fork. The lower river is more attractive, featuring fewer homes and banks lined with rhododendron and hemlock.

SHUTTLE: If you see something you like along CR 5, do it!

GAUGE: None. The Elk River gauge at Webster Springs should be between 5.8–8 feet; call (304) 847-5532.

BIRCH RIVER

MAPS: Tioga, Little Birch, Herold (USGS); Webster, Nicholas, Braxton (County)

BOGGS TO BIRCH RIVER

CLASS	2 (4)
LENGTH	8
TIME	3
GAUGE	PHONE
LEVEL	6.1+ FT. (WEBSTER SPRINGS)
FLOW	FREE FLOWING
GRADIENT	56
VOLUME	VS
SOLITUDE	A
SCENERY	B+

DESCRIPTION: Birch River above Boggs is small with most of the gradient near Boggs, where it achieves the Class-4 rating. A mile below Birch Falls, it tapers off to Class 2. A short whitewater section above the falls could be run with high water, but then you'd probably have to carry 20-foot-high Birch Falls. For the next mile the river runs rapidly downhill over 4–5-foot ledges in twisting current. Undercut rocks and logs are a constant problem. After the first farmhouse, paddling much easier.

DIFFICULTIES: Birch Falls has been run but it isn't the best. Sharp rocks cover the shallow bottom except for a small break on the left side. The steep section has several drops running out under rocks or into logjams, so watch out! Low-water bridges and fallen trees can be a problem in this lower section.

SHUTTLE: Follow CR 1 upstream from the town of Birch River. The road is near the river so you can put in and take out anywhere.

GAUGE: The level shown above refers to the Webster Springs gauge on the Elk; call (304) 847-5532. The 6.1 level is absolute zero. There's a gauge on the Route 19 bridge in Birch River; 0.5 feet is a minimum and 3 feet is high.

CORA BROWN BRIDGE TO HEROLD

CLASS	1–3
LENGTH	6
TIME	2
GAUGE	PHONE
LEVEL	5+ FT. AT WEBSTER SPRINGS
FLOW	FREE FLOWING
GRADIENT	26
VOLUME	S
SOLITUDE	A
SCENERY	A-

DESCRIPTION: This is a gentle stream travelling over cobble bottom for the first 6 miles with Class-2 rapids. Just above Herold rock cliffs close in on the river and the rapids change to ledges. The rapids reach Class 3 and continue for 3 miles into the next section. Your trip could be extended to include these. The scenery is good, although many eddies are decorated with trash. This river was designated the first wilderness river area in the state.

SHUTTLE: To reach Cora Brown Bridge from Birch River, take CR 1 downstream from US 19 to the second bridge crossing to the put-in on Birch River. You have two shuttle choices to get to Herold. You can continue on CR 1 up the hill to CR 2 and take the first sharp right turn. This will take you to CR 40, where a right turn will take you to the bridge in Herold. Or you can return to US 19 and head north, turning left on CR 40. Be careful where you park. Some of the cheery-looking summer homes fail to reflect the true dispositions of their owners. If you want to include the rapids below the Herold bridge, drive downstream from the CR 40 bridge until the road starts climbing away from the river. Park near an overhanging rock and look for a short path down to the river. You can also get to the river opposite Diatter Run, 3 miles farther downstream, on river left. Get out your county road maps and ask a local resident to tell you which roads are passable.

GAUGE: See section C.

HEROLD TO THE ELK RIVER

CLASS	1−3
LENGTH	9.5
TIME	4
GAUGE	PHONE
LEVEL	5+ FT. AT WEBSTER SPRINGS
FLOW	FREE FLOWING
GRADIENT	11
VOLUME	S
SOLITUDE	A
SCENERY	A

DESCRIPTION: This run starts out with Class-3 water at Herold and then changes to flat water within 3 miles. There is nothing harder than Class-1 water in the last 6 miles of the river. The last of the Class 2–3 rapids on the river, which are at the beginning of this section, can be combined with the section B trip to take in all of the whitewater.

SHUTTLE: Take out near the Glendon Post Office, located on WV 4, 3.1 miles south of I-79. This is on the Elk River just below the mouth of the Birch. Herold is reached by driving north on WV 4 to Frametown, then right across Elk River on CR 21, back under I-79, and on to Herold.

LITTLE BIRCH RIVER

MAPS: Little Birch, Herold (USGS); Braxton (County)

A

US 19 TO BIRCH RIVER

CLASS	1–2
LENGTH	3.5
TIME	1
GAUGE	VISUAL
LEVEL	NA
FLOW	FREE FLOWING
GRADIENT	40
VOLUME	S
SOLITUDE	A
SCENERY	A

DESCRIPTION: The Little Birch River has been run for 3.5 miles from US 19 to its junction with the Birch, taking out on the Birch River in Herold. The run is an easy float over cobble rapids runable only in periods of very high water. The scenery is good.

SHUTTLE: From the put-in, go north on US 19 and west on Herold Road, CR 28.

GAUGE: None. Inspect on site.

part**Seven**

BIG WATER FROM THE SOUTH— THE NEW AND THE BLUESTONE

The mighty New River begins high in the Blue Ridge Mountains of North Carolina, crosses Virginia, and enters West Virginia near its southernmost tip. From there it heads north through the Alleghenies to meet the Gauley where it forms the Kanawha. The New is one of the world's oldest rivers. Prior to the most recent Ice Age this river's ancestor, known as the Teays, flowed even farther north to the vicinity of the present Great Lakes. Actually, the Ohio, which didn't exist then, should be called the New, and the New should be called the Old. Some of the oldest rocks in the East are exposed where the New crosses the Virginia State line.

The New passes through rugged country about which even the native people knew little. In 1755 a native war party raided the small village of Draper's Meadows, near today's Blacksburg, Virginia. They killed the men and took women and children captive, leading the hostages across the mountains, bypassing the gorge, into the Ohio River country. Months later two of the women, Mary Draper Ingles and an unnamed companion, escaped from their captors. Starting near present-day Cincinnati, they walked upstream for 40 days with only the clothes on their back. They moved along the Ohio, then up the Kanawha, and finally followed the New to home. They were almost certainly the first Europeans to travel through the New River Gorge! Their story, told in the James Alexander Thom epic *Follow the River,* is fascinating reading for modern river travelers. The New eventually became a major route of exploration and travel, and today a major railroad line follows it closely.

The area has many developed sites for outdoor recreation. The USCOE has a huge flood control dam on the New above Hinton. Bluestone Lake is a popular broad-water recreation area and has private and public campgrounds around it. The backwaters extend up the Bluestone River into a state park bearing the same name. Although the Bluestone itself is a small river tumbling through largely inaccessible country, Pipestem State Park, situated high above it, offers resort activities. Both parks have camping facilities, the former being right on the river. Two other state parks, Babcock and Hawks Nest, are perched hundreds of feet above the

river on the canyon rim further downstream. Babcock has nice camping facilities, while Hawks Nest has a first-class hotel. In addition, most of the 18 river outfitters in the area offer camping.

The New below the Bluestone Dam is one of the most productive warm-water fishing areas in the United States. The river is extremely wide and flows over shallow shoals, creating ideal wading conditions for fishermen. Bass, redeye, bluegill, catfish, and suckers can be caught; farther down, large muskies may be taken. The river is fished hard, but even an inexperienced angler can catch big fish. At Sandstone Falls, another popular fishing spot, the National Park Service has constructed an overlook. Below here, getting down to the water is not easy. Float fishing from rafts is popular, and outfitters employ professionals to run these trips.

The New passes through only one major West Virginia city, Hinton, a former lumber and railroad center. Other towns in the area like Beckley, Oak Hill, and Fayetteville are on the surrounding plateau and cannot be considered river cities. Because there are very few communities on the New, the twentieth-century anachronism of Thurmond stands out. It began as a coal and railroad center at the turn of the century. There were no through roads in those days, so the only way in and out of town was via the railroad. It was a lawless place, somewhat akin to Dodge City of the Old West. The infamous 100-room Dungeon Hotel was host to the longest continuous poker game in history, lasting some 14 years! Prostitutes, booze, dice, and cards were brought in fresh every day, and the unlucky losers of arguments were disposed of in the New. There are two old sayings that describe the town color fully: "No Sunday west of Clifton Forge and no God west of Hinton" and "The only difference between Hell and Thurmond is that a river runs through Thurmond." As you drive down to the Fayette Station takeout, consider that before the New River Gorge Bridge was built, this winding road was one of the state's major north-south highways! It took almost an hour to get from one side of the river to the other, something that today's busy travelers can do in minutes.

Today Thurmond and Fayetteville are tourist centers. Whitewater rafting is big business, and dozens of companies ply their trade on summer weekends. The surrounding rivers are a magnet for some of the best playboaters and creekers in the country, and many call the area home. The cliffs of the Gorge have become one of the East's most active rock-climbing centers. The river from Hinton to Fayette Station is now a National Recreation Area, and on US 19 an impressive National Park Service visitor center overlooks the famous New River Gorge Bridge. People stop here by the hundreds to take in the spectacular river views. The Park Service also has facilities in Grandview and Glen Jean. The third

weekend of October is Bridge Day, and the Route 19 bridge over the New becomes a frenzy of rappelling, BASE jumping, and bungee jumping. Less terrifying activities like mountain biking and horseback riding are always available for regular people, and there are plenty of motels and restaurants in the Fayetteville–Oak Hill area.

The New was dammed for a second time below Hawks Nest, which created the placid lake seen from the overlook there. The scene's beauty contrasts with the sordid history of the place. The 4-mile-long Hawks Nest bypass tunnel was built for the New Kanawha Power Company, a subsidiary of Union Carbide, to divert the New for power production. The tunnel was drilled through solid silica rock under conditions straight out of the Dark Ages. The men who were "employed" on the project were practically slaves. At least 476 men are known to have died from silicosis, some quietly buried in unmarked graves. Attempts to investigate this matter were thwarted for many years. What is most amazing about this heartless chapter in American history is that these events happened as recently as the Great Depression! Today the project, run by Elkem Metals, generates the power needed to run their big metals plant at Alloy. The bypass carries water around what paddlers call the "Dries" of the New.

Appalachian naturalist Maurice Brooks has written of the New River's role as a vehicle for plant species from more southerly regions. The Catawba rhododendron, Carolina silverbell, sweet gum, and Spanish oak are just a few examples of streamside plants that attract the naturalist-paddler, and waterfowl are common on the river's upper reaches. The New is one of West Virginia's most magnificent treasures, and the whitewater paddler can see it all!

BLUESTONE RIVER

The Bluestone River, named Momongoseneka by local American Indians, which means "big stone," meanders a bit in the highlands, collecting water before it carves a deep valley on its way to the New. The best whitewater, rated Class 3, occurs in the 6 miles bracketing Eads Mill, hundreds of feet below the WV Turnpike Bridge. Anyone who doesn't get "stoned" by this creek had better stick to TV football. The Bluestone is now protected as a National Wild and Scenic River, administered by the National Park Service.

MAPS: Athens, Flat Top, Pipestem (USGS); Mercer, Summers (County)

SPANISHBURG TO EADS MILL

CLASS	1−3
LENGTH	10.5
TIME	3.5
GAUGE	PHONE
LEVEL	4.5−9 FT. (PIPESTEM)
FLOW	FREE FLOWING
GRADIENT	20 (2@45)
VOLUME	468
SOLITUDE	B
SCENERY	B

DESCRIPTION: This delightful intermediate run is similar to the downstream canyon, but shorter and more accessible. The first 3 miles flow fast and flat to an 8-foot breached dam. The dam looks runable, but most people will carry on the right. With plenty of play time left, the rest is a solid intermediate run .

DIFFICULTIES: The 5 miles below the dam are a relaxing Class 2 leading into solid Class-3 rapids. The first is a series of vigorous drops leading to a 4-foot pool plunge. The second, Bear Claw, re-quires boaters to work to the right of a pourover, then cut hard left to avoid an undercut ledge jutting from the right bank. The river then tapers down a bit, passes the mouth of Camp Creek, and slips into two curving, fun slalom rapids. The first passes under the West Virginia Turnpike bridge. There is a very danger-ous undercut shelf on river-right below the drop, a few hundred feet upstream of the Eads Mill bridge. The second ends in a juicy hydraulic on the bottom right. Both are easily run on the inside of the curve. Take out on the left immediately below this drop.

SHUTTLE: Spanishburg is on US 19; take the Camp Creek exit from the West Virginia Turnpike (I-77) and follow US 19 South to where Rich Creek joins the Bluestone. Eads Mill can be reached by driving upriver on CR 3 from US 19 at Camp Creek.

GAUGE: See section B.

EADS MILL TO BLUESTONE STATE PARK

CLASS	1−3
LENGTH	19
TIME	7
GAUGE	PHONE
LEVEL	4.5−9 FT. (PIPESTEM)
FLOW	FREE FLOWING
GRADIENT	20 (4@45)
VOLUME	468
SOLITUDE	A
SCENERY	A

DESCRIPTION: This is a delightful stretch of continuous, inter-mediate whitewater flowing through a spectacular gorge. Stair-stepping waterfalls, hundreds of feet high, enter on both sides. Ducks, deer, and beaver live in abundance along its green banks.

DIFFICULTIES: The first 10 miles of the run are continuous Class 2–3 rapids with the most vigorous water coming early. The drops are challenging without real penalties and have lots of playing opportunities. About 9 miles into the trip, a mirage ap-pears: a luxurious lodge and restaurant in the middle of the

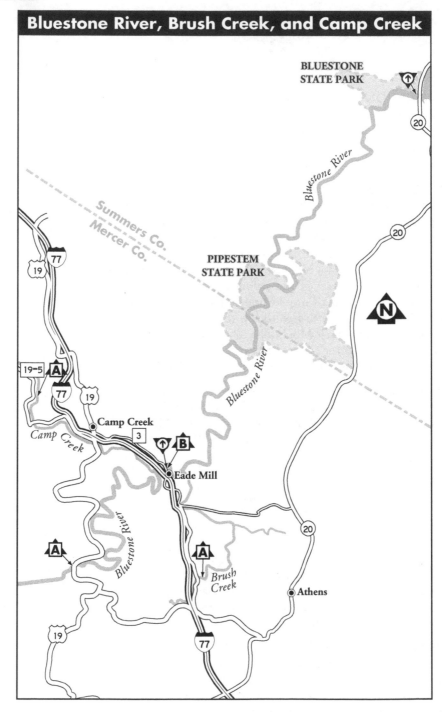

Bluestone River, Brush Creek, and Camp Creek

BLUESTONE STATE PARK

Bluestone River

PIPESTEM STATE PARK

Summers Co.
Mercer Co.

Bluestone River

Camp Creek

Camp Creek

Eade Mill

Bluestone River

Brush Creek

Athens

wilderness. This is the Mountain Creek Lodge, a part of the Pipestem recreational complex. Boats can be pulled out here by prior arrangement; call (304) 466-1880, ext. 394. The freight tram can take four to five kayaks or three open boats on each trip. Operations begin in early April, which is late in the season for this river. Without a reservation you'll have a brutal carry up the hill.

The run beyond the Mountain Creek Lodge is continuous Class-2 water for about 4 miles. At 5 miles beyond the lodge, there's a long pool transected by a gas pipeline. There are 3 miles of flowing water from there to the take-out.

SHUTTLE: Take out at the Bluestone State Park Campground near Hinton. If closed in winter season, you can take out at the boat dock in front of the park headquarters 1 mile down the reservoir. To reach Eads Mill, use WV 20 to the CR 3 turn-off at the town of Speedway. Some folks like to carry their boats upstream, under the Turnpike, to run the last rapids of the previous section.

GAUGE: The Pipestem gauge is reported daily to the USCOE in Huntington; call (304) 529-5127. There is a USGS gauge 1.2 miles downstream from Mountain Creek reported daily; call (304) 529-5604. Paddlers can read the second gauge on site. The river is flashy, rising and dropping quickly after heavy rain. A 4-foot reading is zero; 6 feet is ideal. At 8 feet the holes get sticky, and the difficulty increases one class. At 10 feet all of the eddies are in the trees and epic swims await those who miss a roll. The river is runable about 50 days per year, mostly February–April.

CAMP CREEK

MAPS: Athens (USGS); Mercer (County)

CAMP CREEK STATE FOREST TO EADS MILL

DESCRIPTION: Although it is possible to paddle from the confluence of the Marsh Fork in Camp Creek State Park, most boaters put in at the church yard by US 19 over the Bluestone River. This 2-mile section drops 80 fpm and offers an exciting entrance into the Bluestone River above the Eads Mill Bridge. All of the rapids except the last one are straightforward Class-3 slides. The scenery is good even though the WV Turnpike is never more than a quarter mile away.

CLASS	2–3
LENGTH	4.5
TIME	1
GAUGE	PHONE
LEVEL	OVER 6 FT. AT PIPESTEM
FLOW	FREE FLOWING
GRADIENT	60–80
VOLUME	S
SOLITUDE	A
SCENERY	A

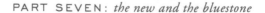

SHUTTLE: Exit I-77 at Camp Creek and look for CR 19-5, which parallels the creek between Camp Creek State Park and Eads Mill.

GAUGE: If there is enough water to get through the first riffle below the churchyard, the river is probably good to go. You should have good water when the Bluestone gauge at Pipestem reads over 6 feet.

BRUSH CREEK

This nasty little cousin to the Bluestone drains the Princeton area, picking up a slight odor of sewage, crosses under the WV Turnpike, and slashes its way down into the Bluestone Gorge.

MAPS: Athens (USGS); Mercer (County)

CLASS	3–4 (6)
LENGTH	5.5
TIME	2.5
GAUGE	PHONE
LEVEL	6 FT. (PIPESTEM)
FLOW	FREE FLOWING
GRADIENT	4.5@71 (1@200!)
VOLUME	S
SOLITUDE	A
SCENERY	A

BRIDGE 1.5 MILES BELOW WV TURNPIKE TO BLUESTONE RIVER

DESCRIPTION: Running through remote, unspoiled scenery, the river begins with Class-2 rock gardens, soon graduating to constant Class 3. The addition of Laurel Creek about midway through this upper section nearly doubles the water volume. The bridge located a mile before the confluence with the Bluestone is the take-out for intermediate paddlers and the weak at heart.

DIFFICULTIES: About 4 miles into the trip a heavy Class-3 ledge is encountered. Scouting may be needed. Within site of that rapid is a heavy Class-4 ledge. This sloping 8-foot ledge, dubbed Brillo Falls, can be pretty mean and may need to be carried depending on conditions. The bridge after Brillo Falls marks the end of the trip for intermediate paddlers. All who tackle the last mile of Brush Creek should be prepared for a great deal of scouting and at least two carries.

Shortly after crossing under the bridge, paddlers find themselves staring at the treetops as a 2-step, 35-foot falls (which has been run) appears. After the falls is a series of long, steep drops that can be run without scouting. With about 0.75 miles to go, the pace slows to a crawl and nearly every rapid requires scouting. The narrow streambed is pinched between valley walls and strewn with boulders, and the rapids are ultracontinuous Class 4.

There is one Class-6 rapid in this stretch—a 4-step drop. The entrance drop is relatively harmless, but the next two drops are

narrow slots, barely wider than a kayak, with imposing VW-sized undercut boulders. The carry is on the left. The final drop of the fourth step is a Class 3–4 sloping ledge, which must be run because the left bank turns into a sheer cliff.

SHUTTLE: The put-in is on CR 14 paralleling the WV Turnpike about 4.5 miles north of Princeton. The take-out for the first section is reached by heading north from the put-in and taking the first right. It's a 1-mile carry up the Bluestone to the Eads Mill Bridge. A trail is on the left side of the Bluestone. It's 8 miles downstream from here to the Pipestem State Park tramway.

GAUGE: You'll want at least 6 feet on the Pipestem gauge on the Bluestone; call (304) 466-1056 for a reading.

NEW RIVER

The New drains a tremendous watershed. It has scores of small tributaries, but only two of them are really large: the Bluestone and the Greenbrier. Because the river flows through a rugged canyon most of the way, much of the route is unsettled. There is little industry other than coal mining and almost no agriculture. Today, the river is West Virginia's biggest tourist attraction. Where small, steep creeks drop from the surrounding plateau to the river, local experts have pioneered some of the most intense runs in the country.

MAPS: Narrows, Petertown, Forest Hill, Pipestem, Hinton, Meadow Creek, Beckley, Prince, Thurmond, Fayetteville, Gauley Bridge (USGS); County: Mercer, Summers, Raleigh, Fayette (County); Virginia State Road Map

GLEN LYN, VIRGINIA, TO BULL FALLS CAMPGROUNDS

CLASS	I–3
LENGTH	20
TIME	7
GAUGE	WEB
LEVEL	2.5–6.5 (GLEN LYNN, VA)
PERMITS	NO
FLOW	DAMMED
GRADIENT	8
VOLUME	5,059
SOLITUDE	B
SCENERY	A–B

DESCRIPTION: This is a long stretch of predominantly flat water interspersed with a few ledges and occasional mild rapids in an isolated valley far from civilization. It is occasionally run as an overnighter. Every rapid in this part of the country is called a falls, but they are really low ledges. They demand some respect, especially at high water. Wylie Falls is right at the state line, so if you plan on a fishing trip you will need two licenses. The reservoir flat water begins near the campgrounds. Do not expect to see Bull Falls unless you are a scuba diver.

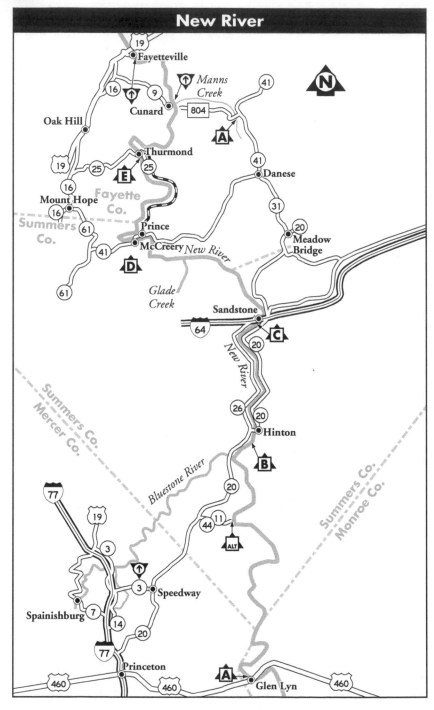

New River

DIFFICULTIES: Shumate Falls, about 2 miles below Glen Lyn, is the most difficult rapid on the whole run. It can be mean in high water and should be scouted by first-timers. Run on the left. Four miles below here is Wylie Falls, easily run on the right. The names of the next "falls," which you might not even see if the river is high, are Sand Bar Falls, Anderson Falls, Harvey Falls, and Harmon's Rapids near the mouth of Indian Creek. Other than Shumate, all of the falls may be run on the right.

SHUTTLE: Brutal—2 hours one way. From Princeton take US 460 to Glen Lyn, Virginia. Put in at the bridge. Bull Falls Campgrounds, a Department of Natural Resources area, may be reached by taking the very steep road toward the river from WV 20 near Pipestem.

GAUGE: The best gauge for this section is on the New at Glen Lynn, VA. Access it through the USGS website. Levels between 2.5 and 6.6 will work; upstream hydro plants release water to generate peaking power and the river rises and falls quite quickly.

BLUESTONE DAM TO SANDSTONE

CLASS	1–3
LENGTH	11 MI.
TIME	3–4
GAUGE	PHONE
LEVEL	2–3 FT. (HINTON)
PERMITS	No
FLOW	DAMMED
GRADIENT	10
VOLUME	7,531
SOLITUDE	B
SCENERY	B

DESCRIPTION: This section begins immediately below the Bluestone Dam and flows through a very scenic valley. The mouth of the Greenbrier River joins the New from the right just below the dam. Gentle, easily negotiated rapids are encountered between flat stretches. About a mile after passing the bridge in Hinton a very long Class 2–3 rapid makes for excellent canoeing. After this there is a rather long flat stretch with intermittent riffles where the river has broadened out to almost half-a-mile wide.

DIFFICULTIES: At the end of this flat stretch a very loud rumble and the appearance of spray warn the paddler of something special. This is Brooks Falls, a vigorous drop over the complete width of the river. You can scout from the Brooks Falls Day Use Access Area, but the river is so wide that scouting may not be easy. Helms Beach Access can be also found on the left, just below the Falls. After several low but powerful ledges the water picks up speed and drops about 6 feet at places over a wide reef. Several passages exist—one on the extreme right, one about a

third of the way from the left, and the most dangerous, the extreme left against the bank. At higher water levels you can go over at almost any place, but the turbulence will be greater. It is probably more difficult at lower flows.

In the 3.5 miles between Brooks and mighty Sandstone Falls there are only three rapids. The first two, within a quarter mile of each other, are river-wide ledges. The first is fairly high, with a deceptive and dangerous recirculating hole at the center. Run just to the right of the island. The second is lower and more easily negotiated. If you are in doubt, each of these may be run safely on the extreme left. The third rapid is relatively minor, but the width of the river makes rescue difficult. The portage at Sandstone Falls is rough, but there are two useful access points. Both are found on river left, across the river from Hinton. The first portage is a half mile above the falls on river left. A wooden ramp and buoys can be seen from the river. The second is a half mile below the falls and the boardwalk area. There's good playing in the run-out of the Falls, but stay clear of the tour boat! There's also a take-out at Sandstone, along a dirt road off WV 20 behind the Sandstone Post Office.

SHUTTLE: Put in just below Bluestone Dam at the USCOE park located at Bellepoint on WV 3 and 12. The National Park Service has provided numerous take-outs off the River Road on river left and WV 20 on the right. These are all noted in the description; pick the ones best suited to your needs.

GAUGE: See section D.

Fuel For the New River Controversy

Well, I just paddled on the Youghiogheny this weekend (9/13–9/14/80). Probably the first time in 2 or 3 years, maybe more. You know what? It wasn't half bad. Not nearly as unpleasant as the New River. The rafters travel in troops and after they pass, you almost have the river to yourself. There really aren't that many paddlers. The put in is clean; the take-out is clean. Very little trash along the river. A nice big parking lot exists at the put-in and take-out for paddlers. What is so terrible about all of that?

We say we don't want the New River area developed. What are we saying? We like the fact that there is

no good put-in at Thurmond? We like to have our cars broken into at Cunard? We like parking problems and traffic jams and trash at Fayette Station? We like to paddle the New River in the winter, so who cares if it is over crowded in the summer? No, I don't think that it is really what we want.

Consider the Grand Canyon. That may not really be a fair comparison but if there were not some controls on the river access then all that makes the river desirable would be gone anyway. Would you rather have a little hassle over something worth waiting for or would you rather have ready access to a low-grade experience? The Grand Canyon system is not perfect and the Yough system is not perfect, but they do work and they do help.

How about state or federal campgrounds? They are clean and well maintained, right? When was the last time you wanted to spend the night in the New River area? What did you do, sleep at Fayette Station amid the trash and bugs and local whoopies throwing beer cans or did you sleep along Rt. 19 with the 18-wheelers rolling by your tent all night?

Do we want sleazy little junk stands and souvenir shops? Do we really believe that the growth in popularity of this sport will level off before the Cheat, Gauley, and New Rivers are saturated out of existence? Unfortunately, I don't see any signs of this happening. Do you?

What are your answers? Surely I have stirred up some opinions. I believe we need an open forum on this subject while there is time to make responses and changes. Burying your head in the sand will not make this go away. The *status quo* now is change for the worse. Do we want the *status quo*?

Ward Eister

Reprinted from West Virginia Wildwater Association
Splashes, January 1981

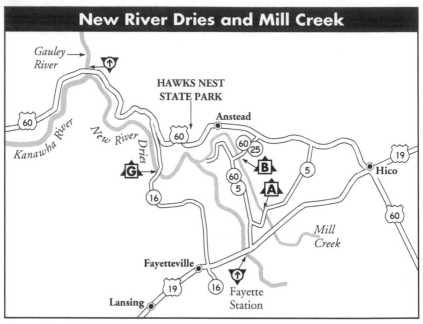

New River Dries and Mill Creek

Gauley River

HAWKS NEST STATE PARK

Kanawha River

New River Dries

Anstead

60

60 25

G

B

5

Hico

19

60

5

A

16

60

Mill Creek

Fayetteville

Lansing

19

16

Fayette Station

SANDSTONE TO McCREERY

CLASS	1–3
LENGTH	15
TIME	4–5
GAUGE	PHONE
LEVEL	1.35–4 FT. (HINTON)
FLOW	DAMMED
GRADIENT	8
VOLUME	7,531
SOLITUDE	B
SCENERY	A

DESCRIPTION: This is a very long run with several nice rapids, but there are long expanses of flat water in between. The rapids are mainly long chutes dropping gently over ledges. Although waves are large, little maneuvering is required. It's a beautiful and powerful river that's always up in the summer. Campsites abound, and it's perfect for overnight trips. National Park Service campsites at Glade Creek and Grandview Sandbar are often used as access points for a popular 5-mile day trip.

DIFFICULTIES: Novices will encounter only two places that may cause trouble. The first occurs at the top of Horseshoe Bend, easily seen from the Grandview Visitor Center. It is located about a half mile downstream from the concrete bridge piers at Glade. The entire river necks down, creating big waves. The river heads to the left and turns sharply back to the right. There's some very heavy water here, including a big stopper. After the rapids push their way to the right, they straighten. There's more very heavy turbulence midstream, including a mean hole large enough to swallow a kayak! Avoid the heavy water by staying far to the right.

    The second potential trouble spot is a delightfully long Class-3 rapid at Quinnimont just above the railroad station. Near the

bottom a huge drainpipe enters from the right. Just before this is a powerful hydraulic in the middle of the river followed, by 20 yards of flat water. Then there's a very deceptive wave that camouflages another hole deep enough to eat a canoe! Fun, but surprising.

SHUTTLE: Put in at the Lower Sandstone Falls or at Sandstone Post Office access areas described in section B. There are several intermediate access points to the river off of WV 41. The McCreery take-out is on WV 41 near Prince and is well marked.

GAUGE: See section D.

McCreery to Thurmond

CLASS	2–3
LENGTH	15
TIME	4
GAUGE	Phone
LEVEL	1.35–4 ft. at Hinton
FLOW	Dammed
GRADIENT	10
VOLUME	7,531
SOLITUDE	C
SCENERY	A

DESCRIPTION: This stretch from Prince to Thurmond contains fewer rapids and longer flatwater pools. The river is wide and powerful at 2.5 feet on the Hinton gauge; it's unwise for unsupervised novices to proceed at this or higher levels. Each rapid is a river-wide long stretch of big waves with few obstructions. Occasionally a ledge is encountered, but it is always eroded in the heaviest current. Although large stopper waves and an occasional hydraulic may be present, very little maneuvering is required.

DIFFICULTIES: Intermediates with heavy-water experience should have no problems, but this is no place for unsupervised beginners. More than halfway down, after a particularly long flat stretch, four sand storage silos appear on the right bank of a left-hand turn. Just below this, there are very large, avoidable waves near the right bank. At low levels the right bank is undercut, so watch out! There's another long flat stretch, two minor rapids, and a zesty chute over a ledge before the take-out.

SHUTTLE: The McCreery put-in is 1 mile downstream of the WV 41 bridge on river left. To avoid a long stretch of flatwater, most paddlers take out at Stonecliff, approximately 2 miles upstream. There's also public access to the river at Dun Glen, opposite Thurmond, accessible via "25" from WV 19. There is a gravel road connecting Prince and Thurmond, but it's slow going compared to the highway. Take WV 41 from Prince towards Beckley, turn right on WV 61 to Mount Hope, turn right on WV 16 for a mile, then right on CR 26 to Thurmond.

GAUGE: Call the Bluestone Dam at (304) 466-1234 for the Hinton reading. It includes both the dam release and flow in the Greenbrier. Anything between 1.25–4 feet is good. Comparable

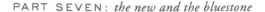

readings for the Thurmond gauge downstream are 1.25–7.45. The river seldom drops below 1.75 feet and is often at this level in the summer. At 3.5 feet (10,000 cfs) the New is very wide and powerful. Skilled boaters float it as high as it goes.

E

THURMOND TO CUNARD

CLASS	3
LENGTH	8
TIME	3
GAUGE	PHONE
LEVEL	1.5–16 FT. (FAYETTE STATION)
FLOW	DAMMED
GRADIENT	12
VOLUME	7,531
SOLITUDE	C
SCENERY	A

DESCRIPTION: This is a nice stretch of intermediate whitewater with fewer pools and more action than the section above. Most of the runs are long, gravel-bar-type rapids with good waves and current. Formerly this was the lead-in to the gorge, but now the National Park Service Cunard Access allows you to get off the river before you get to the big stuff.

DIFFICULTIES: Watch out for Surprise Rapid! From the top it looks like an ordinary riffle, but halfway through, paddlers realize they are in a funnel and all of the water is moving towards a mountainous double wave. There's a hole between the first regular wave and the second curler wave that can stop a 10-man commercial raft dead! Some kayakers like to play with it; others avoid the problem by sneaking down one shore or the other.

SHUTTLE: Access has been improved since the Park Service arrived. To get to Cunard, turn onto Salem Gatewood Road (CR 9) off of WV 16 just south of Fayetteville. Follow the signs to the sanitary landfill, then turn left in Cunard onto the access road. Rusty's Shuttle Service is a great help if you want to save time or have only one car. Call (304) 574-3475 for directions to Rusty's.

F

CUNARD TO FAYETTE STATION (ENTERING THE NEW RIVER GORGE)

CLASS	4–4+(5)
LENGTH	6
TIME	2
GAUGE	PHONE
LEVEL	1.5–12+ FT. (FAYETTE STATION)
FLOW	DAMMED
GRADIENT	15
VOLUME	7,531
SOLITUDE	C
SCENERY	A

DESCRIPTION: The New River Gorge is home to the biggest whitewater in West Virginia. The action starts right below the put-in and doesn't let up until you paddle the last big drop below the New River Gorge Bridge. The challenge is remaining upright while bobbing among the 6–8-foot standing waves and dodging holes, stoppers, and whirlpools. There are big, powerful rapids and many play spots. The gorge itself is immense, and well worth seeing from overlooks. Rugged mountains and cliffs line both sides of

the river for the entire trip. Only the remains of mining equipment left over from a previous era break through the thick forests.

DIFFICULTIES: Upper Railroad Rapid is just below the Cunard put-in. It's a steep drop over a shelf that is best run just right of a dry rock in the center of the river. There's a wicked hole on river right (The Stripper)—play it if you dare! The next rapid, Lower Railroad, cascades through a complicated barrage of boulders. It's normally run down a left-of-center tongue. At low water (less than "0") this drop has several dangerous undercut rocks. Three people have died here, and scouting is recommended. Below are several easy drops that provide excellent big-wave surfing at levels of 4 feet or more.

You are now ready to mix it up with the big stuff, the Keeney Brothers. Regardless of how these rapids look, the best way through them is right down the center. Upper Keeney is marked by a huge, midstream boulder the size and shape of a whale (Whale Rock). The current will take you to the right edge of the rock, behind which is a fine place to eddy out and gather your spirits for Middle Keeney. At higher levels these two rapids merge, so a swim here makes for a long day. Middle Keeney has three large breaking waves in the center channel, but this is the safest route. At low water, head just to the left of a dry rock in mid-channel. At higher water follow the huge tongue out of the pool behind Whale Rock. At a level of 4 feet the waves here are 8 feet high and merge with the granddaddy of them all, Lower Keeney. Larger holes exist to the right and left, so don't try to sneak it.

Even if you're very familiar with the river, it's a good idea to get out and scout the next rapid, Lower Keeney. It cannot be snuck, it cannot be lined, and it would be one hell of a carry over the house-sized boulders, so you may as well go for it. It's a short drop, but the river necks way down, concentrating the action. Look for a rooster-tail wave at the top of the main chute. A run to the right of this wave is pretty straightforward, but a run to the left takes you on a wild ride through huge waves, shockingly close to giant shoreline boulders. Be ready to compensate for the current, which pushes hard to the left the whole way. Swims here are awful! At higher levels watch out for the powerful whirlpools that form in the "little" drop just downstream. At higher levels, this section becomes low Class 5.

The two rapids below here are uncomplicated but powerful. Next is Sunset, or Double Z, a long rapid marked by a chain of rocks extending halfway across the river from the right. Enter the rapid and eddy out right, then head for the right channel. This allows you to avoid a V-ledge and hydraulic in the center. The right

channel takes you diagonally to the left, but it tumbles steeply through a field of holes and boulders. It's Class 5 at higher flows. Avoid the huge boulder on the bottom left, which is undercut and has a powerful current going under it. There are three more rapids (Old 99 or Hook, Greyhound Bus Stopper, and Tipple Rapids), which would be regarded as difficult anywhere else, but here they are a welcome breather.

Next comes Bloody Nose Rapid, a right-hand turn out of a pool. Avoid the temptation to begin at the far right and start just right of center, paddling toward the big rock on the right. Stay to the left of the chute and think left, left all of the way! You'll encounter some enormous waves, but they are fun to ride. Do not begin on the far left; not only is it pretty shallow but there is a nasty hole at the bottom.

Just below the Fayette Station bridge is one of the best rapids on this run. Run on the mid-right side. It's a multiholed roller coaster with some good-sized holers hidden by the big waves. Other than one or two minor rapids, the next 4 miles to the Hawks Nest Dam are mostly flat water and hence are seldom run.

SHUTTLE: To get to Cunard, turn onto Salem Gatewood Road off of WV 16 just south of Fayetteville. Follow the signs to the sanitary landfill, then turn left in Cunard onto the access road. Fayette Station can be reached by CR 82, a steep side road leaving US 19 just north of the New River Gorge bridge. Traffic is one-way from here: cross the Fayette Station Bridge and drive out on the other side of the gorge. The take-out is in the big eddy below Fayette Station Rapid. Rusty's Shuttle Service can be a great help if you want to save time or have only one car. He has camping available, too! Call (304) 574-3475.

GAUGE: The Fayette Station visual gauge has an interesting history. On July 1, 1964, the zero mark was chiseled into the bridge pier at Fayette Station by Jon Dragan. Jon and his brothers founded Wildwater Unlimited, the first outfitters in the river, and most paddlers still make reference to his mark. There is a real-time gauge at Thurmond, which can be reached by calling (304) 465-0493. The Canyon Rim Visitor's Center (call (304) 574-2115) has this gauge reading by 9 each morning.

Here is a conversion table for the Hinton, Thurmond, and Fayette Station gauges. It was developed by the West Virginia Wildwater Association using Dave Bassage's formulas. When discussing water levels on the New, always be sure you know which gauge people are referring to!

FLOW CONVERSION TABLE FOR FAYETTE/THURMOND/HINTON GAUGES

Note: The New River Dries will run above 5.5 feet.

Fayette	Thurmond	Hinton	(cfs)
-3	1.25	1.35	732
-2	2.00	1.5	1,240
-1	2.75	1.78	1,875
0	3.50	2.00	2,580
+1	4.26	2.24	3,472
+2	5.01	2.50	4,516
+3	5.76	2.77	5,820
+4	6.51	3.10	7,415
+5	7.26	3.42	9,300
+6	8.02	3.74	11,460
+7	8.77	4.05	13,710
+8	9.52	4.33	15,960
+9	10.27	4.65	18,880
+10	11.02	4.99	21,900
+11	11.77	5.41	25,650
+12	12.53	5.88	29,980

HAWKS NEST DAM TO GAULEY BRIDGE (THE NEW RIVER DRIES)

CLASS	3–4
LENGTH	6
TIME	2
GAUGE	PHONE
LEVEL	6–12 FT. (FAYETTE STATION)
FLOW	DAMMED
GRADIENT	18
VOLUME	NA
SOLITUDE	A
SCENERY	A

DESCRIPTION: Hawks Nest Dam and its infamous tunnel divert the New River for 5 miles to a power plant. When there is more water than the reservoir or tunnel can handle, the excess is released back into the old riverbed. Paddlers call this section the Dries. The tunnel has a voracious thirst, so the river is empty until the New's flow exceeds 10,000 cfs (3.5 feet) at Hinton or 5.5 feet at Fayette Station.

The Cotton Hill Bridge Rapid consists of long, smooth slides terminating in stoppers. Below Cotton Hill the river is rocky and the rapids are closely spaced. There are many 2–3-foot drops.

Scouting is difficult due to the huge boulders. Some rapids appear completely blocked at low water, and only narrow chutes remain. Boulders the size of the large ones on the Cheat or Gauley are a dime a dozen here. There's a mile-long continuous Class-3+ rapid that ends in a pool dammed behind a massive landslide. The landslide is runable, although finding the best passage is difficult. Usually the second or third slot from the right be run. The last rapids above the railroad bridge are below the power station diversion tunnel, so it has the full volume of the New.

DIFFICULTIES: Landslide Rapid chokes the river into 5 or 6 chutes between house-sized boulders. The second from left is unrunable. The next two to the right are OK. Scout or carry on left.

SHUTTLE: Although some people have put in at Hawks Nest Reservoir via a steep road running out of Ansted, most boaters find the WV 16 bridge at Cotton Hill a more convenient alternative. Take out along US 60, just above Gauley Bridge.

GAUGE: See section D. The readings given at the beginning of the profile are for the Fayette Station gauge. The tubes fill up at 5.5 feet, and 6 feet spills about 1,400 cfs for a low-water run. The section has been run with over 26,000 cfs in the Dries. It was absolutely huge!

GLADE CREEK

This classic stream was "discovered" by West Virginia paddlers in the 1980s. It's tight, steep, and technical, so great care is required. Allow plenty of time if you're unfamiliar with this run.

MAPS: Prince (USGS); Raleigh (County)

PINCH CREEK TO NEW RIVER

CLASS	4
LENGTH	6
TIME	3
GAUGE	VISUAL
LEVEL	NA
FLOW	FREE FLOWING
GRADIENT	127
VOLUME	S
SOLITUDE	A
SCENERY	A

DESCRIPTION: Things start out in a ledgy manner below the mouth of Pinch Creek but quickly change to boulder-choked cascades. Rapids continue all the way to the New River. All rapids are runable, but don't be too macho to stop and scout. Fallen-tree hazards do exist as on all tiny streams, and often many of the rapids have only one narrow passage. The scenery is dense, southern West Virginia rain forest if you have some time to look. But don't look around too long, or you'll get pinned!

DIFFICULTIES: Everything—getting there, getting down the stream, and getting to the take-out. The first and last are described under the shuttle. Primarily, don't try to remember what we say here. Get out and scout every drop of which you cannot see the bottom. This means almost every rapid.

About halfway through the trip, paddlers are confronted with a rapid where a large number of trees have fallen from the right bank. Several of these are cluttering up the rapid, so be very judicious about your route here. Later you will observe the results of a landslide from the left shore. Eddy out above this rapid and scout. This is one of the steepest rapids on the river, steeper than it looks from the top.

Finally, less than a mile from the end, a stone-retaining wall forming the left bank of the stream indicates a falls ahead. You had better concentrate on getting through the next rapid first, however; it's the tightest and toughest on the river. Fortunately, there is a good eddy to take out on the right between this rapid and the falls. The falls, an 8-footer, is scrapy but an easy shot down the middle. If you've made it thus far, the falls are a piece of cake. Chug your way out to the New River from here, but watch out for one more big ledge. Run it far left.

SHUTTLE: The put-in is over a well-maintained dirt road, CR 22 off of WV 307 near Grandview State Park. Follow WV 307 toward the park from Beaver until it Ts with CR 9. Turn right and then left on the first unmarked dirt and gravel road. Follow this road to where it fords Glade Creek at the mouth of Pinch Creek.

You can drive to the mouth of Glade Creek (and the take-out) with some difficulty on Park Service roads. This is a good spot to visually check the water level. You can also continue down the New to the National Park Service's McCreery access point on river right.

One other point: There is no gauge other than the one at the put-in, so the level must be judged from there. If there is any doubt, consider Piney Creek as a second choice. Leave a car at McCreery, which is at the end of Piney Creek, to serve as a shuttle for either trip. This adds 4.5 miles of New River after the farthest upstream take-out for Glade Creek; however, it also adds insurance that you won't have to set up a second shuttle. You might check Piney Creek first, because it is on the way to the put-in to Glade. If Piney is 6 inches or less, then forget the Glade; it will almost certainly be too low.

GAUGE: This creek is hard to catch up. The gauge is an old bridge abutment. At the mouth of Pinch Creek, at the put-in,

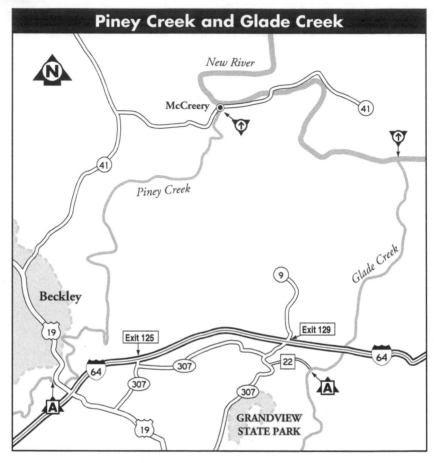

look across the creek. All runs have been made at a level within 2 inches of the bottom of the eighth stone down. One run was made with the level at 8 stones and rising and the group nearly got swept off the river. If there's enough water to get through the first few hydraulics without scraping too badly, then there is adequate water.

The Piney Creek gauge may also be used as a reference. On most occasions, if the Piney gauge is over 0.5–0.8 feet, then Glade Creek is runable. Don't always count on this, because there are three lakes on the upper Glade that can and often do catch runoff and dampen the flow, particularly after prolonged dry spells.

PINEY CREEK

MAPS: Beckley, Prince (USGS); Raleigh (County)

BECKLEY TO MCCREERY

CLASS	3–5
LENGTH	12
TIME	5
GAUGE	VISUAL
LEVEL	NA
PERMITS	No
FLOW	FREE FLOWING
GRADIENT	80
VOLUME	S
SOLITUDE	A
SCENERY	A

DESCRIPTION: This tiny tributary of the New falls off the plateau near Beckley. After passing the Beckley sewage plant, which adds more than volume, only an active coal mine and the railroad tracks indicate civilization. The river, however, is anything but civil. The stream is in a very deep and intimate gorge— the intimacy of a grizzly bear hug! The streambed becomes multiple 3–5-foot ledges with irregular broken-ledge rubble and then gets worse. Near the take-out it levels off to a Class 2–3.

DIFFICULTIES: In one memorable stretch with a gradient of 160 fpm, the river disappears over five, steep, intricate cascades into a narrow, twisting riverbed with 4-foot-high drops that are only 3-feet wide. One rapid shoots out between an overhanging, house-sized boulder and a meat cleaver rock. Soon after, a succession of 3–4-foot Humpty Dumpty ledges ends on the brink of 8-foot Big Rock Falls. The pool on the left side is very undercut and extremely dangerous. Run it on the right. The next rapid has a bad strainer. Watch out. Late in the trip, after an old left-side mine, watch out for a Class 3–4 approach rapid bending right out of sight. This is the Flusher that terminates on a large midstream rock with very narrow passages on each side. Don't go too far; most people carry it from the top. The final caution is that the river water is badly contaminated with sewage. It smells and feels bad and has made some paddlers sick. Hopefully this will be cleared up soon to make this fine run more appetizing.

SHUTTLE: Take out at WV 41 bridge at McCreery. Put in via Raleigh Motor's parking lot off US 19 in Beckley.

GAUGE: None. Examine the river at the take-out. You'll want a low-to-moderate flow.

Exploratory Trip—Piney Creek

Received two reports of exploratory runs on this stream that all of us have been overlooking for years as its mouth is right at McCreery. Bryan Bills reports that he, Leo Bode, and Ernie Kincaid scouted it on Feb. 3rd from the mouth up and found increasing gradient and a couple of nasties as they worked their way upstream.

They returned the next day to be the first to run this hidden gem. Apparently, Bryan waxed ecstatic about this to Charlie Walbridge (who never needs any prompting) who later returned with Paul Singley to run it themselves. Here is what they have to say:

Put-in: Just as you start out of Beckley on Rt. 19/21, you will see Boggs' Tackle Shop. Stop and ask permission to park there. CW mentions such helpful hints as putting in near Raleigh Motors and passing the Beckley Sewage Disposal Works by boat, which added appreciably to the volume. Bryan reports a couple of miles of Class 1–2 and then the first fall, which they carried easily on the left. CW mentioned entering an intimate gorge, its intimacy being compared to a bear hug from a grizzly bear. CW also reports the stream getting very "ledgey" and said it compared favorably with the Lower Middle Fork below Audra. Three 5-foot ledges, boulder gardens, and hydraulic fields (that's a new one!) gave way to a place where the river began to disappear from sight forming five, long, steep intricate cascades in a narrow twisting river bed. Bryan reports that some of the ledges had broken off boulders beneath them forming possible traps for the paddler. Some passages were blocked or made more difficult by fallen trees. CW did a lot of scouting (something he rarely has to do) and reports that your entire path had to be carefully planned as a miscue could cost you your boat. There was one cascade which ended in a 4-foot-high, 3-foot-wide sluice; another shot between an overhanging, house-sized boulder on the left and a nasty "meat cleaver" rock on the right. The most memorable one, reported by both explorers in the same detail, was a succession of 3–4-foot ledges which ended up in a turbulent pool before lunging over an 8-foot ledge, a difficult carry. There then follows more technical water before the gradient lets up to an easier Class 2–3 pace.

Both paddlers reported that it took a lot of time to run this 12-mile stretch with scouting, carrying, flips, etc. CW says they are all runable, but I know he is crazy—

most would prefer carrying a few of these baddies. Bryan didn't want to hang a classification on the middle narrow section since it will change greatly with small differences in water level, but CW said it was the technical equivalent of the (gulp!) Blackwater, except that the gradient was much more irregular. CW advises not to get near it if it looks at all high at the McCreery bridge.

Thanks to Bryan for bringing this to our attention. I know this has to be STEEP as I always thought it was one hell of a climb by car from McCreery up the mountain to Beckley and this is what these yo-yos descended by boat! Congrats!

Bob Burrell

Reprinted from West Virginia Wildwater Association
Splashes, July 1973

GLADE CREEK INTO MANNS CREEK

This is one of the steepest and most dangerous runs in this guide. Its extreme gradient creates an astonishing sequence of Class 4, 5, and 6 boulder rapids. The river cuts its way to the New through a deep gorge of remarkable beauty, but you won't be looking at the scenery. The action is utterly continuous, blind, and intense. Numerous undercut rocks, downed trees, and narrow offset chutes demand respect from the strongest and most experienced paddlers. Much scouting is required and you may want to portage some rapids. The first run took 10 hours!

MAPS: Danese, Winona, Fayetteville (USGS); Fayette (County)

A

BABCOCK STATE PARK TO NEW RIVER

DESCRIPTION: Hiking trails follow the river on both sides for the first 2 miles. A brief scouting hike is always a good idea. Below the second footbridge there are no trails, so if you're in over your head or start running out of time, this is the easiest place to get out. A road parallels the river on the left side along its entire length. Although it's very high above the river, a boater could probably claw his way up and out. About a third of the way through the run, Mann's Creek, the major tributary, comes in and doubles the flow.

CLASS	5–6
LENGTH	7
TIME	8–10
GAUGE	VISUAL
LEVEL	NA
FLOW	FREE FLOWING
GRADIENT	100–280
VOLUME	VS
SOLITUDE	C
SCENERY	A+

DIFFICULTIES: This creek is truly unique and extremely difficult. The action is nonstop and the creek goes through tough boulder drops that we find difficult to describe. Occasionally there's a short stretch of easy water between steep sets of blind boulder drops. Very few, if any, creeks in the world stay as difficult for as long as Manns does. Stamina, skill, and good judgement are prerequisites for a successful descent.

The action starts immediately with a slide into the 15-foot Grist Mill Falls. Most people don't run this falls below -3 inches because of the junky falls lip and the shallow landing pool. Generally try to launch off the middle. There is a 10-foot dam that follows immediately, which can be run on the right with left angle. Some steep slides and boulder drops carry you to the first major rapid, Gladiator.

Gladiator is a steep series of ledges and lets you know quickly what to expect for the next several miles. A little further down, you'll reach Pillage and Plunder, a nasty series of drops through some narrow chutes. After many more steep boulder drops, you'll come to a huge boulder jumble called Goliath. The creek splits on an island here, and you'll want to take the left channel. This leads to a 12-foot boof ramp followed by an intense series of boulder drops. Further down, you'll reach On Ramp and Off Ramp: two closely spaced boulder rapids that should be scouted. Many paddlers portage Off Ramp at lower flows. The next major rapid is Lunatic Fringe, a 10-foot drop into a rock. Run down the left or portage on the right.

Manns Creek comes in on the right during a calm stretch, but it isn't long until the run picks up again. Around the right side of an island, you'll see a 10-foot falls called Ten-Foot Pole; run on the right. Some of the more interesting boulder drops downstream include Mann Eater, Double Dare, Bouncing Betty, and You Ain't Gonna Like This One.

Near the end, you'll reach the toughest boulder drop on the run, Liquid Drano. It is a steep series of boulder drops, a 90-degree turn to the right off a double drop, and a slide. From here to the New the creek slowly starts to calm down, but it packs some punch all the way to the end.

SHUTTLE: The put-in is on Glade Creek, below the well-known and photogenic gristmill in Babcock State Park. Mann's Creek enters the New River just above the Cunard access.

GAUGE: There's a gauge on river left above the bridge at Babcock State Park. Minus 5 inches should be considered absolute minimum. Minus 2 or 3 inches is probably a great first time level. Only paddlers who are very familiar with the run should attempt it above +1 inches You can also examine the first rapid

below the dam, a nice slide. You should be able to run this without scraping too badly. If there are any waves and turbulence, the creek is too high. When the Meadow at Mt. Lookout is at over 2,500 cfs, Manns should be running.

MANNS CREEK (REAL MANNS)

Real Manns is a tremendously steep and difficult test piece for hardcore creek boaters. The run is similar to the traditional Glade/Manns run, but the rapids are steeper and more demanding.

MAPS: Danese, Winona, Fayetteville (USGS); Fayette (County)

RT. 41–CONFLUENCE WITH GLADE CREEK

CLASS	5–6
LENGTH	2
TIME	4+
GAUGE	VISUAL
LEVEL	NA
PERMITS	NO
FLOW	FREE FLOWING
GRADIENT	@ 500
VOLUME	VS
SOLITUDE	C
SCENERY	A+

DESCRIPTION: The run begins placidly, flowing through a marshy area for almost a mile before it gets down to business. Then a long, steep slide leads into boulder drop after boulder drop as the creek cuts its way deeper and deeper through the gorge. There's a trail along the river at the start of the run, but it stays on the rim of the gorge and gets farther and farther away with each drop. Sieves and undercuts are found throughout the run. Trees are also a problem in spots so scouting is a must. A lot of the drops can be viewed in the various *Falling Down Productions* videos.

DIFFICULTIES: Real Manns has some of the most challenging boulder drops found anywhere. Immediately after the opening slide, the run splits on an island, with most of the water heading right and a demanding boulder drop where the channels rejoin. Directly after this there is another small island split (run again on the right) where a 3-foot drop leads onto a 10-foot slide that slams into a brutal pin rock at the bottom. Make sure that you are driving hard left here. Another steep boulder drop, complicated by a downed tree, brings you to Mann-O-Mann. This is a steep series of ledges run on the left leading into an 8–10 foot boof in the center to avoid a heinous sieve on the right. After a small slide, get out of your boat and look at the next rapid, Energizer.

Energizer is one of the steepest runable series of boulder drops anywhere and is one of the most impressive rapids in the entire state. It contains three parts that are linked together, any single part of which would be challenging enough. It starts with a 10-foot slide that pillows off the right bank and over some more

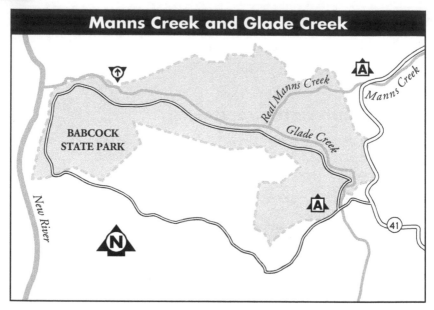

Manns Creek and Glade Creek

small drops. After a very short calm stretch, there is a 6-foot ledge that pillows to the left and off another 6-foot ledge. This leads right into the steepest part of the rapid, a cascade that heads right and then over an impressive double drop of about 12 feet with an almost unavoidable piton rock at the bottom! This rapid is not run very often. Portage on the right if you have any doubts.

More steep boulder drops lead right to Tunnel of Love, a 10-foot drop that lands under an overhanging boulder. Make sure that you boof hard left, then duck or eat rock! Several more challenging boulder drops will carry you to the confluence of Manns Creek and Glade Creek.

SHUTTLE: Put in where Manns Creek goes under WV 41 before you reach the turnoff for Babcock State Park. You can take out at the confluence by hacking your way through the woods on the left bank up to the gorge rim trail. This trail takes you back into Camp Washington Carver, which can also be used as a put-in. It's possible to continue the run down the lower part of Manns Creek to Cunard but paddlers who try this at high flows must be very familiar with this lower stretch.

GAUGE: There is no good gauge for Real Manns other than a painted gauge in Babcock State Park above the Gristmill. This gauge should be +3 inches or higher for a run down Real Manns. For a rough correlation, the Meadow at Mount Lookout should be 3,000 cfs or more.

KEENEY CREEK

Keeney Creek is one of the most difficult creeks described in this book, if not THE most difficult. It is very small, very steep, and incredibly demanding. The creek starts off slow at the put-in, but once it starts dropping there's no stopping until you reach the New River. The action is utterly continuous, with lots of big boulder drops, slides, and waterfalls. There are a number of downed trees that clog the drops, and several deadly sieves that must be avoided.

MAPS: Winona, Fayetteville (USGS); Fayette (County)

CR 85-2 FORD TO NEW RIVER

CLASS	5–6
LENGTH	1.5
TIME	3+
GAUGE	VISUAL
LEVEL	NA
PERMITS	No
FLOW	FREE FLOWING
GRADIENT	466 (1@600, 0.5@200)
VOLUME	VS
SOLITUDE	C
SCENERY	B

DESCRIPTION: This run is only for the best of the top-notch creek boaters. There's a railroad grade on the right side that parallels the steep section of the creek. It's useful for scouting or beating a hasty retreat if you are having more fun than you wanted. The scenery here could be gorgeous, but the railroad grade has allowed people to dump trash (and even a car) down into the creek.

DIFFICULTIES: This creek is extreme! The action starts with a 15-foot cascade that may be clogged with trees and continues through several ledge drops before you reach Accept Reality. This is a huge rapid that drops at least 60 feet. It starts as a long cascade of 30+ feet leading into a 30-foot waterfall that lands on a rock halfway down. After some steep boulder ledges, you will arrive at a horrendous boulder drop. The river drops 10 feet into a narrow notch followed by a 5-foot ledge. Several more steep ledge drops lead to Silver Creek Supper, a 30-foot waterfall with a junky lip and a fairly shallow pool. The next major rapid, Miller Time, is particularly dangerous. It's a steep series of ledges with a nasty underwater sieve just under the surface of the biggest drop. This has been the site of at least one close call and several pitonings. More sketchy boulder drops carry you to the New River, where you can finally relax.

SHUTTLE: To reach the put-in, go into the town of Winona and follow CR 85-2 along Keeney Creek until you reach a ford. Put in here or continue driving downstream on the railroad grade to get closer to where the action starts. There's no take out at the New other than carrying your boat back along the railroad grade. It's probably best to make a high-water run down to Fayette Station.

GAUGE: None. Inspect on site.

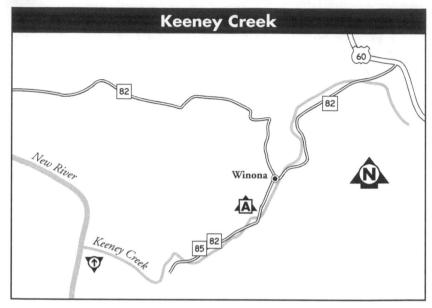

MILL CREEK

The upper section of this delightful, scenic winter run is an excellent warm-up for the craziness that lies below Ansted. From Ansted down, Mill Creek is a short run with a split personality. There is a falls midway down. From Ansted to the falls is mostly Class 4 with a couple of Class-5 drops. The falls is a clean shot into a deep pool. The lower run is considerably more difficult, with several Class-5 and -6 rapids. Several rapids are very difficult and almost everyone portages something.

MAPS: Fayetteville, Ansted (USGS); Fayette (County)

CLASS	2–3
LENGTH	5
TIME	2
GAUGE	VISUAL
LEVEL	6 IN.–2 FT.
FLOW	FREE FLOWING
GRADIENT	40–80
VOLUME	VS
SOLITUDE	C
SCENERY	A

HOPEWELL ROAD TO ANSTED

DESCRIPTION: Most rapids are gravel bars or small boulder drops. Aside from a major logjam midway that must be carried, there are no unusual problems.

SHUTTLE: Put in on Hopewell Road, which can be reached via WV 60. Take out at Chestnut Bridge in Ansted.

GAUGE: See section B.

First Run of Mill Creek: October 9, 1976: Length: 2 Miles; Gradient: 250–300 Feet/Mile; Approx. 400 CFS

Here we were, looking at that stream referred to as unrunable by that famous flatwater paddler—what's his name? It looked like the weekend had good potential. The Gauley and New were flooded and so was this. Bryan Bills was insistent that we look at it. After spending the day scouting and missing all the good runs, he was ready. We were back with the boats the next day. Locked in the trunk were Don Beyer and Scott Mansour. Scott and I knew Bryan, and we knew the creek. Don apparently didn't know either. Bryan quickly convinced him that it was only Class 3 on the Brian Bills Scale (BBS). The Gauley rates a Class 1 on this same scale. Don knew something was wrong when he learned that the easiest rapid was a 20-foot sheer drop. Scott and I just left our boats on top of the car and provided rope and camera support. About half way down, shortly after Bryan declared the creek good class 5, Don joined us on the bank. It should be noted here that Don ran every drop on the Lower Meadow the previous weekend.

Mill Creek is a boulder-choked, severe-drop type of creek. Of the more memorable rapids was the falls (20 foot), which has an extremely deep pool (containing a railroad car). We also named one triple drop. This one has 2, 6-foot drops terminating in an 8–10-foot drop, which we called Dry Falls. The creek ends under Hawk's Nest Tramway, which is reached by the road going under the overpass on Rt. 60 in Ansted.

Ernie Kincaid

Reprinted from West Virginia Wildwater Association
Splashes, July 1977

CLASS	4–6
LENGTH	2
TIME	2+
GAUGE	Visual
LEVEL	7–18 in.
FLOW	Free Flowing
GRADIENT	250–300
VOLUME	VS
SOLITUDE	C
SCENERY	A

B

Ansted to the New River

DIFFICULTIES: Early into the run, there is a 12-foot falls with a scrapy approach and a bad sieve on the left. Run this left of center. Soon, you come to a steep boulder drop, which should be run down the right bank and off an 8-foot ledge. Some nice slides carry you to the big falls halfway through the run. The falls is about 25 feet high into a deep pool and can be run down the middle. Unless you have a good amount of water (over 1 foot on the put-in gauge), the lip of the falls gets scrapy, so it's difficult to get a good launch.

The run steepens below here, with several menacing boulder drops containing some bad undercuts. Headless Horseman, the first major drop, requires a boof onto a slide that ends in a 5-foot ledge. There's a nasty overhanging rock to duck partway down. After another steep boulder drop, you will reach F••••d Up Falls, a 20-foot cascade that slams into the right bank. Soon, you'll see the remains of an old powder mill on the right. There is a tough boulder drop here with a huge undercut at the bottom that was the site of the only drowning on this creek. Please be careful. Not long after there's an unrunable boulder jumble that runs through a nasty sieve/crack. Portage on the right.

Near the end, the river splits around an island. Take the left channel; the right side drops into a nasty undercut where there's been at least one close call. There is one more nasty drop off an ugly fang rock not far above the takeout that should be scouted and portaged on the left.

SHUTTLE: Accessible by CR 60/5 from Ansted. The entire run can be scouted along the road from Ansted to Hawks Nest Lodge. It would be a good idea to use it.

GAUGE: You'll need lots of water to run this creek, but it often comes up after big thunderstorms. There's a paddler's gauge painted on the river right side of Chestnut bridge in Ansted. Seven inches is considered a minimum; 1 foot is nice; 1.5 feet is awfully high.

LAUREL CREEK

Laurel Creek used to be one of the best creek runs in the state. Its steep gradient created steep boulder drops, large waterfalls, and long

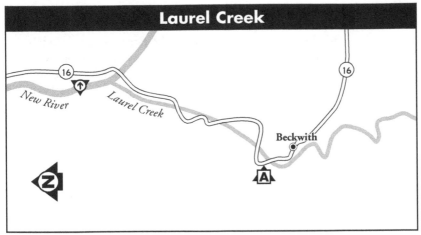

Laurel Creek

New River · *Laurel Creek* · Beckwith

slides. Many drops (like 35-foot Captain Crunch Falls) have been featured in the videos produced by Falling Down Productions. It is unclear when this stream will be paddled again. In the summer of 2001 there was major flooding throughout the Fayetteville area. Record floods flushed an incredible volume of water down to the New. When the water finally came down, there was massive devastation. Houses, cars, and roadways were destroyed. Many streams were badly scoured. Of all the creeks, Laurel suffered the most. Its rapids were changed and, in many areas, piles of rocks and trees were left in the streambed. New channels were cut and some of the major drops were destroyed. Debris from highway reconstruction added to the problems. The streambed is now extremely unstable and many changes are likely to occur here in the coming years.

MAPS: Fayetteville, Ansted (USGS); Fayette (County)

DAM AT BECKWITH TO NEW RIVER

DIFFICULTIES: The creek runs right along the rebuilt Rt. 16 so you can view most of it before deciding to make an attempt. Not far below the dam, there is a long slide that ends in a 12-foot falls onto rocks. This is followed by Windy Falls, a 20-footer into an extremely shallow pool. This falls was usually portaged before the flood. Below here are the remains of Roadside Attraction, one of the more famous rapids on the creek before the flood. The rapid is completely changed, with most of the channel swinging to the left of where the rapid used to be. The remaining drop is an ugly

CLASS	5-6
LENGTH	1
TIME	3
GAUGE	PHONE
LEVEL	NA
PERMITS	No
FLOW	FREE FLOWING
GRADIENT	400
VOLUME	VS
SOLITUDE	C
SCENERY	B

12–15 foot boof on the left that should be scouted on the left and portaged on the right.

Further down into the run, you'll find the remnants of Vandalizer and Captain Crunch. Both are significant waterfalls, but with all the boulders that have moved around immediately above and below them they probably shouldn't be run. This run has been badly damaged and future attempts are not recommended. Hopefully Mother Nature will repair herself in the coming years and kayakers will once again enjoy paddling here.

SHUTTLE: Rt. 16 snakes along the entire run. The put-in is just below a dam in the town of Beckwith. The takeout is on the other side of the New River, where there is a pull-off on Rt. 16.

GAUGE: You'll need a heavy rain to get this creek up. It usually runs when the other creeks in the area are going. If the Meadow at Mt. Lookout is over 3,000 cfs, there is a good chance that Laurel will have water in it.

INDIAN CREEK

MAPS: Greenville, Forest Hill (USGS); Monroe, Summers (County)

CLASS	1–2
LENGTH	16
TIME	5
GAUGE	VISUAL
LEVEL	NA
FLOW	FREE FLOWING
GRADIENT	10
VOLUME	VS
SOLITUDE	B
SCENERY	B

A

RAINS CORNER TO RED SULPHUR SPRINGS

DESCRIPTION: This is an easy run. There are a couple of small rapids between Raines Corner and Greenville, but mostly the stream is slow moving, with only a low-water bridge above Red Sulphur Springs to watch out for. Below Red Sulphur Springs the river flows into the backwaters of Bluestone Lake.

GAUGE: None. Inspect on site.

LICK CREEK

MAPS: Meadow Bridge, Meadow Creek (USGS); Summers (County)

GREEN SULPHUR SPRINGS TO THE NEW RIVER

CLASS	3–4
LENGTH	5
TIME	1.5
GAUGE	VISUAL
LEVEL	NA
FLOW	FREE FLOWING
GRADIENT	66
VOLUME	VS
SOLITUDE	B
SCENERY	A

DESCRIPTION: Lick Creek runs along WV 20 north of Sandstone. The last 3 miles have a 75-fpm gradient and are the most exciting. There's continuous downhill action here through narrow chutes and over 3–4-foot ledges. The last mile of the creek is the steepest, and the biggest drops are located about 0.75 miles above WV 20's Lick Creek Bridge. Here the river rushes over 2 ledges, about 6 and 10 feet respectively. These, and most of the rest of the creek, can be scouted from the road.

SHUTTLE: Take WV 20 north out of Sandstone. Put in wherever it seems appropriate; take out under the railroad bridge just before entering the New River.

GAUGE: None. Inspect on site.

part**Eight**

TROUBLED WATERS DRAINING THE WEST

Almost everything bad you have ever heard about West Virginia and almost every picture you have seen depicting Appalachian poverty or land abuse is reflected in the southwest portion of the state. This section of the Mountain State is very rugged and has been isolated throughout its history. Coal is the unquestioned king here, and nothing else counts. Since the days of the Hatfield-McCoy feud (they're folk heroes down here), this part of the state has also been associated with lawlessness. The area has traditionally been poorly represented in the legislative halls, and the bleak countryside looks it.

The area drains into three main rivers: the Guyandotte, the lower Kanawha with its spectacular falls, and the Tug Fork-Big Sandy along our western border. Most of the watersheds are in terrible shape. Uncontrolled strip mining has ruined vast areas. More recently, mountain top removal has made things even worse. Valley fills have buried over 220 miles of headwater streams in the Coal River Drainage alone! Erosion and siltation have fouled many other streams. Pools, once 30 feet deep, are now quite shallow and barely paddleable. Flooding is common and becoming more severe. Huge rocks have been dislodged; some roll down hillsides and damage homes in the narrow valleys. Wells are drying up or becoming fouled. In some areas the coal companies are simply buying everyone out and evacuating vast areas. Many segments of the population have been terribly mistreated by the coal industry, but there is simply no other way for them to make a living here. And, since strip mining requires a small fraction of the workers that the deep mines did, the population continues to decline. There is great apathy about the environment and streamside littering is atrocious. But here and there you find dogged, even inspired resistance to this environmental mayhem.

Roads didn't enter this isolated area until the late 1920s, so conventional history and progress bypassed the area. No famous Civil War battles or American Indian skirmishes are associated with the region, but that doesn't mean it hasn't seen its share of war and bloodshed. Some of the bloodiest encounters in American labor history were waged in this area between company-hired

thugs and labor hooligans. Cabin Creek and Paint Creek, both of which drain into the Kanawha only one ridge apart, were the scenes of many murders during labor strife over 80 years ago. Matewan and Welch saw murders in broad daylight in the 1920s. A pitched battle at Blair Mountain involving thousands of men armed with machine guns took place during a bitter coal strike in 1921!

Dams around here do more than just hold water! In the 1970s a tributary of the Guyandotte, Buffalo Creek, made national headlines when a coal slurry dam burst during a period of heavy rain. The slurry, which has the consistency of wet cement, roared down the valley below. Over 130 people were killed and hundreds more were left homeless. Politicians called it an "act of God," ignoring the shocking land abuse that preceded the disaster. In October 2000 another huge slurry dam broke in Kentucky, dumping its contents into the Tug Fork. The effects were seen on the Ohio, over 70 miles downstream! Extensive strip mining and deforestation was partly to blame for the massive floods that occurred in the summer of 2001, which took a terrible toll on the area's infrastructure. With this sad history of land abuse, it's easy to see why the building of the R.D. Bailey Flood Control Dam on the Guyandotte generated little opposition.

TRIBUTARIES OF THE KANAWHA RIVER (LOUP CREEK, ARMSTRONG CREEK, PAINT CREEK)

LOUP CREEK

MAPS: Powellton, Beckwith (USGS); Fayette (County)

A

NORTH PAGE TO DEEPWATER

DESCRIPTION: Regardless of what mapmakers say, locals insist on the "Loup Creek" spelling. Paddlers will be "thrown for a loop" by two sets of ledges encountered early in the run regardless. This juicy ledge/hole-ledge/hole combination can be seen from the shuttle road south of Robson. Below here there's a ford, then the river starts picking up. The rapids are mostly small slides and boulder drops, nothing over Class 3, until the paddler sees treetops at eye level.

CLASS	2–3 (5)
LENGTH	9.5
TIME	3.5
GAUGE	NONE
LEVEL	NA
FLOW	FREE FLOWING
GRADIENT	50 (1@90)
VOLUME	VS
SOLITUDE	B
SCENERY	A, D

DIFFICULTIES: You'll see treetops appearing in the mist below a major drop. The mist is formed as the creek drops over an 8–10 foot ledge into a shallow pool, then screams down a cheese-grater slide for 20–25 feet more! The only other problems you'll encounter are at the numerous railroad bridges, which collect debris. Many of the bridges occur at bends in the creek, in the middle of rapids.

SHUTTLE: Easy! Find deepwater on WV 61 upriver from Montgomery on the south side of the Kanawha River. For the put-in continue south on WV 61 to the small communities of Page and North Page. Put in wherever it's convenient.

ARMSTRONG CREEK

MAPS: Powellton, Montgomery (USGS); Fayette (County)

MacDunn to Kimberly—8 mi.

DESCRIPTION: When everything else is too flooded and you need an hour of mud and chills, try this! At medium flood the Armstrong and both forks are amusing streams. It ranges from 5–30 feet wide. At high flood it has lots of flotsam, including outhouses, Christmas trees, and dead chickens.

DIFFICULTIES: The Powellton Fork has several good rapids and a hairy bridge near the junction. The Eldridge Fork is quieter, but it has a nasty 3-foot backwave at a pipe within eyesight of the junction.

From the junction to the Kimberly take-out, numerous undercut banks and trees are hazardous. A fallen footbridge 3 miles from the junction can be snuck on the right, but a low, wooden bridge less than 1 mile farther downstream cannot be passed. Because this bridge comes immediately after a severe right-hand bend, eddy out immediately or you'll smash your skull on two, low, 8-inch posts. The current is very fast from here on.

SHUTTLE: Turn off WV 61 at Kimberly up CR 6. Because the road runs beside and sometimes under the stream at a runable level, getting there is half the fun. The take-out is a grassy bank between the railroad bridge and the WV 61 bridge.

GAUGE: Flooding.

PAINT CREEK

The upper part of this run down to Westerly is isolated and scenic. Below Milburn, Coal tipples, slag piles, junkyards, garbage dumps, red dog heaps, and other eyesores create an unattractive scene throughout the run. The best that can be said about this section is that it provides some interesting sport very close to Charleston when other rivers are too high.

MAPS: Pax, Powellton (USGS); Fayette, Kanawha (County)

PLUM ORCHARD TO BURNWELL

CLASS	2–4
LENGTH	15
TIME	5
GAUGE	VISUAL
LEVEL	0–1.5 FT.
FLOW	FREE FLOWING
GRADIENT	35
VOLUME	S
SOLITUDE	B
SCENERY	A, D

DESCRIPTION: In the first half-mile, a power pole and a transformer on the right indicate the start of Stone House Rapids. There are remains of two old houses on the right. The rapid consists of a series of many intricate ledges and hydraulics with a long rock garden. Another similarly complex rapid among the many others is named Dreaded Drop. It is about 2 miles from the low-water bridge below Mossy. Below Milburn, Paint Creek continues flowing down to Burnwell in a Class-1 to Class-3 manner.

DIFFICULTIES: There are several low-water bridges between Westerly and Milburn that must be avoided, so take-out here and have a car available to carry your boats to the bridge below the falls where you can put in again. Other hazards include strata of undercut rocks protruding over the main channel, but these are easily avoided. Keep a careful watch for ties, logs, and metal trash in this desecrated stream. Work on upgrading the WV Turnpike changes the stream daily, so be careful.

SHUTTLE: Take the Mossy exit from the WV Turnpike. Get on CR 23, drive past the turnoff for Plum Orchard Lake, and put in near the Laurel Grove church.

GAUGE: There is a low-water bridge a quarter mile downstream from the Mossy exit along "15." The top of the bridge is zero but the lower section can be run to -0.3 feet.

COAL RIVER

MAPS: Whitesville, Sylvester, Belle, Racine, Julian, Alum Creek, Saint Albans (USGS); Boone, Kanawha (County)

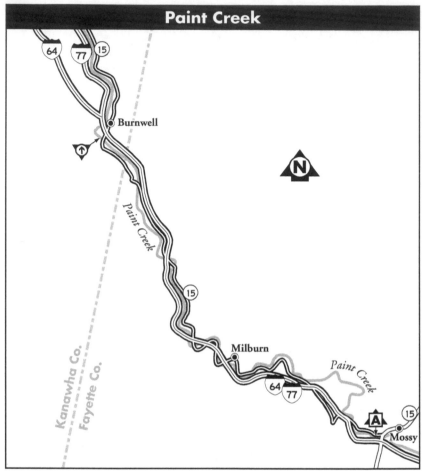

CLASS	I
LENGTH	8.5
TIME	3
GAUGE	VISUAL
LEVEL	NA
FLOW	FREE FLOWING
GRADIENT	6
VOLUME	S–M
SOLITUDE	B
SCENERY	C

A

WHITESVILLE TO ORGAS

DESCRIPTION: Marsh Fork and Clear Fork combine just above Whitesville to form the Coal River. After merging, the gradient slacks considerably. The water is Class 1 with fair current and some tricky eddies, making it a good beginner's section. Pools are not too long and move between riffles. Scenery is mixed.

SHUTTLE: The usual put-in is on the east side of Whitesville; the take-out is on a side road at Orgas. WV 3 parallels the river.

GAUGE: See section B. Observing the river from the road should tell you all you need to know.

Coal River

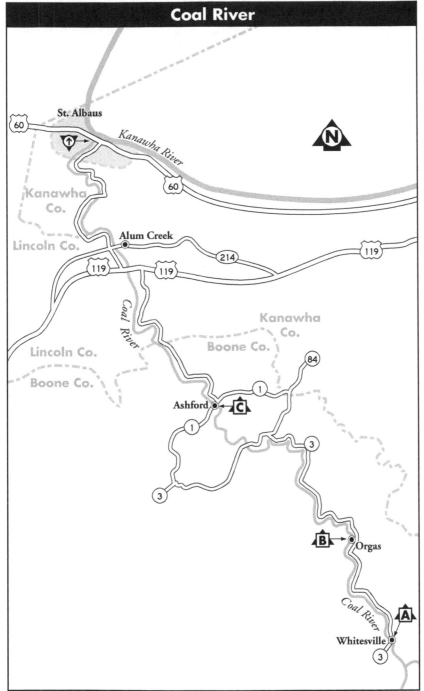

St. Albaus

Kanawha River

60

60

N

Kanawha Co.

Lincoln Co.

Alum Creek

119

214

119

119

119

Coal River

Kanawha Co.

Boone Co.

Lincoln Co.

Boone Co.

84

1

Ashford

C

1

3

3

B

Orgas

Coal River

A

Whitesville

3

CLASS	I
LENGTH	I 7
TIME	NA
GAUGE	VISUAL
LEVEL	0–3 FT.
FLOW	FREE FLOWING
GRADIENT	I 0
VOLUME	496
SOLITUDE	B
SCENERY	C

B

ORGAS TO ASHFORD

DESCRIPTION: This silted, fast-flowing section of the Coal River has the occasional Class-1 rapid. Its muddy banks are bordered throughout by backyards and railroads. An alternative put-in may be made at Seth or at several bridges along the route.

SHUTTLE: From Orgas, take WV 3 west to WV 94 north (this was US 119 on old maps), to CR 1 west to Ashford.

GAUGE: A canoeist's gauge exists at Racine on the "119/18" bridge.

CLASS	A–I
LENGTH	29
TIME	NA
GAUGE	VISUAL
LEVEL	NA
FLOW	FREE FLOWING
GRADIENT	3
VOLUME	I,24I
SOLITUDE	B
SCENERY	C

C

ASHFORD TO THE KANAWHA RIVER

DESCRIPTION: These sections are flat and flowing. There is good fishing for bass and catfish, although the quality has dropped off due to silt from upstream mining operations. The Little Coal enters just above Alum Creek, doubling the flow. The only difficulty is Upper Falls, a 4-foot dam above a crumbling 10-foot ledge. Lower Falls, 6 miles below Upper Falls, is a Class-1 gravel bar.

SHUTTLE: County roads parallel the river most of the way. Consult your county maps for the sections that you wish to run. Alum Creek, 12 miles below Ashford, seems to be a convenient break point.

GAUGE: Water level doesn't matter here.

MARSH FORK

The section from Fairdale to Arnett is one of the best and prettiest intermediate runs in West Virginia. The scenery is just beautiful; the lush, wooded banks and high sandstone cliffs create a feeling of wildness. From Arnett to Rock Creek, the scenery is fairly remote and quite pretty, with few signs of civilization. The trash increases proportionally to the degree of "civilization.

MAPS: Arnett, Dorothy, Whitesville (USGS); Raleigh, Boone (County)

Marsh Fork, Sandlick Creek, and Clear Fork of the Coal River

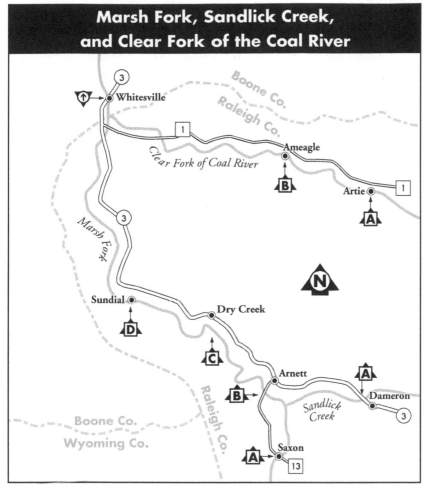

FAIRDALE TO ARNETT

DESCRIPTION: The river is flat and placid at the put-in, but within a half-mile the current picks up, the creekbed narrows, and streamside boulders appear beneath the thick rhododendron. The next 2 miles contain a series of small drops through tight chutes and boulders. All but one rapid can be boat-scouted and none exceed Class 3. Soon a pool marks the approach to the Saxon Bridge. Below here the creek gets wider. The rapids are mostly Class 2 with a few Class-3 ledges.

CLASS	2–3
LENGTH	8
TIME	3
GAUGE	WEB
LEVEL	12-15 FT. (TORNADO)
FLOW	FREE FLOWING
GRADIENT	60
VOLUME	S
SOLITUDE	A
SCENERY	A

Somehow these sections of the river are generally free of trash. However, to make up for this otherwise uncivilized and natural state of the river valley, locals have dumped a huge pile of cans and cars in one spot between Rock Creek and Dry Creek.

DIFFICULTIES: About 1 mile downstream from the put-in, the river makes a left bend and then straightens. Just below here is a rapid that first-timers ought to scout from the right bank. It's a stairstep drop with offset chutes created by large boulders with a very short runout pool at the bottom. There's a large amount of streamside wood from here to the confluence with Sandlick Creek, so paddlers need to be able to catch side eddies! You may need to make several portages through thick rhododendron.

SHUTTLE: Easy on, easy off. CR 13 connects Saxon and Arnett. Find Arnett first on WV 3, then turn south on Saxon-Bolt Road, and continue a quarter mile to the Coal River Volunteer Fire Department. Take out there. Then continue south to the Saxon Bridge, where you can put in for a 5-mile trip. To do the full 8 miles, continue on CR 13 across the Saxon Bridge. The road leaves the river, then goes over a hill. Look for a convenient put-in when it returns.

GAUGE: See section C.

ARNETT TO DRY CREEK

CLASS	2–2+
LENGTH	6.5
TIME	2
GAUGE	WEB
LEVEL	11.5–14.5 FT. (TORNADO)
FLOW	FREE FLOWING
GRADIENT	35
VOLUME	S–M
SOLITUDE	A
SCENERY	A–C

DESCRIPTION: The river consists of pools and shoals from Arnett to Rock Creek. Below Rock Creek, the rapids become steeper, about Class 2+. Scenery becomes more civilized but is still quite pleasant. For those who want a little more intermediate water, this section may be a good finish for the section above (Saxon to Arnett), or it may serve as a warm-up for those paddlers going on to the heavier and much more difficult section from Dry Creek to Sundial.

SHUTTLE: Put in at the Volunteer Fire Department in Arnett. See section A for details on how to get there. For the take-out, follow WV 3 through Rock Creek to Dry Creek. Watch for Dry Creek Post Office and General Store on the north side of the road and the private bridge across Marsh Fork immediately below there and on the south side of the highway. You may park near the bridge but do not block the road. This is a private road, which means that it's owned by someone—someone who may not like you parking there!

GAUGE: See section C.

Dry Creek to Sundial

CLASS	3–4
LENGTH	4
TIME	1.5
GAUGE	Visual
LEVEL	12–15 FT. (Tornado)
FLOW	Free Flowing
GRADIENT	64
VOLUME	S–M
SOLITUDE	*
SCENERY	B–C

DESCRIPTION: Behind the small town of Naoma lurks a short whitewater section with rapids up to Class 4 in high water (1+ foot). The river starts out with easy Class-2 rapids and then enters a small canyon with shallow ledges, rock gardens, and a small falls. One of the more challenging rapids on the river is encountered about a quarter mile below the CR 10 bridge on a right turn. The course is fairly obvious from the boat until you encounter a river-wide, 3-foot ledge several hundred yards later. This is best run at left center. The take-out is about a mile beyond here.

DIFFICULTIES: Flats Falls, the first drop encountered, is a rapid with a total drop of about 8 feet, but it's primarily a 4–5-foot ledge with most of the current running over the right side. Watch for a stern-crunching rock in the middle of the chute. The next major rapid, just after an undercut cliff, has been known to trap trees, so keep your eyes open. Finally, after another half mile, "civilization" returns and a house is sighted on the left. Watch out for a cable dangling completely across the river and drooping into the water.

SHUTTLE: The shuttle is all on WV 3. Put in at Dry Creek on the small, private side road where the gauge is located. This is a private drive, so park off the main road. The easiest take-out is at Pettry Bottom, just before Sundial. This is approximately 1.2 miles below Naoma on a sharp right turn. There is a side bridge across the river here and a dirt road down to the river at the middle of the turn. We were advised not to leave a car along the road after dark, because, as one of the locals put it, "there ain't no law in these parts."

GAUGE: The Coal River gauge at Tornado is the best reference we can give. This gauge is 60 miles downstream and it is hard, during summer thunderstorm season, to determine which fork the water is coming from. Sometimes the water has passed by the time you get there. All of the visual gauges mentioned in previous editions are gone now, as bridges have been replaced or destroyed by floods during the past several years.

SUNDIAL TO WHITESVILLE

CLASS	1–2 (6)
LENGTH	9
TIME	NA
GAUGE	VISUAL
LEVEL	NA
FLOW	FREE FLOWING
GRADIENT	20
VOLUME	S–M
SOLITUDE	NA
SCENERY	C

DESCRIPTION: This section just isn't worth paddling. There are several coal company bridges and dams that could be hazardous. There's an especially nasty dam at Montcoal. We haven't run it because it's not very exciting, except for the above-mentioned problems. The road parallels the river allowing for easy scouting and shuttling.

SANDLICK CREEK

MAPS: Arnett, Eccles (USGS); Raleigh (County)

DAMERON TO ARNETT

CLASS	2–3
LENGTH	6
TIME	3
GAUGE	WEB
LEVEL	13–15 FT. (TORNADO)
FLOW	FREE FLOWING
GRADIENT	50
VOLUME	VS
SOLITUDE	B
SCENERY	A–C

DESCRIPTION: Sandlick Creek runs along WV 3 for several miles, gathering volume before wandering off through semi-wilderness to join Marsh Fork. This section begins as fast-flowing water with riffles then turns into continuous Class 2–3. After merging with Marsh Fork, the rapids become heavier and pushier Class 2–3 for the next 2.5 miles to Arnett. If you continue on, it is 4 more miles to Rock Creek and 6.5 more miles to Dry Creek. The river here has Class-2+ rapids, but the scenery runs hot and cold. (See section B of Marsh Fork, p. 302.)

SHUTTLE: Shuttle may be made about anywhere along WV 3 as water levels permit. Sandlick leaves WV 3 about 2 miles below Dameron for 3 miles and reaches Arnett at CR 13. Take out here, at Rock Creek or at Dry Creek, or continue to the next section around Naoma for bigger, heavier water.

GAUGE: The Coal River gauge at Tornado is the best indicator. This gauge is 60 miles downstream and it is hard, during summer thunderstorm season, to determine which fork the water is coming from. Sometimes the water has passed by the time you get there. All of the visual gauges mentioned in previous editions are gone now, as bridges have been replaced or destroyed by floods during the past several years.

CLEAR FORK OF THE COAL RIVER

MAPS: Pax, Dorothy, Whitesville (USGS); Raleigh, Boone (County)

A

CLEAR CREEK TO AMEAGLE

CLASS	2–3
LENGTH	9.5
TIME	3
GAUGE	WEB
LEVEL	13–15 FT.
FLOW	FREE FLOWING
GRADIENT	46
VOLUME	S
SOLITUDE	B
SCENERY	D

DESCRIPTION: Though it is a major tributary of the Coal, Clear Fork can only be run when the Coal is at very high levels. Ledges, cars, and furniture form most rapids. It was noted while sitting in an eddy behind a sofa that the rapids here come in both white and coppertone. Because this is a very small stream, footbridges, fallen trees, and playground sets can be problems.

DIFFICULTIES: Watch out for a low dam at Ameagle. The railroad bridges upstream of the dam can be a real problem. They are often jammed with debris, forming strainers.

SHUTTLE: CR 1 follows the stream its entire length. Put in at the confluence of Toney Fork across from a church. Take out above the dam at Ameagle as the banks get steeper near the dam.

GAUGE: The Coal River gauge at Tornado is the best reference we can give. This gauge is 60 miles downstream and it is hard, during summer thunderstorm season, to determine which fork the water is coming from. Sometimes the water has passed by the time you get there. All of the visual gauges mentioned in previous editions are gone now, as bridges have been replaced or destroyed by floods during the past several years.

B

AMEAGLE TO WHITESVILLE

CLASS	1–2
LENGTH	8
TIME	2
GAUGE	VISUAL
LEVEL	2+ FT.
FLOW	FREE FLOWING
GRADIENT	33
VOLUME	S
SOLITUDE	*
SCENERY	D

DESCRIPTION: Once past the bridges at Ameagle the river provides good beginner whitewater with the usual fallen-tree and foot-bridge hazards mentioned under "Difficulties" in section A.

GAUGE: See section A.

LITTLE COAL RIVER

MAPS: Lorado, Wharton, Williams Mountain, Madison (USGS); Boone (County)

CLASS	1–2
LENGTH	8
TIME	3
GAUGE	VISUAL
LEVEL	NA
FLOW	FREE FLOWING
GRADIENT	12
VOLUME	S
SOLITUDE	*
SCENERY	B

UPPER POND FORK—10+ MI.

DESCRIPTION: The far upper reaches of Pond Fork, on Guyandotte Mountain, contain several good ledges. By the time the river passes Bald Knob, it has settled down to no more than Class-2 water. This section, down to Van, is fairly continuous moving water with several low-water bridges and culvert hazards around the many coal mines in the area. The West Fork joins in at Van to increase the volume considerably, making the Pond Fork runable most of the early spring.

GAUGE: None. It's runable only in very high water.

CLASS	1–2
LENGTH	8
TIME	3
GAUGE	VISUAL
LEVEL	NA
FLOW	FREE FLOWING
GRADIENT	12
VOLUME	S
SOLITUDE	*
SCENERY	B

BIGSON TO PRICE HILL

DESCRIPTION: Pond Fork joins Spruce Fork to form the Little Coal River and flows down a narrow valley. It's a good place for beginners to become accustomed to moving water. The rapids are mostly rock gardens with lots of maneuvering and good eddy lines. The scenery is usually attractive on one side, where the banks are too steep to live on, and cluttered and junky on the other. One side or another is always nice, so look that way.

SHUTTLE: The river runs along WV 85. Put in at the downstream end of Bigson where a hundred-foot dirt road crosses the railroad tracks before reaching the river. At Price Hill, park between the car wash and Dales Grocery. A bulldozed trail leads to the river.

GAUGE: None. This river holds its water well and can be run through June and into the summer during a wet year. It's best at low water; at high water, the rapids wash out, forming lots of bouncy waves and few eddies.

SPRUCE FORK—10 MI.

At Madison, Spruce Fork joins with Pond Fork to form the Little Coal. Spruce Fork is very similar to Pond Fork in that it has very little gradient, a mostly sandy-muddy bed, and mostly Class-1 riffles. WV 17 parallels the Spruce Fork during most of its runable length.

MAPS: USGS: Clothier, Madison; County: Boone

LITTLE COAL RIVER FROM MADISON TO COAL RIVER—27 MI.

There's little good that we can say for the Little Coal from Madison to Julian. From Julian to McCorkle and from McCorkle to Alum Creek, just below the confluence with the Big Coal, the river used to run through a partially isolated section with McCorkle being a fairly good midpoint of a 19-mile trip. New highway construction downstream from Julian is changing all of that, however, and at this time it is not known what effect it will have on the river.

MAPS: USGS: Madison, Julian; County: Boone, Lincoln, Kanawha

GUYANDOTTE RIVER

MAPS: Baileysville (USGS); Wyoming (County)

ABOVE BAILEYSVILLE AND SIMON TO R.D. BAILEY LAKE

CLASS	I–3
LENGTH	8
TIME	2.5
GAUGE	PHONE
LEVEL	5–7 FT.
(BRANCHLAND)	
FLOW	FREE FLOWING
GRADIENT	I 7
VOLUME	736
SOLITUDE	*
SCENERY	B–D

DESCRIPTION: Above Baileysville the Guyandotte does not exceed Class 1 and has little to offer a paddler except easy accessibility. From Simon to the R.D. Bailey Lake, there is a short section of Class 2–3 water, with the scenery changing to sheer sandstone cliffs. Unfortunately, most of the run is lined with discarded car bodies, tires, and garbage and trash piles. Relocation of the railroad and highway to make way for the lake has added to the scars. The USCOE has cleaned up the riverbed somewhat in preparation for the rising lake forming behind the R.D. Bailey Dam, but this good deed is offset by the fact that the Class-3 water that used to exist is now under the lake.

This is one of the most depressed areas of West Virginia. Twin Falls State Park is right in the middle of this and presents the odd contrast of state-supported grandeur in the midst of poverty.

SHUTTLE: Put in 3 miles below Baileysville where WV 97 leaves the river. To reach the take-out, continue to follow WV 97 west to "9/1," then right on "9/1" to R.D. Bailey Lake Overlook. The take-out is made from the old road down to the river near what was once called Cub Creek Junction.

GAUGE: Call the Huntington River District office, (304) 529-5127, and ask for the Branchland reading. You'll want at least 5 feet of water.

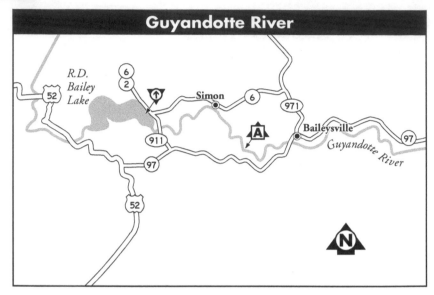

CHAPMANVILLE TO RANGER—21 MI.

DESCRIPTION: This section of river can be floated at quite low levels. It is mostly flat with occasional riffles. At minimal water levels the river is often less than a foot deep for great distances, making the paddling tedious. Luckily, the current is swift in the shallow spots. The scenery is par for the area, with the once pretty slopes of this narrow valley offset by trash and old tires in the riverbed.

About 2 miles below Atenville, the houses disappear and the river becomes remote and semi-wild. Trash still lingers to remind paddlers where they are.

MAPS: USGS: Chapmanville, Big Creek, Ranger; County: Logan, Lincoln

RANGER TO ROACH—20 MI.

DESCRIPTION: High mud banks and a wider flood plain hide a lot of houses from the canoeist, and there is much less fresh junk on this section. There are also some coal dredges. The river is still narrow to West Hamlin but widens and shallows out below there.

MAPS: USGS: Ranger, Branchland, West Hamlin; County: Lincoln

TRIBUTARIES OF THE GUYANDOTTE RIVER

PINNACLE CREEK—11 MI.

A nice 11-mile trip may be made from the road bridge 9 miles southeast of Herndon on CR 18 to the Guyandotte at Pineville. Some less than desirable mileage may be cut off the end by driving up "12/3" as far as you want or can. Water levels must be very high elsewhere before this is runable. The first 5 miles are beautiful and remote in a wooded canyon. Rapids are plentiful and Class 1–3 until a large mining operation appears. Then the rapids ease off and the scenery deteriorates.

MAPS: USGS: Mullens, Pineville; County: Wyoming

CLEAR FORK—9.5 MI.

Clear Fork is formed high on Guyandotte Mountain, but it doesn't get big enough to paddle until Oceana where the Laurel Fork and Toney Fork add significant volume. From Oceana to its junction with the Guyandotte at Simon, a 9.5-mile run, it is mostly just floatin' and driftin' water with a few Class-1 shoals between long, slow pools.

MAPS: USGS: Oceana, Baileysville; County: Wyoming

MUD RIVER

This tributary to the Guyandotte is appropriately named. Flowing through Lincoln and Cabell Counties, it offers little in the way of excitement or enticing scenery. It is, more often than not, muddy, at least in the Cabell County section. It offers some afternoon entertainment for flat-water paddlers a short distance from the heavily populated Huntington area. In Lincoln County, above Hamlin, the Mud is a very narrow creek, often blocked by trees and logjams. There is a fair current, and you will even encounter a few riffles. The scenery here is of a thinly populated river valley with moderate streamside trash.

MAPS: USGS: Hamlin, West Hamlin, Hurricane, Milton, Barboursville; County Lincoln, Cabell

MISCELLANEOUS STREAMS

TWELVEPOLE CREEK—12 MI.

*From Wayne to Lavalette (about a 12-mile stretch) the river is flat
with two dams. The first one, 10-feet high and located beneath
the CR 52 bridge on the downstream end of Wayne, has a terminal
keeper. Carry on the right. The second is a 5-foot dam at a secondary
road bridge located around the bend from the CR 52 bridge above
Lavalette. The scenery is fair but trashy, banks are very high, and
there are no good take-outs in Lavalette.*

MAPS: USGS: Wayne, Lavalette; County: Wayne

WEST FORK OF TWELVEPOLE CREEK—24 MI.

*Above Wilsondale the river appears runable but the road is poor.
Below Wilsondale the passage through Cabwaylingo State Forest is
mostly attractive with narrow bottoms, forested slopes, and many riffles. Below the state forest the river becomes flat but fast flowing.
Trees grow in the streambed and many logjams are encountered. Expect to carry a few. The valley itself is attractive, but too often the
views from the river are mud banks, run-down dwellings, and trash.
The trip from Wilsondale to the mouth of the West Fork is 24 miles.*

MAPS: USGS: Wilsondale, Webb, Radnor, Wayne; County:
Wayne

TUG RIVER

*"The Mighty Tug" runs through the "Billion Dollar Coal Field."
Don't waste your paddling time on any of this shameful desecration
with the exception of one good segment described below. This river has
no redeeming cultural value and should be stamped with an XXX
rating. At one time it may have been a river. Now it's a big ditch and
a depository for the refuse of the southwestern border area of the state.*

   *In McDowell County, where the gradient indicates that it once
was a whitewater river, it has been dredged straight to make room
for railroad yards and depressed company towns along the narrow
river benches. These hardscrabble towns are populated by tough, re-
sourceful people forced into generations of serfdom by an inhumane,*

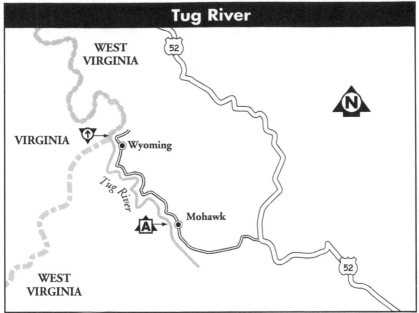

extractive, absentee-controlled industry. The riverbanks serve as open dumps. Garbage is smeared along the valley each spring by the flooding, leaving plastic-bag festooned riverbank shrubs. The banks are silt stabilized by cans, glass, and brightly-colored plastic bottles. If you decide to paddle this water, your primary problem will be to avoid being pinned across the broken-out windshields of the cars abandoned in midstream.

After the Tug enters Mingo County, it flows with minimal gradient for a hundred miles as the border between West Virginia and Kentucky, merging with Kentucky's Levisa Fork to form the Big Sandy River. The latter is mostly flat. It is here that the senseless backwoods violence of the Hatfields and McCoys was replaced by the lawless violence of the labor union wars 100 years later. It is along this section that the spring rains run off the denuded strip mines and smoldering slag dumps to flood the area. The locals predict the crest of the flood when the bleach bottles are no longer floating down the center of the river.

MAPS: Wharncliffe (USGS); McDowell, Mingo (County); West Virginia Road Map

MOHAWK TO WHARNCLIFFE

CLASS	A–2
LENGTH	6
TIME	2
GAUGE	VISUAL
LEVEL	NA
FLOW	FREE FLOWING
GRADIENT	20
VOLUME	559
SOLITUDE	A
SCENERY	B

DESCRIPTION: Somehow the ravagers overlooked one little piece of this once beautiful river between Mohawk, West Virginia, and Majestic, Kentucky. After leaving Mohawk it is just you and the railroad down in a deep, steep-walled forested canyon periodically decorated by large, intricately weathered sandstone cliffs. There are a few houses at War Eagle, but otherwise the only reminders of the world outside are the incredible plastic jug jams stranded at the sites of flood-stage eddies. The stream tumbles down numerous easy, gently-graded rapids formed by gravel and small boulders. The water at moderate levels is murky gray from coal dust but is clean enough to support fish. You can extend this trip an additional 2.5 miles to Glen Alum or even 6 additional miles to Devon on a slower river with only a few more scars. But don't consider floating past Devon because the ensuing degradation will depress you.

DIFFICULTIES: The only problem is getting there and finding a place to stay. There are no places to camp and precious few motels. Move on as quickly as possible.

SHUTTLE: Go as fast as possible, remembering, of course, that the roads in this part of the world are crooked, crummy, and have 50-ton coal trucks coming toward you. Put in 1.2 miles downstream from Mohawk, at the CR 1 bridge, shown as Wyoming on the McDowell County map. Getting to Mohawk is not easy. Take CR 1/1 north to CR 13, right on "13" toward Gilbert, then left on CR 10 to Wharncliffe. Consult your Mingo County map for downstream take-outs.

GAUGE: None. Inspect on scene.

Tug Fork River—November 13, 1976

Normally I have no reason to question the credibility of Davidson's and Burrell's fine guidebook, *(Wildwater West Virginia)*, but the tempting picture suggested by the topographic maps just didn't jibe with their description of an ugly, repulsive river. An investigation was imperative.

The Tug drains the southwestern tier of West Virginia counties in the heart of the coal fields. It is incredibly rugged country where every river and creek valley is really a canyon with at best a narrow strip of bottomland at the foot of the always precipitous slopes. And into each and every one of these valleys, strewn linearly along the bottoms and chiseled into the hillsides are crammed an endless procession of dwellings to house the throngs of humanity that inhabit this region. The dwellings range from mobile homes (I've never seen so many) and miserable shacks right next door to beautiful houses that would be at home in a plush big city suburb, all competing with a road, a railroad, and mines for precious room. All this became painfully obvious when we drove into the area Friday night.

Now the normal procedure for late night arrivals on canoeing trips is to pull the car over in any quiet spot, be it campgrounds, picnic areas, church yards, side roads, etc., and go to sleep. However down there, there were no such places. We drove for miles down narrow valleys, through small towns and hollows looking for a spot and found none. We finally ended up camping in the parking lot of the Majestic Collieries Store and Post Office, complete with street lights, barking dogs, and midnight dragsters. Saturday morning dawned with a dismal fog and a 20° F temperature. We finally found enough privacy to change into our paddling clothes at a roadside–riverside trash dump where our arrival awakened a pair of mongrel dogs from their bed atop a heap of smoldering garbage. We left a car at Edgarton, WV, and proceeded to our put-in at Panther, not particularly enthusiastic about the day's prospects.

Things turned out all right though. The sun burned off the fog, leaving behind a blue sky to contrast with the snow-covered hillsides. When we pushed off from Panther we left behind most of our civilization except for a

strip mine, the railroad, and occasional houses at the mouths of side canyons. The river cut through a steep and deep canyon similar to that of the Dry Fork of the Cheat, flowing about the base of numerous tiered sandstone cliffs. It tumbled over a 20 foot/mile gradient in a Class 1–2 manner down frequent rapids formed by gravel and small boulders. The water was rather murky but local fishermen claimed to be pulling out (alive) plenty of catfish. About the only negative aspect of this run was the incredible volume of trash that washed down from points upstream. Trees decorated with shredded plastic, and Clorox and milk jug jams forming highwater marks were very much a part of the scenery. But this blight is common to too many streams, including our Potomac and I didn't feel it overshadowed the basic beauty of this section of the Tug. So we floated rather pleasantly down past Mohawk and War Eagle and finally to Wharncliffe where the dismal reality of the coal fields began to reassert itself. By the time we reached the misnamed hamlet of Majestic, KY, the river was once again lined by houses and trash dumps and the air stank of coal fires and burning garbage. The most beautiful object in the neighborhood was the road out of there.

Ed "Boulderbuster" Gertler

Reprinted from Canoe Cruisers Association of Washington
Cruiser, December 1976

part**Nine**

AND A COUPLE FROM NEIGHBORING STATES

Although this is supposed to be a comprehensive guide to the rivers of West Virginia, it just doesn't seem right not to include several outstanding rivers from nearby states. Whitewater sport knows no political boundaries, and second, the rivers in question, the Youghiogheny and the Savage, are paddled often by area paddlers. And what the heck—they sort of are West Virginia rivers anyway! The Yough rises in Preston County and is a part of the Monongahela Basin, and the Savage is right there on the state line and feeds the North Branch of the Potomac.

YOUGHIOGHENY RIVER

The Yough is one of the most popular rivers in the East, being supplied from a large reservoir through the dry summer months. It is one of Pennsylvania's prime recreational areas and is known nationwide among paddlers. Four commercial firms offer guided trips and rent rafts to the general public, and the run gets quite crowded in the summer. Permits are needed to float the river, and these can be scarce on popular summer weekends. The Lower Yough can be rather unforgiving in places, and has taken the lives of several paddlers in recent years. Maryland's Upper Yough, home to plenty of Class-5 action, has become increasingly popular as paddling skills have improved. Today hundreds of canoeists, kayakers, and rafters enjoy the river during summer releases.

George Washington was probably the first white paddler on the Yough, having paddled the Confluence-to-Ohiopyle run in 1754. He reported that "not even an Indian whith a pistol to his head could be pursuaded to go below the falls in a canoe." George traveled through the area frequently and had a rough time of it. First, Lord Fairfax sent him to Fort Duquesne (the site of today's Pittsburgh) to deliver a message ordering the French to vacate the area. They politely turned him down. Then, in an event seen by many as the spark that started the French and Indian War, he ambushed a group of French officers in nearby Jumonville Glen. Pursued by the French, he built a "fort of necessity" at the headwaters of Meadow Run.

There he was surrounded and forced to surrender. Later he returned as an officer under British General Sir Edward Braddock. They were ambushed while crossing the Allegheny. Braddock was killed and his army destroyed. Washington had several horses shot out from under him that day, but he got away in one piece. This was the "experience" that got him the job of leading the continental army!

MAPS: Oakland, Sang Run, Friendsville, Confluence (USGS); County: Garret, MD, Fayette, PA (County); Pennsylvania Road Map

TOP YOUGH: SWALLOW FALLS STATE PARK TO SANG RUN

CLASS	3–5
LENGTH	6
TIME	2
GAUGE	PHONE
LEVEL	1.5–2.8 FT. (UPPER YOUGH)
PERMITS	NO
FLOW	FREE FLOWING
GRADIENT	36 (3.5@90)
VOLUME	M
SOLITUDE	B
SCENERY	A

DESCRIPTION: The first 3 miles of this section is the "Top Yough." After putting in below the bridge at Swallow Falls Road, the river moves quickly over low ledges to the brink of Swallow Falls, a 20-foot-high, sloping ledge. The next mile is in Swallow Falls State Park. This is one of the most beautiful stretches of river land anywhere, with many waterfalls and miles of hiking trails. The first 3.5 miles are steep, blind, technical Class 4–5 boulder rapids. Hoys Run Generating Station dumps in below here. The last 2.5 miles are Class-1 riffles that are very scrapy at low levels.

DIFFICULTIES: Swallow Falls itself is a big, runable, sliding ledge. The route is tricky and the consequences of a miscalculation are high. Carry on the left. A short distance below is Swallowtail Falls, an abrupt 8-foot-high ledge. At medium to high water a vicious hole is formed, so carry this one on the left also. Over the next 2 miles you'll find a series of steep, blind boulder rapids in a narrow gorge. Most of the rapids can be scouted by boat, but watch out for Suck Hole, a very complex, ugly drop toward the end of the run. Several paddlers have washed under the big boulder halfway down the rapid on the left. Anyone good enough to get this far can stay clear of Suck Hole, but the lower part of the drop is wickedly difficult. Anyone with normal survival instincts will scout this rapid; a useful portage trail can be found on the right. There are several more good drops between here and the powerhouse, then easy riffles continue a few hundred yards to the halfway take-out at Hoys Run. Downstream the river flows gently through riffles and pools at the boater access above Sang Run Bridge.

SHUTTLE: Swallow Falls Bridge is easy to find: follow signs for the state park off Route 219. There is a boater parking area at the

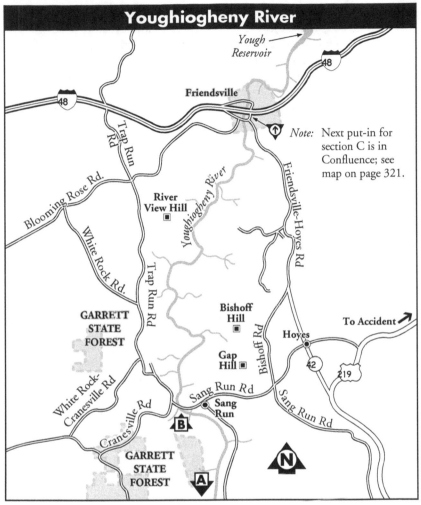

Swallow Falls Road bridge. To find the take-out, head east on Swallow Falls Road and turn left on Hoys-Sang Road. Most of the Hoys Run area is private and the residents are VERY protective. State owned land can be found on the downstream side of Hoys Run, located at a sharp bend in the road on the north end of the settlement. There's a pullover that you can expect to share with fishermen and a trail leading to the river. Be quick, quiet, and don't even think of changing clothes here. If you're heading downstream, continue down Sang Run Road to the Upper Yough put-in.

GAUGE: The readings refer to the Upper Yough gauge at Sang Run when the Deep Creek turbines aren't generating. The Friendsville Gauge gives a rough approximation; call (412) 262-5290 and deduct 1.3 feet from the reading. The river is rocky but boatable at 1.5; most drops can be run without scraping or bashing. A nice low level, 1.7 is noticeably easier and is a good choice for introducing people to technical paddling. Small amounts of extra water push the difficulty up fast. By 2.5 the river is full, wild, and pushy. It should only be attempted by those familiar with the run. It's often "up" in late spring and after hard summer rains.

UPPER YOUGH: SANG RUN TO FRIENDSVILLE

CLASS	4–5
LENGTH	10.5
TIME	3
GAUGE	PHONE
LEVEL	1.7–2.8 FT. (SANG RUN)
PERMITS	NO
FLOW	DAM CONTROLLED
GRADIENT	48 (3.5@116)
VOLUME	632
SOLITUDE	B–C
SCENERY	A

DESCRIPTION: The renowned "Upper Yough" is one of the finest expert runs in the entire country. Dave Kurtz and a group from Penn State ran it for the first time in 1959. Nowadays hundreds of rafters and kayakers attend scheduled releases there in each summer. The run begins with 3 miles of flat water to Warmup Riffle, an easy Class 3. The first significant drop, Gap Falls (Class 4) is a sliding ledge that drops you down the left side into a stopper. Then, after a mile of Class 3–4 boogie-water you enter the pool above Bastard Falls (Class 5). This is the first of the hard rapids. Start down the center, eddy right to avoid a nasty pourover, then ferry left to clear an ugly rockpile. Charlie's Choice (Class 5) is complex and blind. The easiest route is on the left. This is followed by two solid Class 5s: Triple Drop (run down the right) and National Falls (sneak the big hole on the left). Enter the next rapid on the right to avoid Tommy's Hole, then cut to the left to catch a tricky route over Little Niagara, a 4-foot ledge. The river mellows out momentarily, and Trap Run enters over a beautiful waterfall on the left. The upper part of Heintzerling Falls (Class 5) is nasty and obstructed, so most paddlers duck into an obscure right-side channel to run a narrow chute called the Gun Barrel before cutting back into the main flow. Below here, paddle directly onto an impressive pillow and ride it toward the center of the river. At high levels this section and the rapids below are very pushy! At Meat Cleaver (Class 5), go to the left of a ship's prow rock, being careful not to spin out, and run the next ledge on the far left to avoid some nasty hidden boulders. Powerful Popper (Class 4) is a narrow, playful chute. Enjoy the surfing holes downstream, but don't get careless! Lost and Found (Class 4+), just below, has one chute blocked by a tombstone rock. This was the scene of a fatality and several close

calls. If you don't know the line, please stop and scout! After Cheeseburger Falls (Class 4) you'll encounter several small hydraulics above the infamous Wright's Hole (Class 4); sneak by on the right. In Double Pencil Sharpener (Class 4), the last major rapid, you'll have to cut between two juicy holes. The last 3 miles are easy. Yough Lake begins just a mile below town.

DIFFICULTIES: Are you kidding? You'd better go with someone who knows the way!

SHUTTLE: Large numbers of paddlers taking out in Friendsville have caused friction with local residents. The Mountain Surf Shop on Main Street maintains parking and changing rooms for paddler use. Use them! To reach Sang Run, drive south on MD 42, turn right on Bishoff Road, then right again on Sang Run Road. The put-in parking lot is on the left, a quarter-mile before the bridge.

GAUGE: The gauge is at the Sang Run Bridge. The USGS Friendsville gauge is reported daily to the National Weather Service in Pittsburgh; call (412) 262-5290 and deduct 1.3 feet for the Sang Run reading. For water release information, call Deep Creek Hydro at (814) 533-8911. Releases are usually on Fridays and Mondays, but one Saturday release a month is scheduled from May through October. At a normal summer water level of 1.1 feet at Sang Run, the release adds 0.8 feet of water and takes 2 hours to reach the put-in. River difficulty increases significantly with each additional inch of water, so beware of a release on top of runable natural flows! Any level over 2.5 feet is very serious business!

CONFLUENCE TO OHIOPYLE

CLASS	1–2
LENGTH	10
TIME	3.5
GAUGE	PHONE
LEVEL	1.2–6 FT.
PERMITS	NO
FLOW	DAM CONTROLLED
GRADIENT	10
VOLUME	1,899
SOLITUDE	B–C
SCENERY	A

DESCRIPTION: This is a good novice run passing through a beautiful winding gorge. Aside from the railroad tracks on either side, the river flows through an unspoiled setting. If there is not enough discharge from the dam, put in downstream beyond the mouth of the Casselman. For about 2 miles below the dam, there are only occasional riffles. About a mile below the outskirts of town, the river turns away from the broad valley and heads left into narrow confines. Ramcat Rapids (Class 2) begins here. It is easy to read and delightful to run. The Riversport paddling school's camp is located here. Soon the rapids recede and the river broadens out considerably for 3 or 4 miles. On a windy day

this section can be tough in canoes and rafts. The wind always seems to blow upstream. Soon, however, the canyon walls begin to squeeze the river in and rapids return for the last 3 miles of the trip.

DIFFICULTIES: A half mile below the road bridge in Ohiopyle is a 15-foot falls with a treacherous half-mile-long rapid leading into it. The fast water begins above the Route 381 bridge. While stopping below the bridge is not usually a problem at low water, at high levels people have been swept downstream and over the falls to their death. The preferred takeout is a few hundred yards upstream of the bridge on river left. Experienced paddlers may want to run the Class-2 rapid just downstream and take out below the bridge. If the water is under 2 feet, an upset at this point is not serious; just stand up and walk to shore. Running the falls is illegal and paddlers will be heavily fined. If you want to try it, wait for the Falls Race in late September!

SHUTTLE: Put in on the left side of the river in Confluence, anywhere from the USCOE recreation area downstream for 2 miles. Heading back to Ohiopyle, take the first right beyond the cemetery. The takeout is between the two parking lots at the train station.

GAUGE: See section D.

CLASS	2–3+
LENGTH	7
TIME	3
GAUGE	PHONE
LEVEL	1.2–5.5 FT. (OHIOPYLE)
PERMITS	YES
FLOW	DAMMED
GRADIENT	13 (1 @ 100)
VOLUME	2,494
SOLITUDE	B–C
SCENERY	A

LOWER YOUGH: OHIOPYLE TO BRUNER RUN

DESCRIPTION: This is one of the most popular whitewater runs in the East. After putting in below the falls, paddlers will encounter a long, ledgy rapid known as Entrance Rapids. Half of the upsets on the Loop take place here! Most paddlers run down the right center and regroup in an eddy below Entrance to retrieve paddles and gather courage for the next rapid, Cucumber. Here a long rock garden precedes a vigorous drop through a narrow passage. You should stick to the far left, carefully avoiding anything resembling a broach, and gradually move more to the right where huge boulders compress the river. Watch out for a bad pourover at right center! The next rapid is a minor surfing hydraulic divided in midstream by a boulder. Following is an interesting drop into an S-shaped curler (Camel and Walrus). Next is a long, steep rock garden, which can be run in a variety of ways. The far right is the most direct except for the extremely sharp left-hand turn at the bottom. Another vigorous but

Youghiogheny River

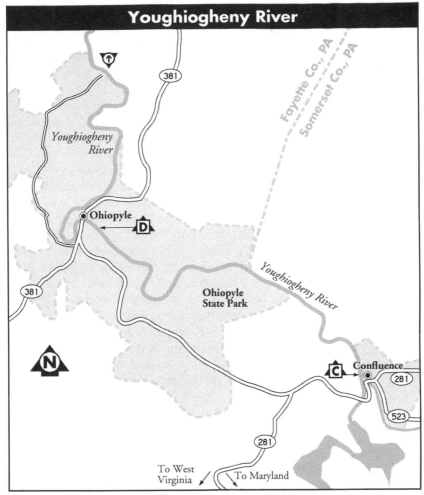

straightforward rock garden, known as Dartmouth Rapid, follows. Whitewater slalom races used to be held here.

The final Loop rapid, Railroad, is an infamous boat basher. Several passages exist over the steep drop. The most vigorous one is slightly left of center, but you won't recognize it until you are right on it. If you go too far right you drop into a nasty hole known as Charlie's Washing Machine. It may all be over very quickly! Immediately after dropping the ledge, you have several options, depending on the water level. If the water is low, you will have to immediately make a sharp left to avoid the next set of boulders. In high water it's a straight shot. The loop take-out is marked below. Carry out up a very steep bank on the right and follow the trail up to the picnic area.

Generally, paddlers spend a lot of time playing around the Loop before they continue down to Bruner Run. The first 2 miles below the Loop are called The Doldrums. These are uncomplicated, open, Class-2 descents with only one that drops sharply.

Soon the river narrows and appears to end, but a loud roar warns the paddler that there is trouble ahead. First-timers should always scout Dimple Rapids, considered to be the most difficult rapid on the Lower Yough. The current is choked down into a bulging filament, smashes directly into a large boulder, and veers off to the right. The boulder is very undercut and there have been several fatalities here. Immediately below is a dazzling combination of reefs and boulders. Trouble at Dimple Rapids makes for very long swims, so take your time. The rapid can be snuck at river center (except at very low water) or carried on the river-right bank.

At medium to high water Dimple runs right into the long line of haystacks and the gaping, river-wide hydraulic that is Swimmer's Rapids. The hydraulic and waves below create the most popular play spot on the river. Other gems before reaching the take-out include Bottle of Wine, the next rapid below Swimmers. Double Hydraulic is just what it is; if you don't punch the first, forget about the second! At River's End, huge boulders seem to dam up the river but actually funnel it through a sharp left turn. Schoolhouse Rock was named because of the expensive tuitions that have been collected over the years in broached boats and battered bodies

SHUTTLE: Ohiopyle State Park regulates access to the Lower Yough. This is not a problem during the spring, fall, or summer weekdays. On weekends from mid-May to mid-September the river becomes rather crowded. Commercial raft traffic is heavy, and since the park is popular for biking, hiking, and sightseeing, the place gets very crowded and parking is tight.

All boaters are required to sign-in at the put-in. Permits are needed on summer weekends; check with park personnel at the launch area. Reservations are recommended for rafters, but kayakers and canoeists who come early and are flexible about their launch time almost always get a slot. Shuttle fees, quotas, and other regulations are subject to change, but at present, river use is regulated by permit until 3 p.m. Paddlers may sign in and launch after the permit window, but they must be off the river by sunset. For the most current information about access, write the Superintendent at Ohiopyle State Park, Ohiopyle, PA 15470 or call (724) 329-8591.

Drive south from the parking lots of Ohiopyle State Park on PA 381, crossing the Meadow Run Bridge. Turn right and follow signs to the parking lot above Bruner Run. A road leads down to

the river, and during the off-season the gate is left open except when snow or ice create problems. At other times you must park in the hilltop lot and use the park shuttle. Shuttle tokens should be purchased beforehand at the put-in.

GAUGE: The Ohiopyle Gauge is now online! Call the Pittsburgh Weather Service at (412) 262-5290 for a reading. The reading is posted at the launch site and the gauge can be read on-site. The river is never too low to float, but is run often between 1.5–6 feet. Levels between 2–3 feet offer the best playing. The Confluence gauge is a good indicator of river levels; it reads roughly 0.4 feet higher than Ohiopyle at moderate flows. Call the Pittsburgh Weather Service tape at (412) 262-5290.

TRIBUTARIES OF THE YOUGHIOGHENY

DRAKES CREEK

DRAKETOWN TO YOUGHIOGHENY RIVER

CLASS	4–5+
LENGTH	1.8
TIME	3
GAUGE	PHONE
LEVEL	NA
PERMITS	NO
FLOW	FREE FLOWING
GRADIENT	240 (1.3@300)
VOLUME	VS
SOLITUDE	C
SCENERY	A

DESCRIPTION: Drakes Creek is a pretty mountain stream that drops steeply into the Youghiogheny River just below Confluence. It flows along at a Class 1–2 pace for the first half mile with the only complication being a low metal footbridge. Soon you reach the first of several good slides. After the slides, the run alternates between ledge and boulder drops. There are several nasty undercuts to avoid. The action is fast and continuous with only small eddies in which to stop.

DIFFICULTIES: The metal footbridge near the beginning can be a major hazard depending on the water level. After two good slides, get out and scout Ignorance, the biggest rapid on the creek. Ignorance starts with a long, shallow approach that leads into a right bend. At the bend, the creek cascades 25 feet with a huge piton boulder right in the middle of the channel. The water is pushing left which will set you up to run down the slope and off a drop that lands hard on rocks. The right side drops into a pool but you have to stroke hard to get there.

After about a half-mile of small boulder drops there are three steep ledge rapids that are pretty close together. The first one is a wide 6-foot ledge onto a small slide that's best run left of center with some right angle to avoid a rock that sticks out from the

bank. The second is a slope into a ledge that has nasty undercuts on both sides. A tricky approach makes it challenging to walk the tightrope between the undercuts. The third rapid is a narrow double drop of 4 feet, then 8 feet into a deep pool. Watch out for the undercut on the left! Next you'll come to an island split. When the channels converge, there is a nasty 8-foot ledge that should be scouted and possibly portaged on the right. Just before you reach the Yough, there's a beautiful 8–10 foot falls landing in front of a boulder; boof on the right.

SHUTTLE: Put-in at the Draketown bridge. The takeout is at the Riversport camp near Ramcat Rapid on the Middle Yough. After running the creek you'll need to walk upstream on the tracks for about a mile to reach your vehicle.

GAUGE: There is no solid gauge for this creek, but it flows from an area similar to the headwaters of the Big Sandy. If the Big Sandy is over 7 feet and rising, you have a good chance of catching Drakes. If the creek looks runable at the put-in there's enough water to do the creek.

MEADOW CREEK

This is a great stream flowing through a beautiful gorge that has some really fine rapids. It is ideal for the paddler who is just starting to run creeks. There are several fun slides, ledges, and rock garden rapids that provide constant action throughout the run. Because it's short, it's often combined with a high-water Yough run or a nearby creek like Fikes Creek.

MAPS: Confluence (USGS); Fayette, PA (County)

CLASS	3–4+(5+)
LENGTH	3
TIME	1–2
GAUGE	VISUAL
LEVEL	NA
PERMITS	NO
FLOW	FREE FLOWING
GRADIENT	88
VOLUME	S
SOLITUDE	C
SCENERY	A

DINNER BELL ROAD TO YOUGHIOGHENY RIVER

DESCRIPTION: About a half mile into the run, you'll come to the Cascades. Here, the creek drops 30–40 feet over a 100-yard-long slide. It's a straightforward run down right or center, but scout it regardless. About three-quarters of the way through the run, you'll come to a fairly steep rapid that leads into an 8-foot ledge with a nasty hole at the bottom. This can be scouted on either bank. As you approach Ohiopyle, be on the lookout for the Meadow Run Slide. This is a long, narrow, twisty slide almost 200 yards long. Sharp undercut edges on some of the turns make it very dangerous and people have been hurt pretty badly here.

But it has been run successfully many times, including once in a Topo Duo! Scout and portage on the left.

SHUTTLE: Put in at the rafter parking lot at the bridge on Dinner Bell Road. You can take out at the mouth, which is just below the put-in for the Lower Yough or continue down the Yough for a high-water run down the Loop. There's also a parking lot at the Slide that can be used as a takeout.

GAUGE: There's no good gauge for this run, but the water comes up after rains during wet periods. If the Yough at Ohiopyle is over 4 feet or if the Big Sandy is 6.5 and rising, the Meadow should be running. If it looks runable at the put-in then you have plenty of water.

BEAR CREEK

This spunky little screamer provides excellent entertainment when everything else in the area is too high to run. A road coming out of Friendsville parallels the run so that the water level can be inspected on site. Downed trees are a constant problem, so watch out!

MAPS: Accident (USGS); Garret, MD (County)

ROUTE 219 TO FRIENDSVILLE

CLASS	I–4
LENGTH	7
TIME	3
GAUGE	PHONE
LEVEL	4+ FT. (UPPER YOUGH)
PERMITS	NO
FLOW	FREE FLOWING
GRADIENT	81
VOLUME	S
SOLITUDE	A
SCENERY	B

DESCRIPTION: The river can be divided into two sections. The upper part drops about 60 feet fpm and is Class 2–3. Its biggest dangers are the usual small stream hazards: downed trees, low bridges, and other assorted strainers. Three miles above Friends-ville the river nears the road and starts to pick up speed, throwing itself over several medium-high sandstone ledges. Most of this can be scouted from the road. The run from the confluence with Little Bear Creek down to Friendsville is fast Class 3. In town the river has been channelized; there are some eddies and a few interesting waves. Take out at the park on the north edge of town.

GAUGE: You'll need at least 4 feet on the Upper Yough gauge at Sang Run. Call (412) 262-5280. From the Friendsville reading subtract 1.2 for an appropriate level. The Bear Creek Reading, found on the USGS Maryland Web Sit, should be over 300 cfs. People running the creek have reported many strainers in the past few years, so it's best not to go much over 500 cfs.

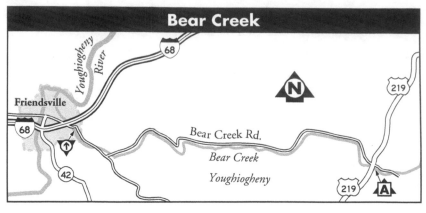

CASSELMAN RIVER

This is a very pleasant run for intermediates at medium water levels or for advanced paddlers at high water. It is up during most of the winter, and it comes up fast after rainy weather. This is an excellent second choice if you find the Yough too high. The water is acidic, but the action is pretty constant and varied.

MAPS: Confluence (USGS); Pennsylvania State Road Map

MARKLETON TO HARNEDSVILLE

CLASS	1–3
LENGTH	11
TIME	4
GAUGE	PHONE
LEVEL	2–4 FT. AT MARKLETON
PERMITS	NO
FLOW	FREE FLOWING
GRADIENT	25
VOLUME	649
SOLITUDE	A–B
SCENERY	A–B

DESCRIPTION: Many of the rapids in the upper part of the course are very long. However, you can usually find sneak routes if you prefer to avoid the big stuff. The river below Fort Hill becomes easier and is interspersed with flat water, but the scenery remains good, giving way to more settled farmland. Most of the rapids occur at wide places in the river and many are straightforward, open descents. A few more are large, straightforward rock gardens that do not require too much maneuvering.

DIFFICULTIES: The rapid immediately after the easy opening rapids below the put-in bridge is a rather sharp left-hand turn. At the outside of the curve there is a large boulder that creates a mean hydraulic at higher flows.

About 3 miles into the top run, the river appears to be dammed by boulders. This complex drop could be tricky for inexperienced

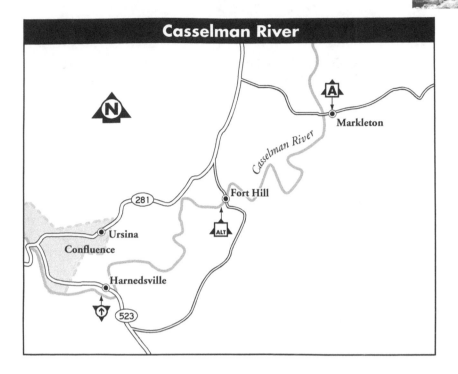

Casselman River

paddlers. Stay to the far left if in doubt, but remember that it will still be a double drop. In very high water, a sneak route exists on the far right. At any level, the most entertaining descent is through the center and requires a sharp right-hand turn.

As you approach the second railroad bridge, avoid the extreme left side as there are some good-sized holes in high water. In low water, it's a sharp, dry drop.

There are no difficult spots below Fort Hill unless you choose to make them so. About midway there is a nice rapid that turns sharply to the right as a fantastically beautiful waterfall enters from the left. Here a large boulder divides the river. An easy, but wavy run is to the right; a very interesting fandango lies on the left!

SHUTTLE: The take-out is the bridge right below Harnedsville, which is only 1 mile south of Confluence on PA 53. This road goes on out to US 40 only a few miles away. To reach the put-in, go north on PA 53 through Ursina and turn right. The river you cross is Laurel Hill Creek. In about 5 miles the first right takes you down to the midpoint for a take out at Fort Hill. This is the most popular option for whitewater paddlers. The next right

(4 more miles) takes you into Markleton where there is a PA Fish Commission access point across the bridge on River Left.

GAUGE: Call the Pittsburgh Weather Service at (412) 262-5290. The Markleton gauge should read between 2–4 feet.

SAVAGE RIVER

The Savage was first paddled by Joe Monahan in 1968. It is dam-controlled, but the reservoir is not large enough to accommodate regular paddling. The river was the site of many important slalom and wildwater races. US Team Trials, Olympic Trials, National Championships, and North American Cup Races have been held here. In 1989 it was chosen as the venue for the World Championships. The Savage Races were the biggest reason why the quality of whitewater paddling improved so much during the 1970s. Releases have not been scheduled for many years due to pressure from fishing interests. We hope this will change so that more people can paddle this great run.

MAPS: Westernport, Barton (USGS); County: Garrett, MD; Maryland State Road Map

SAVAGE RIVER DAM TO THE NORTH BRANCH

CLASS	2–4
LENGTH	5.5
TIME	1.5
GAUGE	PHONE
LEVEL	350–1400 CFS
PERMITS	NO
FLOW	FREE FLOWING
GRADIENT	63 (1 @ 100)
VOLUME	S
SOLITUDE	B
SCENERY	A–B

DESCRIPTION: The Savage is small but fierce. It might be considered a 5.5-mile-long rapid, completely white except for two very small pools (one just above the old Piedmont Dam, the other 400 yards from the mouth). The water is going downhill all the way and is in a big hurry to get there. The river was the site of the 1989 World Championships and numerous national and regional events in the decades preceding it. Due to opposition from fishing interests there has been little racing since then.

At 800 cfs the water is mostly continuous Class 3. The waves are fairly high and little maneuvering is required. It is just one haystack after another, and it gives you the impression of riding a rocking horse instead of a whitewater craft.

At 1200 cfs, the river is something else. Most of the rocks are completely covered and well padded, but the force of the current and the size of the waves are greatly increased. The hydraulics are almost keeper-sized, and several waves are absolute stoppers. Paddlers will find their attention glued to the action and many demands will be made on their paddling abilities. The river is relent- less Class 3+ to Class 4 at this level due to the continuous heavy water that gives few breaks. Other than avoiding the larger holes, not much maneuvering is required. Above 1,200 cfs the river can get very nasty and the hydraulics very dangerous. Consider it a Class 4+.

There is an iron bridge crossing about a mile above the Potomac. Paddlers looking for a taste of the upper river usually put in here.

DIFFICULTIES: The whole river has continuous action, and the chief difficulty is rescue. Swimmers can usually make it ashore without losing too much skin, but it's extremely difficult to recover boats and gear. There are no really dangerous spots before reaching the Old Piedmont Dam about a mile downstream from the first bridge. There is a sluice on the left that can be run, but you tend to submarine into a mean hydraulic at 1,000 cfs or more. The dam is also broken out on the far right bank and is occasionally run there. The section below here is where the best slalom courses of previous competitions were laid.

A half-mile below the dam the river begins a steep 100-foot-per-mile descent around a long right-hand bend. When the river abruptly leaves the road and swings to the right there is a wild drop called Criss-Cross that creates a long set of heavy breaking waves. Below here are some solid holes, followed by a boulder on the left side of the river. Run this one as close to the right side of

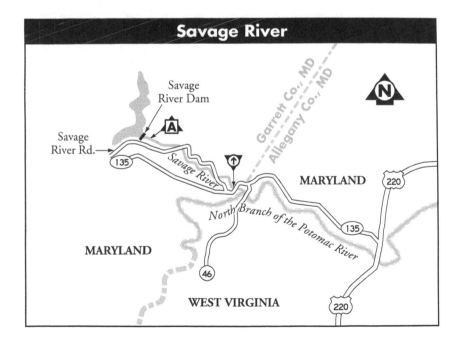

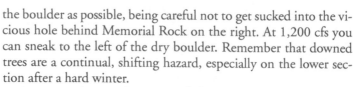

the boulder as possible, being careful not to get sucked into the vicious hole behind Memorial Rock on the right. At 1,200 cfs you can sneak to the left of the dry boulder. Remember that downed trees are a continual, shifting hazard, especially on the lower section after a hard winter.

At every release a few misguided tandem paddlers show up with their lake canoes and feed them to the river. The boats come out looking like a monster chewed them up! But advanced to expert solo canoeists with full flotation and a defensive attitude can paddle this run with style.

SHUTTLE: The Savage River Road out of Bloomington, Maryland, follows the river closely to the Savage River Dam. It offers several steep put-in/take-out possibilities. To run the entire river, put in below the big dam (reached from a dirt road forking up on the river left just before the second bridge). At the end of the run, take out on the North Branch just downstream

GAUGE: Savage River runners depend on releases from the Savage River Dam. Due to pressure on the Potomac River Basin Commission from fishing interests no recreational releases have been scheduled for years. Most recent runs have come when the lake overflows the dam and "spills" into the river. Release information from the Savage River Dam is available from the USCOE in Baltimore at (410) 962-7687; 350 cfs is minimal; below 800 involves lots of boulder dodging; 800–1200 cfs is great. Above that the river is screaming fast, with miles of big, continuous water. Swimming is not a good option. The Savage River reading at Bloomington is reported to the National Weather Service in Washington DC; call (703) 260-0305. A reading of 2 feet is minimal; 3.8 feet is a good high level. CFS readings and trends are available on the USGS website.

CRABTREE CREEK

This is as entertaining a stream as you are likely to paddle. The creek never stops coming at you as it flows continuously over slides and small ledges. It's a real gem of a run, but hard to catch up. It runs through a pretty area; there's a road along the creek with a few houses but they are hardly noticeable when you're down in the streambed. Stay on the lookout for strainers!

MAPS: Westernport, Barton (USGS); Garrett, MD (County)

Spring Lick Run Road to Savage Lake

CLASS	3–4
LENGTH	1.8
TIME	1
GAUGE	VISUAL
LEVEL	NA
PERMITS	No
FLOW	FREE FLOWING
GRADIENT	110
VOLUME	VS
SOLITUDE	B
SCENERY	B+

DESCRIPTION: Although the stream moves very fast, you can probably pick out trouble spots while you drive the shuttle. About halfway through the run a waterfall pours in off the left bank. Just below is a very entertaining sloping ledge drop with an overhanging rock on the right and a juicy hole at the bottom.

SHUTTLE: Put-in where Spring Lick joins Crabtree Creek. This is where the road goes away from the creek for good. Takeout at the lake just past the bridge on Savage River Road.

GAUGE: The Barton gauge on the Savage River should be 2.8 or higher (over 500 cfs). If the rapids along the road look runable, there's plenty of water.

Index

SPECIFIC RIVER DIFFICULTY RATINGS FOR RIVERS OR RIVER SEGMENTS ARE
LISTED UNDER CLASS (E.G. CLASS 1-2)

Printed in the USA
CPSIA information can be obtained
at www.ICGtesting.com
JSHW082150140824
68134JS00014B/159

9 780897 325455